creativeCOMMUNICATION'S

Spring 2010 Poetry Contest

This Certifies that the poem written by

Chandra Bergmann

was selected as one of high merit
and was chosen for publication

CO-DUR-391

A CELEBRATION OF POETS

WEST
GRADES 10-12
SPRING 2010

creativeCOMMUNICATION
A CELEBRATION OF TODAY'S WRITERS

A CELEBRATION OF POETS
WEST
GRADES 10-12
SPRING 2010

AN ANTHOLOGY COMPILED BY CREATIVE COMMUNICATION, INC.

Published by:

creativeCOMMUNICATION
A CELEBRATION OF TODAY'S WRITERS

1488 NORTH 200 WEST · LOGAN, UTAH 84341
TEL. 435-713-4411 · WWW.POETICPOWER.COM

Authors are responsible for the originality of the writing submitted.

ISBN: 978-1-60050-374-0

FOREWORD

I am often asked why we create a book of the best entries to our contest. We started this project when the internet was in its infancy. It was a time when the written word was less electronic and recorded the old fashioned way: written on paper. Now in 2010, with email being the primary form of personal communication and classroom assignments often existing only between computers, this project takes on new meaning. We often say that our project helps record literature that would have been lost in the bottom of a locker or a backpack. However, with electronic books becoming increasingly popular, our books also create a historical and permanent record. We create an actual book that can be handed down and read and re-read for generations.

I also reflect upon the letters from poets, parents and teachers I receive each year. This year the most meaningful letter came from a teacher who had a student that was not interested in school and was a member of a gang. This student had received little recognition in school. However, she wrote a poem, sent it into our contest, and it was accepted to be published. With this small bit of recognition, the teacher stated that this student quit her gang, changed what she was wearing to school, and now has an interest in writing.

Why do we create a book of the best entries? We create a book to motivate and inspire today's student writers. We create a book to record poems that would be lost to history. We create a book, and in the process, change lives.

Enjoy what these students have created.

Sincerely,

Tom Worthen, Ph.D.
Editor

WRITING CONTESTS!

Enter our next POETRY contest!

Enter our next ESSAY contest!

Why should I enter?

Win prizes and get published! Each year thousands of dollars in prizes are awarded throughout North America. The top writers in each division receive a monetary award and a free book that includes their published poem or essay. Entries of merit are also selected to be published in our anthology.

Who may enter?

There are four divisions in the poetry contest. The poetry divisions are grades K-3, 4-6, 7-9, and 10-12. There are three divisions in the essay contest. The essay divisions are grades 3-6, 7-9, and 10-12.

What is needed to enter the contest?

To enter the poetry contest send in one original poem, 21 lines or less. To enter the essay contest send in one original non-fiction essay, 250 words or less, on any topic. Please submit each poem and essay with a title, and the following information clearly printed: the writer's name, current grade, home address (optional), school name, school address, teacher's name and teacher's email address (optional). Contact information will only be used to provide information about the contest. For complete contest information go to www.poeticpower.com.

How do I enter?

Enter a poem or essay online: OR   Mail your entry to:
www.poeticpower.com   Creative Communication
                                                       1488 North 200 West
                                                       Logan, UT 84341

When is the deadline?

Poetry contest deadlines are December 2nd, April 5th and August 16th. Essay contest deadlines are October 19th, February 15th and July 19th. Students can enter one poem and one essay for each spring, summer, and fall contest deadline.

Are there benefits for my school?

Yes. We award $12,500 each year in grants to help with Language Arts programs. Schools qualify to apply for a grant by having 15 or more accepted entries.

Are there benefits for my teacher?

Yes. Teachers with five or more students published receive a free anthology that includes their students' writing.

For more information please go to our website at **www.poeticpower.com**, email us at editor@poeticpower.com or call 435-713-4411.

TABLE OF CONTENTS

STATES INCLUDED IN THIS EDITION:

ARIZONA
CALIFORNIA
HAWAII
IDAHO
MONTANA
NEVADA
NEW MEXICO
UTAH
WYOMING

Spring 2010 Poetic Achievement Honor Schools

Teachers who had fifteen or more poets accepted to be published

The following schools are recognized as receiving a "Poetic Achievement Award." This award is given to schools who have a large number of entries of which over fifty percent are accepted for publication. With hundreds of schools entering our contest, only a small percent of these schools are honored with this award. The purpose of this award is to recognize schools with excellent Language Arts programs. This award qualifies these schools to receive a complimentary copy of this anthology. In addition, these schools are eligible to apply for a Creative Communication Language Arts Grant. Grants of two hundred and fifty dollars each are awarded to further develop writing in our schools.

Abraham Lincoln High School
San Francisco, CA
Elizabeth N. Gladding*

Animo Leadership Charter High School
Inglewood, CA
Amy Belier*

Bradshaw Christian High School
Sacramento, CA
Shelly Burg*

Calvary Chapel Christian School
Murrieta, CA
Terry Do*

Chandler Preparatory Academy
Chandler, AZ
David Allen*

Cinnamon Hills School
St George, UT
Fred Rogers*

Coronado Middle School
Coronado, CA
Ananda Dejarnette
Jennifer Landry

Cypress High School
Cypress, CA
Pamela Lightner*

Diamond Ranch Academy
Hurricane, UT
Ashley Riddle
Kristy Stratford
Jordan Williams

Duchesne High School
Duchesne, UT
Mona Farnsworth
Lori Ann Potter

Emery High School
Castle Dale, UT
Valene Wakefield
Wendy Whittle*

Encore High School for the Performing Arts
Hesperia, CA
Nicholas Gaspar
Lindsey Lewis

Fountain Valley High School
Fountain Valley, CA
Patricia Muñoz
Steven Schultz
Minnie Zeigler

Golden Sierra High School
Garden Valley, CA
Liz Ketelle*
Edward Larson

Grossmont High School
El Cajon, CA
Joann Phillips*

Iolani School
Honolulu, HI
Dorsey Gibson
Dr. Michael F. LaGory
Mrs. Okino*
Mrs. Shim*

La Serna High School
Whittier, CA
Shelly De Simone
Karen Lantz

Lincoln County High School
Panaca, NV
Sherrin McHenry*

Lucerne Valley Jr/Sr High School
Lucerne Valley, CA
Cindy Lazenby*
Linda Schlenz*

Madison Sr High School
Rexburg, ID
Amy Leatham
Diane Madsen
Janene Marcum

Merit Academy
Springville, UT
Jodi Meyerson*

Mililani High School
Mililani, HI
Jennifer Laxton*
Jeni Nishimura*
Lisa-Anne Tsuruda

Monte Vista Christian School
Watsonville, CA
Devin O'Connell
Janice Renard*

Mountainair High School
Mountainair, NM
Sue Waid*

New Plymouth High School
New Plymouth, ID
Paula Leppert*
Pierrette Madrid-Harris

North Hills Christian School
Vallejo, CA
Carol Garcia
Trina Miniano*

Oakley Jr/Sr High School
Oakley, ID
Karma Archibald*

Orem High School
Orem, UT
Kerry Downs
Neil K. Johnson*

Pine View High School
St George, UT
Nancy Endsley*
Kendrik Snow

Pioneer High School
Carson City, NV
Charity Graff*

Preston High School
    Preston, ID
        Brandon Ormond*
        Julie Tueller

Red Mountain High School
    Mesa, AZ
        Rachel Kaminsky
        Mrs. Lemon-Saquella
        Jan Saquella

Sequoia Village School
    Show Low, AZ
        Amy Benzon
        Paul Cryder*
        Mona Doyle
        Linda McAteer
        Kristi O'Riley
        Kim Robinson
        Mindy Savoia

Shelley Sr High School
    Shelley, ID
        Teresa Dye*

St Francis High School
    La Canada, CA
        Rudy Trujillo*

University Preparatory School
    Redding, CA
        Romney Clements
        Andy Hedman*

Valley Christian High School
    San Jose, CA
        Brianna Hori
        Katie Isaacs*
        Judy Marc*

Viewmont High School
    Bountiful, UT
        Lou Bean
        Kristin Friederichs
        Michelle D. Smith*
        Kristin van Brunt

Wilson High School
    Santa Clara, CA
        Miquileen Correa
        Christine Elgin
        Karen Jones
        Lisa Weiland*
        Liz Winslow

Woods Cross High School
    Woods Cross, UT
        Mrs. Blackham
        Brooke Gregg
        Virginia Riley
        Jessica Wilson

Youngker High School
    Buckeye, AZ
        Heather Romito*

Language Arts Grant Recipients 2009-2010

After receiving a "Poetic Achievement Award" schools are encouraged to apply for a Creative Communication Language Arts Grant. The following is a list of schools who received a two hundred and fifty dollar grant for the 2009-2010 school year.

Arrowhead Union High School, Hartland, WI
Blessed Sacrament School, Seminole, FL
Booneville Jr High School, Booneville, AR
Buckhannon-Upshur Middle School, Buckhannon, WV
Campbell High School, Ewa Beach, HI
Chickahominy Middle School, Mechanicsville, VA
Clarkston Jr High School, Clarkston, MI
Covenant Life School, Gaithersburg, MD
CW Rice Middle School, Northumberland, PA
Eason Elementary School, Waukee, IA
East Elementary School, Kodiak, AK
Florence M Gaudineer Middle School, Springfield, NJ
Foxborough Regional Charter School, Foxborough, MA
Gideon High School, Gideon, MO
Holy Child Academy, Drexel Hill, PA
Home Choice Academy, Vancouver, WA
Jeff Davis Elementary School, Biloxi, MS
Lower Alloways Creek Elementary School, Salem, NJ
Maple Wood Elementary School, Somersworth, NH
Mary Walter Elementary School, Bealeton, VA
Mater Dei High School, Evansville, IN
Mercy High School, Farmington Hills, MI
Monroeville Elementary School, Monroeville, OH
Nautilus Middle School, Miami Beach, FL
Our Lady Star of the Sea School, Grosse Pointe Woods, MI
Overton High School, Memphis, TN
Pond Road Middle School, Robbinsville, NJ
Providence Hall Charter School, Herriman, UT
Reuben Johnson Elementary School, McKinney, TX
Rivelon Elementary School, Orangeburg, SC
Rose Hill Elementary School, Omaha, NE

Language Arts Grant Winners cont.

Runnels School, Baton Rouge, LA
Santa Fe Springs Christian School, Santa Fe Springs, CA
Serra Catholic High School, Mckeesport, PA
Shadowlawn Elementary School, Green Cove Springs, FL
Spectrum Elementary School, Gilbert, AZ
St Edmund Parish School, Oak Park, IL
St Joseph Institute for the Deaf, Chesterfield, MO
St Joseph Regional Jr High School, Manchester, NH
St Mary of Czestochowa School, Middletown, CT
St Monica Elementary School, Garfield Heights, OH
St Vincent De Paul Elementary School, Cape Girardeau, MO
Stevensville Middle School, Stevensville, MD
Tashua School, Trumbull, CT
The New York Institute for Special Education, Bronx, NY
The Selwyn School, Denton, TX
Tonganoxie Middle School, Tonganoxie, KS
Westside Academy, Prince George, BC
Willa Cather Elementary School, Omaha, NE
Willow Hill Elementary School, Traverse City, MI

Grades 10-11-12
Top Ten Winners

List of Top Ten Winners for Grades 10-12; listed alphabetically

Skye Bear, Grade 10
Carroll High School, IN

Sarabeth Bernyk, Grade 11
Melbourne High School, FL

Mélanie Evans, Grade 11
Collège catholique Franco-Ouest, ON

Helen Liu, Grade 10
Bayard Rustin High School, PA

Alexander Norton, Grade 11
Klein High School, TX

Kelley Oliva, Grade 11
Cape Coral High School, FL

Ivan Pyzow, Grade 11
Los Angeles County High School for the Arts, CA

Rebecca Reichenbach, Grade 12
Dwight D Eisenhower High School, MI

Linda Trujano, Grade 11
Stratford High School, TX

Carla Worley, Grade 11
Avondale Girls Academy, PA

All Top Ten Poems can be read at www.poeticpower.com

Note: The Top Ten poems were finalized through an online voting system. Creative Communication's judges first picked out the top poems. These poems were then posted online. The final step involved thousands of students and teachers who registered as the online judges and voted for the Top Ten poems. We hope you enjoy these selections.

Addiction

Addiction
Quit, give it up, why hurt again?
They shout at him and plead.
There is no chance for you now.
How can you possibly believe?
Too many old friends against him
just because of one mistake.
He tried to stop but the drive kept him going.
He was nothing but a fake.
Each time was easier than the last.
No feeling left inside
except helpless cries of selfishness.
He thought he would survive.
Yet now he sits waiting
for some help from up above.
He asks for help so earnestly
to feel and hope and love.
Quit, give it up, why hurt again?
They cry for him and plead.
He turns toward heaven for
he knows only there can he succeed.

Naomi Snow, Grade 12
Emery High School, UT

Little Moments

The first meeting
Awkward and shy at first
Fun and friendly after a while
Little moments — a small amount of time
But grow to last a life time
That night on the beach
You held me in your arms
And told my you loved me
Little moments — treasures in time
When the whole world stands still
And time stops
That rainy day we spent at your house
Where you told me I meant the world
And you'd never let me go
Little moments — they take my breath away
And plant their memories on my heart and soul
The way you've been on my mind
Since the first moment I saw you
And I know you were the one
Little Moments —
Life in it's most basic and unforgettable form.

Sondra Forsberg, Grade 12
New Plymouth High School, ID

Magnet Love

Magnets attract together,
It's love at first sight,
Leaving positive and negative alone,
'Till they attract to other ones

Nia Chea, Grade 11
Hughson High School, CA

When He Left

Hi mom, it's me
The littlest boy
I went to war today
I don't know if I'll return
Pray for me
For someone to keep me safe
Don't I look good in uniform? My cap is set so neat.
Will my uniform get dirty? Ripped and torn, with blood?
Will I be a hero?
Will I have the courage to save someone's life?
Would I have the courage to lose my own?
I'm scared but I'm proud
To know I belong to you
I tried to look serious, and all grown up
But inside, I'm scared
I love you
You must know you brought me up well
Now, goodbye don't cry
For if you do I know I will
I love you
Your son.

Corissa Johns, Grade 11
Twin Falls Sr High School, ID

Autumn Rush

Nobody forgets their favorite memory.
Nobody forgets the vivid splashes of color
of the trees shedding their leaves,
draping the green grass with touches of flames
of burnt brown and golden reds.
Autumn, that glorious season
where bonds are made over pumpkin faces
and warm flames flicker as a beacon of hope;
of laughter intertwining with the apple-scented air
and long walks on a royal carpet of leaves.
Sunrises painted golden and sunsets setting pink,
two people, standing in solidarity admiring
the untouched beauty of their war ravaged world,
forging new beginnings and forgetting about the end.
Even now, standing in the midst
of the same leaves,
yellow, red and golden tornadoes
spinning down to grace my head a year later
the crisp autumn breeze reminds me of everything I had,
and everything I lost.
Nobody quite forgets the day they fell in love.

Samantha Chong, Grade 10
Valley Christian High School, CA

Life

Life is like a bed of roses
That often gives us thorns
But still life has its seasons
By which thorns come and go.

Melissa Cook, Grade 10
Idaho Distance Education Academy, ID

His Joy

Here in the rain forest, I listen…
The rain is falling as I tilt my head
Up to heavens,
And I close my eyes
The joy of my Father makes me smile.
His joy is the best in the universe.
I feel like laughing with happiness,
But crying at the same time.
I remember that I should
Make Him happy more often.
I feel free in the rain.
Let His rain fall to water the earth,
The earth that He made
I want to take off my shoes,
Run in the mud and dance,
Dance with delight.
I thank Him for this masterpiece,
For my life, for every breath.
Stephanie Abraham, Grade 11
Hawaii Preparatory Academy, HI

The Sea

Born on the Earth
Meant to die with the sea,
I knew you'd get away,
You'd swim away from me
someday; you could never stay

I could wait for you to sway,
To change your mind
I'd waste my life away,
Rooted to the ground,
I wouldn't make a sound,
earthbound, 'til you came around

I'm held to the Earth;
I wasn't made for the sea
All these scars that you've carved,
I wear them, don't you see?
You've changed me
Claire Wright, Grade 10
Cypress High School, CA

Peace and Harmony

What is racism?
What does it do?
Does it hurt people?
Is it a self hatin' Jew?
You be what you want
and
I'll be what I want
But I just want you to see
that
We can live in peace and harmony.
Peter Zeuz, Grade 12
Prospect Continuation High School, CA

Take Me to the Time

Take me to the time,
When my life was great,
And I was fine, until that one date.
That sent you away this place,
Without one single trace.
Did you know I said goodbye?
Because when I was by your side you were already gone,
And now I can't I can't say hi
Because you're not buried in some lawn.
Do you know I miss you?
Or do you see me cry at night?
I want to know where you've gone to,
So I know everything's all right.
I try to hold it in
So people won't think anything's wrong.
I feel like I'm being poked by a pin
That tries to make me speak out, since I haven't in so long.
Yet day by day I know I'm getting close to eternal sleep.
My eyes will be shut and I won't make a peep.
But for now take me to the time, when my life was great, and I was fine until that one date.
Ashley Zembower, Grade 10
Cypress High School, CA

Illuminated

It was never my intention to presume,
to contemplated whether it was a facade,
or to knock myself down because I was pretentious.
But the idyllic nature of it all never compensated,
for the facetious tone I had to endure.
Imposing questions made you sinfully smile as you refuted,
"innocence is fragile,
and to be naive is to be pure."
For the lack of knowledge did not bear resemblance,
to what he confided was true.
As it blurred into view,
I realized it had been a euphemistic denial.
Chains broke and I was free to go,
to wander with what bittersweet had laid.
A bit more revealing, a lot more wounding, and completely barricaded.
Anna Le, Grade 10
Abraham Lincoln High School, CA

Skipping Rocks

The soft breeze rustles my hair, leaving goosebumps on my neck.
A rock is resting in my hand, cool and smooth.
My thumb traces circles against the grain of the rock.
My eyes lower over the water, watching the calm water pulse back and forth.
The rock slips between my first two fingers,
My elbow pulls back ready to sling the rock into the water.
I force my arm forward.
The rock dislodges and flies over the water.
1, 2, 3, 4, 5, 6, 7,
finally, it slips beneath the water.
Not bad for my fist time skipping rocks.
Ashlynn Tomkinson, Grade 10
Orem High School, UT

I Lack —

I
Lack life —
Experience.
Wisdom slips through —
My fingers.
Self identity,
Do I know it?
What sophistication of
Living,
Have I mastered?
Accelerate,
Advance
Toward childhood?
Reverse to adulthood?
I lack —
Enlightenment.
Give me sufferings.

Anastasia Fenald, Grade 12
Paraclete High School, CA

Paradise

I'd like to believe that there's a place

A perfect place for you and me
A private place where no one else can go
A hidden place where no one else can see
Yet everybody knows of this place
Or at least it's a place he'd like to be
It could be hidden in forests
Under rocks, protected by trees
What it looks like, I'm not sure
And frankly, I don't care
It's more the fact I'm not alone
It's more the fact I know you're there
But I have no proof, just confessions
This might be just a fantasy
And if it is, I don't care
Our place can have the best of me

Matthew Kaufman, Grade 10
St Francis High School, CA

Dreams

I have dreams when I am asleep.
I have dreams when I am awake.
Some dreams are not dreams.

Some are nightmares.
Mostly dreams are good.
People dream about the future.

Some dream about the past.
Most dream about fantasies.
A lot dream of people on their minds.

Brianna Krummes, Grade 10
Pioneer High School, NV

Waterfall Canyon

The sky was still
The wind had stopped breathing
The trees guarded the meadow —
Standing as lonely sentinels
Crying for the world they once knew —
The air was still, the animals silent
The only sound is the labored breathing
Of four humans out of place
The waterfalls' tears were dried
And the remaining snow was
Melting from the heartbreak
Lo! Another sound to break the monotony
The streams cry as they fall
Down the lonely, silent mountain

Darren Cole, Grade 10
Shelley Sr High School, ID

Evil Letter

He told me to take responsibility,
in that evil letter.
He lied to his best ability,
and my night did not get any better.
I gave up and know he was bluffing.
To my surprise he called me a brat,
and said I was nothing.
I still cannot believe he said that.
My tears fell from my face
I was hurt to the core.
All I wanted was some space.
Minutes later I heard a knock at the door.
An angel of hope and laughter.
She helped me remember and laugh at her.

Shaun Heim, Grade 10
Youngker High School, AZ

The Beginning Rush

It's the start that matters,
It's how you take the lead.
It makes your team better,
it makes the others worse.

The beginning is what matters.
Without it, how is there an end?
If you don't take the opportunity,
There is no way you can win.

It's not the end that counts,
It's how it starts that matters.
All of it just depends,
On the beginning rush.

Jayson Brandner, Grade 10
Orem High School, UT

Actor's Facade

I am not one person, I am many.
I live a facade.

To please those who watch,
I flit from emotion to emotion,
Like a hummingbird or a fickle breeze,
Yet my emotions are not my own.

I laugh, yet I am not truly happy.
I cry, but I do not feel sad.
I scream, yet I do not feel fear.

I am loved by all.
Everyone knows my name,
But I wonder to myself,
Who is it that they love?
Is it me? Or one of my masks?

No one truly knows who I am,
But somehow, this does not bother me.
For I thrive on their love,
No matter how shallow it may be.

I am a facade.
I am not one person, I am many.
And quite content to be so.

Sarah Dickson, Grade 11
Merit Academy, UT

A Horrific Tale of History

As it starts the bombs burst
What happens is the worst
Millions of people are dead
Two alliances blood is shed

While this cold war is on
The war efforts are strong
Italy and Japan do wrong
By joining the enemy making him strong

Meanwhile the harbor is bombed
When it's over waters are calmed
While many soldiers are hurt
Nurses do their best work

The enemy does his best to dominate
We do our best to kill this hate
And politicians debate and communicate
What we do with all this hate

Now the destruction is done
And it's all up to fate
Now I will communicate too
This is the horrific tale of World War Two

Dakota Gochenour, Grade 10
Lucerne Valley Jr/Sr High School, CA

Everlasting Torment

I know that he
    knows,
He remembers,
My past, His past,
    OUR past
His guilt, My lost innocence
A hazy, dark cloud

I want him to regret it,
I want MY revenge
from him, from life,
from this corrupt world,
I want HIM to suffer.

Larissa Donikian, Grade 11
AGBU Manoogian-Demirdjian School, CA

Perseverance

Perseverance, a word for many,
    Athletes call it Endurance,
    It runs, swims, and plays.

Lawyers call it Patience.
It talks, persuades, and informs.

Artists call it Motivation,
It sparks hope, love, and ideas.

But I call it Courage,
People in my life have given me plenty.
Perseverance, a word for many.

Liana Bak, Grade 10
Cypress High School, CA

The Dreadful Snow

You walk out the door,
and to your surprise it's snow galore.
There's two ways to react,
    With great joy,
Or…the way I would with complete dread.
The snow is wet and cold.
Don't get me wrong. It's beautiful
    but, to love the snow is crazy!
Snow makes the whole day boring
    and lazy.
As it melts away it gets muddy and groggy.
Now it's slushy everywhere,
but why does everyone seem not to care!

Alyssa Huska, Grade 12
Lincoln County High School, NV

Chasing After Greed

Born in the slums, I would look up and see,
Billboards of the rich and famous, but none seemed to look like me
I looked around my home, at the faces of my struggling parents
At the emptiness of things that clung to the walls
Having things, that seemed the most important
And so, I grew and left the wrinkled faces of my parents, wrinkled by years of worry
I left my friends, I would make more where I was going
Their hard eyes bore into my face, and I vowed that I would never return
I was nothing at first; fake smiles adorned my face, pleasing those above me
Stepped on, crushed, tangled in the webs of wanting, needing
But slowly, I became the one doing the crushing
My eyes now targets to fake smiles, my hard, powerful eyes
I rose on the ladder to success, I rose, and I rose, until…
My face beamed from every billboard
And those who had previously doubted me, who mocked me, they craved to be me,
To have the power I had, the money I had
My pockets full of lies, deceit, money
I greedily climbed the ladder, gripping every rung with gold encrusted hands
And finally, I reached the top of the world, and my name itself was a force
And as I gazed down from the top of the world,
I realized, that I had nothing at all

Ava Abuchaei, Grade 10
Palisades Charter High School, CA

Snowball Fight

The battlefield is pure white and unmarked.
The armies face each other.
They eye the hands of the other with anticipation of what is to come,
Their breath smoky in the cold air.
Once one moves, they all rush screaming with glee,
Grabbing perfect cold spheres, their weapons of choice.
As they snow down on one another, crystals embracing them with cold energy,
You can hear their shrieks of joy, shock, and delight.
How strange, these warriors are not filled with fright
But thrilled with the joy of this white campaign.
They fight 'til dinner, and then they hear
Commanding voices calling them to eat.

Not a soul died, but lived a little more in that moment,
Each one a victor in their own way.
The perfect war where no one loses, but a treasured instant is seized,
The battlefield, no longer pure white, but colored in the bright hue of happiness.

Nicole Rodriguez, Grade 11
Mercy High School, CA

The Devil's Advocate

Most people don't even know the devil had a kid
But you will know when you're laying on your back looking at the roof of the church
The preacher saying the truth but it hurts
Your family is crying, oh how they miss you now you're on the news
But how long will they mourn you?
I sometimes feel as if I were Dr. Faust or Mephistopheles bargaining for the devil's power
But it's what you get in return now that's the fun part.
Do you want vengeance or clemency?

Jedediah Blythe, Grade 12
Pine View High School, UT

Menagerie of Plastic

In my menagerie of plastic
You'll find ponies, pink and blue.
You will even find a lion
And a dinosaur or two.
There are dragons, cats, and dogs,
A fairy and a pig,
And my playing field, though it's small,
To me seems very big.
So I'll escape to my closed bedroom
And let every creature free;
They run around my playing field
And seem to speak to me.
Though as many years have passed,
My toys have gone away,
And my menagerie of plastic
Is someone else's form of play.
So as I sit here plain and true,
I will tell you one last thing:
In this world of bland realism,
You must hold tight to your fantasies.

Alexis Crandall, Grade 12
Woods Cross High School, UT

Money

It is spelled,
M-O-N-E-Y,
Money can make,
You fly,
Money is made of paper,
You work for it,
And get it later,
Money kind of,
Rings a bell,
I also love,
How it smells,
Money is nickels,
Dimes, quarter, and dollars,
If you need money,
Give me a holler,
Sometimes it is,
Even in plastic.

Money is,
Quite fantastic

Maximillian McNab, Grade 10
Cinnamon Hills School, UT

Butterflies

Life stopped.
Butterflies
Fell in love.

Alexandra Rosario, Grade 10
Ernest Righetti High School, CA

Lines Composed Whilst Marveling at an Oncoming Storm

Tepid gray water that stings the clouded sky,
Warm like the arrows that stir the blood
Of a million doleful dreaded hearts,
With their inscribed wisdom, bind the celestial sheets
And shoot them into the far-flung distance of the sleeping sun —
Past the drowsy waxing moon; the torpid fiery stars
The blossoming ivory roses of dust and light — ,
Making dreams and fears melt into fledgling stardust
Of crystal clarity and obscure shadow;

Shadow in which the most base creatures lie in wait while,
Above the crust of the mortal sphere,
Wisps of opulence converge on the zenith of oblivion
Ebbing and flowing to conform to the face of the celestial dome
Morphing into a heavenly atrium pulsating with the lifeblood of a burgeoning storm,
A network-like honeycomb of shapes and evanescent whorls,
Sweetening the sky with nectarous and awful dew;

The lifeless hills that are the epicenter of the palpitating nebulae
Leap to welcome the brooding and dreadful tempest,
The dry honeyed blades of grass, thirsty, slice the static air for a sip of dew;

All this for but one drop of divine elixir
That mimics the fate of an unloved race.

Mitchell Winter, Grade 12
San Gorgonio High School, CA

It Wouldn't Have Been as Bad, if I Didn't See It Happen

It wouldn't have been as bad, if I didn't see it happen,
But I did and it makes it that much more worse.
Man's best friend it is often called,
But my dog was a whole lot more to me.

I often watched my dog chase after cars, and bit at the tires,
But this day he wasn't chasing cars, he was just sitting on the edge of the driveway.
I was about to call him in,
When his life came to an end

An SUV drove on the curve,
and hit my dog
I ran over to him,
But by the time I got over, he was already lost.

The driver who had hit my dog,
Did it on purpose, and didn't see fit to stop.
After his funeral I was in bed for a week,
And it took over a month to get me to talk.

The hole in my heart was large and fragile,
And it took days at a time, to fill a small part of it.
People say that a dog can be replace,
But for me, I can't stand to have another dog for fear of more loss.

Trevor Holmes, Grade 10
Orem High School, UT

The Measure of a Man

He is not poor who has a friend
To share his sorrow till the end
Who daily does some little thing
That tends to make a sad heart sing.

He is not poor who gives away
The gift of laughter every day,
Who shares the pain and yet can smile
Because he knows that life's worthwhile.

He is not poor who dares to fight
For what he feels is true and right
The unsung hero, at his best,
The Unknown Soldier laid to rest.

He is not poor who does these things
Although he has no diamond rings,
Because his wealth is stored above and
Measured by God's staff of love.
Robert Estrada, Grade 12
Riverside County High School, CA

Forged from Freedom

I'm building a poem
It's a lot like a home.
Brick by brick. Line by line.
I think both will turn out fine.

Wait, a window!
So I can see out
and others peer in,
without chagrin.

A chimney I think.
So my poem won't stink.
Words of my poem absorbed by senses,
onlookers admire my home sans fences.
Tyler Goulden, Grade 10
Trinity Pacific Christian School, CA

Nightmare

Impetuous nightmares,
    seizing me in the darkness
    leaving me to clutch the oblivious
    stifling sweet dreams
    as I succumb to this nightmare
Agony strikes,
    dragging me back and forth
    like a rag doll
I glance one last time
    at the crescent shaped moon,
    the clock croaks the midnight hour
My mind is bound
    depleted by nightmares.
Teresa Ortiz, Grade 11
Schurr High School, CA

Footprints

She sits alone in the kitchen, knows there's no one there to listen
So she dishes about all her latest news
Lived alone for the past years, given into all of her fears
But it's okay, cause it's all she ever knew

And the people, and the places, not remembered by their faces
Still linger, still leave their small traces

But he doesn't want to be one of them
And she doesn't want to be one of them
So they leave it all on the pages
And they leave it in more than small traces

And he doesn't want to be one of them
And she doesn't want to be one of them
So they put themselves on the pages, and hope we remember the faces

Died alone in her small bed
Just a name and two dates left, but it's okay because no one really knew

And some pass through, never look back. All the others cover their tracks
And they decide to let meaning slip away

But he's refused to be one of them, and she's refused to be one of them
So they write what they are believing
And they give us all something worth reading
They've given us something with meaning, something worth remembering
Marina Polites, Grade 12
Foothill High School, CA

Championship Softball Game

The time has come for the game to start; we are pitching first,
We get three outs in the second inning, and we are up to bat.
How can this be possible? We just started then again we are good at what we do.
One person bats, then another.
I am so nervous. Will I hit it? Will I make it home? I take a breath and see my family
smiling. They're cheering me on and I calm down.
I can do this. My team is counting on me.
I miss once, twice, and then a ball.
I see it coming. What can I say? Will it hit me?
I swing; my hit is a Grand Slam. We are ahead 13 to 5
My hit is a triple! My friend's up to bat.
I yell, "GET ME HOME!" She hits a double
I am caught between third and home. What will I do?
I run back and forth and I run for half of the game. Will it ever stop?
I fake a run to third, I make it. I get my power run. I need to steal home I run before they
can get me.
I slide. I get burned on my way to the base. I hit base.
We are in the end of the game
My team Blue Jays we won
WE WON THE CHAMPIONSHIP! WE WON!
Put your mind to it and you can do anything.
Cami Green, Grade 10
Orem High School, UT

Looking For You

I liked you;
You liked me;
But somewhere
We got lost.

We tried to find our way back,
But it was just like
Going in circles.
It was very tiring
To be looking for you.

We thought we found each other,
But it wasn't so.
Why couldn't we be?
We just couldn't.

We looked around forever;
It just wasn't going to happen.
Now we ended up
Lost from each other

Tanner Mieure, Grade 10
Orem High School, UT

If I Had One Wish

It's hard to begin this journey,
it's even harder to keep consistence.
One must remain calm,
and do this at a distance.

Lift off and soar,
it gets easier; this task,
to look upon the world's troubles,
to gaze into its distorted mask.

If everyone could,
they too would try,
to leave the pain behind
and learn how to fly.

Brittany Bartholomew, Grade 12
Lucerne Valley Jr/Sr High School, CA

Rain

The dark dreary skies, the booming thunder
The tears of God are felt down under
These drops of water that drench the world
They make grass greener, the flowers unfurl
Some call these waters a perfect bliss
The showers that call for a true love's kiss
Though the air around us may be grim
And the light that was, now is dim
The world goes on, it doesn't stop
So enjoy the downpour, every last drop
You might be alone, drenched in pain
Live through this blessing. We call it rain

Colton Richins, Grade 11
Viewmont High School, UT

The Man Out of My Life

You play the game like you know what you're doing,
while it's obvious that you're losing.

A broken spirit with an upside-down smile,
trying to hold back my tears as they begin to pile.

Puddles form from my own rain,
traumatized by the thought he might forget my name.

I guess my tears don't matter to you, hmm…such a man.
But I'm afraid nobody can push that button more than you can.

Love is always devious, future and previous.
No matter how hard I try you always end up leaving us.

You probably think this is another hopeless love story,
but everyone does, so try not to worry.

But instead, it's about the one who's supposed to hold me in the dark
and play with me at the park.
The one who's supposed to save me from my troubles, not start them…
and still consider himself my father.

Brittney Horton, Grade 12
Desert Hot Springs High School, CA

For You

To just talk with you of
Where we've been, or about former mistakes we've made
I'll promise to throw away the past
And your hand I will take

I've shared more with you than can be said
Of many secrets ill-spoken
I promise to give you everything
But it's only a small token

Compare it to what you have given me
And it's nothing
I'll list the things I'll give
And all of it to you

I give to you my
Patience, humility, thoughts, love, being, love, secrets, emotions, heart, pride, breath,
Time, strength, insecurity, love, love, love, love, love, awkwardness, dreams, past, talent
Perseverance, sweetness, all love, love, love, sanity, dedication, triumphs, opinions
Body, lips, my all, joy, stories, love, love, and most of all I give you all of me, the
Love in my soul,
The real me, who I am supposed to be on the real

Lauren-Ashleigh Castro, Grade 11
Mililani High School, HI

Community

If you take a look at the world today,
You might see that things are not quite the same.
People walking fast past one another,
While afraid to speak a word to bother.

So much of our problems, all on one plate.
All left with nothing, so why do we hate?
People pulled apart with hatred violence,
Solved with bad actions, our words left silent.

We are all different, never the same,
Discrimination we can never tame.
Our laws cause justice, as well as these wars.
We keep our thoughts locked with unopened doors

Our world is wild and crazy, yet unique.
People trying to find good ways to seek
What ways must we change to break ourselves free?
Or are we just one false community?

Marlon Dela Cruz, Grade 10
Jesse M Bethel High School, CA

Ebb and Flow

Whistling winds from distant horizon blow,
Wafting the pungent salt spray through the air
As frothy waves ebb and flow, ebb and flow.
Stretching as far as east to west will go,
When sea meets land, waves crash without much care
And whistling winds from distant horizon blow.
Born on west coast sand, fair haired babes will grow
And splash gaily at the shore, bottoms bare
As frothy waves ebb and flow, ebb and flow.
Rocky cliffs afar, raging waves below,
Maiden, in tear streaked lace, looks with despair
As whistling winds from distant horizon blow
Hand in hand, heartfelt question to bestow
His love, on this white sand, he shall declare
And frothy waves ebb and flow, ebb and flow.
People pride themselves on uniqueness, though
To find a thing constant like waves is rare,
Whistling winds from distant horizon blow
And frothy waves ebb and flow, ebb and flow.

Claudia Nunez-Eddy, Grade 10
Chandler Preparatory Academy, AZ

There Is No Wanderer Like the Mind

There is no Wanderer like the Mind
To take us to our Fears,
Nor can the fastest plane like sleep
Bring us to wanted dreams.
Everyone experiences these Desires
Without the need to pay
How powerful is the magnificent brain
That allows us to dream day by day.

Jonathan Ho, Grade 11
Valley Christian High School, CA

Moving Forward

You can never tell when life will knock you down,
all I can tell you is it's easier to smile than to frown,
so hold your head up high,
and just look up to the sky!

Attitude is where it all starts,
and then slowly you'll acquire the smarts,
keep on plowing on no matter the resistance,
if you do this then I'm sure you'll make it the distance.

If you forget to be humble,
you'll almost surely take a tumble,
but if you do you must get up and carry on,
and if you do you'll finally see the light of dawn.

Even when you think you've finally reached success,
there is almost certainly more you can do to progress,
it's on you to take that step up,
and make sure you don't ever give up!

Cody Chiarelli, Grade 10
Diamond Ranch Academy, UT

Lead Me On

Quick switch like a lever and gone goes the endeavor,
I must admit you're quite clever to have me thinking forever,
When the reality is never, so now's time to cease,
to keep the mind at peace
away from your tactics
to maintain my frantic
no more turning, no more panic,
no more being your fanatic
'cause you were the kind of girl
whose mind was smartly obscure
made guys feel insecure
you're a leech, you're a lure, sadly spectacular
no true vernacular
stayed constant with yourself
a true faker itself, so I'ma put you on a shelf
cause you're worth no wealth with a mind like stealth,
so hidden so cryptic, making ways elliptic
you're like a drug that's addicted and you need to be restricted
from any guy convicted to your facade inflicted.

Alastair Sison, Grade 11
Carson Sr High School, CA

Summer

Clear summer day
Birds flying low under trees
Wind blowing up leaves
Children wearing swimsuits
Running along shoreline
Sound of laughter echoes in distance
Old rusty boats sway in rhythm
Fish scurry underwater.

Joel Murillo, Grade 12
Redwood High School, CA

Starry Night

Seemingly adrift, she waits and watches
Feeling every current and wave
Trying to find a reason to swim
Barely floating, she dreams
The moment takes her away…

Soft footsteps across the threshold
A sanctuary
She closes the door, sighing in silence
All is dim
Moonlight filters through the open window
Soft lamplight glows to life

Pulling gently on the dark ribbon
The book falls open…

Stark emotions course to her fingertips
As the bold ink webs across yet another blank page
And so she writes…

Jessica Arnold, Grade 11
Viewmont High School, UT

The Highlight of Our Lives

Walking, marching, the buzzing of the crowds.
The buzzing of my lips in the mouthpiece,
the constant beat of the drums behind me.
Boom, boom boom, boom.
The sharp rat-a-tat-tat behind each boom.
I have to focus as we start the turn.
Keeping it straight, keeping the focus.
As my line finishes the turn, I can't help but give a start.
The crowds are amazing!
Bleachers at least 30 feet high, lining both sides of the street.
Cameras suspended from cranes swiveling to and fro.
The speakers blasting out who is coming around TV corner.
I know we have to step up the intensity, so I blast out the notes.
The whole band does the same. We're so loud.
But I still hear the speaker blast out,
From Omaha Nebraska, the Millard West Marching Band!
And I know that this is what we have spent hundreds of hours on.
The moment hundreds of kids like me have been waiting for.
The time we were in the Rose Parade.

Josh Nelson, Grade 10
Orem High School, UT

Moments

We all wait for these times
They take your breath away leaving you speechless
After they pass we wait
Hoping that it will return again
It always happens when I am with you
When your eyes catch my gaze
Your eyes tell me all I need to know
The words that you never will say
And this feeling that fills my heart
There is no denying something is there
Something much bigger then the two of us
And your smile makes me weak
Easily healing my bruised and battered heart
I know you're everything I want
But everything I can't have
You will never see me the way I see you
My eyes tell you the truth
I want no one in this wide world
No one but you

Kayla Knight, Grade 12
New Plymouth High School, ID

Dear Mama

Dear mama you seem like nothing
more than a picture in my imagination.
The memories of us are not enough.
There are times I wake up looking for you.
Dear mama you said you'd be around forever.
Guess nothing could ever be that long.
I miss those hot summer days
we would go out and play.
Those cold rainy days we would
watch movies.
Those days I could go to you
for anything.
I miss you mama.
I need direction.
Guidance
An angel over me.
Dear mama watch over me.
Even though you're not here.
I know you're there.

Erika Tellefsen, Grade 11
Newark Memorial High School, CA

Dear Father…

With a mighty caring heart
And also very smart
A stern voice
Yet always rejoices
Brown love is what I get
Works so hard for me, I must admit
As old as he is,
Always a daughter of his

Cheryl Romero, Grade 10
Shelley High School, ID

Life

Life through my bloodshot eyes
Would scare a normal person to death,
Poverty, murder, violence
And never a moment to rest.
Fun and games are few
But cherished treasures to me
Because I know I must return
To my spot in poverty.

Jose Campos, Grade 12
Redwood High School, CA

Road to New Life

My birthplace remains a faint remembrance
Of Grandmother, ice skating, and shopping
When I heard the news, I started to dance.
Once we moved, I saw no importance,
The Chrysler is slowly deflating,
My birthplace remains a faint remembrance.
Is it possible we moved to France?
Six long treacherous hours and waiting
When I heard the news I started to dance.
New surroundings, I had a small glance,
My new lifestyle struck me as exciting!
My birthplace remains a faint remembrance.
Classrooms with toddlers; they are a menace
Are filled with energy without stopping,
When I heard the news I started to dance.
My home and I; close as a small romance
New life, my family is rejoicing
My birthplace remains a faint remembrance
When I heard the news I started to dance.

Kruzhencka Ovando, Grade 10
Chandler Preparatory Academy, AZ

Shades of Marine

Long, long ago it was carved by a glacier
Now, it's protected by our legislature
The good times I've had there with my favorite cousins
As I reminisce, they pile up in the dozens
Spending our time in the icy cold water
Oh, how I wish it was just a bit hotter!
Riding our bikes along the white shore
Is richly engrained in our family folklore
We leaped from great boulders of impressive height
Falling to the water, you could see our delight
The stars at night are the brightest I've seen
Reflected with the mountains in the shades of marine
A place like this could easily be fake
But all of these wonders are at Redfish Lake!

Joshua Fuller, Grade 12
Madison Senior High School, ID

The Sound...

The ringing of the phone you won't answer.
The voice on the other end of the line.
What whispers in your ear as you dream.
Who calls your name.
Singing, laughing, sometimes it just all feels the same.
You're the one song I can't get out of my head.
A constant melody and rhythm that drives me through my days.
The unstrummed note.
The verse without words.
Trying to keep good measure.
But my heart beats out of time.
If I had a name for this song I'd call it.
The Sound.

Dustin Jones, Grade 12
Pine View High School, UT

The Great Betrayal

This is a story of a great betrayal
Who would've known of this devastating tale
More than 2,300 people deceased
May all of them rest in peace

This happened on a nice Sunday morning
On December 7, 1941 with no warning
Planes soaring, dropping bombshells on the ground
So many people listening to the terrible sound

Although they were outnumbered
They fought with pride
The Americans were proud
But many died

This is a story of a great betrayal
Who would've known we would prevail
All these men died with honor
And now we remember the story of Pearl Harbor

Rita Correa, Grade 10
Lucerne Valley Jr/Sr High School, CA

The Unicorns

A herd of unicorns visited me in my dream
Their wavy hair blew beautifully in the wind
They stood tall and graceful, an amazing team
Their glistening eyes connected with mine as they grinned.

At once, they seemed frightened, their eyes filled with fear
Like they had been struck by lightning and thunder
Stomp, stomp, stomp! They dashed away like deer
Disappearing in the thick forest, no time to wonder.

It was then cold and quiet, I was as lonely as ever
Small leaves crackled as they flew in the breeze
To keep warm, I held tightly to my soft, silky sweater
Hoping to visit the unicorns in another fun dream.

Sherry Li, Grade 10
Cypress High School, CA

My Name

Trevor James Setzer,
My first name comes from a famous guitarist named Trevor Rabin,
My middle name is James after my uncle James,
The definition of my name is prudent,
Careful and sensible,
But my name has a lot of different meanings,
I'm always going,
Love the outside more than inside,
Always smiling,
Constantly laughing,
Some say loud,
Others say quiet,
Sometimes shy.

Trevor James Setzer, Grade 12
Pine View High School, UT

Hurt

You broke my heart
you lied to my face
what am I?
a huge disgrace?
What we had
in the start
is now a pain
in my heart
What can I do
to make you see
that you and I
aren't meant to be
I can't look at you
but yet I stare
with loving eyes
and you don't care
I'll forget you
you forget me
my heart will break
but I'll be free

Kayla Ricker, Grade 12
Frontier High School, CA

Flavor of the Day

If your day was a flavor of ice cream,
What flavor would it be?

Vanilla…plain and simple?
Chocolate…rich and dark?
Strawberry…sweet and fruity?
Oreo…crunchy but creamy?
Rocky Road…a little bumpy?
Chocolate Mouse Royal…extravagant?
Burnt Almond Fudge…really nutty?
Bubble Gum…childlike and chewy?
Neapolitan…not sure?

Whatever flavor it is…
Just don't let it melt.

Nathan Brown, Grade 10
Orem High School, UT

My Mother

My mother once told me
I shouldn't make fun of people
Or climb on top of church steeples.
She told me not to pout
And tried to teach me what life was about.
My mother told me not to stay out late
Or go on too many dates.
She told me not to jump on my bed
And said it's rude to hit people on the head.
My mom told me to be myself
And break from the pages.

Morgan Harrison, Grade 10
Preston High School, ID

Battling Reality

As I walk into the world with my arms out and free,
I set and prepare for the battle that has yet to await me.
With my soul exposed as I open and close my eyes
as I realize the real lies that hide behind these alibis,
I begin to face the harsh realities that I despise.
Pot heads pressuring people into smoking weed,
while kids drive illegally finding their need for speed.
Gangsters and alcoholics abusing their own souls
with teenage girls walking out wearing less clothes.
Temptations hitting me up and down, side to side,
as I continue to fight through the furious rip tides.
Coming home to a broken family, always mad at me.
I wish this was all a dream with fiction full of fantasy.
The shield that once guarded my heart is now shattered,
scattered into places of my body that have been bruised and battered.
These battle scars I wear upon my tainted soul,
shows nothing but the determination when I'm giving it my all.
Among all the influences I choose nothing but the best,
because I know deep within my heart I'll rise above the rest.
So I set my sword aside and cry for just a while,
because deep inside this armor, the warrior is a child.

Bryle Tayag, Grade 12
Ronald E McNair High School, CA

Darkness

The darkness is closing in on it.
The hopes and dreams that used to be, are gone.
Everyone has given up on it.
It is never coming back; no one will miss it.
The room begins to spin.
It seems as if it was never there.
The only remains are faded scars.
Time keeps ticking; life goes on.
The world has suffered no loss.
The room spins faster and faster.
It gets darker and darker.
They have destroyed it.
It has slipped into insanity.
Yet it is still not noticed.
Everyone continues living their pointless lives, without a second look.
They are completely content with never knowing the truth.
They make humanity look like a sick joke.
Mindless drones walk the streets.
While those in the know, are buried underneath.
Well to hell with them, to hell with the light.
It is safer here, in the dark.

Jacquelyn Little, Grade 12
Westlake High School, CA

I Am the Sinner

Before the sin was hidden
Under breath and skin

Now revealed as whole
All that is left
The feeling of freedom

The admission of guilt
My sins let go

Now known to all
No longer guilty
The sin is forever a part of me

I am the sinner
Though she is the sin

Now both to live together
Absent of guilt
Not hungry for regret

Moira Hill, Grade 11
Grossmont High School, CA

Suffocation

I'm suffocating here
Can't even exhale
My vision is hazy
Darkness, creeping in
Drowning in my loneliness
But through the gasps I find a voice
Breaching the silence around me
With every sound I hear
The pressure on me weakens
Until finally my own voice joins the melody
Screaming with emotion
The light quickly floods everything around
I have found my salvation
From this past suffocation

Michael Nickles, Grade 11
Ironwood Ridge High School, AZ

Richard Nixon

Tricky Dicky Nixon
Came 'Nam fixin'
And Commie huntin'
Rose from the ashes
Battled the fascists
And conquered the moon
But recordings he took
Though not a crook
Hastened his exit
And Jerry Ford
Smart as a board
Sworn in at noon (tomorrow)

Jonathan Kachiu, Grade 12
St Joseph Notre Dame High School, CA

Tonight I Understand Juliet

Without you with me, the night emerges.
Seeing my pain, the diminishing horizon, grimaces, in a bleak sigh.
Our family's ancient feud divides a love that holds only the purest innocence.
Each is waiting for the other to make restitution for a blunder not quite remembered.
Tonight I understand Juliet. But hope is lingering.
I will not give in; submission is a word I refuse to learn.
Our love will endure time's scheme; the hours away can only bind us closer.
They may lock us away but confinement is for the weak of heart.
Separation cannot harm destiny.
I look away, turning my back on the families plotting our love's demise.
They cannot understand. They have not tried.
Battles and blind hate fill their souls; their eyes are blind to the turning of time.
So, tonight I wander the vacant streets.
I am following empty breaths into a frozen night.
With the sun's blessed glow shadowed in twilight's mask,
the colorless world lays in restless slumber.
Every silvery breath stolen, by night's frosty grasp, draws us closer.
Be strong in faith. For you, tonight I walk, alone.
Tomorrow's welcomed dawn brings the promise of a new day.
Daybreak will lure our severed bond together once again.
With you in my sight, my heart will beat anew.

Brianna Howard, Grade 10
Orem High School, UT

The Mystification of a Deity

I can't believe nor trust
— or can I?
I speak of religion you see, and time after time I ponder on it.
How can it speak of so much wisdom and still cause so much problems?
People take religion into their lives reaping any benefit, to get near
or to have some connection with their God.
God?
who is God?
surely to believe, you must have seen.
— but who needs to see?
He is all powerful, all knowing all great.
It is uncanny to believe how our mind works to get an answer.
But at the end of the day, I'm still left with
Questions.
But who are we to judge on how we came to be?
To be given the gift of life and still wanting more
I sometimes feel ungrateful.
Maybe there is no answer, maybe there is no God.
Maybe all I need is to believe, in myself.
Can I?
Yes I can.

Javier Juarez, Grade 11
Animo Leadership Charter High School, CA

Nat Turner
A mystic
A preacher
Longing for the true taste of freedom
but swallowed up by men who hate
His plan
derived from those who failed before
To begin a bloody march
and refresh a
pale panic

From fighting to
hiding to
corners and capture

From dying to…

Living on
A symbol of courage
but largely a symbol of fear
To those who could not contain him
or chain him

Fear will hold masters
Shannon McHatton, Grade 11
Golden Sierra High School, CA

Bees
Bees. EWW!
Bees. Hooray!
They get real close to you.
They sting you
They make honey.
They pollinate flowers.
Bees.
Bees.
I don't see the point of having
They do good things.
bees around. They hurt with their
Ouch! (slap your thigh) it stung
sting and make that annoying
Me!
buzzing sound.
Jamie Norlander, Grade 11
Pine View High School, UT

Two Words
Two little words
That's all I have to say
Just two little words
Take them as you may
Two little words
Just two
These two little words
Thank you
Acacia Lain Peers, Grade 12
Lucerne Valley Jr/Sr High School, CA

How Could I Have Loved You So Much?
How could I have loved you so much,
And now hate you this much.
You were the one with the broken heart,
'Till I showed up and fell in love.
Thought you were one of a kind,
Would have done anything or given up anything of mine.
For you to be mine, so I did.
Gave you my love, gave you my perfect heart.
I felt so alive when you were mine,
I felt so loved when I was yours.
Felt everything was perfect.
And you, you seemed to be happy.
But all of a sudden everything changed,
I don't know what happened or where it went wrong.
I guess it was 'cause I gave you too much love,
That you just did not care for.
Or maybe cause you no longer had that broken heart,
'Cause I remember I gave you my perfect heart and you gave me your broken heart,
How could I have loved you so much,
And now hate you this much?
Yorlin Hernandez, Grade 10
Crossroads School, CA

Disillusion
You've gotta wonder why the sky is blue.
They say it's the wave of refraction —
But it's gotta be more magical, doesn't it?

What kinda world do we live in when the end of the rainbow never comes?

And wishing upon a falling star
Merely allows you to reflect on your innermost desires?

That will never come true.
Why? Why?

The mind of man
Has created God.
Why, then can't we create our own Elysium?
Anna Benham, Grade 10
Palo Alto High School, CA

Like the Night, My Sight
Stars so bright like glitter being thrown into a black sky,
Mists of rain spraying the ocean,
Making tiny, almost undetected splashes.
A purple ocean swaying with the light waves,
And a moon so bright that it makes shadows beneath the willows.
Fierce wind like a tornado amongst the bushes, scaring them into hiding.
The layer of cool dampness amongst the leaves.
Hiding in the shadows is a howl like screech.
Crying into the wet air like a child cries on a shoulder.
Sand that glistens under waves, as if scared to come out.
Stars so bright that the night is now my personal light.
Marrisa Avila, Grade 12
Wilson High School, CA

Uncle

You would try and be there to visit me,
That I could see
I'd do anything for one last hug,
And to hear that laugh
When I think of you I can't speak,
There is only a tear down my cheek
I wish I could write a letter to where you are,
But there is no address in the stars
I wish my heart would mend,
The night has come again
I never thought it would be this hard
Now I see you in my dreams,
And it always seems harder to wake up

Emily Schafrick, Grade 10
Dobson High School, AZ

Jungle Life

The life in the jungle is never dead
The movements of the tiger on the prowl
As he hunts for his food among the grounds
Then he strikes for his prey as he's fed
He climbs through the trees looking for a bed
If you disturbed him in his sleep he'll growl
Beware to not wake him you'll die you shall
You will believe as you start to see red

He defends his territory as he goes
Taking each step like a beast in the jungle
Anyone that enters is now his foe
He fights his enemy as they rumble

DeMaree Lowe, Grade 10
Calvary Chapel Christian School, CA

L'arbre

A scent, sprolluping light
Upon the faerie-breath wind
Tickling, tangled
And dribbles down my chin
Hidden behind that white
And rose-petaled moon kiss
Perched on the mangled
A face of mischievous bliss

A wafting call, light and warm
And a voice I cannot seem to hear
Falling in and out of branches
Beckoning without fear
But my footsteps have become worn
Faltering as I draw close
All the while she dances
A flickering, fantastical ghost

And left? I, only here to gaze
Merely mortal in this moonlit haze

Emily Zwier, Grade 10
Xavier College Preparatory School, AZ

Winter

Like a flower;
Whose petals,
Have long past wilted.

My limbs hang loose,
With no energy; or want
To move them.

Like the trees,
In winter;
Bare and cold.

I stand here naked,
So vulnerable,
So alone.

The wind whistles,
And whines
Crossing paths with my ear.

The night hours,
Telling stories;
Of triumph,
Of fear…

I sit here alone,
Staring out at the night…

Sydney Wright, Grade 12
Independence High School, CA

Believing to Succeed

Believing.
Succeeding.
Guileless.

Never gave up,
Or had a doubt.
Just kept searching,
Through the long drought.

Believing to fail,
Was not the dream.
Having to rebel,
Was the big scene.

Walking along the trail,
Meeting new people;
Driving in the car,
With a big ego.

With her head held high,
And the pride in her eyes,
Made her believe,
A body goes far.

Jatice Payton, Grade 10
South Ridge High School, AZ

I Am

I am the storm.
Rushing into things,
Crying over where my lightning
Accidentally strikes.

I am the river.
I move forward, never looking back.
I become clean as I rush.

I am a bird.
Soaring, gliding,
Painting the sky with my colors.

I am a candle.
Illuminating the dark,
Giving and giving and giving
Finally gone by a breeze.

I am red.
Sometimes a rose,
Most times a blush.

I am clear,
Shimmering invisibility.
Seen only by a few.
Colored only by light.

Ashley Stilson, Grade 10
Emery High School, UT

Time Is of the Essence

I look through the window
I watch through the blinds
I've seen it
I saw it,
A moment in time
you've given to yours
as you've taken from mine

Your painful thoughts
destroy my innocence of mind,
Through all of the time, I'm left behind,
as I search to find,
a reason, to smile

In my head
these thoughts they disappear
to wait, in the wake, of the mistake,
of everything I fear

By the end of the day
we, anticipate, a new chance
to start again
as we fear
the inevitable, end.

Andrew Rodrigues, Grade 10
Cypress High School, CA

Puddle Magic

Look down
Standing in the sky
Smile becomes a frown
Clouds close by

Twinkling stars
On the ground
Farther than Mars
Swirling around

Jump in
Stars dance
Waves begin
Bright romance

Moon of the night
Grounded light

Amanda Loosli, Grade 12
Virgin Valley High School, NV

A Lover's Wish

Don't buy me a bouquet of flowers,
Give me a packet of seeds.
Don't buy me chocolate,
Bake me something sweet.
Don't give me a card,
Give me a hug, kiss, or just
simply say 'I love you'.
Don't spend lots of time or money
preparing something special,
Just spend some time with me,
let's walk and talk.
Love is simple, powerful, and
affectionate.
No need for the extra ordinary.
So give me simply this:
time together,
you and me.

Maggie Blount, Grade 10
Moscow Sr High School, ID

An Imitation of Dickinson

Oh so I shall see the world—
    Oh what of wondrous design—
I can't help but see God's hand—
    No one else on such high demand—
I look out upon God's land—
    With its checkered fields quietly laid—
And the animals calm upon the day—
    And some waltz by without a care—
And pause not at all to see the land—

Oh so I see the world (when others do not).

Cassandra Killion, Grade 11
New Plymouth High School, ID

My Mother Once Told Me

My mother once told me
Look before you cross.
She said to never doubt my intuition
And my ambitions, not to toss.

She told me with scissors do not run
Teddies are there to make me smile
Cleaning my room can be fun
And to heal my heart may take awhile.

But the most important thing
My mother ever told me
Is no matter where I am or what I did
She will always love me.

Kodi Shirley, Grade 10
Preston High School, ID

Home

A blade of grass
A grain of sand
A raindrop in the sea
Oh where, atop this face of earth
is there a place for me?
In cities, men
Are cultured strong
In country, work is key
I'll live on mountains, anywhere
that has a place for me.
Am I a blackened butterfly?
Am I a burnt out tree?
There has to be a reason why
there is no place for me.

Jacob Tonks, Grade 11
Viewmont High School, UT

Dead

My life is consumed by school,
But I have passions I want to follow.
I'm stuck inside studying,
Who knows, I could die tomorrow.

But I'm trapped inside this routine,
Of wake up, work hard, study all night.
I hardly get sleep, I hardly eat
But in this society, that's what's right.

I might be getting good grades,
But I'm really dying inside.
Quenching a passion for tennis,
You could say half of me already died.

Jake Trinh, Grade 11
Valley Christian High School, CA

Now I Believe Families Are Forever

You have left me all alone which
Makes the world seem dismal
Although you left with a smile on your face
Mine had none to bear
I miss you terribly
Why did you have to go
My days go by in shades of gray
No light
No darkness
Just gray
Then one day I realized
You left to our Heavenly Father
He said it was your time to go and
You willingly obliged
By your willingness I remembered that
Families are forever
Only now do I truly believe
Natalie Baantjer, Grade 12
Emery High School, UT

You Caught Me

Every time when I try to hide,
you always appeared with your smile.
Don't be sniffing for me,
for my eyes will ocean wide,
and my heart will balloon and dynamite.

When I walk towards danger and death,
leave me be alone on my path.
No one should care,
nobody should have to know,
but you came and awakened me to be alive.

You won't let me jump into the hole,
or hate you to the foot.
Tight in your arms,
I've decided to burn my wings,
so I could be trapped in the world of us.
Tina Chang, Grade 11
Hiram W Johnson High School, CA

Montra

Summer storms will soak
Spicy Thai food always chokes
My heart never broke

Today it is raining
My hasty smile feigning
Gloomy friends chaining

Chance is so fickle
When you're in a pickle
Stars shine like nickels
Jessica Fuller, Grade 11
Lone Peak High School, UT

Dreams

A tractor
A warehouse
A big scary tree
A castle
A palace
A big scary bee
A lake, a pond
A tiny stream
A boat, a raft
It's all the same thing
Dreams, dreams
Where can they lead
A field full of grass
Or a cup of smoked tea
Dreams, dreams
Where can they lead
These are my recent but
Let's see more things
Marissa Minocchi, Grade 11
Red Mountain High School, AZ

Everything About You

I love your eyes
The way they match the color of the ocean.
I love your smile
How big it gets when we see each other.
I love your laugh
It makes me high.
I love the spaces between your fingers
Where mine fit perfectly.
I love the way you look at me
It gives me butterflies.
I love it when you hold me tight
It makes all the pain inside disappear.
I love how you say all the right things
To make me feel better.
I love that feeling when we kiss
When nothing else matters.
To put it simply
I love you.
Stefanie Greene, Grade 10
Mountainair High School, NM

Thank You

I did not have a clue
That you would be the one
To make me unblue
Yes it is true
Because of you
I am a happier person
I was hurtin'
For a long time
Thank You for all
You've done.
Rashele Hoffman, Grade 10
Pleasant Grove High School, UT

When You Say My Name

When you say my name,
My heart skips a beat.
When you smile and wave,
I smile back, and when you
Leave my sight, it grows.
When you laugh at my jokes,
I laugh in relief and joy.
When you give me a high-five
I wish, if only for a moment,
I could hold your hand.
When you say my name,
I melt inside,
But, inside, I know
Though I wish it weren't so,
I can never be
With you.
Janessa Armstrong, Grade 12
Viewmont High School, UT

If

If you asked me out,
Would you go with me?
If you said you love me,
Would you mean it?
If we went to the movies,
Would you hold me?
If someone said that I am ugly,
Would you stand up for me?
If I said I love you,
Would you say it back meaningfully?
If a guy said you aren't worth it,
Would you prove you are worth it?
If this happened to you,
What would you do?
Would you answer at all?
IF!!
Sarah Xanthos, Grade 12
Flowing Wells High School, AZ

Face Painting

I walk through the gallery
And gaze at the portraits.
Hundreds of faces staring back at me.
Hanging on the walls.
So many expressions
Painted on fresh canvas.
Many created with meticulous care.
Others with strokes of natural skill.
Then some with hurried smears of color.
Yet each expression unmistakable.
I walk through the gallery
And gaze at each familiar portrait.
These faces, these paintings,
Painted by my own hand.
Rachael Alley, Grade 11
Viewmont High School, UT

Ascending

A breeze carried by the sea
Brings itself to her
Passing over her skin lightly
Pulling her close

Embracing her
Who is only eighteen

With two children
And family
Also friends across the sea

Holding tightly
Making her let go
Of the life before

Casting her into the air
Where she grows wings
And ascends
With the breeze
To a peaceful land
Made for joy

Davelyn Reyes, Grade 12
Waianae High School, HI

The Photograph

Photographs
Take you back
White and black
New and old
Some are dull
Some are bold
Some have smiles
Others frowns
Some have children
Act like clowns
Grandmas, babies, friends and fun
Photographs are never done
Laughter, sadness, joy and tears
Memories that last for years.
The photograph.

Gabrielle Bruggeman, Grade 11
Seton Catholic High School, AZ

Erased

I forgot who I was
A long time ago
Who I am I really don't know
I think of Shay
As only mind and body
She's only a memory
She's only a face
The rest of her
I guess was erased

Shay G., Grade 10
Casa Pacifica School, CA

A Beacon of Light

When you look into the eyes of a child,
It is like looking at a beacon of light.
They show us the innocence, love, and future of our world,
Like a looking glass of hope.

They will see and learn so many things as they grow,
With fascination and creation.
Through their eyes, we see the changes to come,
The presidents, artists, teachers, actors, and doctors,
Some parents, athletes, soldiers, or builders.

Their eyes immersed with the colors of the seasons,
Without realizing the impact they have on the future.
Parents guiding them in the right direction,
Witnessing the fire lit in the eyes of their child.
They too were beacons of light, unsuspecting the true meaning of life.

Eyes shining so bright, laughing and playing, their smiles a symbol of light.
Looking into the eyes of a child reminds us of the times of our childhood days,
When we envisioned the world in a different way, beautiful, carefree, and timeless.

As we grow older, our beacons of light tend to burn out and we now view the world,
In a totally different light: stressful, hectic, exhausting, and like time is running out.
Until, we look into the eyes of a child and are reminded of the beacon of light,
Helping to guide us back into the right direction.

Kyle Logan, Grade 11
Sierra Charter School, CA

Wander

Every moment's growing warm but we can never stop getting old
We come out, as is the norm but the nights are never to be cold

I've walked alone through the brush and I stumble upon the sledge
The slab of waste, the reasons laced with crushed dreams on the edge
I decide to stay and concentrate at this place I find a mess
But this could also stimulate quick heartbeats in your chest

But I fear not as I stare across the nature sits below
I see my life not as a loss but now I truly know
That I may be a wanderer, but one more comes up next in line
And now I know where I should go to start this newfound life of mine.

Soon comes another youth to wander just floating as the days go bye.
We bring him in for we don't ponder if he's one of us, never question why.
The last one who completes us the new leader of us all
Unknowingly the biggest heart knowing he'd protect our fall

As we'd do the same for each other never looking back again
We stand as one group never another we are syphistos until the end.
And when it ends we will never part 'cause we'd meet at the edge again
Where the wanderers had their start we won't forget that we are friends

I dare you to find the edge, literally and mentally you can
Walk as one up to the ledge and find another, united you'll stand…

Bijan Shoushtarizadeh, Grade 12
Huntington Beach High School, CA

Not a Love Poem

I won't write a love poem
On the way I think only of you
When I hang longingly from your neck and
You cling to my waist and we lie on the floor, our breath all gone
As our laughter travels on a night that seems to go so fast

I won't write a break up poem
With vivid words of hate and agony
For the maroon in my tears or the blue in my heart
With the cliché revenge and ironic declaration of freedom
Of the way you slit my throat or snapped my ribs or crushed my lungs
Or mostly broke my heart with lengthy lines and clever rhymes
And the nights that seemed to congeal together in snotty tissues and melting, drippy cartons of ice cream

I won't write a sappy sad poem
About the way I miss you, despite what you've done
And the things I long for, of which, you are number one
About the chick flicks I watch and imagine it's you and it's me
Or the way the moon looks all lonely in the sky with all her lonely stars and their lonely song and my lonely sigh
And I'll never admit the secrets I whisper to them
On the nights that seem to drag way too long

No, I won't write a love poem.

Corinne O'Donnal, Grade 12
Merit Academy, UT

Do You Know What It's Like…

My parents woke up, not knowing if they were going to make it through the day. Just a little kid, I didn't know what to say. Went down to the basement for 12 hours of the day, avoiding the barbarians or the "dogs" as they say. Old enough to know what a bomb was but too young to be killed by one. Unfortunately, it is the sound of the bullets that makes the soundtracks to my nightmares. Far away from the battle field, but I can see people's tears, imagine their fears, I cannot. So I cross the border, go to my neighbor, to them we're just ghosts, walking around without souls, Failed our goals and lost our hopes. It's time to start all over, no home, no money. This ain't life, this is poverty. Yeah, I've been there, done that. No food, no clean water, this ain't life, this is poverty. Yeah, I've been there, done that. But do you know what it's like?

Do you know what it's like to look into the eyes of your parents and see fear?
Do you know what it's like to work as a seven year old?
Do you know what it's like to not go to school until you are ten years old?
Do you know what it's like to wake up in the middle of the night and cry for food?

I do, 'cause I woke up one night, walked around in the dark, went to the food basket, nothing but crumbs of bread. An empty stomach, I go back to bed. Nothing to do. I lay and think about the day ahead.
That's not life, that's a tragedy and I know what it's like. Yeah, I've been there done that but, I ain't ashamed of it. 'Cause that's the past and it's over. If all good things come to an end then so do the bad.

You got to keep your head up and never give up. That's no cliché, that's a motto. You got to believe, because in life, you are defined by how well you deal with adversity. I dealt with it and continue to deal with it to this day. Like a soldier, never switching up my colors 'cause I am proud. I am proud to have survived a world where the smoke rises high. Yeah, I am proud to have come from a world where freedom doesn't have a key. Yeah, I am proud to have survived a world where poverty, homelessness, and death are all old news. I know what it's like 'cause I've been there, done that. But you tell me, do you know what it's like…?

Musadiq Bidar, Grade 12
The Athenian School, CA

Lonely Is Routine

He gets out of bed, to take a shower. He looks at the clock, he still has one sparing hour.
So he makes his way to the kitchen. Where to eat a good breakfast is his mission.
He chows down, and says his goodbyes. It's time for reality, minus the long drive.
He rides his bike because he lives blocks away from the school, where being out of shape never felt so cruel.
His life is boring and lonely, some people have no clue. They're too busy lusted in popularity to notice who is who.
So he's in the background, watching everything go by. No place for him in society, no reason for him to try.
And after all the loneliness at school, it's straight back home. Where he gets to wonder in his own drool.
He thinks about this…and he thinks about that. He wonders if he was noticed today or if he was just another gnat.
His mind is filled with visions of his lonely walks in the shadows. Just trying to get noticed but instead he gets even more shallow.
Every day it's a battle to get a glance in his direction. He tries so hard but ends up staring at his own reflection.
Wandering in the quiet, by himself, with no sound in detection.
He knows he's the lonely guy with no life and plans for the future. He needs a wake up call like farmers get from a rooster.
And all he really has is his family and the smile he keeps on his face. He's a bright kid but deep down he's insecure about his place.
And at the same hour of each day life comes bluntly to his senses. It whispers in his ear to live life and to climb over his stresses fences.
He then realizes life isn't just a walk in the park. Its viscous to us all and its got a loud bark.
But he knows that his life will always remain. While he sits in the dark praying to God in vain.

But at the end of the day he's still by himself aching from his empty heart. No happy ending, just time for him to sleep for his routine to restart.

Dominic Gomez, Grade 10
Thunderbird High School, AZ

Don't Forget

When you least expected, it happened.
When you were in search of yourself you found him.
When you were at your highest, it dropped;
As if he had forgotten all about you.
And now you're left to forget about him.
So you question yourself.
Where did we go wrong?
Do you regret ever standing by my side?
You stay up late at night, blaming yourself for once falling in love.
Trying to explain to yourself why he was your priority and you were just an option
So where do you go from here, when you know it hurts you
But you just can't seem to let go.
And you're lost, with no way out and all you hear is silence.
Wishing you could disappear because your world is black and white once again.
And the love you and him once had seems to have been banished all away.
With no return back.
And even though it might never be the same
Your love is like a song, that you hope he never forgets.
And at last all the memories have been burned, all the past is just a lesson that you've learned.

Maria Avila, Grade 11
Animo Leadership Charter High School, CA

Reality

Reality is what it's expected to be,
life without chances without regrets is life with no disgrace,
knowing you could survive in this world with nothing but yourself is a chance we gotta take,
forget those that made you feel like a failure,
ignore those who don't live up to your expectations and hold on to those who you just can't go without,
because one day those who made you fail will embrace the truth,
that your reality was and forever will be better than theirs.

Maria Cortez, Grade 11
John H Francis Polytechnic High School, CA

The Belief of Existence

…But what is believing? Is it something you do?
Something you see? Or something that's you?
Something you know? Or something you feel?
Something that's true, but not really real?

What IS believing? That's a question to answer.
Believing is dancing when you're not a dancer.
Believing is jumping while knowing you'll fall.
And believing is living when you've lost it all.

Believing is hurting and still getting up.
Believing is loving when you've had enough.
Believing is seeing and doing and thinking.
Believing is jumping and falling and sinking.

Believing is simply all that you do.
All that you see, and all that is you.
It is all that is true, that you know, that you feel,
Even if it all is not really real.

Tara Howard, Grade 11
Madison Sr High School, ID

Poetry

Is it an art?
Perhaps, a simple beauty
A way to let it all out
A time to shout for joy
Spreading happiness, sadness, humor or love?
An old language? A new one?
Do you share it with another or hide it deep within?
Will it sway another or perhaps yourself, one day?
Required by your teacher? Love to do some more?
Rhymes and rhythms.
Sounds and slurs.
For a loved one? For a foe?
I don't think I want to know.
So tell me, what is poetry?

Amanda McNeece, Grade 11
Merit Academy, UT

The Amazon

A mazon is filled with **B** ees buzzing
C ausing the **D** ragonflies to dance
E ver so **F** reely.
G orillas **H** aving a gourmet **I** n the trees.
J aguars are jumping
K nowing **L** eopards are leaping
M ating together **N** owhere in sight.
O ver mountains and treetops
P lants are growing **Q** uickly and calm.
R eaching out to the Amazon **S** unsets setting and rising
T ogether the **U** niverse comes as one.
V arious plants and animals **W** elding together
X -citement bringing **Y** ou God's very own creation of a **Z** oo.

Allyson Stowers, Grade 12
Red Mountain High School, AZ

Addictive Love

You're the one that makes me smile.
You're delicate gait makes my thoughts fragile.
My love is a provocation for your desires.
The abyss in your heart has no room for those liars.

Your silence has yet to be golden.
For I can't bear to see your voice get stolen.
Your apathy for love is nothing but an illusion.
Your doubt in love stirs up consternation.

But who cares if romance can't be our catalyst,
In the end, you will always be the true idealist.
I have a fervent thirst for your laughter.
But my desires avert from your stories of disaster.

Our attraction is a gyration that has no ending.
Your refusal, is what you are constantly defending.
Why must your answers always be questions?
Your irrevocable thoughts are your only suggestions.

Zain Madha, Grade 11
Cerritos High School, CA

When You're a Teenager

When you're a teenager, nothing seems to be going well
No one seems to be on your side
Every goal seems to be out of sight

When you're not quite a kid and not quite grown up
You can make bad choices or make good choices
You can either follow the crowd or lead the crowd

When you're in high school
And everyone around you is going in the wrong direction
And no one seems to care
And every day you wonder if you will make it through
You have to stay true to yourself and do what you know is right
Because in the end, that is all that matters

Jennifer Zagorski, Grade 11
La Serna High School, CA

Darkness' Loss

Midnight comes as a dawn of the dark,
Whilst Morning has his own light,
Yet Night comes softly in stillness bleak,
And strikes fear in Morning's bright heart.

Darkness speaks to Night in a whisper,
And causes Morning to redden,
But Morning shimmers with glorious victory,
And sparkles with courage never ending.

So you see, my friend, Morning may have an end,
But Darkness shall always be the latter,
And that, my friend, is all that really does matter.

Sarah Yackey, Grade 11
Temple Baptist Academy, NM

Life Is Better With…

The holder of wisdom
Found in a square
Who might have thought
True knowledge found there

Withered with age
Heavy to hold
Delicate in thy fingers
Wonders behold

Turn back the wall
And one may find
A world of fiction
Truth benign

A moment's insight
The mind's eyes adjust
Images emerge
Vanquish the dust

Seth Miller, Grade 11
Weber Institute, CA

Lonely

As he walks down the street,
In the midsummer's heat,
He looks up to the sky,
Where birds and planes do fly.
So beautiful in flight,
Like many stars at night,
They all stick together,
Birds of the same feather,
But no one's by his side,
He's frequently denied.
Always he is single,
Never has he mingled,
He's crying all night long,
Singing his same old song.
But really who needs them,
All they do is condemn.
They walk around like drones,
He's better off alone.

Alexander Najarian, Grade 10
St Francis High School, CA

Blind

Eyes are cold and glazed over
Skin pale and shivering
Spin the chair, she won't see it
Skies are black, no light shown

Fight to feel colors inside
Lips quiver, showing fear
Hips can be seen from afar
Sight is now within reach

Crysta Tankersley, Grade 11
Pioneer High School, NV

The Insomniac

He lay there gazing into the infinite:
     at intricately forming and dissolving pseudo-dreams
     dancing in His mind.

He lived whole lifetimes in the passing minutes:
     lives of new and old pain laughs and madness
     all washed away by a new wave — gone.

His open eyes saw nothing but singular dark:
     a stage for thought-actors to play
false scenes of hate and love.

and as He laid in the still cradle dark
     His body was shattered sick and feverish
     with restless light.

He wandered the desolate wastes of His being
     as cool darkness tricked out of the world-oasis
     blown away in the shifting dunes ticktickticking.

slowly the hateful sun arose bright-blazing
     illuminated ugly reality and banishing the dream-plays of glamour
     it burned away the stage.

He lay there gazing into the fascist finite:
     trapped in flesh weak and weary. His eyes saw nothing
     but hostile light.

Alex Zhang, Grade 11
Ironwood Ridge High School, AZ

(Tragic) Love

Valentine's Day is coming soon. It makes me feel alone.
But I don't think I'd feel that way if I had a clone.

My clone could be my Valentine, we'd give each other stuff
Like candy hearts and heart-shaped cards, and pink heart-scented fluff.

My clone would be just like me, so I know we'd get along
Because, of course, I'm wonderful: so handsome, smart, and strong.

I love the way I jump about, I love the way I grin,
And when I play monopoly, I love the way I win.

But please don't think I'm shallow, now, I love me for my mind.
I'm brilliant, I'm creative, I'm unique, one of a kind!

My clone, O my true love! O my dearest, can't you see?
There's no one in the world who I love as much as me!

I wish my clone was with me, I wish my clone was near,
I wish my clone existed, and I wish my clone was here.

Alas, there is but one me. I do not have a clone.
And that is why on V-Day, I feel so all alone.

Chandra Bergmann, Grade 11
Valley Christian High School, CA

Past, Future, Present

Up late, thinking how in the world
You
   and
I
Can make each other feel
Like our insides belong in outer space
Like an ocean doesn't seem so vast
And a day seems…
Short
(Yeah that's right. Short)
Up early, marveling how in the world
You
   and
I
have possibly blundered upon the foundations of love
In the many millions of people that make up the world
Up in the middle of early and late, wondering how
You
   can make
"I" (me)
Feel so loved

Farah Schumacher, Grade 12
Mililani High School, HI

One Man's Best Friend Is Another Man's Greatest Fiend

In my home you stay alive
Our neighbors fence, a battle line
Obnoxiously barking from three to five
The neighbor's swimming pool, where you dive
Barbecue invite, they decline
Oh little dog of mine
My constant wonder, how you survive!
The neighbor's backyard, bone shrine
Obnoxiously barking from three to five
Paperboy comes, six o'five,
Their newspaper shredded, very fine
Oh little dog of mine
My little dog, don't you mind?
The neighbor's shotgun is quite fine
Still, obnoxiously barking from three to five
You offer me a little high-five
As you're leg-lifting habit, sends chills up their spines
Oh little dog of mine
A hammer is heard, while we dine
"For Sale By Owner," reads the sign
Still, obnoxiously barking from three to five

Samantha Robison, Grade 12
Layton High School, UT

Snow

The coldness dampens the morning of day.
The soft, frozen earth gives off no warmth yet
Snow glistens — as it drifted slowly set
Is beautiful watching this white array.
This blanket of wonder sent as it may —
Is a gift of truth and promise God set.
Snow is here to enjoy, our pleasure met
To show power through His nature to stay.

The breeze of cold winter is everywhere
The signs of it's coming is again here.
It is something that the weather will share
Though some might see and praise — or see and fear.
He made this world for us with love and care
And shows Himself in His nature near.

Anna Marsh, Grade 10
Calvary Chapel Christian School, CA

Midnight

I am to confess my unique delight:
Look at the cabin by the beach with sand
From a place sky high, a magical land.
And I can see the fire's twinkling light,
When I am part of the dark, dark, dark night.
And I can witness the girl in dreamland
Sleeping as the tides come in strand by strand.
All this in the silent night, I recite.

I see the moonlight, I see the shadow,
I see the remainders of the fire.
It is now midnight, only tides make sound.
The stars all around me shine with a glow
Dawn will come as night will now retire.
I close my eyes, lean back, come back to ground.

Angela Wang, Grade 10
Calvary Chapel Christian School, CA

Returning to Oahu

I can hear the waves lapping up along the shore.
I can feel the energy and warmth of the sun as I bask in its light.
I can sense the beauty of nature all around me.
And when I wake up it's not a dream, it's real.
I would be so happy to be home,
at the beach playing in the waves.
That would be the perfect spring break
On Oahu in the warmth,
Seeing old friends and making new ones,
just being glad to have finally come home.

Trenton Talbott, Grade 10
Orem High School, UT

Amber

Our name on everyone's mind,
The two of us are one of a kind.
The name we share,
Everyone knew me before ever walking in the door.
Twins are we,
Two peas in-a-pod.
You and me,
One and the same.
Blood sisters forever,
Remember — till the end.

Amber List, Grade 12
Wilson High School, CA

Stop, Look, Listen

The slender woman,
Standing
By the tree, tendrils hanging all around,
The wind whipping a silent song,
Smelling
The blossoms blooming in the air,
Looking out at,
The river's banks as blue as the morning sky,
The burning,
Of the sweet sun upon her face.
When the day comes
She'll soon be wed,
And evening so serene,
People she loves all around, wishing her the best.
Walking
Up the aisle,
Looking at the groom.
People stand and stare
Not a word to be spoken,
Until they say I do.

Carri Elder, Grade 12
Pine View High School, UT

Deception

I find it quite hard for me to conceive
Of all objected to things that may change.
I find it quite hard for me to believe
The concepts and words that all must exchange.
But how shall we know when we find the truth
In words that some may perceive as disdain?
If spoken words are then tainted like youth
Used only to express and entertain.
What problems soon revealed by deception
How must we understand what all they mean?
But do not worry about perception
Because to you it will only demean.
Embrace what you have and think of no more
The trouble with words and their waging war.

Akela Oania, Grade 10
Chandler Preparatory Academy, AZ

Vicious Harmony

How sweet the vicious harmony.
Melodic, the clashing cacophony.
Musical discord trips and twirls;
Slipping and twisting bombardments of chaotic liberation.
The brilliant crashing of fortissimo noise
Rumbles and tumbles in a cascade of sound.
It swirls, bends, rushes forward — a tremendous throb
Reaching insanity!
Oh that turbulent, trembling, voluminous sound
Dancing in celebration, salutation, aviation
The barbaric rhythm
The beautiful sparkling tune!

Becky Watkins, Grade 11
Madison Sr High School, ID

The Key

The key to my heart is a priceless gift I own
My Father in heaven gave it to me from His throne
He told me that it can't be lost
But to always remember to count the cost
Before I chose what to do
Should my options be many or should they be few
I thought awhile and then replied
"Father, it's by Your will I wish to abide"
"I know that child, so here's what I'll do
To make the way easy to follow for you
Keep listening to My voice and trust in My word
And with your hopes you'll fly like a bird
And in time you'll know what to do
Because you followed Me all the way through"
When He had finished, I thought long and hard
Then said a thank you and left the yard
And as of today, I still don't know
Exactly which way He wants me to go
But I'll keep following wherever He leads
And always try to do as He heads

Bethany Hadley, Grade 11
South Bay Faith Academy, CA

As Night Falls

The sun has rent his breast
And bled upon the sky and sea
In arching bands he's stained the firmament
And cast a reddish world

The moon has dipped her silver brush
Into the shimmering oceans
And with splendorous strokes traced the image
Of everlasting grace

As I gaze into the sky above
The celestial beauty unfolding
I cannot help but thank the heavens
For giving me this sunset

Sara Rama, Grade 11
Jewish Community High School of the Bay, CA

Seed of Hate

We ourselves have sewn the racism seed
It's grown tall, it has grown high
What we really need is for this to die
And through the course of history
I could see all the hate in front of me
Another way to show that, nothing is make believe
We need to put an end to this
Do not let a victim fall to it
Stand together and rid the problem
If we do something now, there's a chance we can solve them
So come with me
I won't let this be.

Lo Saelee, Grade 12
Prospect Continuation High School, CA

TV

Watching TV I pay a fee,
who pays it, not me.
$25.99 they ask,
25 brain cells they take and never give back.

Who cares if mom calls,
I cannot miss Megatron's fall.
So what if sis has a stroke,
Shopaholic's main character is broke.

Someone help put my legs on the coffee table,
just don't disturb the wires for my cable.
I need help turning the volume to ten,
my finger's too big for the remote button.

I'll pay you ten bucks to make me food,
I must see Bella ride with the biker dude.
Movies over, and nothing good on,
I should go sleep.
I could see the sun,
it's about to come up.

Brain to life, brain to life.
Status: battery low,
signal lost.

Angiealina Tiaseu, Grade 10
Home School, HI

Classroom

There are the people in the classroom
that you see every other day
The ones that make you crazy
or the ones that brighten up your day

There are the people in the classroom
who may be smarter than you
or the ones who don't pay attention
but excel at everything they do

There are the people in the classroom
who are shy and undemanding
or the people loud and bright
but still they are understanding

There are the people in the classroom
and not just the students too
there's the silly outrageous teacher
who participates too

There are the people in the classroom
who groan at the sound of homework
or the nerds in the front who want more
and who makes me want to go berserk
There's the people in the classroom you can't help but love

Kelsey White, Grade 11
Encore High School for the Performing Arts, CA

Goes to Show

Irritated at what?
The world may never know.
So many questions and no answers,
Sometimes it just goes to show.
I'm mad at the world
But don't quite know why…
Can somebody tell me?
So angry about to cry
Friends? No such thing.
Love? Non-existing
Respect? Only for a few
Mother of mine?
The best in the world
Through my lifetime has always been there for me
Father of mine?
Nothing but a coward
I guess sometimes it just
Goes to show…

Norma Romero, Grade 11
Wilson High School, CA

I Don't Understand

I don't understand
Why people can't be friends
Why people fight
Why they don't listen to other people
But most of all
Why I'm always thinking about you
Why I'm falling in love with you
Why I get so excited to see you
Why I'm scared to let you know what I feel about you
What I understand most is
Why I get nervous when I'm with you
Why I don't talk much about my life with you
Why I get this really cute feeling when you smile
Why I think we will be together someday you and me.

Lupita Sanchez, Grade 10
Preston High School, ID

The Wound That Doesn't Heal

I look into her eyes;
They glisten like shining stars.
Sadly it's not happiness.
It's the sign of tears;
her tears trickle down her face.
Her knees slowly begin to buckle.
She falls into my arms,
Weeping and moaning.
My mind is boggled.
Then it hits me;
Another has broken her heart.
I wrap her in my arms.
The only words that come out of my mouth are,
I'm here for you.

Austin Price, Grade 10
Orem High School, UT

The Disguise

How am I constantly searching
For a trace of meaning
You tell me I have to "be better, constantly better"
Your strong high standards
Hidden in my mind.
I'm pretty, I'm smart, I'm modest
But why does it feel like
There's clogged chlorine in my brain
With deathly pesticides.
Now I can't dress up in pink dresses, tightly bounded bows
I can't please the Ivy League
Disappointment from you, I have to sow
Doomed to be in a disguise
To be only a part, a percentage
Of those pretentious perfect minds
All this was wasted time!
It was to please you,
But to lose me.

Kayla Niu, Grade 11
Ironwood Ridge High School, AZ

Summer's Tryst

So long as men can breathe or eyes can see
Or my own hands can write another word,
So long my tongue is able to run free
And all my words are able to be heard,
I shall love thee. In all the binds and chains
The language is subject to, I shall sing
In whispers to thine ears my own refrains
Of happiness that makes thee everything.
So long as thou shalt draw a laughing tear
Or fall into this breast that holds my heart,
Thou art my joy, my mind, my lady dear.
And in this act shall we two play the part:
The tenderness that makes the whole earth ours
And the love that moves the sun and stars.

David Lee, Grade 12
West Ranch High School, CA

Superhero

You orbit around my heart
Like you were Superman
Keeping it from falling apart
Something I cannot ban
My heart wakes up to your smiling face
Like you were some kind of super human
You make my heart race
If you go crazy I will still be holding your hand
You are the superhero of my world
You keep me by your side
The way you make my head twirl
No need to run and hide
There is no way you are a zero
You are my SUPERHERO

Sara Sidwell, Grade 11
Preston High School, ID

My Brother

The few, the proud, my brother
A marine like no other
Trained for months at a time
Each day working and progressing to his prime

Stationed in a modern day hell
You can see where one, two, three marines fell
Under fire from the enemies shell
He may die from what he can tell

Back at home he is a hero
Yet in his mind he feels like a zero
Because of the blood on his hands
Left over from those war torn lands

I'm filled with pride
That I cannot hide
For my brother, a marine

Jordan Magyar, Grade 10
Cypress High School, CA

Spring

As winter starts to disappear,
The snow starts to melt from the ground,
The dark gray sky fades as the blue appears,
Then the world knows that spring is coming around.

The first flower of spring blooms,
The grass and trees turn a bright shade of green,
As beautiful rays of light fills up the room,
Then sweet spring starts to show.

We start to awaken from winters sleep,
As our energy starts to arrive,
We start to see springs wonderful sight,
Spring makes us glad to be alive.

Eric Nguyen, Grade 11
Valley Christian High School, CA

Perfect Memories

When I look at our pictures the memories flood in
Back to when our story begins
I look in your eyes, and you know what I see?
I see where I want to be for eternity
There in your arms, I felt safe and warm
My lips told you secrets that my heart had formed
You touched my face, and gently you stared
You kissed me softly, and I knew that you cared
You pulled me in closer, and you whispered in my ear
"I'll be waiting by our hammock in two short years"
You tucked my hair behind my ear, and we began to dance
Staring into each others eyes, that was true romance
I keep thinking to myself, how lucky could I be
That this amazing, perfect guy would take a chance on me

Amber Geddes, Grade 12
Preston High School, ID

The Death of a Dream

I know how it feels to dream, for I once did.
I once aspired to be the greatest there was, but aspiring is never enough.
Fame, fortune, and prosperity were once mine, but that was when I dreamed.

I used to have knowledge as fathomless as the sea,
And friends as numerous as the sands of its sun-baked shores, but that was when I dreamed.
Oh, I know how it feels to dream, for I once did.

My dreams were to me a solace from reality; a place where true happiness was found.
But that was when I dreamed. My dreams were as invincible as me, my stronghold in times of despair.
Yes, I know how it feels to dream, for I once did.

There are no more dreams. No more fame, fortune, or friends.
I now have no place for which to reside in times of remorse and despair.
My dreams were murdered in cold blood by greed, malice, and bias.
My soul was buried with my dreams.

Do not dream, for dreams are not meant for this world.
The grandeur, fame, fortune, and prosperity; the friends, knowledge, and happiness of dreams…
Are no match for reality.
I know how it feels to dream, for I once did…

Luke Plaizier, Grade 11
Viewmont High School, UT

The Ties That Bind

Displace the promises that were never kept and drown them in the tears that I forever wept.
Burn the images of the life once endured, let go of the heartache that will never be cured.
Release the memories that haunt my soul and leave them to perish in a disillusioned hole.
Relinquish the tears that wouldn't stop, purge me of the wounds that have yet to rot.
Unhinge my heartstrings which were selfishly torn, forget the wretched joke which was the day I was born.
Wash away the lasting pain, relieve myself of the unjust blame.
Abandon my sad and tortured past and of the love once thought would last.
Deprive the ones who beg for redemption, maybe my words will force their attention!
Reminisce no longer, suffer no more, because my words are not merely an articulative lore.
They are the truth, an endless truth, listen to them I pray, for fear that I will die and will no longer be left to say;
these misfortunes I experienced were in no shape or form kind, raped with the travesties of corruption and of lies.
Keep thine demons away for my spirit they will find, keep your ignorant perception for I'd rather go blind.
Your eyes, are they saddened or are they dry from the horrors you hear which are drunk with rhyme?
These words you hear which are in no way kind, do they come from a mad mind, a mind that of which could only be mine? No!
These words come from a pure and lucid mind, because I cut away the ties that bind!

Cruz Moore, Grade 11
La Quinta High School, CA

The Minority

I young Mexican American who comes from the city of Lennox
I attend a school full of minorities
Yet at the young age of 16 have already fallen into the minority stereotype
Ruben my son already going on a year is starting to walk
Day in day out I sit and think of what path I will walk through to take my young one out of the ghetto
I love to play baseball, hoping that, that will be my way out
Will I make or will I not?
If I don't at least I know I tried and set the expectations for the younger generations higher than it was.
I am a rose who grew from the concrete
I am the underdog, the "THUG" one who will make something out of nothing.

James Barraza, Grade 11
Animo Leadership Charter High School, CA

Gratitude

I'm going to bed with little on my mind, been at work all day and people weren't too kind. Plug in the iPod and try to relax but there's still that awful pain in my back! Finally I begin to doze off, forgetting my day and the problems aloft. Hoping to have a really good dream, thoughts in my mind of what it will be. Then the picture appears, crystal clear.

Everyone around me is wearing black. Standing in a line, I'm afraid to look back. I finally do and I'm upset that I did, how could this happen? He's only a kid. I burst into tears, how can this be? My little brother's just barely thirteen. I put a hand on his face; it's hard as stone. People all around, but I feel so alone. Looking for my family, and I see my dad, shaking his head and folding his hands. My mom is sitting; she can't bear to stand. Realizing she'll have to put her son in the ground.

Terminal illnesses all end the same. It's not by chance, but predetermined fate.
We knew this would happen and had for years. That didn't stop the sadness and tears.

Moments later I awake in my bed, sweat and tears, I hope he's not dead. I rush into the hall and up the stairs. Repeating, repeating my silent prayer. I get to his door and open it a crack, I see him asleep, snoring on his back. Slowly I drop to the floor, and I'm crying once more.

I won't waste my time, his life I'll enhance.
Thank you God, for my second chance.

Erin Gates, Grade 11
Woods Cross High School, UT

This is Me

Surely everything in this world deserves a decent amount of respect and kindness.
Even though I am forever bound to roam the rough earth,
the wonderment of the magic in the sun, moon, and sky forever transfix me.
If those shining orbs of crisp gold and that window of beautiful sapphire were so lovingly painted high in the heavens,
Surely, drops of paint must have fallen from the artist's canvas, glistening down into earth.
Perhaps, by wind or rain they failed to scatter here in this treacherous jungle.
Perhaps, this is why neither respect nor kindness abounds.
When others look at me,
Although they don't truly see,
They race away with hearts and pulses thudding, so quickly that all that remains are
torn green brush and quickly fading prints in the ground.
Am I truly that revolting, so disgusting?
Does my limb-less body frighten them?
Or is it my dry, scaly viridian skin that blocks their vision?
I am so much like them,
Constantly changing skins,
Ceaselessly trying to fit in and rise up,
Instead of crawling and slithering below.

Chanelle Dayrit, Grade 11
Palos Verdes Peninsula High School, CA

Of Myself

On days when I've nothing to do, or need an escape, I find myself retreating to a small tree house where I can peacefully savor every moment while others continue at their irrationally fast pace. Here time stops, and I can do as I may on any whim which so moves me. This is a land where spontaneity is the norm and where dreams live. I bear testament to the existence of this land with my scepter of creativity, my pen. My pen can capture the elusive thought by use of the written word or illustration. She allows me to open the floodgates of my mind, and let the spirits whom I house to roam free. The mind turns inside out, and the imagination is imprinted on the physical world where they are seen as exotic creatures. If only men were to pause for a moment, they would find that these children of mine are ordinary, and that each mind has a set of its own.

Michelle Montrose, Grade 11
Grossmont High School, CA

Family

Who is my family, I don't know
Too many different people
Too many different ideas
One world, different aspects

Who is my stepfather, I don't know
I see him every day, I don't know
Is he like I think, who knows
He is what I see, could be

I think of my sister, I don't know her
Is she happy like I think?
It is her life, and I don't know
If I see her, I probably cry

Where am I, don't know
What is my life, I am going.
Alicia Miguel, Grade 10
Pioneer High School, NV

Summer Rises, Summer Calls

Summer Rises, Summer Calls.
The morning comes, faces fill the halls.
In the quad, people all around
By my friends, I am found.
And Summer Rises, Summer Calls

Class begins with work and all
Learning is the student's duty call.
Wishing their brains could go to sleep,
Teachers pack the work on deep
And Summer Rises, Summer Calls.

The bell rings; students wait near the halls
And run quickly, for the summer calls:
It is time to go have fun, and nevermore
Shall homework bore,
As Summer Rises, Summer Calls.
Carmen Farhat, Grade 11
Valley Christian High School, CA

Winnie the Pooh

My love,
Where are you?
My honey,
I long for your tenderness.
I yearn for your velvety sweetness.
Descending in
An amber cascade,
You alleviate
My longing.
You are my amber mistress.
You are my saccharine consort.
Oliver Dam, Grade 12
St Joseph Notre Dame High School, CA

Life Is a Playlist

I wish my life was controlled by a DJ, controlling the beat with a light touch.
Simple enough to maneuver, simple enough to comprehend, but harder than double dutch.

I wish that choices were easy as scrolling through a list and picking it with bliss
For every scratch and fade is the same as every time and day I reminisce.

Hoping that every step I take is as easy as dancing to the beat.
Downloading my friends and settings to life like creating a verse with a music sheet.

Cross fading from song to song is another transition from event to event.
Remixing my song, my life, to the rhythm of the music, it gives me a feeling of content.

Slowly changing the pitch and speed to adhere to the sound of our choice.
Turning the bass higher, helps me fill in the monotone parts of my voice.

Effects show my characteristics, as they begin to unwind when the beat drops combined
With those moments in life that I will always remember, are on an endless loop in my mind.

Life runs itself track by track, and for the first time good and bad won't have irony.
Music simply molds my life and universe together in immense harmony.
Timothy Nguyen, Grade 10
Cypress High School, CA

Books, Books, Books

Sitting in a classroom
Reading aloud like a monotone goon;
One tone, no emotion, total blandness —
How can you stand this absolute madness?
These beauties are to be read with full vigor,
Utter emotion like exuberance, anxiety or fiery anger.
A book is good for the soul;
It teaches us how to act in scenarios we can't control.
A book is where I go when my real life isn't satisfying.
When I want more, when I'm greedy, when it's all that I'm desiring,
It is my confidant; it relaxes me and never gets sick of me.
It has no criticism, no outright arguments, and doesn't act like a nasty-she;
It acts as constructive entertainment, enriching the brain and soothing the mind.
It makes you aware of things you've never seen; for no longer are you blind.
I love books, regardless of what people say;
For they have shaped me into the person that I am today.
Leslie Tay, Grade 10
Bradshaw Christian High School, CA

One Window

One window is all I need
To show my inner soul, my darkest dream
My hidden desire shed through the light of a fire

One window is all I need
To be myself, to show my feelings
To dance and to sing, even if off-key

One window is all I need
To show others the true me
Kayla Parnin, Grade 11
Preston High School, ID

Waiting

Today is a special day.
The one I have been waiting for.
Sitting at my desk I silently pray.
Oh, how I can't wait anymore.

Anxiously I look all around.
Over here and over there.
Wondering where you'll be found,
With your perfect face and crazy hair.

I see you in the corner staring off into space.
And I silently wonder with a smile.
What're you thinking with that smirk on your face?
Is it something worthwhile?

Please turn around and share your secrets with me.
Share your secret world with me.
Lady-Lyn Dasmarinas, Grade 10
King Kekaulike High School, HI

Grandpa

Every day I think about you
and think that just a year ago you were gone
the tears still flow
but my heart beats slow
I always think maybe you'll be back
but there's no use of that
I love you so much
but I know I'll never feel your touch
without you in my life I feel something
but I'd rather feel nothing
if it meant for the heartache to go
I will never forget seeing you on the hospital bed in peace
the feeling I had was so horrible
but you always told me I was adorable
you'll always be somewhere special in my heart
but your memory will never depart
I miss you Grandpa you're my everything
Adeanna Sturdivant, Grade 11
Encore High School for the Performing Arts, CA

Pretending

You show people what they want to see
You never show them how you feel
When you feel sad, unwanted, dark inside
You show them what they want to see

You are fake to them and to yourself
Pretending to be happy, when you're lonely
Like an actor cleverly playing his role
You show people what they want to see

Stop pretending and show your true side
Show them how you really feel and not what they want to see
Cynthia Rojas, Grade 10
Delano High School, CA

Success

The key to a happy life is maintaining trust,
Having this trust is a definite must.
People just desire to feel accepted no doubt,
And when you're rejected don't cry or pout.
Take this rejection as an opportunity for learning.
Try to succeed again and you'll subside your inner burning.

The feeling of success makes a caged man feel free.
Departing life's distractions brings successful men pain,
Often from these distractions, knowledge is to gain.
Success will result from valuing yourself,
To be successful never put your values on the shelf.

When life gives you lemons, what can you do?
Be sour like lemons or make lemonade and pull through.
Success is discovered by overcoming inner frustrations.
Surpassing these struggles reveals true determination.

Problems in life frequently overload you with stress,
Finding solutions to these problems will guide you to success.
The game of life is portrayed as one giant struggle,
Becoming successful reveals the key to this puzzle.
Jon Sanders, Grade 12
Diamond Ranch Academy, UT

Steven

I told myself no,
You broke me without any effort.
I didn't want anything from you,
Now I see everything in you.
I'm honestly afraid,
I see potential.
I fear loss.
I want to make you mine,
I want you to call me yours.
As I pour my heart out I can't help but wonder,
What are your intentions of this all?
The other girls that want you,
Make me want you more.
Jealousy of hers will drive me harder,
I have become determined because of more than a few things.
You'll have a name with me soon. Count on it.
Kathryn Creekmore, Grade 12
University Preparatory School, CA

My Beacon

Cracking twigs beneath your toes,
Feeling the breeze continually flow.
With the river you feel your problems floating away.
Without nature I would not be functioning as I am today.
Majestic beauty, hidden always in plain sight.
Heaving itself upon our lives no matter how we may fight.
Embrace the beauty, let it cradle your soul.
Without this blessing I may have already let go.
Cheyenne Rinne, Grade 11
California High School, CA

The Curtain Has Closed

The curtain has closed,
The play of emotions is gone.
There will be no encore.
No bowing or applauding.
No, the main act in life has
    forgotten its lines.
And I'm left with just me.
I could be anything,
I could be nothing.
Furious, excited,
Depressed, or hysterical.
Whatever it is,
You can't see it.
Because I'm closed,
Shut down,
Locked away,
Hiding.
I can't hide forever,
But for now,
It will have to do.
Adriana Diaz, Grade 10
Orem High School, UT

Light Fills My Eyes

Light fills my eyes
Perception never dies
Through life it may change
Even seems so strange

Beauty that fills the sky
Life I would not exchange
Take life's first flight
To the road of possibilities to be rearranged

My distorted eyes
Seemed to lie
Not to me
To the person everyone wants me to be
As the light fills my eyes
Dennis Wahl, Grade 12
Pioneer High School, NV

Herd Mentality

Hooves beat the ground,
    tails held high,
All of these mustangs proud,
    as morn turns to night.
Listen to the mares and foals,
    whinny, whine and neigh.
they roam the dusty prairie,
Free, independent and fierce,
they gallop and prance so gently,
    it's obvious they are free.
This is the herd mentality.
Alannah Leavitt, Grade 10
Orem High School, UT

Being

It is dark.
One timid foot tip taps after the other,
Playing an unsure game of "Follow the Leader."
My eyes flutter open and close, seeking light
Even if it is just the briefest, dimmest flash.
    Tip —
            Tap —
    Tip —
            Plick!
The tender flesh of my fingertips taps metal.
I blink, "Huh?"
I give an experimental push
And something shakes.
I shove…
Falling through a door, entering the universe.
Plummeting by Saturn's rings, submerging into a pool of stardust,
I spot something bright, precious —
Something that has lasted for centuries and centuries and centuries to come.
The sun's gentle flames caress my being, sinking me into exquisite, toasty warmth.
I open my eyes, grinning.
It is bright.

Kristen M. Mesa, Grade 11
Schurr High School, CA

You're Gone

You're gone
where do you go?
When the smoke dehydrates your lungs and poisons your veins.
Do you walk amongst the devil?
Do you hide from your fears?
Where do you go?
When you intoxicate your intelligence and seal away your heart.
Do you burn your angels wings? Do you envelop the habits of a liar?
Where were you?
When my walls were falling down and I was drowning in my tears.
Were you laughing in the glass mirror of fake happiness?
Were you forcing yourself to believe I never existed?
Where were you?
When I gave myself to you and you burned away the best part of me.
Were you in a dream so tainted you actually believed I was beautiful?
Were you lost so far in the depths of your mind your forgot the law of humanity?
Where do you go?
Where were you?
Where are you now?
You're gone, you're gone, you're gone.
A stranger with no existence.

Madison Fawcett, Grade 12
Pine View High School, UT

Frightful Insecurities

It's simply Life. It's not an intricate word but behind that word is something you will definitely face for the rest of your years to live.
People talk rich, people talk happiness, people talk success,
Where do I fit in? Will I ever fit in?
I let them fall, but you can't see these tears because I am my only comfort.
I'm no genius, just human; having that bleeding pain in your gut every day thinking will I ever make it? Kills me,
With nobody to run to, nobody to cry to, nobody to complain to, my inner soul cries more in search of that security and happiness.
I feel alone. I am alone.
A young adult with 16 years in this universe, what have I really learned about life?
The fact that you're not always happy,
The fact that it's intimidating,
The fact that you must burn your eyelashes out in order to make it,
The fact that screwing up will screw you over,
The fact that money is always the issue, yes, nobody ever said that life was easy but then why does everyone seem so happy except for me?
Am I missing something? Who knows?
It frustrates me to know that I'm not good enough,
Every day I feel as if I fall deeper into this black hole we like to call "life"
But that one day I thirst for will come soon, I hope.

Mayra Rodarte, Grade 11
Animo Leadership Charter High School, CA

It's Just Me

It is 10:00 in the night, my eyes are still wide open.
I fear to go sleep and hold my bear tight.
I don't want to live a dream full of happiness and have to wake up and face a complicated world that is not right.
Been there done that, heard this heard that.
No difference.
Life is dangerous, people can poison you
You can cry or you can die or just survive.
This world is full of missions, full of problems that make me feel this fear. Then again I want to wake up because it's my world, because it is me, my life and only mine.
Not yours, not hers, not his, just mine.
I will ignore you or her or him unless you're right.
Unless you can prove me wrong. My life is not perfect and it will never be.
I am human and I make mistakes but I move on. I have my ups and downs
and I should always keep my head up. I now feel the fresh air blowing through my hair. I am now enjoying life like there is no tomorrow, we live it once. My happiness will leave you speechless
Reasons for my happiness are, I stay in my bubble, you will not burst it.
In other words I live in my own little world. And one day your life will flash, before your eyes make sure it is worth watching.
The way mine did.

Gennesis Tamayo, Grade 11
Animo Leadership Charter High School, CA

Loyalty

Loyalty is the Virtue of the strong willed and brave
Loyalty is what you are to those close to you
Those who remain loyal through thick and thin are those true few that are there no matter what
Those whose loyalties change on whims and wishes will be hard pressed to find themselves at peace with their lives
To remain Loyal is what one must do to keep those chosen few close and Loyal in turn
As long as you are Loyal you will find happiness as well as find yourself on the right path for your life
Always Loyal

Calvin Anthony Ruiz, Grade 10
Arcadia High School, AZ

Quiet

I'm quiet. Often.
Quiet in my room on my bed,
Letting my mind swirl like the ends of my hair
As it sprawls against my pillow.
I listen to my heaving sighs
Of a contented mind.
My sighs of big "hhhmmmmmssss"
That reverberate in my chest
And breaks some of the quiet in my heart.
The simplest sound.
The most beautiful music.
Like guitar strings echoed against walls.
My mind
Spirals and sprawls
And I keep quiet for that.
Quiet to fulfill the empty bowl inside my chest
That is the soul.
It's with great bravery that I speak.
With quiet,
I retreat to safety.

Maricela Guardado, Grade 11
Los Angeles County High School for the Arts, CA

Scars

Sitting by my window I glance at my feet
Worn and scarred from everything they have carried me through
Burns from ice packs, scratches from braces
Gashes from rocks, and marks left from my stitches
Previous battles overcome or lost
Every single mark on my body
Right down to the freckles
Telling a story of its own
Or a memory lost with time
But both worn to carry as reminders
Of times in the past
Or what I am
Never to lose myself along the way
Encompassing a life that should be lived without fear.
The fear of a scrape or the fear of what is to come
I carry the scars along to keep in mind
What I was
What I am
And what I will be
Without forgetting me.

Lauren Arnzen, Grade 12
New Plymouth High School, ID

Rest on Wings of Caterpillars

Beside the winding path their lay a grove
of trees that nestled inside of its trove
was bounty that life would change to beauty
and would through its metamorphosis free
the little one from its callous cocoon
so it could fly up to the sun and moon
and learn the secrets of all space and time.
Teach me O wise one of air, hear the pine
that walks forth boldly from trembling lips,
soft lips that seek to tell of what we missed.
For none attain your stature, you alone
are crowned the Monarch upon the sky's throne
You have mastered this Earth. You will fly
until the sad day that you too will die.
Yet death to you is naught but a false road
for in the eternal is your abode.
Teach me O Monarch, raise me from the sod,
teach me to turn from a worm into God.
I would go to the grove and be a lord of the air,
but somehow I doubt that the grove is still there.

Matthew Horner, Grade 11
Iolani School, HI

Not Just Now

Before I lie down,
I've never had horchata.
Tomorrow will you get me some? No —
today is a good time to start
everything we said we'd do
right?
Now we've got forever to
endeavor:
so much time to
start, right?

But what about sunset?
End of day, a
faceless denial for every
observation we wanted to make.
Ridiculous to think things really must end

And before their time — lives
grabbed up against their will.
Easy to accept when it's not happening to you.

Chloe Madison, Grade 12
Encore High School for the Performing and Visual Arts, CA

Why Do You Judge Me So?

Why do you judge me so?
Have you ever lived my life?
Spent one moment in my loneliness?
Have you ever walked in my shoes?
Then tell me why do you judge me so?

Nicholas Porter, Grade 11
Redwood High School, CA

Water

W aves crashing on the shore
A rush like never before.
T eetering in the tide
E nding the day with pride.
R ocks or not, water is in my heart.

Bailey Hopkins, Grade 10
Mililani High School, HI

The Storm

Peak breaks cloud
Storm breaks cloud
At the top a thin wind
Clean wind
Roughs the earth
The mountains stand
The storm stays
Flashes of light
Break the clouds
And more light
Comes crashing down
A sickening crack
Lets loose a wave
Of light, that falls
Burning the cage
Of life
That encases the earth
Releasing it
To climb a peak
And breaks the wet cloud
To bring life

Ryan Pea, Grade 10
Shelley Sr High School, ID

April Lamb

April Lamb slips on her neon pink rain boots and lily pad sun hat
She walks gingerly toward her garden and digs her hands in the soil
So moist and cool, she fantasizes the life of a seed
Submerged in the darkness, pushing its soft slender body out of a hard shell,
Reaching upward to the kaleidoscope sun and the brilliant shimmering moon

Snapping back to reality, she begins to gather her magic paraphernalia into her basket
April embodies a kind of magic that tickles the senses and feeds the soul
She concocts crystallized violets and frosted honeysuckle,
Tulip bulb teacakes and lilac jelly,
Sweet intoxicating aromas consume the air —

One bite of her red rose velvet cake glazed with dark chocolate
Envelopes you with feelings of tenderness and passion
Just a sip of her pumpkin spice tangerine tea
Engulfs you in a state of pure ecstasy
She surfaces emotions so thick you can cut them with a knife
Emotions you thought you'd never feel again

April does more than bake petal pastries,
She restores memories, feelings and hope.

Elmast Kozloyan, Grade 10
Schurr High School, CA

Realization

Smell the chamomile
Filtering through the airways.
We, the trampled twigs,
Converse.
As our cracking amplifies.
Tremulous and shimmering,
The lake saunters…
Waiting, flowing, resiliently caressing
The dipping cormorants
They come, they sit, yet they do not trust,
They pass through
Believing the water
Does not giggle
Or cleverly cackle.
Yet it comes, filtering through the canopies
Touching the drenched waters
Embracing the leaves
Making them green
Creating the shimmer
On lashes
With laughter of lakes.

Gladys Martinez, Grade 12
Mercy High School, CA

Confusion

Always in the race
Perplexed mind in the working
Still knowing little

Ashlyn Mace, Grade 10
Temecula Valley High School, CA

Summer

I awake to the chirping of birds,
sun shining through my window.
I glance at the clock,
9:00 a.m.
I lay my head back down,
no work for the day.
10:30 a.m.
I finally muster the strength to drag myself out of bed.
I walk upstairs to the kitchen to eat the most important meal of the day.
7:00 p.m. rolls around.
Dinner time,
Mom makes my favorite, hamburgers and Tater Tots.
I continue watching movies.
12:00 a.m.
my eyelids slowly slip as I drift off to sleep.
Summer

Jessica Huffaker, Grade 10
Orem High School, UT

True Opposition

Conflicting feelings,
Conflicting thoughts,
Our minds fight on a battlefield of consciousness.
Unable to determine our individual fates, it continues.
Decades pass and the war still rages,
Until our final days it settles on one event.
And as we draw our last breaths we realize the truth:
True opposition lies in ourselves.
And as suddenly as the truth lightens our minds, the light flickers and dies.

Brett Loree, Grade 11
Youngker High School, AZ

Best Valentine's Day Yet

I took a step off her porch, into the cool damp night.
I started walking to my house, with a feeling of delight.

I hadn't driven, for I cannot drive quite yet,
But I am old enough, to know that my feelings are set.

We had just had a long talk, and to me it was surprising,
That I could even walk, and my temperature wasn't rising.

She told me that she loved me, and that she wanted to be with me.
I told her that I felt the same, and she stared at me with glee.

We hugged for, — like eternity, I wouldn't have it any other way.
After she let go of me, I started slowly, on my way.

This day was such a day, as I'd never had before,
And that was when I realized, I would have a whole lot more.

I replayed what happened, and I felt that in a way,
This was by far the best of all my Valentine's days.

Ben Lemley, Grade 10
Orem High School, UT

A Passing of Time

A newborn, ocean sky begins to match the Autumn trees.
Clouds, painted by some unknown being, blush in the warmth.
The bright guardian descends countless rays of light,
covering the land.
A calm wind grows fierce and parts the clouds
to view another world.
The sun kisses the earth,
in their tender embrace they share a short farewell.
When the light departs, a celebration begins:
one to celebrate the setting of one world,
and a dawning of another.
Beings known as Orion and Scorpio,
Gemini and Libra,
illuminate an unknown darkness.
They dance in the night, protecting the world below them.
The guardian once again rises,
Relieving the beings of their duty.
A familiar light returns,
bringing new life,
it starts the cycle again.

Jennifer Serrato, Grade 11
Encore High School for the Performing Arts, CA

Weather

Breezy cold wind flows
Boring skies never fading
Want the warmth and shine

Chantel Cargeeg, Grade 11
Viewmont High School, UT

Late Night Silence

As the dark sets in
noises seem to slow
the busy movements end
and voices become soft and low

The sky is now dark
stars only bring dim light
I am silently sitting on my porch
thinking of the past day that seamed so bright

The silence brings about thoughts
only known when by one's self
the stars seem so distant
as if mere dots

This solitary moment
how peaceful it can be
the decisions set before me
now sit on my mind like sweet bread
with a cup of bitter tea

Ashley Cooper, Grade 10
Oakdale Charter High School, CA

Eternity

dirty feet sliding in brown sandals
a long journey through the woods
sun beating down
so tired
so thirsty
towels flung on bushes
sandals kicked off
glorious hot springs meet sore muscles
babbling ice water rushes past just beyond the rock wall
I watch crazy kids jumping in
coming out refreshed and renewed
as I stand next to the edge uncertainty takes hold
he reaches out his hand
palm up
his blue eyes, so kind, know everything

I am over the wall now in the freezing flow
hesitant and excited
the dip seems to last for an eternity yet it is fleeting
the eternity continues in my soul

Kelsea Breton, Grade 12
New Plymouth High School, ID

Winning at Basketball

Jump up to get balls
When you're playing basketball
So you can slam dunk

Trevor Mertz, Grade 10
Wilson High School, CA

Christmas in the Air

Six days before Christmas
I can feel it in the air
We make a big fuss
And get presents to share

The smell of pot pies
And cake in the oven
Puts a sparkle in our eyes
And fills us with lovin'

After we eat
And open our gifts
We sit in our seats
And watch snow drifts

Once the show is at its end
We get onto our feet
And say bye to our friends
'Til the next time we meet
Jessica Johnson, Grade 10
Shelley High School, ID

I Am

I am cute and quiet.
I wonder when I will see him again.
I hear his voice.
I see his face.
I want to be with him.
I am cute and quiet.

I pretend to be here.
I feel happy.
I touch his heart.
I cry when I remember.
I am cute and quiet.

I understand that he's not here.
I say that I will see him again.
I dream about being with him.
I try to forget with no success.
I hope he's in my future.
I am cute and quiet.
Dalila Carrillo, Grade 10
Shelley High School, ID

Rain Will Dry

shards of shattered rain,
smash against the window, pain

the fire inside,
burns on joy and humble pride

soul will be tried, rain will dry
Westin Porter, Grade 12
Woods Cross High School, UT

Nat Turner: A Slave's Elegy

May the breath of poppies kiss your corpse
And celebrate your freedom
You are freed my brother

Death has no prejudice
The angels have lifted your chains and healed your wounds
You are freed my brother

The God in heaven that will seek damnation to our heathen masters
Has born witness to the hope you have instilled in us
You are freed my brother

Let the white man walk in fear
Let your presence fill every field of the oppressed
Every house of the forsaken
Every heart of the enslaved
And we shall hope that though your life has passed
You soul shall guide us to a time when we shall break the bonds of slavery
And join your soul in its current state
For you my brother
You are free

Alex Dukes, Grade 11
Golden Sierra High School, CA

Invisible Wound

It hurts like an open sore,
Throbbing and bleeding nonstop.
If anyone talks it hurts even more.
Hour by hour my smile continues to drop.

No one truly knows why,
No one really knows who.
They only know I cry,
But can't figure out what to do.

My heart has been broken,
It's laying in pieces, too destroyed to mend.
I wonder why I ended up with this unlucky token,
To not accept the help, people try to lend.

I will tell you who gave me this pain,
The ones who hold the weapon are my friends I thought lucky to gain.
LaReesa Sorensen, Grade 12
Madison Sr High School, ID

Two Hearts That Beat as One

As he walks out the door to defend his country he felt his heart break,
A single tear ran down her face for the war in her heart has just begun,
She wishes time would go back just for love's sake,
He promised her he would come back from war and take her hand,
She remembers the moment they first met and their eyes locked on one another,
Little did he know she just found out she is going to be a mother,
Something in her heart tells her everything will be okay,
The heartbeat in her stomach gives her hope for another day.
Ashlee Gist, Grade 12
Lucerne Valley Jr/Sr High School, CA

Battles

In this empty room our showdown presides
Like two known enemies we circle each other
Sizing up our opponent knowing their weaknesses.
The first move is mine
And I defile your pride
No retaliation instead you study me.

So I lash out again
This time attacking your integrity
No return fire and I am still studied
Once more I strike
This time ambushing your heart
Your weakness shows and I know one more move will mean victory.

Yet I hold back and idolize my work
Amidst my distraction
You begin your assault.
Your moves are small
Barely noticeable
But eventually
I fall.

As your evil grin comes into view
I now realize I am only fighting my reflection.

Shelby Cron, Grade 12
Home School, CA

One Secret

Sweet pieces, your soul hides from others' eyes,
Trimmed with lace, like the flower once in vase.
You wish to keep secret, never to obliterate,
Never to pass lips of steel.

But why do I wish to imbibe?
This one secret you wish to hide.
Am I some being deserving more than I receive
Or do I push patience over into the sea of deceitful fools?

If so, conflagration will consume me,
Skin shall turn dark as coal, bones as charcoal,
Tissue: ash
You may dispatch me to my deplorable death.

But if not, don't be so rash
You will rule my annihilation, with such determination
Your shrouded knowledge will be, trapped in your perception
It may seem miniature to the minister
But to my merit mentality
You may discharge your secret
Tell me, tell me my chum
So you will no longer have sweet pieces
In your soul to be hidden.

Breanna Stockwell, Grade 12
Merit Academy, UT

Papa

— Your old red Baretta
the windows down
Paul is in the front seat, I'm behind you
The blanket you put on the seat is falling
I really don't mind the dog hair on my jeans
— I cried when I thought you couldn't make it
to my concert or my birthday
but you always knew how to turn my tears dry
and make me giggle
I'll always love the way you did.
— I saw you lying in a hospital bed
Your "Hey man" sounded painful
It smelt like sick people, not like Papa
From there, we watched your hair turn gray
and I knew nothing would be the same
— If you were here now, you'd wipe my tears
I'd throw my arms around your neck
the smell of your cologne would be bitter sweet
I will never forget your love I can't
and I will always miss the way your kiss felt
on my cheek when you didn't shave.

Corine Bender, Grade 11
Twentynine Palms High School, CA

The world around me

The human mind is like a baby.
Always observing something new.
You think you know it all and then,
you find something new.

The world is like a rose,
it can be a beautiful place,
but sometimes the world is a cautious place.

I believe to never back down.
This is my truth because I,
always do what I say,
I live my life as an adventure.

It is important to do what
you think is right and what you believe in.
Power lies within my world and my mind.

Kathy Carreon, Grade 11
Animo Leadership Charter High School, CA

Gone

How can one be so close but yet so far?
You give your heart and soul one day,
and then the next day it's like it didn't count.
It's all uncalled for;
Everything is gone: your true love,
your heart, your better half, everything gone forever...

Cindy Gonzalez, Grade 11
Orem High School, UT

If I

If I were gone would you miss me?
Here one second and gone the next.
Would you cherish the moments?
Our life is short and like the fog,
Hold on to the memories...

If I was no longer yours,
Would you feel pain and cry?
Or would you let the feeling die?
Would you care if I walked away?
Would you want to rewind to yesterday?

If I was no longer with you,
Would you consider me at loss?
Only time can tell,
If our paths will again cross.
If I was gone would you realize something was wrong?

If I said good-bye would you stop me?
Would you try to hold on to what we have?
Today our love is all we can see,
But we can't be blind to reality... good things end.
And in an instant, in a breath, we've lost a friend.

Ericela Ruiz, Grade 11
Connecting Waters Charter School Modesto Learning Center, CA

A Tree

I am a tree
Towering over all
Yet reflective and still
I yearn for the sun
But my life comes from rain

When I'm pulled
My branches break
But my feet remain still
That branch I'll give, that branch you'll take
For in life and death, a new branch will fill

When the harsh winter comes
And it comes down to naught
My leaves fall, my disguise lost
My soul naked in thought

When the sun comes again
A disguise I may wear
Of beauty and grace
Of humor unfair
But if you really, truly look at me
I am only a tree

Ethan West, Grade 12
Glacier High School, MT

I've Never Been to the Moon

What makes me different?
Why am I special?
I've never been to the moon
or signed the Declaration of Independence.

I didn't fly the first plane
or deliver presents to every good child in one night.
I've never eaten my weight in chocolate
or dug to the center of the Earth.

I wasn't the one who invented the light bulb,
and I definitely couldn't end world hunger.
But, I have flipped a burger before.
I hope that you will hire me.

Nicole Smith, Grade 10
Orem High School, UT

Here I Lie Because I Am Weak

Here I lie as life passes
Because I am weak I do nothing to stop it
Time goes on while I stand still
Only growing older, never any wiser
Here I lie wishing this away
Because I am weak I only sit
How I wish it would leave me alone
But here it is and stays forever
Here I lie cold and alone
Because I am weak I ask no one for help
Time is the enemy and I am powerless against it
It creeps by as I try to crawl
Here I lie
Because I am weak

Stephanie Bryant, Grade 11
Viewmont High School, UT

The Feeling of Music

Your instrument
Who you are, how you sound
The way you choose to express yourself
The notes flow through you out through your fingers
Music fills the room at your command
It reaches people's ears and they feel how you feel
You tell them with distinct dynamic and articulation,
and when you're done playing,
you leave an echo not only in the room,
but in the hearts of your audience
They applaud in approval and you feel complete
You feel the feeling of love without a lover,
and this is why you are a musician.

Lindsey Bellefeuille, Grade 11
Encore High School for the Performing Arts, CA

Self-Pity Is Self-Destruction

I just realized here I am looking down on
myself. Literally living off my own self-pity.
Drowning myself with my memories of all the people
who have hurt me. I was literally sitting in a pool of
my own self-pity.

Me that's all I seem to think about. I spent so
much time just thinking of things to drown myself
with and reasons why the whole world should feel
sorry for me. I realize I seem to have forgotten why
people wanted to hurt me.

It was because all my life I took on a role of
protecting people. The very people who later turned
their backs on me. Everything I went through was for
a good cause.

I was standing up for people who had long lost
their own voice. I protected them and I built them
up. I stood with them and sometimes when it got hard
I carried them through it.

Now that I remember I can hold my head up
high and live my life with now knowing that if I
could go back in time I would change nothing.

Offiong Effiom, Grade 10
High Desert Academy of Arts & Sciences, CA

Life of the World

In this world so full of chaos and hate
I close my eyes to clear my mind
And remember the good before it's too late
Our souls are taken and we're forever blind
The days of happiness are lost and forgotten
What's left is a sorrow that will always remain
And never again will we stand as men
But cowards too weak and afraid to bear the pain
We hide ourselves alone in the dark
To escape the creature lurking outside
Faces full of fear have lost their spark
Memories of better days lost in the tide
They'll just wait for the end to waste away
No more pain on their face or light in their eye
Alone in this world no longer will they stay
The end is here, time to say good-bye.

Ashley Wilde, Grade 12
Pine View High School, UT

Wish

I wish I was your skin, so I could hold you forever.
I wish I was the world around you, so I could take your breath away.
I wish I were your lungs, so I could give you a breath of fresh air.
I wish I were your coat, so I could keep you warm on cold days.
I wish I were your heart, so when you go so will I.
I wish I was your boyfriend so I could make you happy
My wish came true

David Kaeding, Grade 12
Salisbury Continuation High School, CA

You Without I

You without I,
A hand touching mine.
Eyes on my face, filled with undeserved desire.
Imperfections and flaws,
You leech to them with lovers vigor.
I sit.
Longing, adoring, grasping, for you.
No light pierces the darkness
Until, your witty phrases.
I sit. Indifferent.
Why don't I long for you always?
Why only sometimes?
Is it my heart or mind telling me not to adore you,
Not to beg you for your crimson words.
Turmoil, like an ashen beast.
Numbing my soul. I sit. Finished.
Done with wondering.
You without knowing,
The melodrama of I.
Blissful in your ignorance.
Friends and lost lovers, you and I stay.

Sarah Ashcraft, Grade 12
Merit Academy, UT

You Can't Fail

What would you attempt if you knew you could not fail?
The possibilities are endless
Times only a figment of your imagination
The fear of failure will no longer…
Gnawing at my insanity
Something like a ruthless disease
I seek for my demise
In this time of need
Where do I hide?
Do I fall or do I fail?
A mislead success
Attempting to do the rest
Going up against the best
This is what I'll attempt to do
I walk away knowing I cannot fail
Hoping tomorrow will be a better day to prevail

Tessie Dominguez, Grade 10
Silver High School, NM

Melt Me Away

Like candy dwindles away on my tongue,
As ice-cream is melting in the heat of the sun,
Like snow evaporates from the ground,
As the uranium core melts in an atomic power plant,
Like solid is reduced into fluid state in tons,
In times is exactly what to my burning heart,
You have done.

Lisa Anna Maria Meyer, Grade 11
Merit Academy, UT

Requiem

The gray sky weeps, bathing the bloodied earth with her tears,
Washing away the stains of red from the trampled turf.

A banner flutters in the cold drizzle, the only movement
As it is clenched in the dead hands of the flag bearer.

A sigh, a guttural groan, an agonized cry of inexpressible fears:
These are the sounds of the figure that stirs on the cold turf,
His hands reaching, yearning to find something lucent;
But his eyes are burned, sightless orbs that now weep and fester.

Yea, he seems yet to be the only survivor of this bloody battle;
And, despite his sightless eyes, life gives him the face of an angel.

But his groans are as a dirge, a final croon to those who lie dead.
Aye, and as a croon it bears the weight of all the vain bloodshed.

No more can his eyes see the light; a small blessing in such pain.
His breath slows and his eyes shut, bringing in the darkness.
Ah, and as the darkness of the mind encroaches again,
So comes cold relief that no more will he live life so grievous.

Jeanette Nadeau, Grade 11
Home School, UT

Winter Winds

The days have become so cold since you left.
Now I stand as stone as cold as the winter winds.
With shaking hands, tearful eyes, and a broken heart.
The blistering, heart-wrenching wind on my naked back.
Like needles as sharp as the ice holding my heart hostage.
My once hot red blood now frozen as the frosted ground on my feet.
A knife's penetration that seems eternal.
Like a bite from a wild beast so sharp, and aggravating.
As I lie my head to sleep I see your face.
I am overwhelmed with happiness.
Back to the warm summer days when you hold me.
The look in your eye warms the ice from my frozen heart.
I feel the way I have always missed.
And then it is gone as fast as it comes just as it always does.
Back to the lonesome cold, hard stone I have become.
Just waiting for the day that we can be together again.

Billy Jake Anderson, Grade 12
Cinnamon Hills School, UT

The Warlocks

The warlocks dance in the dead of night,
whistling silver tunes from lips and bone flutes.
They drink cocktails of dew and blood
and feast on dreaming dust.
They cast divinations through smoky quartz,
and curse their enemies through voodoo dolls.
Their eyes look like fire, and their fingers are like velvet.
Beware, my dear, their revels after dark.
Like faerie lords, they keep who they catch.

Sara Hendricks, Grade 12
St. Maries High School, ID

Moon Light

This is why the wolves howl
This why they prowl
Through the shadows and in the dark
Through the streets and in the park.

When the cities light and glow
When off to sleep you go
The sun is gone and the air is cold
The shimmering light is millions of years old.

Surrounded by billions of sparkling diamonds it stands out
A shimmering glow surrounded by too many diamonds to count
And in the woods where you can really see
It's pitch black, but look up past the trees.

Like a moth drawn to flame
Its affect on me has been the same
Its beautiful light and grasping shine
Has always made me feel the night is mine.

Johnathan Cordova, Grade 10
Mountainair High School, NM

You

No matter the distance,
No matter the wait,
No matter if you anticipate,
I'll always care for who you really are,
I think I could fall in love with you
If you'll go that far,
When the days go by
It seems so lonely without you here
I wish I could have you in my arms
Then everything would be clear
I think about you night and day,
Wishing and hoping my feelings won't go astray,
When I see you again
My heart feels so happy and that is the end.

Anjie Pineda, Grade 12
Oakdale Charter High School, CA

Time Machines

Take me back to that fall
with that time machine of yours you call memories,
tell me how he was
and what funny things he'd say.

Let me ask you as many questions as I can,
I'd like to know him
as if he were still here.

My grandfather died
before I was born,
so please take me back
with that time machine of yours.

Hiram Sahagun, Grade 10
Orem High School, UT

Heart of Content

She looks like me, but it's okay.
In his heart I know I'll remain.
With a letter of rejection,
and a heart of content,
I know my time was well spent.

He's got a spot in my memories,
and a spot in my thoughts;
Forever I know my love for
him and his family, will never stop.

I've not forgotten, nor lost, all of the memories.
My love was once given, but I took back that key.
He was everything my heart had desired;
but the only things I will keep,
are the memories and the laughter…

So I have respect to the woman who shares him in this present,
only a love lost once, costs a fortune…
Because the moments in our life that we allowed,
makes up the man who she has now.
…I can gladly say my time was well spent,
forever our moments will remain,
in my heart of content…

Ashley Robertson, Grade 12
Walnutwood High School, CA

Birds

Birds go flying by
Soaring in the air
Flying in the sky

As if saying hi
Grouping together in a flock
Birds go flying by

I watch them and say my my
Either flying down or up
Flying high in the sky

Landing when one sees a fry
Some waddle and some run
Birds go flying by

I feel sorry for one when it dies
Thinking what it's like to be a bird
Flying high in the sky

Wondering if one could talk what would it say
Bird watching is a good hobby
Birds go flying by
Flying high in the sky

Daniel Cabrera, Grade 11
Pioneer High School, NV

Lost Boys

I am lost and cold
I own nothing to my name
Wandering, waiting every day
To the world it doesn't matter, it's all the same

I am lost and hungry
I travel all through the day
Over the hills and rivers
Searching, seeking for a place to stay

I am lost and alone
Traveling on aching feet
Running from the bad
Only wanting something to eat

I am lost and tired
A refuge far up ahead
Just above the hill
A safe place to lay my head

A chance for a better life
They all say
To be positive
There will be a way

Jordan Greenhalgh, Grade 11
Viewmont High School, UT

In Love with Chance

Among the flowers shall she dance,
Her laughter full of silver ring,
For she's in love with chance.

Soft touch on skin, a fairy prance,
Awakens beauty like the spring,
Among the flowers shall she dance.

Soft curve of lip and confident glance
Reveal envy in peasant and king,
For she's in love with chance.

Her joyous heart sounds a grand romance.
On her brow lie beads of faith upon a string.
Among the flowers shall she dance.

Glittering eyes only do enhance
Her daring leap and spread of wing;
For she's in love with chance.

Beware of her, for 'tis like the trance
Upon those who listened to the Sirens sing.
Among the flowers shall she dance,
For she's in love with chance.

Jessica Lawson, Grade 12
Spanish Springs High School, NV

Time

When the time is right
You then will know

The reason behind
This façade I show

The reason why
I chose to hide

And fight my way
Even though I lied

The walls come down
When the time is right

And bring a dawn
To this endless night
Jennifer Terry, Grade 12
Borah Sr High School, ID

Changing

I used to be a piano
People played and my strings obeyed.
But now I am a writer,
My story is my own.

I used to be gray and white:
The colors of winter.
Now I am green and yellow:
Full of spring.

I used to fear caves
Full of darkness.
But now I take a light
And push through.
The darkness disappears.
I can see what's ahead.
How could I be afraid?
Emily Donaldson, Grade 12
Woods Cross High School, UT

Haiku

Waves crashing on shore
Salt's aroma sifting through
White foam receding

Stalking through the brush
A feline eying his prey
Pouncing and success

Wind whispering past
Flowers peaking clear of grass
The world seems to sigh
Sydnie Wilson, Grade 11
Wilson High School, CA

Today, I Met an Angel: A Tribute to Beck

Today, I met an angel; he stayed for just a blink.
And yet he caused my heart to race, my thudding mind to think.

Today, I met an angel; he lingered for a while.
But in those moments, I was his — he caught me in his smile.

Today, I met an angel. What color are his eyes?
The bluest blue, the deepest blue, that shame the endless sky.

Today, I met an angel. I held his little hand.
He smiled and told me silently who I am, and where I stand.

Today, I met an angel. He's torn down all my walls.
Now he builds a kingdom; he's answered Heaven's calls.

Today, I met an angel, who gave me all of him.
But the more he gave, the more he had — And now, for him, I'll live.

Today, I met an angel — A sign I'm not alone.
Today, I met an angel.
He's come to guide me home.
Kimber Jenks, Grade 10
American Fork High School, UT

The Person in the Mirror

Your face.
That face in the mirror, so full of curiosity
It looks back at you.
Your various colored eyes seemed excited with some other hidden emotion.
You have some form of a beautiful figure,
Though you wish you were skinnier.
Your hair flows with the wind like light brown thread in the wind,
And once it hits contact with something,
It feels like silk against your skin.
However, you wish for something more.
Something that you're not.
A picture of someone who is not you.
You know that you yourself are beautiful
But once you step out that door, you're someone else.
Another you.
A different you.
Someone who's not real.
McKenzi Luther, Grade 12
Red Mountain High School, AZ

What Is Love?

Love is a word you cannot define
Love can be something little to someone and something big to someone else
Love is not always perfect, you have your ups and downs
Love is so powerful
It is something that has a lot of meaning to it
Some people find love and others don't
You can't describe your love for someone
Love is just that one word that means a lot and can't be defined.
Krystal Ulrich, Grade 11
Prospect Continuation High School, CA

The Shadow of My Life

I was brought to this world with nothing to do
Living my life, having dreams to pursue.
So I was a kid, very rowdy and fun
Hating that school has already begun

So I go to school and start to excel
Waiting for recess — oh soothing bell
To play b ball at lunch was oh so amusing
Ruing to stop while all is refusing.

Now I grow older, better, and strong
Wondering why life is taking so long
Not knowing that time has already gone by
Announcing my childhood a happy goodbye.

So now I know a few years have passed
Reading out loud to my new high school class
Letting them know of the shadow of my life
I have nothing to hide my life has no strife.

My shadow is my twin I can't say anymore
It is me all the time in any shape, way, or form.

Sean Ross Lazaro, Grade 10
Cypress High School, CA

Every Time

Every time I see those eyes,
Every time I see that smile,
It makes my day,
A perfect day,

Every time I feel you near me,
I don't want you to go away

I need to see you,
I need to be near you,
You are my medicine that I need to take every day,
In order to survive,
In order to be alive,

In your eyes I see my future,
Our future,
That one day will come,

Every time seeing you is what keeps me alive,
You are my life and if one day we are not together,
The last thing I want to see are your eyes.

Marisol Haro, Grade 11
Merrill F West High School, CA

On Your Toes

Dancing in moonlight
Quite a new feel in the air
Softly music plays

Terra Tolentino, Grade 11
Encore High School for the Performing Arts, CA

Monster

Converse shoes slapping pavement never rest,
Rising from bed before the blazing sun.
Rush Rush by the spry monster I am pressed.

Biting my heels before I'm fully dressed,
Out the familiar door at a swift run,
Converse shoes slapping pavement never rest.

It waits in corners, an unwelcome guest
Plagues me even after school has begun.
Converse shoes slapping pavement never rest.

Frantically fleeing from the sly pest,
Hurry home to get dreaded homework done,
Rush Rush by the spry monster I am pressed.

Nighttime sleep conquers me without protest,
In morning again it will have begun.
Converse shoes slapping pavement never rest,
Rush Rush by the spry monster I am pressed.

Victoria Howell, Grade 10
Chandler Preparatory Academy, AZ

Water Adventure

Rushing down the raging river
I row with my paddle keeping time
My heart pumping inhumanly fast
Although it was cold I didn't shiver
It was so loud we could only mime
I was so fast I couldn't be passed
The beauty of it all was enough to make you quiver
Glad I could do this in my prime
The smell of this river is a blast
Of fresh water and pine
Everything was amazing down in the water
Even if it felt like we were being brought to the slaughter
We were all at the mercy of the rapids
Then we were there at last
In the smooth clear water.

David Butler, Grade 10
Shelley Sr High School, ID

Ode to My Bed

Oh soft and soothing spacious sack,
The infrastructure of comfort that rests upon my back.
You've been my friend for all this time,
Not once have I offered you a single rhyme.
I'd like to take this time to say it
Whenever I lie upon your mattress.
And I'll never ever doubt your softness.
You are the shifter of my dreams.
Of you I hold in high esteems.
No one can estimate the value of your true worth,
At least with you, I'm not lying on the earth.

Phillip Green, Grade 11
Merit Academy, UT

It

It's gone.
It was but is no more.
I cannot light a fire,
I cannot see at night.

Where does It hide,
Why has It gone?
Must I be blind,
Must I be cold.

It's gone, It's gone, It's gone.
Where does It hide,
Can It be far?

It must find me,
It must find Her.
For It I hunger,
And I weep,

How can It be,
How can It not.
Oh Lord, help me find It.

Brigham Kmetzsch, Grade 11
Viewmont High School, UT

This Feeling

This feeling I'm feeling,
Is like no other!
I feel like there's not another…
This feeling I'm feeling,
Has got my mind so cluttered!
I feel like spacing out into nothing…
This feeling I'm feeling,
It's got my heart to singing!
I feel like busting out into song!
This feeling I'm feeling,
Got my mind to thinking
I feel like dreaming of only you…
This feeling I'm feeling,
Has got me going insane!
I feel like strappin' into a straight jacket!!!
I feel your stare is so breathtaking,
So my heart is always racing,
I feel your thoughts are so amazing,
So your presence I'm always craving,
I feel your soul is Oh! So brightening,
So your love, for it, I'm always fighting.

Athena Staggs, Grade 11
Lucerne Valley Jr/Sr High School, CA

Morning

Brooklyn eats waffles
spreading syrup on pancakes.
Delicious, she says.

Elsie Reyna, Grade 12
Pine View High School, UT

Mirror Mirror

Mirror, Mirror, Lie to me,
Show me what I want to see,
A girl dying on the inside, a girl trying to be something she's not,
She tries to be like everyone else,
The words she throws out our untune, not caring whether she hurts a soul,
But the only person that she's hurting is herself,
She doesn't realize that she is perfect in Gods eyes,
But yet she wants to be perfect in the eyes of others,
Shell do almost anything to be perfect in the eyes of others,
She's 16 and weighs 80 pounds,
She has a pale face and thinks she's pretty
She thinks she's skinny enough to be a model,
The girls she hangs out with weigh less then a feather,
And she thinks that's normal, and she wants to be like them,
They all have this fantasy that being 80 pounds is beautiful,
She goes through the bulimia and starving herself,
She thinks that will help her chances out as being a model,
In her mind she thinks that she's perfectly healthy,
She doesn't mind being the prissy, snobby Barbie,
Mirror, Mirror Lie to me, show me what I want to see,
Because I hate the girl, staring back at me!

Victoria Cairns, Grade 11
Valley Christian High School, CA

My Mother

My mother who shows her precious love it's like no other,
There can never be, will never be anyone above her.
She is a symbol of strength. For her happiness I will go to any length.
She is divine, yet she is no myth.
She has overcome the storms of life.
Walked through the rain defeated strife, I thank her for the gift of life.
I'm sorry for the pain, all the memories, forgive my evil ways.
I was lost. My vision was blinded by a windshield of frost.
Now I'm sitting here. I'm paying the cost.
The world was so bright. I was in the sunshine, yet I ignored the light.
Now that I've seen it, it fades from my sight.
Mom, you've been so strong. Through this difficult road.
Fought the pain for so long.
never doubted me even when I couldn't hold on.
For you I'm gonna take it before the day turns black.
Mom, I promise I'm gonna make it.

Juan DeHaro, Grade 10
Crossroads School, CA

It Was Me

She runs around and plays all day, the boys have cooties, stay away!
Patty-cake and duck-duck-goose, she doesn't car if her clothes fit loose.
Her hair is a mess, her shoes are untied,
Scraped elbows and knees were the only reasons she cried.
Her mommy is her best friend and her daddy is so strong,
Her heart is never broken; no one ever does her wrong.
That little girl is lucky, but little does she know,
That one day she'll look back and see,
That little girl was me.

Caitlin McCullough, Grade 10
Preston High School, ID

Game Time

Butterflies in my stomach, concentration.
The adrenaline rises.
Ready, or maybe not.
My feelings are confused.
The referee whistles:
It's game time!
Walk onto the court,
Everything around me seems to move slowly.
Jump, touch the ball.
The game has started.
Nothing else is important now,
Just your team and the ball.
Run, dribble, pass, and basket!
Excitement just for a moment
Time to run again
I try hard, my best.
It's not always enough
But I'm not alone, my team is here.
We try hard, our best.
And we win as a team.

Alessandra Botta, Grade 12
Merit Academy, UT

Spring Rain

The rain
It reminds me of you
Pouring down from the heavens
Like the sky is crying
Now I'm sitting in my room
Looking outside and listening to the rain
As I cry
For what we had
For losing you
I think about the summer and the memories we made
I step outside into the cold rain
As it falls on my head, my face and arms
I remember the way you made me feel:
The rain washes away my pain
Free from worry
Like nothing in the world could ruin what we had
But in the end you got bored of the rain
Such a simple thing as me
You needed something more to make you feel that free
Like the rain could do for me

Jackie Olsen, Grade 12
Viewmont High School, UT

Dream Place

Many colors of sand
Water and shells beneath my feet
Gorgeous flowers
Bitter salt water
Roaring waves, chirping birds, many laughs

Heather Beebe, Grade 11
Merit Academy, UT

How to Write a Poem

Find a paper, blank and clear
And go somewhere, nothing you can hear
Pick up a pencil, with an eraser, for sure
Think of something you love strongly, and pure
What is it about that thing
That made it touch your heart and sting
What made it come to your mind
Was it the first love you could find
Now don't think too hard, don't stress out
Put your pencil to the page, and just let it out
Let the words in your heart escape to the page
Let those words dance, on their paper-like stage
Let them glitter and twirl, around and around
And hope that they make a beautiful sound
Reread and reread, changing small things
Until to one's heart, happiness brings
Then read it aloud, to a friend or a mom
And watch their face, as they try these words on
If it brought a smile, tears, or laughter, no less
Then you'll know for sure your poem's a success

Stacey Penman, Grade 12
Red Mountain High School, AZ

Flower Ways

Covered in polar and bright sunlight
Brushing the summers air with rainbow delight
Mooshing into Earths core, never widening the open door
No need to travel, for the roots feel all
Painted in yellow, purple, and blue awe
Sucking the life from every which way
A flower turns its attention to the suns rays
Even in the coldest of winter days
Petals be plucked, but never of thought
That your pulling on your own root, letting it rot
Feeling their colors tug at your inner being
Grass is greener when flowers are singing
Their hours of staring at the sun is magical
For we can't look for three seconds, its only rational
The tallest daughters of the father trees
Flowers only have a few irreplaceable leaves
Cut and be cut, you're making your own world
Flourish and be flourished, on this beautiful world
Flowers though unnoticed for wisdom of all land
Only seemingly, look beautiful when plucked in our hand

Danielle Dunn, Grade 12
La Mirada High School, CA

Dolphin

Peaceful
A free spirit
Beautiful animal
Bubbly personality
Graceful

Delaney Burdick, Grade 12
Red Mountain High School, AZ

Stranger

A Stranger in the Night
A Stranger in the Dark
A Stranger silently waiting
as the Shadows leave their Mark

He listens ever closely
to the sounds that they make
the tears fill his eyes
for it's you they will take

He reaches out his hand
hoping you will grab
your fingers slip through his
the Shadows take their stab

You slowly slip away
into the Shadows Unruly ways
He listens ever closely
in the dark, A Stranger stays

Hannah Crawford, Grade 11
Academy for Careers and Explorations High School, CA

The Night Stars Truly Shine

Dresses and shoes, Halters or straps, heals or flats,
Hair and make up, straight or curled, fluorescent or pastels
Oh my oh my
It's not just any night, it's the night
It's not just any event, it's the event
It's almost as important as my wedding day will be
I have to look just as good as I would for that day
It's like the cherry on top of my sundae of high school events
I will share the night with many friends
But most importantly my special guy
Who will be wearing a suit of amour
And will arrive to pick me up in
A beautiful white Cinderella carriage
With a driver wearing a tall white top hat and
Gorgeous white stallions guiding our way
The night will be filled with love and magic
While the stars shine over our heads
We will dance the night away
Duh it's my prom night

Tiffanee Zamora, Grade 11
Bell Gardens High School, CA

Days Go By

The ice is melting as days go by.
From the blue to orange to black, gleams in the sky.
The sun is forgotten, but there are still stars in space.
Just like the sun, in the world I know my place.

My thoughts grows dimmer as days go by.
All my words and looks inspire fear in my children's eyes.
A castaway rose without a spot of luster or beauty,
a blown hue all weak and weary.

It grows unbearable as days go by.
In my head there are tears, but in reality I cannot cry.
The children are nice and caring, but I know I scare.
The ice has melted, leaving a lifeless puddle there.

I see the end as my days go by.
The darkness comes when the blue sky dies.
What is this feeling I cannot bear?
The ice has gone and dissolve in the air.

Marion Eng, Grade 10
Abraham Lincoln High School, CA

Sitting, Watching, and Waiting

The world is moving, spinning, revolving.
The people are learning, gaining, changing.
Cities are growing, spreading, advancing.
But families are screaming, leaving, breaking apart.

Friends are betraying, lying, hurting.
Children are rude, mean, and nasty.
Parents are lost, hopeless, and desperate.
People worry, cry, scream, and sigh,
Laugh, play, debate, and die.

The only things peaceful seem to be the trees,
But even their lives are being cut short.
I don't understand.
All this moving, changing, and gaining
Seems like chaotic madness.
But what dumbfounds me the most,
Is that I still sit here, silent as can be.
Simply sitting, watching, and waiting…

Danielle Davis, Grade 10
Bradshaw Christian High School, CA

Smile

one's smile tells a life story
A smile means the world
Happiness can be shown through a smile
Brighten a day —
Forget the worries of today
Just turn that frown upside down
A smile is a wonderful gift
Smile with the world, always

Danielle Rubino, Grade 11
Valley Christian High School, CA

The Joke

The children all gathered 'round
To hear their teacher's joke.
They urged him to get started.
Their little fingers they did poke.
The teacher wove a pattern of words,
Delivered the punch line with success.
The children burst out laughing,
"Oh teacher you're the best!"

Mahonri Tukuafu, Grade 11
Merit Academy, UT

Hate

I pick myself up
only to be knocked back down
I am falling and falling
into a place far, far removed
where fantasies and fairy tales are reality
and happiness is everywhere yet it melts away
I fall onto the ground as pain impacts
but in some unexplainable way
my head lands in your hands, the light all around you
the sight fills my eyes
the pain diminishes into yesterday
I lay determined not to lose
I stand only to be hit again
I am beyond pain
with you dominating my thoughts
deflecting the blows of depression, pain, hopelessness, anger
I walk out of this fiery pit
onto the plains of happiness and fairy tales
knowing that I have won today's battle
knowing that I have defeated the hate that surrounds me

Jason Bellegante, Grade 12
New Plymouth High School, ID

Faith, Hope, Love

F ear of wanting something more
A lways trust when you have no reason to
I nternally is where you look for guidance
T heatrics you do not pride yourself in
H ostile, but only at your will

H appiness is knowing there's reason
O ptional, but worthwhile
P otentially harmful, like anything
E xpected to never come down, so foolish

L avish and beautiful all while rude and ugly
O pen doors to anywhere but not taken for granted
V icious in its fight, but humble if defeated
E ternally yours, forever and always

Alexandria Nelson, Grade 10
Harlowton High School, MT

The One For Me

I walk up to him
He looks at me and grins
I hold my arms out open wide
You can tell that he is shy
He grabs my waist and holds me close

In his arms I start to tear
His pounding heart is all I hear
I look up in his eyes and smile
We were in each others' arms for quite a while
I knew he was the one for me

Colleen Hara, Grade 10
Cypress High School, CA

Droplet

Eyelids cover my eyes
My tender eyes
Never can see nothing

Delicately opening,
Black lashes pull a liquid chain
Glistening and forbidding deserved happiness
Instead, I see blurred pleasure
I see duplicated anguish
Through the kaleidoscope droplet
Where glasses offer no support

I recognize the liquid
Wet, heavy, saturated.
I recognize the warmth
With no comfort

And I blink
With unclosed eyes;
Water chain broken
Multiples erased
Comfort restored

A solitary tear glides down my lonely cheek
Ashamed, I wipe it away

Dustin Atlas, Grade 12
San Dieguito Academy, CA

Running in Circles

You and I were both lost,
Lost far, far away,
With no maps or instructions, nowhere to stay,
And somehow you found me.

I was alone on the road, after the storm had ripped through,
With nowhere to go, but it led me to you,
So I stayed.

You saved my lost mind, recouped my lost soul,
You gave me everything back, but it came with a toll,
And I left.

I was so lost before, now I was running away,
From you who had saved me, told me everything was okay,
I was scared.

I had bled for these feelings, that I now felt for you,
And I knew all too well, what these feelings could do,
So I saved you.

And I ran,
I ran far, far away,
With no maps or instructions, nowhere to stay,
Someday I'll find you.

Brett Spadaro, Grade 12
Thousand Oaks High School, CA

Invisible

There's something there between us, something we cannot hide
It fills my heart with sorrow and glee, fills my stomach with butterflies
We smile and laugh and make time for each other
While I keep these feelings locked inside, hiding undercover
Everywhere I go his face is all I see
It kills me somewhere inside when he looks right through me
I'm as invisible to him as glass in a windowpane
But it is not his fault; my heart is the one to blame
I keep my hopes up, willing to hurt myself and try
To make him see, I never want him to leave or say a permanent good-bye
His hugs feel right and his simple jokes cheer me up
But it must be that my endless love is not enough
No matter his decisions or paths of life he ends up choosing,
Whenever he needs anyone I will have open arms and be soothing
Whenever I'm around him my heart cries and my stomach aches
Every time I see him my nerves tremble like an earthquake, I need him to love me, my heart is only surviving on hope
The very breath inside my chest lets me know I can't just cope
There is no reason for me to still have feelings for him
I want to just tell, to go out on a limb, because these feelings will never end, this time it's completely true
I want to just say, "I am totally, truly, irrevocably in love with you."

Kellie Erickson, Grade 11
La Serna High School, CA

Butterfly

I stumbled upon your broken wings while
I gathered up the little yellow flowers in the garden.
I nearly missed you because you tried blending in
To hide from your attackers, but I saw your special markings that shone through your surroundings like diamonds.
You looked up at my lonely little face, with the glimmer in my eye asking to be needed.
You held still while I scooped you into my miniature palms.
I held onto you tightly as I ascended the tree house ladder to the highest point I knew.
I carefully stretched my arms, raising you into the sky and nudging you gently into the air.
You reluctantly gave a few weak flaps and lay sullenly in my hand. I tossed you gently into the breeze. I saw you flutter your inept
wings and give up, falling solidly to the ground.
I clambered down after you and plucked you from the grass.
I tried again and again to toss you
To life, but time after time, you dropped to the earth.
I pleaded for you to try for me, but you
Plummeted again to the soil. Crying out in frustration and confusion, I picked you up and threw you from the lofty setting.
As I saw your body
Lying lifeless on the dry dirt, I screamed in anguish. My heart dropped almost as fast as the tears. I looked into the clouds for aid.
I held your battered body on my fingers and cried in despair.
Would one last chance have been the key?
— or were you just a stupid butterfly?

Caitlin Lyman, Grade 10
San Juan High School, UT

Life

Life is a test to see if you pass, Life is a game to see if you win, Life is a chance to make something out of it. Life goes on so keep moving on. We are always moving on, so make something out of it. As a youngster kicking back and ditching school and having fun is what we all want in the moment, but later is when it all hits you. You go down and may lose your chance for an education and if you do not start hitting the textbooks, you're going to keep going down, so start hitting the textbooks and get an education. This test we live is to see what we make of it. This game we live is to see what we can do and this chance is to make something out of it. So get an education and live your dreams.

Alex Schmidt, Grade 12
Cinnamon Hills School, UT

Numb

I'm laying here tired just tryin' to get some sleep.
Got too much on my mind I'm in way to deep.
We reap what we sow and my seeds, they're no good.
I wish I could fix things if only I could
I screw up everything, no stone left unturned
My soul it's been stained it's been beaten and burned.
From the people who messed me up to the girl who fixed it all,
I'm sorry for what I've done. Ultimately in my own downfall.
I'm a wonderful magician I fool you every day.
Putting on a mask making things look ok
But inside I'm rotting and my hearts in despair,
It's broken and shattered no chance of repair.
Made out of stone yet it burns like a fire,
Reckless and pure, my love won't expire.
I've told myself again and again, to stay away from things calling me in,
But just today I've been crushed worse than before, I feel weak and torn, my heart's out the door.
I'm not worth no ones love. Not their time. It's just me.
Not sure I'll come back from the major k.o. think
I'm down for the count, it was my final show.
I'll just have to close up shop, put up the guarding walls.
Just to be shot down again, by the things calling me in.

Nick Hiteshew, Grade 11
North Hills Christian School, CA

…Won't Somebody Please?

Color blue, color green, color pink, color red.
These are all colors you can use to describe a feeling.
I feel many colors trapped inside.
To the naked eye these colors are much too complex to distinguish.
How does one know what colors are within you, when you don't even understand how you feel?
When for oh so long all you've seen and experienced
is the paleness and sadness of the color blue.
How can you assimilate to other colors?
Such as pink, that stands for love and affection?
Or green that stands for life?
Can there be more to this life, or is this it?
How can you ask for help, a hand, to let people know you're hurting?
Would someone even care? Or is it just a waste of words?
Things are just so confusing when we don't understand how to explain or accept that we're just human, weak, and vulnerable.
For this stubbornness there's a price to pay — drowning one self in your own thoughts and despair.

Alma Zendejas, Grade 11
Animo Leadership Charter High School, CA

I Am Back

Before I dug myself into a deep whole, I didn't care about school/family
I didn't care about school or graduating and I was just concerned about NOW, living my life to the fullest
But now I'm back and I'm back for good.
No one is getting in my way of reaching my full potential
I am now going to school for the right reasons, instead of cutting class or skipping school completely
I don't need anybody besides my parents to get through high school
The less friends I have the better
I've learned my lesson and from now on I give my word that I will no longer be the family disaster

Briana Lopez, Grade 11
Bell High School, CA

Fighting for Love

White skin, tan skin, black maybe purple,
all on the Earth, all in the same circle.
We breathe the same air, fight in combat together,
who's to tell us, we're not all equal?
We're all different, yet the same at the heart,
We're all pieces in a clock, just ticking away,
trying to survive every day.
Trying to keep families together, and kids away from drugs,
it sounds tough but it must be done.
Our Lady Liberty stands strong and proud,
we cannot let her down.
All the prejudice and hate, seems to disappear,
when we are carried out to war.
We fight a battle every day....
it's a battle between love and hate.
Every breath we take, is another day gained,
every word we say, can be taken any way.
Whether you fight for a sister, a brother
or maybe a mother, we fight for who we love,
and love one another.

Anna Marie Greenwood, Grade 10
Arlee High School, MT

She's My Princess

It started off when Mommy and Daddy fell in love
Then 9 months later she came out of Mommy's tummy
And the precious little girl has finally come to this world
We accept her ever so wonderful, while others just look and stare
She is special to us but to others she is just handicapped
They say she wouldn't go very far but she really did
They say she wouldn't walk 'til after she was two
But now she's walking two hundred and two steps
They say she wouldn't do much but now she's doing way too much
They say she couldn't rule a kingdom
But now she's a princess, my princess
And who may this princess be you may ask…
Her name is little Sue
And she has
Down Syndrome too

Kimberly Morales, Grade 11
Preston High School, ID

Caps and Gowns

We're graduating, and we know
Our lives will be different and new;
We're going out into the world,
Our goals and dreams to pursue.

Cheers and applause from all the people you know.
Moments to come and places to go,
A new experience of your life to come.

The start that will define your future,
As the adult you've become.

Claudia Jimenez, Grade 12
Woods Cross High School, UT

When We Were Us

Sunny days, spent out in our own little world
We were strong then
heroes in that world,
noble, courageous
The legends, we made
The mysteries, we solved
We were confidants
and vigilantes
We were knights on white stallions
We were healers in white robes
We were the conquerors of our bold world
We were free to be ourselves
who we wanted to be
But that was then
That was before
we chose divergent
paths through life
Setting off to make
a name for ourselves
as if the ones we shared
weren't good enough

Kyra Nelson, Grade 12
Billings West High School, MT

God Paints the Sky

As evening comes and the daylight fades away,
    The sun goes down beneath the horizon.
On a nice cool beach where the tide is risin',
    Over the waves the many colors display,
    As God paints the sky in a brand new way.
By day blue, but filled with color near night.
Red, orange and pink, the colors so very bright.
    The beauty of God is shown every day.

Through creation and nature such as this.
    As I watch the sunset by the ocean
    My mind is free of all the commotion,
As thoughts that I think of every day dismiss.
    All I can think to do is lay and rest,
My thoughts are filled with all God's holiness.

Amanda Pirot, Grade 10
Calvary Chapel Christian School, CA

Alone*

I sit alone.
I don't see clearly anymore.
I feel sad, trapped, and paralyzed.
I've been here long enough for flowers to bloom.
Blood on my hands, but I'm afraid of death.
The locks are broken.
The barriers are broken.
Nothing but me.
Alone.

Erin Trawick, Grade 10
Helix High School, CA
*Inspired by "Undergrowth" by Robert and Shana Parkeharrison

Without You There

You said you would be there,
I thought you would.
It was you who was with me,
When I received the gifts.
It was many precious things,
From money to clothes.
You would treat me like a king,
Which I thought was nice.

But one day, the incident happened,
When I lost all those things.
I woke up one morning to find
You with a bag.
The bag was full of my new things,
Which you were taking.
You broke every picture,
Of you and me.

But what you really broke,
Was my pride.
You went out the door and
Never looked back.
I thought you would be there, but I thought wrong.

Luis Rios, Grade 11
Weber Institute of Applied Sciences & Technology, CA

In the Summer Time

In the summer time,
nearly every day we feel a deep embrace,
from the sun's rays of light reaching down on our face.
It is a beautiful time,
to many the best time of the year,
in which we can all sit back, relax, and jeer.

Amongst each other we enjoy ones company,
For as though it seems it will last forever,
The very thought of it is short to be,
Throughout the year people cannot wait,
for this special time in which many elate,
and feelings tend to escalate.

For many it is a time when emotions erupted,
particularly that of love and happiness,
which are known to surprise people and
make them feel as if they were corrupted.
While we live and bask in summer time,
fun is cheap and in abundance,
sometimes costing less than a dime.
But as it ends we cannot help, to look back on what had happened,
in the wonderful season of summer.

Seth Petee, Grade 10
University High School, CA

My Favorite Color

Today I am red. Soft like a rose,
Strong like a lion... Braver than ever

Today I am orange. Persistent like a butterfly,
Calm like a sunset... Always spontaneous

Today I am yellow. Shining like a star,
Shy like a newborn duckling... Showing who I am

Today I am green. Exceptional like lucky clover,
Identical like a blade of grass... Being myself

Today I am blue. Predictable like the sky,
Secret like the ocean... Hidden within

Today I am purple. Majestic like towering mountains,
Small like a crayon... Starting anew

Today I am the rainbow. My color never constant.
My heart always seen. My appearance unexpected.
My life always changing.

Today I am me, something you'll never expect.

Amy Parker, Grade 11
Viewmont High School, UT

The Open Door

You walk through that open door
Not knowing what to expect

Falling into the darkness
Yearning to seek the light

The mirror image shatters before you
Each glistening piece piercing your skin

You gaze into the broken shards
Making out the unfamiliar face before you

Who is this person?
For I do not recognize myself

My body is frail and insipid
My face expressionless

For the thoughts and opinions of those around me
Have completely taken over

I look into the shattered glass once more
And set eyes on a stranger before me

Jennifer Hendricks, Grade 11
Augusta High School, MT

Ode to My Sketchbook

Oh sketchbook, oh sketchbook
My book of sketches
You make me forget
All the world's wretches.

You expand my talents
You absorb what I feel
You're there when I'm weak
Or as strong as steel.

Oh sketchbook, oh sketchbook
Through thick and thin
I've got so many ideas
And you're filled to the brim.

You take what I give
You're there to look back on
You show me my best
And what I've done wrong.

I love you it's true,
I'll be there for you too.
Maren Fuller, Grade 11
Preston High School, ID

Cars

I remember
Working
And playing
With Dad and Mom
I remember
Building a track
Mud, bricks, sticks
Making mud angels
I remember
Racing, modifying
Cars going Vroom
Mud flying
Tires squealing
I remember
Childhood
Kevin Call, Grade 12
Westwood High School, AZ

fear

fear is a towering mountain
that never moves or sways
it blocks the sun
and stands in the way

and brave must be the traveler
that sees the looming thing
and begins the upward climb
that can change everything
Marissa Higdon, Grade 10
Los Alamos High School, NM

An Account of the Sun's Lovely Children

Let's run away to a very sunny nowhere.
Let's divide the sea and the stars to bleed with meaningless movement
and give light to the grassy areas where stories are left for us to find.
Remember when we made albums with the exact time our fingers touched?
When we made up new ways to smile with our toes
and you told me that my feet were beautiful?
We met where the shade complimented your magnificent flaws.
(cameras were criminal to capture this.)
You wrote this all down, and called it
"Familiar Present"
(or something like that).
We were the principles of delight at its best.
And on a Tuesday morning, you had your boxes painted
you had every page filled out with our names.
You told me not to look at clocks.
You told me, "No one will ever know the colors on your toes
if you don't walk barefoot in the dirt for a while."
You told me, "You're nature's greatest competition."
You told me, "I'll be seeing you in all the familiar places."
"Familiar Present."
Page fifty-four.
Katie Brunner, Grade 11
Marymount High School Los Angeles, CA

Not My Reality

The reoccurring dreams of you control my conscious life
Where you and I live and love as Romeo and Juliet once did
Where you and I share our thoughts and feelings
As if this will better the world somehow
The dreams of you and I cannot be changed
They are always the same like the chorus of a song
They excite my every cell and I pray for them to stay
After dreams of you and me, I feel as if I can hold the world in my hand
Although our lives are small and minute like my hand,
Our love is as big as the world
If I could only grasp that love I know I would never it let go
I hope for the day that my dreams become reality
A place where we can share them together
A place where you will take me as I am
But for now I just stay in this motion
And dream of you whenever I can
Nicole Farquar, Grade 11
Grossmont High School, CA

Your Eyes

The shine in your eyes is far more beautiful than anything in the sky!
So I distract myself by holding your hand,
But then I feel like I just can't stand.
Because the beautiful sounds of both our hearts beating
Creates this one spark and it stops me from seeing,
When I'm about to look in to your eyes
My heart begins to race,
So then I just breathe in deeply and say freely,
I love you and your eyes!
Fatima Allahalib, Grade 10
Wilson High School, CA

Unborn Child

Tiny shoes,
For tiny feet —
of a child unborn.
As I look at them,
Just laying there,
My heart is tearing from my chest.
Tiny shoes,
For a tiny child —
Never taken its first breath.
Tiny shoes,
They are gaping holes —
In a sister's heart full of meaning.
Though the baby,
Never wore them,
They hold a story all their own.
Tiny shoes,
For tiny feet —
Of a child unborn.

Kacie Reilly, Grade 10
Whitefish High School, MT

Strangely Reminiscent

Of fedora-donning men
With a spring in their step
To the jazzy blues,

Of black and white films and
Vinyl records, iconic photographs
And classy Sinatra,

Of art manifested by impulses,
Hidden in the magnificence
Of drips, dashes, and splatters,

Of cries for freedom, for
Brilliance, for potential so
Suppressed and withheld,

Of the glorious thing we
Term the human spirit.

Kathy Zhou, Grade 11
Skyline High School, UT

Yellow

They say "Silence
is golden" and a
breath
of fresh air
is sweet.

BUT what I found in
FAVOR:
The rays illuminate the lilies.
Yellow.

Samantha Brand, Grade 12
Viewmont High School, UT

Ghosts of War

Sitting indoors by the window
Praying to God they'll take me slow
Me and my men are about to ship out
Taking the orders, hiding all doubt
Following the plans laid about

Killing is what we had to know
We were accustomed to fight in the snow
The cold felt like home
Yet we were the dethroned

Our country calls us traitors
For taking out those corrupt dictators
The actions have left craters

To ensure there are no wars
For the future of mine and yours

Jeremy Howard, Grade 12
Lucerne Valley Jr/Sr High School, CA

Blind Men See No Faults

Blind men see no faults
They see the beauty we all pass by
They hear the bird sing and enjoy
What we so quickly despise
Yet is that how to truly see beauty?
Deaf men hear no faults
They see the beauty in everyday life
They judge by feelings instead of words
Yet is that how to truly hear truth?
So much do we take for granted
So much do we pass by
That it is us who are blind and deaf.
Blind men may see no color
Deaf men may hear no music
Yet it is us who live dark, silent lives
It is they who find true happiness in life
It is us who only find sorrow

Blaiklee Cook, Grade 12
Madison Sr. High School, ID

The Next Day and Forever After

Like the winning horse in the derby;
Like the sun rising on the horizon;
Like the wind blowing across the beach;
Like the hummingbird singing a melody;
Like the seashells sinking into your palms;
Like the waves crashing on the shore;

My heart races;
Your breath quickens;
The fire is lit, and the spark is fueled.
There's no turning back.

Margaret Liu, Grade 12
Phoenix Country Day School, AZ

The Women Behind the War

Neighbor against neighbor.
Brother against brother.
Yet they are the ones affected most.
They are the unseen soldiers.

Soccer fields turned into execution areas.
Goal posts used for hanging.
They are as strong as diamond.
They are the unseen soldiers.

Their faces can't be seen.
Still they fight
Hidden behind the dark veil.
They are the unseen soldiers

A dream.
A will.
A power very few people have.
They are the unseen soldiers

Sabrina Romero, Grade 10
Mountainair High School, NM

Water Does Not Come From the Faucet

the color of the sky changes
from black to gray
from light clouds to heavy rain
through any temperature
through any disaster
from home to rivulet
from dry to drenched
I stride make my way back
through the fearsome weather
with nothing but a pail
to carry down water that will last
from the crack of dawn
till the very next day

Shirley Fong, Grade 10
Abraham Lincoln High School, CA

The Ball Rises, The Ball Falls

The ball rises, the ball falls
It hits your forearm like a wall
Bouncing off in perfect form
Let's hope this point will go the norm
The ball rises, the ball falls
The setter has his eyes on the ball
His hands are up, focused now
On where he will pass and how
The ball rises, the ball falls
He takes his gather, hearing the call
It's coming to him, he begins to fly
Hopefully his hit will break the tie
As the ball rises, the ball falls

Alex Hodges, Grade 11
Valley Christian High School, CA

All Alone

Why am I standing here, alone?
When outside you are knocking
I cannot come to you for
My feet are glued to the floor.
Forgive me, but I fear you.
Would you if you could open the door?
But I have locked it.
What a sham.
How you shout,
And beg to enter
And how I want you to enter,
But you have no strength to break the door.
Therefore I cannot see you again.

Kiley Phillips, Grade 11
Golden Sierra High School, CA

Why Do I Feel Empty?

I wake every day feeling emptiness
Thinking why I feel
This chronic emptiness
Wondering where or what
I did to feel this I ask my self
What can I do or change
To take this emptiness
Away is turning into pain
I look at myself in
The mirror and see
Noting but emptiness
Until I turned and saw
The light that took me out of this emptiness

Barbara Valencia, Grade 12
Highland High School, CA

Why...

I will forever caress the emotions spilled.
but why, why must it end?
for our feelings were immense.
the words that remind us will forever feed
our friendship from what is left of it.
and we drowned ourselves in the
confusion of why,
I walk on water,
I breathe fire
invincible it may seem
I am the girl that completes your life.

Lorisha Timbresa-Richardson, Grade 10
Mililani High School, HI

Party of My Life

There's people talking, they talk about me
They know my name and they think they know everything about me,
Forget what they say because I need to go need to get away tonight
Because perfect didn't fell so perfect trying to fit a square into a circle was my life
I want it to rain want the rain to fall down and wash away my sanity.
Because I want to scream so people could hear my pain,
But it seems no one is listening
If it's over, let it go I'm just a bird that's already flown away
I am laugh it of and let it go haven't you heard I'm going to be okay
Thank you, you made my mind up for me when you started to ignore me,
Do you see a tear? It's not going to happen today or here
How can you hang up if the line is dead?
If you want to walk I'm one step ahead
Not worried about anything else, I'm wake up and let it all out
Now I am back on the start, I'm up from my down
And I'm turn it around
In a moment everything can change, for a minute all the world can wait
Open a part of you that wants to shine
All your worries, leave them somewhere else
Reach out for something when there's nothing left,
And the world is feeling hallow.

Eileen Diaz, Grade 10
San Diego Met High School, CA

Moving On

Completing another day,
Living through another desperate night,
Yearning for the dawn, for the sun, for the forgiving light.

Craving redemption,
Learning to accept who I must become,
Yielding to the pain caused by you who were never there.

Deciding to forget, unable to forgive,
Realizing the nature of true destruction,
Suffering rebirth through intensity of loneliness, of heartbreak, of betrayal.

Caring no more,
Surviving once again,
Moving on.

Cara Palmer, Grade 12
Bishop Gorman High School, NV

The Fight Against Cancer

The thoughts of fear and denial,
My mind filled with sadness of the unknown.
The pounding of blood flow, pulsing through every vessel,
Giving life to something unwelcome, growing and twisting within.
The darkness clouded the light.
The thunder storming gray skies, shaking every part of my being,
Longing to hold on to brighter and sunnier days,
Looking forward to walking through a valley of meadows, other than the shadow of death,
Oh so hopeless, but faith remains, love and mercy follow me.
When I close my eyes to this storm I will soon open them to a rainbow of peace and eternity.

Elaine Chavez, Grade 10
Mountainair High School, NM

Hope Rises, Fear Falls

My hope rises, my fear falls
The thought of pain, written on these walls
The flashback in my mind, replaying all the time
As I try to escape, the thought of joy is so divine
My hope rises, my fear falls

I begin to recall the moments, my hopeless smile
Not able to erase the sadness, not even for awhile
But remember, in all time of grief
Love and peace is your relief
My hope rises, my fear falls

The morning sun shines on this place
Receive it with open arms and your embrace
Beyond the shadow lies the light
So be rid of all your fright
My hope rises, my fear falls

Alejandra Alvarado, Grade 11
Valley Christian High School, CA

A Face for the World

I look in the mirror to see a face.
A face in which the world sees me.
I may look like a timid, quiet girl
praying with all my might
that the attention won't be on me.
But truly there is another,
screaming to get out.
Her eyes peer through mine
to look at the world around her.
But to her dismay,
her voice cannot be heard.
For too long she's been hiding;
hiding in this face that the world chooses to see.
Day by day she goes through life
living like it's not her life to live.
She is trapped, and longing to be free.
Free from this face the world wants to see.

KaLin Barnes, Grade 12
Viewmont High School, UT

My Life After the War

Born in a time only allowed to serve the country
I dreamed to be free and live with my family
a woman like me didn't have education
or else my family would be just like before.

Marriage with him was to fulfill my dream
thinking I could live with my family
then I had a son and a daughter
a peaceful time in my life
until the disappearance of my husband
I raised my child working day and night
but I was happy to see my grandsons before I disappeared.

Kevin Fukumoto, Grade 10
Abraham Lincoln High School, CA

To

To live to presence history,
To talk, to feel, to hear and make the difference,
To yell and be noticed,
To run and reach your goals,
To hug and united,
To forget and welcome the new,
To jump and be seen,
To smile and save a life,
To laugh and to have joy,
But to love is to become the reason for someone to live,
To cry and have someone,
To fall and to stand up,
To write and make a reason,
To think and accomplish,
To breathe and to know the world,
To sleep and to dream,
To walk and continue,
But live to become the reason to make a change,
To live is to become the reason for someone to love.

Arely Jimenez, Grade 11
Calexico Mission School, CA

When I Reminisce...

I am alive again, under the ragged roof,
the eyes of beggars bore into me with hope,
the new born peasant shall be full of proof,
I carry the wealth for my family to grope!

The proof leads hard labor, in which I perceived,
I commit to my work until my back starts to ache.
In spite of the struggles, I strive to succeed,
but I will bring wealth despite how long it will take.

At last I am recognized by the king of our land,
the rewards that we received were much more than a few,
I have waited so long to be a man,
I have continued the generations anew!

Kelly Huang, Grade 10
Abraham Lincoln High School, CA

Shyness

I am Shyness...
I am filled with brilliant ideas that can't be heard
I am often burdened with new places
I can't stand up for myself infront of the boss
I am surrounded by talkativeness
I try to change and it slowly works
I am learning...
I am a new person
Now I am confidence
I make friends easier
I compliment
I talk and I am heard
I am happy

Mikaila Johnson, Grade 10
Ponderosa High School, CA

Remembering Those Forgotten

Scavengers,
They hunt among spilled leftovers of the wealthy.
Phantom outcasts —
Defeated shadows hidden by night.
Tormented by hunger,
No one to see their plight,
They cling to survival.
Forgotten thieves,
Desperate, wild in their ways
Because Destiny, Cruelty chose it.
No hand extended or thought of offer,
These ghosts are cast aside.
Invisible and ashamed,
Their pleading eyes make no sound.
They live without hope,
Dreams ravaged by reality.

But with a closer look,
We are able to see
Their great strength
And remember
They, too, are human.

Rachel Kaneshiro, Grade 12
Mililani High School, HI

Decisions

Born in a world without light
searching for my true destiny
will anyone accept me for who I am?
Oh why, cruel fate, have you given me this life
for my soul cannot bear it.
Why must I follow the red strings of the wheel
instead of making my own?
Forever cursed to walk in eternal darkness
and follow the path laid out for me
by my ancestors' holy plan.
Do I dare defy it
or listen to its iron fist law?
Two paths lay before me.
One that is my own,
Another given to me.
Which one shall I follow to my happiness?

Kaihe Fisher, Grade 10
Mililani High School, HI

Death

The dread settles over me like a grim rain cloud
My throat burns as though seared by a hot poker
My insides seemed to disappear altogether
And in their absence, they have filled with lead
Emotions race like startled pigs struggling for an escape.
Then finally the numbness clouds my brain.
And I welcome it with open arms,
Desperate for any escape from this agony.

Katelin J. Allen, Grade 11
Viewmont High School, UT

Let Us Go

Come, let us go
Hand in hand
Into the darkness of the streets,
To walk the path of the eerie moon,
Like lovers with intent.
The windy cold hands
Envelop us,
Yet we continue.
Heat and warmth flee.

Into a tear and blood
Drenched land we tread upon.
Here we lie deathly still,
Awaiting the inglorious morning dawn
To carry off our centuries old souls.
Lusty and bloodthirsty killers are we.
Soul reapers that invade the land,
Evade death like a cancerous tumor.

Yet we found each other
And together we shall travel the undiscovered,
The heavenly hell.

Wendy Robles, Grade 12
South El Monte High School, CA

Some Stuff for Snow

The boots go on
Trucks are slow to fire
Traffic is slow but doesn't stop
Wet snow
Boots, coveralls go on
You walk to school
The clear morning holds a glare in your eyes
Deep snow
Heavy Jackets, gloves, boots go on
The world is sideways with wind
Pull your head down tight
Blown snow
Jeans go on
Trucks come to life with a pop
Windows down, radio on
No snow

Matt Jones, Grade 12
Lincoln County High School, NV

Beauty

Beauty is the dark side of the moon.
Unknown to the people, who desire it the most
A light in the end of a black tunnel, hard to see from far away
Once close it's witnessing color for the first time.
New rain on a flower bed, making the world clean once more
Fresh strawberry scent, almost too sweet
Music being sung by a choir
Feeling of a new born baby, held in your arms.

Zoe Bradford, Grade 12
Wilson High School, CA

Behind It All

Behind every poem there is an author.
    My name is Jacob.
Behind every name there is a person.
    I am a respectful person.
    I am a trustworthy person.
Behind every person there is a personality.
    I am fun.
    I am nice.
    I am intelligent.
Behind every personality there is a potential.
    There is the potential to be great.
    There is the potential to love.
    There is the potential to hate.
    Above all, there is the potential to be a friend.
Behind everyone friend;
    There is a person,
    There is a personality,
    There is a potential,
    But above all, there is a name.
I hope you don't forget my name.

Jacob DeChant, Grade 11
Grossmont High School, CA

Flowing Water

We must learn to be one with flowing water.
Learn to take the path of least resistance.
Take life easy and not take it harder.
Find the weak spots and pass the interference.
For water may shy away from boulders.
It knows against a boulder it will die.
Slipping between the cracks it makes rivers.
Water, for seeing this weakness is wise.
Water does not flow against gravity,
But flows with it being ten times stronger.
With that it flows with apathy, for all.
Beings in its path, live no longer.
The water's edge has always haunted man.
The tide changes the fate of the legged man.

Jonathan Nguyen, Grade 10
Campbell High School, HI

Surprise Birthday Party

I receive anticipation while waiting for my special day.
I receive curiosity while wondering what the decorated boxes hold.
I wish for many different presents.
I receive hope for a fun, memorable day.
I dream about how my special day will go.
I also become curious about who will even show.
I fantasize about what type of food,
Or even what flavor of cake and ice cream.
I decide I need to relax,
But the excitement just won't escape me
And my mind carries on.
Still wondering what unexpected things have yet to come.

Tessa Summers, Grade 11
Pine View High School, UT

An Ode to Love

It's time someone recognized you
For all the widespread things you do
Like take a life and spin it anew
Or wreck a heart or two

Love, you give angsty teens a taste of themselves,
You put beautiful mementos on the shelves
You make philosophers quietly delve
Your year runs from one to twelve.

Love, you destroyed the Berlin Wall
Yet made roman architecture hearts fall
Made one long for that one call
Made all great minds feel small.

Love, your power is omnipotent
Made up or heaven-sent
Although the seasons came and went
None of your true energy was spent.

And so I salute you, oh bearer of my heart
In hopes that you won't start
To impart a taste tart
Otherwise I shall depart,
Sit down, and play *Mario Kart.*

Alex Ekmalian, Grade 10
California Academy of Math and Science, CA

Pain's Purpose

Pain can be crippling at times
Or just a small annoyance
Whatever it is, pain is always there

Pain, however unwanted it is, has a purpose
This purpose is always unknown
And always unwanted at the time that it appears

Pain is an ever-constant presence in life
It is always lurking in the shadows
Always showing up at the most inopportune of times

Pain, however unwanted it is, has a purpose
This purpose is always unknown
And always unwanted at the time that it appears

Pain grants experience and strengthens the body and soul
Pain draws us closer together
Pain inadvertently creates friendships

Pain is here to stay as long as were are here
Pain will continue to thrive
And we will continue to grow stronger and learn

Pain seems to have a good purpose in this world

Ethan Barnett, Grade 12
Bakersfield Christian High School, CA

Shining Armor

When the lights go down and the city frowns,
You're still there holding my crown.
My knight in shining armor,
You stand tall above all others.
Hold your head high for one day you'll be mine.
You climb those mountains,
The ones my heart had built,
To keep out all evil, but let in all guilt.
Like a soldier, you march right in.
With your shield on my heart,
And your sword in his head.
Your army of one is no match for his crown.
With my heart on the ground,
And my head in the clouds,
It's an easy win all around.
The defeat was easy; you have the crown,
But I'm not sure if I'm ready to settle down.
Take me to your castle,
There I will be yours forever.
All I ask is that you protect me from evil.
Because who knows what lurks around the corners.

Emily Wright, Grade 12
University Preparatory School, CA

Meadows

Running through the meadows in the early spring
Walking with the river fish by the stream
Feeling life's simplicity in a sun beam
Listen to the wind and hear the blue birds sing
Humming with the bees careful they may sting
It should not go away like a nice dream
But winter approaches like moonlit beams
Flowers all gone left in a dead ring

The night is coming the day is over
I suddenly found a four leaf clover
To my cozy warm house I must go
No more meadows to frolic to and fro
So when I am down I think about this day
I will come back I'm waiting day by day

Nolan Plano, Grade 10
Calvary Chapel Christian School, CA

Change

There are some things that happen and never end
There are some things that happen over and over again
There is one thing I know, and I know for sure
In my life things go by like a blur
The trials we face are usually hard
I feel as though I am randomly dealt the worst card
Often times the situation ends in debt
I cannot say there are things I don't regret
There are many good memories that unfortunately cannot be kept
Change is a thing I am going to have to learn to accept.

Julisa Fielding, Grade 10
Shelley Sr High School, ID

Be the First

Against a stark gray sky, a single unnoticed snowflake floats —
peacefully down to the world,
 And the ground isn't fun —
because without others, it soon melts.

As a single note begins to play —
 it ends soon as it begins,
For without any others — no song can begin to be sung.

But…snowflakes above —
 one by one look on down,
And joining their friend — they hop down to the ground.

And the single note played —
 soon is joined by the others,
Creating a melody — none can sing without another.

Creating a song together —
 is worth any sorrow,
So have courage, be the first —
 Soon others will follow.

Brandi Moon, Grade 11
Duchesne High School, UT

Of Sea and Stone

The fog and mist dulls dark red seaweed, splays
Cascading limply over spray-slicked rocks,
Their soft shine blended in the salty glaze,
Providing me with my own earth-hewn docks.
I cross familiar boulders, and over channels leap,
To find that place, all sea-washed and embrined,
Where I can sit and watch the water seep,
My thoughts, as waves, eddying through my mind.

As foam swells up, then slides away, drawn back,
This pleasure in a secret world, alone,
A comrade in contentedness does lack;
To share this misty place of sea and stone.
To whom can I my sentiments acquaint
When only lonesome rock will hear complaint?

Tracy Brandt, Grade 10
Chandler Preparatory Academy, AZ

My Everything

My shoulders are sore due to the baggage I was carrying,
My mind is burning due to the pain and suffering,
My eyes are red due to all the crying,
My heart is mourning because you are leaving.
My friends kept on saying,
"Time will pass so just keep on going…
You'll find another guy that's going to make you his everything."
But I'll be waiting,
For more memories with you smiling,
Because you will always be my everything…

Kristine Moje, Grade 11
South Pasadena High School, CA

Voices

I hear voices,
Different kinds of voices saying different things.
But they all pressure me to do things.

They say,
"You want to smoke?"
"Son, be good."
"If you want to succeed, go to college."
"Want a drink?"
"Be careful and behave."
"Plan your future now"

I try to escape, and I do.
I escape all voices except one,
A glorious one
A strong but sweet one
It says to me,
"I am the way, the truth and the life."
This is the voice of God.

Alejandro Lopez, Grade 11
Animo Leadership Charter High School, CA

A Great Rain Forest

There was a rain forest teeming with life.
Luscious green, insects, and different species,
Lived in harmony, perfection, and no strife.
Everything worked from the ground to the trees.
Balance is key and it mastered it well,
But this could not be without anyone's aid.
God created this scene and one could tell,
There's nothing more gorgeous than what He made.
But there are those men who steal God's glory,
And tear everything up from the green ground.
There's been many times and this one story,
Of another great forest with no more sound.
 But just as it seems, nothing left is there.
 A small flower sprouts up to the moist air.

Taralyn Johnson, Grade 10
Calvary Chapel Christian School, CA

Experiencing the Southern Blume

The smell of sage brush hovers in the cold, crisp air.
As the blue sky darkens,
It happens.
Almost as if you are in a painting, an explosion…
Of orange, red, and yellow,
The brilliant explosion of colors
are reflected from the clouds.

As the colors slowly fade
and the moon emerges from the dark abyss
you feel peaceful.
You will never forget the exuberant colors of
The Southern blume.

Daniel Spencer, Grade 10
Orem High School, UT

White Strings

The sky that falls upon my face
Dark clouds swollen and full
Drip at a fastening pace
onto strings with a gentle pull.

Slide down the strings,
enticing a simple melody,
and listen to what it brings,
sun emerging in serenity.

In a flash of bright light
floating above the sea,
Trying with all its might
to break through and be free.

Can you not see the white dove,
that filters on hearts' strings for my love?

Kortney Ward, Grade 10
Encore High School for the Performing Arts, CA

Ode to the Sun

Warm my chocolaty brown skin with your rays!
Teach me that there is hidden beauty in this world!

Nurture my body with your vitamins and minerals!
Brighten my mood with your welcoming cry!

It is your ultimate duty to value this world!
How can I ever thank you for it?!

Guide me with your specified spectrum —
Show me what I have been missing all along!

Identify the virtues and the immorals in this world.
Show me what is attractive and repulsive of the hidden objects!

Thank you for all that you've done,
For, without you, the world wouldn't proceed.

Saidah Wilson, Grade 11
North Canyon High School, AZ

Death Grip

Disaster strikes leaving devastation in its wake.
How many more souls will this quake take?
 Bodies left across on the ground
 Still hundreds more to be found.

 Children lost and without place,
Parents burying their offspring with haste.

 And as many take one last breath,
They are not seized with thoughts of death,
 But where their mind lay is far away
Lost in the events of their lives yesterday.

Micah Byerly, Grade 10
Bradshaw Christian High School, CA

Hidden Lies
Thanks for the promise, for others before you cheated me by and by,
and now you're the one that protects the truths, hidden beneath each lie.

Lies that hide awakened under lips concealed, God only knows when they will be revealed;
though on earth time will only tell,
the meanings portrayed deep within thine eyes own cell.

Eleven o' five a crime was committed, yet no objects were hidden.
Only words unknown lurked around each smirk,
and caution was all set about them.
But what we see can be deceiving, that we know, and still no leaving.
What justice did it do, for the hidden,
one for them and zero for us…no one was kidding.

An eye for an eye, or heart for a heart, whatever it is,
it's a lie no doubt.
For an eye blinks a time too many, and a heart will skip a beat.
Only our mouths can win by a cheat.
What goes around comes around, and what's hidden, is bound to cause a pout.

So where can these hidden lies be disclosed?
The truth is exactly under your nose.
That mouth of yours, or his, and even hers, speaks with a tune so quiet, only they shall discern.
What others around you don't know, won't hurt,
Unless you can protect me from the end of no return.

Ileana Leon, Grade 10
Xavier College Preparatory School, AZ

For the Girls
Curse the butterflies that entered my stomach the day that I met you.
Three million objects in my peripheral vision
but when you walked towards me,
they all blended to the center,
and all I see is a beautiful man.
Stopped beating of the heart.
I resurrected to cloud nine
Fell off of cloud nine,
bounced to the top of Mount Everest,
and fell to the floor with you standing there with your arms open wider than an obtuse angle
Still you have yet to catch me.
This is for all the girls
the girls who've been here before.
You rented out every romantic dictionary, every cheesy pick up line movie,
Asked your english teacher to translate a Shakespearean Love Sonnet so you can speak the words to me,
But they were ever so sweet just because they came from you
Even if they were just lies,
I hated you.
Your love is like an epidemic effecting me the most
Running through my body, Flowing through my veins,
So contagious like your laughter
That I try to take seriously
Like a staring contest between the one who loves, and the one who just likes
Still I can move on,
Even If I still love you.

Katrina Arbis, Grade 12
Palo Verde High School, NV

Underwater Friends

I am the underwater life, filled with urchins and anenomies.
The beauty of the coral reefs, giving shelter to sea horses.

I am the fishes that live in the sea,
Swimming and playing and being friendly.

I am the sharks that hunt for prey,
Seeking for the mean fish and chasing him away.

I am the humpback whale, floating through the water,
Looking for my soul mate, hey I think I found her!

I am the seaweed growing on the ocean floor,
If you pluck me up from the ground, I'll just grow some more.

I am the underwater caves, fun to go explore.
I'm so full of life, you will never get bored.

I am the ocean trenches, so deep you cannot see.
Hiding things inside me, acting mysteriously.

I am the giant submarines, sinking below the surface.
Disappearing into the sea, searching for hidden treasures.

I am all your undersea friends, playing, having fun underwater.
Taking in the scenery, the pleasures of the water.
Adam Fahring, Grade 10
Pine View High School, UT

I Am Not Jealous

Do you see that cute amazing guy over there?
The one with deep blue eyes and a dazzling smile?
He is my best friend, but he just got a girlfriend.
Do not worry, I am not jealous.

We used to be together all the time.
People called us the inseparable pair.
But now he is always with her, and I hardly see him.
I am not jealous.

He said that he would love to stay in this class all day,
But by the way he looks at the clock every five minutes,
I know he is counting down until he can see her again.
I am not jealous.

He was the one that I talked to and tried to understand.
We were comfortable with each other.
Nowadays, they only share thoughts.
I am not jealous.

You may think I like him,
And am hurting inside,
But I do not, so it is all okay.
Besides, I am not jealous.
Hailey Sipe, Grade 11
Merit Academy, UT

The Train

A sallow face wrinkled with
Fatigue and love
She leans back against the window
As the scenes flit by

Too tired to hide
Her mouth hangs open
She's ready to leave
Her ragged shell
Clothed in filthy hand-me-downs

No one knows
No one cares

But her arm so graceful
Beautiful in its arch
Tenderly encircles
A child with porcelain skin

His eyes are bright
His clothes brand new
He pats her rugged hair
Smiles with delight
As they ride away

Into the night.
Erika Nakagawa, Grade 11
Los Angeles County High School for the Arts, CA

Acoustic

In my ears the Spanish dance still lingers,
Pouring from my heart, soaking every fret;
The strings are tangoing with my fingers.

They bend and pull off like failing romance —
Drawn back to the charming strings with regret;
In my ears the Spanish dance still lingers.

Parading over the six string expanse,
Spiraling down the neck in a duet;
The strings are tangoing with my fingers.

Interrupted by a blunder's entrance
On the wood stage; fingertips wince, upset —
In my ears the Spanish dance still lingers.

Engulfed by the deaf applause of silence —
Plucks, twangs, strums paint a cadenza sunset;
The strings are tangoing with my fingers.

Stray, lost thuds a mumbling amp enhances —
Dancers against the wood are silhouettes.
In my ears the Spanish dance still lingers;
The strings are tangoing with my fingers.
Karyn Peyton, Grade 10
Chandler Preparatory Academy, AZ

God of Mine

For the pressure oppression
For the release from bondage
To cease poverty and to be equal
Is God's will to be

To love others
To teach others
The mercy in your hands
Is God's will to be

To be free to worship
To unite, and see God
For it is to be America set free
For God's people of color

to bring together
to break from oppression
to seek freedom
is for God of mine
Cody Tarver, Grade 11
Compton High School, CA

Everywhere

I feel your arms around me.
Your hands close over mine.
I hear you whisper softly,
The quiet words divine.

I feel your piercing gaze,
Searching through my soul.
A fire within me turns to blaze
And fills the empty hole.

I feel your adoration,
Moving throughout space
The love I feel is golden,
I can see it in your face.

In your eyes, your heart, your being
Your smile so debonair
In everything I'm seeing
It's you, you're everywhere.
Mallory Scofield, Grade 12
Merit Academy, UT

Flower

As the sun smiles bright
The flowers arms spread
As their petals catch the light
When it gets out of bed
And grins at people that pass by
As you are trapped by the flower's smell
It releases oxygen into the sky
It's like being in an endless spell
Janeth Quijada, Grade 10
Lucerne Valley Jr/Sr High School, CA

I Made It

The improbability of it all was all to familiar,
Every breath of overwhelmedness beating down on my shoulders,
So I strive, strive for the impossible,
Proving not only to others but to myself as well,
That the world is in my grasp and everything is ahead of me nothing lies behind,
Forgetting all that I once thought, such as I can't, not good enough and no chance,
Remembering that everything that you thought would hold me back made me stronger,
Knowing that the friendships I made today will always be there tomorrow,
Praying that the choices I've made and will make not only lead me to success and happiness
But to the incredible future that was once a dream,
And when it gets hard, because I know it will grace me with its presence every so often,
I will just think about how beautiful it was to see Randell Lynn Pezoldt class of 2010.
Randell Lynn Pezoldt, Grade 12
Columbus High School, MT

This Town

Light the match and run
Run from all the pieces
That were left behind
For fire's light to claim

Small towns and huge secrets
We run from all those days
We loathe the waiting fate
Where sleeping dogs may lay

Dirt, rocks, and suffrage
Kids full of crunk and grime
Those sleeping dogs woke to find
Kids won't make it out alive

Town full of deceit
Emotion rattled in our chest
This town could only bring us down
While we're fighting out the rest
Desiree Walker, Grade 10
Lucerne Valley Jr/Sr High School, CA

Heartbreak

The pain in my heart!
The cry of my soul!
The tears of my eyes.

The music in the distance,
Once calming and soothing,
Only brings heartbreak.

It's gone now
The warmth, the peace, the love.
Gone.

This pain,
No music can heal:
The loss of love.
Paige Benson, Grade 10
Bradshaw Christian High School, CA

Prometheus Legacy

Strike the spark
in living hands
to create the ember
in the night.

instantaneous flare —
vast is the air
fitting, feeding
the passion of my light.

flutter in the conflagration
a reaction to —
the chilling wind
exercising its will in my sight.

burnt out and the
scattered ashes
become dust and resurrect —
love, a man's right.
Brandon Kim, Grade 11
Diamond Bar High School, CA

Dreams of Discoveries

I slowly drift into a deep, long sleep.
Dreaming of the winds dancing around me,
I soar in the sky, I dance with a tree.
Nothing makes a sound not even a peep.
Then I soared over to the oceans deep.
As I keep on sleeping, I begin to see
All that God has planned for me to be
and God will take care of all of His sheep.

For God loves His creation forever.
When we turn away, we have to discover
His arms are open to His beloved.
To see this we don't have to be clever.
During my sleep, this is what I uncovered
In His arms, we will never be unloved.
Summer Hackett, Grade 10
Calvary Chapel Christian School, CA

Hiding in the Crowd

I may not seem like other high school students,
You see I don't like to drive or hang out.
It's not that I am shy or depressed,
I just like being invisible and observant.
While others blithely chatter on,
I read between their words to the true emotion.
You say it hurts, but you are really indifferent,
You say you're mad, but just feeling your impotence.
Driving is a chore for me,
It is only a way to get from point A to B.
I can hardly stay focused on the road,
Because of all the knowledge outside.
If you see one such as me, don't feel bad.
We may seem cold and indifferent,
But that is simply so we can fade away
And acquire the knowledge needed.
We can blend into any crowd,
We know what happens before others,
We see things others only give a passing glance.
So if you feel your missing information,
look for one of us in the background.

Elizabeth MacDonald, Grade 12
Woods Cross High School, UT

Imaginary Rock Star

I pulled out my air guitar for this one,
threw my hand in the air and gestured my rock sign.
The plain ground wasn't enough,
so I climbed onto my bed and started to jump.
I ran my hand across the imaginary audience.
I bobbed my head up and down,
spewing my hair into a crazy circle.
I closed my eyes and they were all there,
screaming for more, chanting as I took over the guitar solo.
The lights were dim on the audience,
but it shined bright in my eyes as I closed them.
But when I opened my eyes again, there sat my
plain
boring
old
room.

Kate Thompson, Grade 10
Orem High School, UT

Earthquake on the Pier

Sitting, eating, and laughing.
Having a great time with family and friends.
Soft swaying, heavy swaying,
This is an earthquake.
Out in the middle of the ocean,
Frightened and scared,
Everyone screams, everyone runs.
The swaying slows down,
Everything is fine.

Britton Green, Grade 10
Orem High School, UT

Poetry in a Byte

O ancient Muse, holy heavenly sprite
Here with your great art, now do I indict,
To challenge the corrupted world, a fight,
One that will be great in every man's sight;
For all unholy powers of dread night
And the great legions of radiance bright
Shall then loose their unfathomable might.
That wondrous battle will be flooded tight
With the bodies of the dead, who yet bite,
E'en being dead, the living in foresight,
For they know that all these enemies'll right
Their enmity by joining this quite
Distressing army, carrying forth a kite,
Emblazoned with our Master's sign, His white
Banner, showing the universe aright
His cross, the burden, pestilential blight
Hope of the devil, the dark parasite,
Which he alone bore, our souls to unite,
To bear us to His holy and blest height,
So all mayest e'er enjoy His happy light.

Michael Haeuser, Grade 12
St. Michael's Preparatory School, CA

Love Chimes and Old Times

They say love is friendship set on fire,
The night I met you, the embers were lit.
According to friends, we're a perfect fit.
First they said you're a player and liar;
Now, it's coming down to a thin wire.
I guess it's what they call being love bit.
I get butterflies when we talk and sit.
I'm simply floating, never been higher.

Hoped one day this wouldn't end in heartbreak,
Thought what we had was really true this time.
When you got sent away, my heart just ached.
Together all the time, partners in crime.
Our first kiss was magical at the lake.
Now it's over, but "I love you" still chimes.

Kelsey Reilly, Grade 12
Pioneer High School, NV

Reality Is Better Than Dreams

I fight to stay awake at night but,
My eyes keep getting heavier,
The more I fight the quicker I fade,
As I sleep alone tonight,
Something just doesn't feel right,
When the sounds of the alarm clock awaken me,
I know then soon I will be by your side,
You will hold me in your arms,
The butterflies will be back,
Then I will realized,
Reality is better than dreams.

Laura McCoy, Grade 12
Lucerne Valley Jr/Sr High School, CA

Captured

War breaks out.
Alone, running away.
Planes tailing from behind,
soldiers running from both sides.
I see two fallen comrades,
One dead,
one missing an arm,
desperately calling for help.

As I grab on to his wounded body,
POW! POW!
I've been hit!
My arm and leg!

I fall on my stomach,
and I turn on my back.
Surrounded.
I have lost all hope in meeting my family again.
Captured.

Kevin Slen, Grade 10
Abraham Lincoln High School, CA

Canvas Escape

The friendly sound of a still summer night,
As warm as the glow of an autumn sky,
Is peaceful and clean like the wintry sight
Of snowflakes gliding through the wind. And I,
A silent watcher, am trapped and apart
From the art of the sunny spring meadows.
The skip in my step, the warmth in my heart,
The summer sunset orange and yellow,
Captured within the walls of my canvas.
Greedily, I paint my man-made landscapes
In attempt to rid me of the stillness
And indulge in my one natural escape:
The oceans and seas, the earth and the trees,
The beauties of nature and it's harmonies.

Jake Winter, Grade 10
Cypress High School, CA

Ode to a Cashew

O thou crescent moon of savory delight
Golden brown and glistening like sunlight on still waters
You come to me in vacuum packaged tins
And with a rush of air the room is filled with thy sweet fragrance.
Turn not away nor reject my salivating lips.
But let me welcome you to me
And taste the blissful salt
As oil on water troubled tongue
And let me delight in thy flavorful crunch.
First one, and then another
And another even more.
I am powerless to stop, slave to thee
Oh master of my hunger.

Aimee Cobabe, Grade 11
Viewmont High School, UT

Back in the Days

Each morning I awake
in my little house made of bricks,
with the same old clothes on me.

There was barely any food to eat.
Only on special occasions,
is when I could have some meat.

There was no electricity,
So we had to use fire.
There was no clean water.
So we had to boil unclean water we find.
There was only enough
to drink and to cook with,
and showered once a week.

I wanted to go to school,
but my parents couldn't afford it.
Instead I stayed home and did what I was told.

Tina Shao, Grade 10
Abraham Lincoln High School, CA

The Journey Ahead

Hot, mosquito infested, and dry…
this is Vietnam, I say.
Eat, work, sleep, and repeat.
On some days, there is business.
on others…no customers at all.

I take my clothes and kids,
and look back at my house, good-bye.
I board this boat holding all three with a tight grip.
I think about this place to come.
Are these stories true?
I keep looking and thinking,
about the journey ahead,
for the American Dream.

Peter Lee, Grade 10
Abraham Lincoln High School, CA

Passing Period

The bell rings and kids head to the door
It doesn't take long before one drops to the floor
The kids pass by and ignore the fall
Pulling out their cell phones and answering their call
It's like they don't have time to help or care
Now you tell me? Is this fair?
It's no wonder we lost friends and forget to share
Time rushes by as kids go zoom
Dodging and weaving to their classroom
Here and there we see a fight
Everyone crowds and beholds the sight
Until it's broken and everyone leaves
The bell rings and being late is her pet peeves.

Hogan Zahid, Grade 12
Redlands High School, CA

Childhood

Child's laughter, shiny new toys
Little girls, little boys,
So naive, so young
Remember all the songs we sung,
When the world seemed so big, so scary
Back when there was still a tooth fairy,
When all that hurt was a simple scrape
Remember your favorite superman cape,
Where playing just meant hide and seek
It was so difficult not to peek,
Where playing with dolls was your whole day
Saying anything we wanted to say,
Now the world isn't so big, but still so scary
There is no longer a tooth fairy,
Now it's worse than a simple scrape
You lost your favorite superman cape,
Where playing is now different from hide and seek
And you no longer feel the need to peek,
School is now what consumes your whole day
You may no longer say what you need to say.

Sammi Dutcher, Grade 10
Woods Cross High School, UT

What Is Winter?

It's as cold as death
The wind howling and snow flying in the air
The stillness in the night
It gets colder
The wind keeps howling
Just keep walking home
You're almost there
Don't be blown away
You're not meant to fly
Don't let the cold win you over
Don't sleep forever
The stars twinkle for you
Follow them home
Don't forget about us
Please come home.

Diana Pepper, Grade 11
Merit Academy, UT

The Key to Originality

Epiphany!
Rainbows and mazes and poems and thought!
Design, devise, imagine!
Give it a shot, it comes to those who try
So start using your imagination!
Lions and tigers and bears, oh my!
Witness Alice and the Mad Hatter at a zany tea party,
Go down the rabbit hole to a mythical new world
Of singular creatures like Gibbli Gobbs and Zango Zeas.
Voilà! My special ingredient,
Creativity!

Omar De La Cruz, Grade 11
St Joseph Notre Dame High School, CA

Guardian Angel

Waking to the sun, birds chirping, flowers blooming...
Skipping along fluffy fields of cotton candy...
Smelling the fresh scent of red roses in the garden...
I live singing in my own enchanted world.

The cut of a golden thorn captures my desire,
    Hauling me into the shadows of darkness,
    Rupturing every bone in my body.
Lost am I in a realm believed to be the gates of hell,
    Drowning in my frost of pierced tears,
    Running barefoot amid shattered glass
    Leaving an endless bloody trail from open wounds.
Embers burn my flesh; pain rips my heart to shreds.
Collapsing sanity makes my vision fade into vapid dust.

Hearing a whisper in the wind,
Feeling a teardrop reborn,
Wings of faith feather my misery away.
A mother's halo reaches out with open arms,
Grasping my soul — pure and precious.
I now see...
My guardian angel.

Victoria Hernandez, Grade 11
Schurr High School, CA

Baseball

It all started when I was eight.
I loved it and took the bait.
I started out at shortstop.
I loved being the center of attention.
Fielding ground balls,
Even when there was rainfall.
Then one day I threw it fast.
My coach had a blast.
He said I should try to pitch.
I didn't like the idea an itch.
I tried it out and was good.
I got better and better and improved.
I then came to love pitching.
The curve was my favorite, holding the stitching.
I also could hit the ball,
So if you want to play, give me a call.

Jake Ailstock, Grade 12
Diamond Ranch Academy, UT

Fallen Soldier

The authority of a vase of flowers
Central in their standing
Tulips, heather, statice
Embellished with a wide, violet ribbon
Their container gleams as the sun reflects
its crimson heart about the room
One fallen soldier droops over the rim
as the rest look on with calculated indifference

Morgan Brown, Grade 11
Pacific Grove High School, CA

Saturn in the Sky

Soaring over metropolis alone,
Majestic figures reign uncontested.
In lens, magnificent cape brightly shone.
Gliding miles away, above human moans,
Cleaving vast fields leaving stars in its stead,
Soaring over metropolis alone.
Fugitive, fleeing the scope, approaching home,
Impossible to catch, through sky it sped;
In lens, magnificent cape brightly shone.
Of stars and planets, Saturn lies alone,
No projectile from the cape seems to shed,
Soaring over metropolis alone.
Our later actions early in the morn,
While beneath horizon Saturn is fed,
In lens, magnificent cape brightly shone.
Day after day, never is Saturn gone,
For always, nightly, the same path it treads,
Soaring over metropolis alone,
In lens, magnificent cape brightly shone.

Paras Mehta, Grade 10
Chandler Preparatory Academy, AZ

Her Eyes Were Truly Windows

Her eyes were truly windows leading to
her soul, transparent through the malachite.
A probing gaze revealed her pain; you knew
to take advantage. Be the parasite.
You did do that and broke her heart; you saw
a lonely child, not hard to terrorize.
And on her heart you'd mercilessly gnaw
away and hush her with your horde of lies.
Now beaten, battered, down on both her knees,
but you won't hear of the pain to lessen,
she whimpers, shakes, and desperately pleads
to leave her be; That's all she asks — Listen!
You noticed then she resembled you so:
In her eyes, a look you knew long ago.

Elizabeth Naameh, Grade 12
La Sierra High School, CA

La Profondeur (Depth)

You burn inside my head
eruptive, enthrall me in your endless embrace
run through my body like an endless string of light
intoxicated, yet frozen by that last word you said
Electrify.

You, my almost Huckleberry friend
rhythmically pumping the blood
with that silken hair running soft against your neck
Come catch, as I make my way across the bend…

Bolden our soul
in the light of the deep.

Laurel Pecchia, Grade 10
Palos Verdes Peninsula High School, CA

Sleep

A sneaky monster arrives every day.
Careless of my tasks it slips in with ease.
It overcomes me without any say.
Knocks at ten, rapidly I become prey.
Homework plus chores! I can't let go in peace.
A sneaky monster arrives every day.
At eleven my thoughts begin to stray.
Growing weak, chances of winning decrease.
It overcomes me without any say.
All lights run away. Silence won't delay.
My dogs been conquered. It's like a disease.
A sneaky monster arrives every day.
Timeless day, it keeps stalking me as prey.
Books away, my last choice is to appease.
It overcomes me without any say.
Ambushed and helpless I quietly lay.
Gripping last moments, I'm forced to release.
A sneaky monster arrives every day.
It overcomes me without any say.

Andrea Torres, Grade 10
Chandler Preparatory Academy, AZ

Nature

A minuscule butterfly in tempest,
With extravagant wings, hamper flailing,
Pulled by beauty into the large abyss,
Unhelped, torn by an unyielding power.
Fighting with muscle, brute force through the gate
Without hope, blown away by howling wind
When, by chance saved by an unknowing fate,
Saved by the intangible, unknowing
The invisible hand that brought safety,
Safe in a blossom quickly forgetting
The idea of weakness, now happily
Living life easily without caring
The unyielding evil in the tempest
Falls to the good that will eas'ly prevail.

Jeffrey Mohr, Grade 10
Chandler Preparatory Academy, AZ

Ode to Dad

Ever since I was little I've been a true Daddy's girl.
You have that kind of love only a truly amazing dad can have.
Sarcasm is as important to us as breathing.
And that makes life all the more enjoyable.
Hard work and endurance have shaped you to who you are.
Although we are almost always laughing,
You can be serious when you need to be.
As a father, it's your job to also be a teacher,
And I, as your student, have learned a lot.
Thanks for taking the time to listen,
And help me when times get tough.
I adore you so much,
And I know we will always be close!

Kayla Butler, Grade 10
Shelley Sr High School, ID

Never too Weak

There's nothing that puts a smile on my face
Like hearing you say you love me.
Our relationship is going so well,
Everything is exactly how I want it to be.
I've never known anyone to make me so happy.
From now on my life will feel forever complete.
I cherish every moment with you by my side.
There hasn't been one moment where our love has felt too weak.
When I say I'll love you forever,
The forever I believe in never ends.
You always know how to make me laugh.
There's never been a problem our love can't mend.
I can't express my love enough
Even though I've said it before.
I'll say it over and over with every day.
Each day my love grows and means more and more.
I absolutely love everything about you.
There isn't one thing I would change.
Our love has no boundaries,
It's not limited by some stupid range.

Carly Turley, Grade 12
Viewmont High School, UT

God's Creations

God's wonderful creations He has made,
I cannot see them all before I die.
This world will cease and still He will not fade,
Angels lifting me up into the sky.
Up to heaven to where the Father lives,
I pray to Him for my salvation now.
His love and mercy He constantly gives,
When Jesus comes back all will have to bow.
Defeating Satan and taking my soul.
Forgiving me of my transgressions here,
Everlasting peace will be my one goal.
The time for God to come is drawing near,
    And in that hour God comes back to earth,
    All will believe in Christ's miracle birth.

Caleb Watts, Grade 10
Calvary Chapel Christian School, CA

Walk On

I walk, walk, walk on,
From all of the hurt,
And avoiding contact in the process,
I walk.
Those words you used,
Were only meant to hurt,
I chose to stand tall,
Now I walk on.
I'm much more than you thought,
I can be anyone, do anything,
It is now your turn to feel, to hurt,
Watch me walk, walk, walk right out of your life.

Lauren Henderson, Grade 11
Grossmont High School, CA

Red

A color of various meanings
Interpretation left to what's inside us
Some pulled from the depths of darkness
Through the blazing flames of hell to show their pain
The blood pulsing through the veins
The only reminder of a stolen heart
Fighting to find the meaning of love and life
The hope that the pieces of a broken heart can be mended
Trying to forget the past but learn from its mistakes
For every rose has its bloody thorns
From those who tried to pick it and make it theirs
This color of which I write, so beautiful yet violent
Shows the pain and trials of those put through hell
But not all is dark and evil of this majestic color
Showing the love of a beating heart
The unspoken spark that draws us together
For it will always be all around us
In the love of intertwined hearts
Or the flames that envelope us in times of suffering
The lustrous red will forever flow through us

Mike Covington, Grade 12
New Plymouth High School, ID

A Child's Wish

Take me away to a world clear and bright
Where wishes come true and dreams always take flight

No more pollution and no more disease
Away with the jerks and the meanness and sleaze

Where hearts never break, they stay whole and intact
And true love is no longer a myth, it's a fact

There, everyone's story ends with "Happily Ever After"
And the streets are filled with happy people and laughter

People call me a dreamer, I won't deny it, it's true
But it's better than this world of hate, money, and rue.

Christina Martinez, Grade 12
Folsom High School, CA

Over You

I used to say I never met a girl like you before,
    I still don't have a clue of who you truly are.
You used to say all you wanted was for me to be yours,
    but I was only a bounce-back for you.
    When you left and slammed the door,
    a lot more other doors were opened.
    So were my eyes so I could see
    that you were never worth my time to be with.
    I'm not writing this to help myself,
    I'm writing this to tell you I'm over you.
    But the day I thought I'd never get through this
    I got over you.

Austin Carter, Grade 10
Orem High School, UT

Look There

Look within the seas.
Feel the breeze
    and see the tide
    swiftly come in and leave.
Look within
    and you shall see
    all your doubts, fears, and dreams.

Look beneath your feet.
See the remnants of your deeds —
    all times of happiness, sadness and joy
    left never to be seen

Look beyond the seashore.
There you will see
    visions of the future
    that may or may not be.

When you look out,
    then you will see.

Jasmine Gerritsen, Grade 10
Schurr High School, CA

God's Love

This vast love cannot be explained by man
It is forgiving of all man's evil
No man will never understand how He can
Save us from the evil one's upheaval
Yes this love is bigger than the mountains
A love like this cannot be found on earth
But this love keeps flowing like a fountain
He died to give us a chance for rebirth
You may wonder who owns a love such as this
This love belongs to our God in the sky
Such a love can be really hard to miss
This extreme love went on the cross to die
Now we can spread such a love to others
We can display this love to one another

Gabrielle Rendeiro, Grade 10
Calvary Chapel Christian School, CA

Beauty

As I left the cradle of all my entire residences,
My home, society of man, and into the Garden of Eden,
A plethora of beauty had caught my senses
Much faster than anything else ever had; and off guard even,
For I hadn't known such magnificence ever existed.
And inside of me a fire was sparked, which I had never
Felt once before in my lifetime. It was a fair flame —
A happy inferno, which I could graciously keep forever.
However, it was hard to imprison such ecstasy all the same.
And so, that flame was released unto the field of beauty,
And every tree and fern and blade of grass burned,
And I discerned that it had been because of my own mutiny.

Devin Cunningham, Grade 11
Valley Christian High School, CA

Open Sea

I know what the dolphin feels.
Where the sea gulls dive for fish
And where the children come to play
Where the sun shines bright and melts the coldness away
Where flying fish fly and whales swim with their young —
I know what the dolphin feels.

I know why the dolphin parts with her mother.
For she cannot live with her forever
She must learn to swim in a vast open sea, without any security
She must learn to be brave and never give up
To catch food and sleep in the dark —
I know why the dolphin parts with her mother.

I know why the dolphin swims.
When anger or frustration builds inside
Swimming comforts her all the time
When the sky turns to gray and light begins to fade
Her emotions are controlled by the cool open sea —
I know why the dolphin swims.

Melinda Sue Chinen, Grade 10
Mililani High School, HI

Heart's Snow

Pale death dwells in the tender heart of love
Rarely receiving a kiss on stone lip
A white shadow trailing, in spite of
the burning heart's desire for sweet courtship
A snowy, hungry wolf waits patiently
Through love's dark trials and its red desire
Until dust filled veins pray not to take thee
And the need for more is yet still dire
Joyous memories cannot keep for all time
No matter the grandeur of love's first kiss
No matter a wedding bell's single chime
Never ending, you thought, would be this bliss?
Not so, death's shallow bed, oh so cold
Earthly love has now been finally sold

Tyler Brisbee, Grade 11
Jefferson High School, MT

Bitter Reality

A crisp, fresh leaf once fell to the ground,
Within seconds it was crushed without a sound.

A cold blooded fish once went back to sea and drowned,
Not knowing it was weak against the cold.
A child once fell down
When he did as he was told.

A daughter once held her head high,
Now, at night, she could only hold it and cry.
A girl once wore her heart on her sleeves,
Within seconds it was torn apart with ease.

Katie Khuu, Grade 10
La Quinta High School, CA

Love

Love is a small word with a lot of meaning, it just takes time to find it.
Once you have fallen in love you won't be able to ignore the feeling.
I have been in a relationship for sixty-two weeks and I have found that feeling.
It took thirty weeks to be sure and now sixty weeks later that love has grown to something indescribable.
He gives me the feeling of being someone incredibly special and the one for him.
He is the one who knows everything about me and the only one who sees the true, complete me.
He accepts me for me and expects nothing else.
He is the one I would do anything for at any time.
He is the person I feel most safe around.
He is the one I feel most beautiful around when I am in sweats and my hair isn't done.
He is the person who stands out to me when in the largest crowd of people.
He is my first boyfriend; he is the one I will love forever and always.

Kendra Toelle, Grade 10
Bradshaw Christian High School, CA

Your First Born

As I look back to see, you weren't always there for me
When it came to my deepest fears, you weren't there to wipe my tears
But as the years started rushing by, I'll have to say with a sigh…
You needed me just as bad and those times were so sad
And now that I'm older, I now know why you left me and mommy with such a heavy boulder
So I accept your apology because I know you're sorry
You always seem to know when I need a smile, especially when you haven't seen one in a while
We know how to make each other laugh and it makes time fly past
Dad, that's why I'm so thankful for you, I would never ask for anyone new
I love you very much because you try to help me with problems and such
I know you wish you could give me the world, but I'm proud enough with my title
"Your first born"

Korina Serrato, Grade 11
CK McClatchy High School, CA

Melodic Robotics

We are each different
And yet the same
We think the same things
And play the same game

We walk the same path,
Eat the same food.
We do exactly as expected too.

We each move alike
And walk with robotic legs.
We walk past the beggar.
As he cries and begs.

We think we know all
When we have so much to learn.
We know what's around every corner we turn.

We try not to glitch
And we hate to fail
We hide from the new
And pretend there's no hell.

Addie Wimmer, Grade 11
Merit Academy, UT

God's Legos

The sun is the golden Lego
and Legos were never meant to imitate metal,
it is the brightest beam radiating from
the bottomless bucket of regular Legos.

The moon is the newest white Lego
the unbuilt white Lego,
the just unwrapped Lego
until now sealed from the Earth,
sealed from the air
sealed in a vacuum,
its minted luster intact,
its edges lethally sharp.

The sky is the teeming infinity
of all the blue Legos to have ever been made in the Lego factory
all the blue Legos retrieved from every household
every drawer they are lost in
and liberated to build themselves unto the vault of the sky,
every newly forged blue Lego joining them
to expand the universe,
the Lego set never to be complete.

Jackson Vanfleet Brown, Grade 11
Ruth Asawa School of the Arts, CA

Island

From the sands of the island into the sea,
Sharing each other just you and me,
It's the dancing of the waves,
And the darkness of the causes,
A wondrous sunshine caresses the sky,
Sharing each other just you and I,
Island time playful and new,
Did you ever think it would be me and you?
The places we come from are brutal not fair,
Your mind's at ease not even a care,
I will take you there to see with your eyes,
Forget the past life, forget the lies,
There is plenty to see both dolphin and whales
The storytellers and wismen's tales,
The fog some days you can cut with a knife,
But remember to breathe it is your life,
The mom has settled and now it is time,
To lie under the stars and wish you could climb,
Into the havens we'll soon fall asleep,
It's in your heart this memory you will keep

Jacob Swisher, Grade 10
Cinnamon Hills School, UT

Hermes

Hermes, God of shepherds and thieves,
at a very young age did what he pleased.
He slipped from the cave where his dear mother slept,
and down to the pasture Apollo's pets kept.
The fifty best cows he quickly did steal,
knowing how angry Apollo would feel.
His Plan did work out, for him and his mother,
for soon he made up with Apollo, his brother.

The other ten gods were amused to see,
such tricks pulled off by one young as he.
For this crafty prank, pulled on his brother,
was a spot in Olympus for him and his mother.
No longer they slept in a dirty old cave,
but now a throne, of gold it was made.

Brittany Kemp, Grade 11
The Learning Choice Academy, CA

Mixed Emotions

Belief and emotion are deep inside.
Something you keep and try to hide
and con faces to tell a lie.
To set free is to be true with yourself
and doing this will give true wealth.
Feelings run deep in the root of the soul
it's a great story that's never been told.
As life is a game and game is to be fun.
To weight your choices is more then a ton.
To keep in emotion is more then despite
you look yourself in the mirror and know its not right.

Meranda Marchese, Grade 10
Cypress High School, CA

The Game of Life

Walking, running,
They're all the same.
Moving forward,
Now that's the game.
The game of life, it goes up and down.
It's all just a big strife.
Some days you may feel sad and want to frown,
But we have to remember to keep our heads held high.
Sometimes it may seem like bad days will never end,
They do, and that's no lie.
When it's all over, our wounds will mend.
As for other days they may seem like it's going good,
And everything goes according to plan.
Life will run smoothly once again.
As long as we live, there will always be ups and downs,
The good days and the bad,
We just have to remember to turn those frowns upside down.
And to always keep moving forward,
With our heads held high not always looking at the ground.
Because in the game of life,
There is no turning back!

Giselle Rambaud, Grade 10
Mililani High School, HI

Framed

Trying to forget the past and how I lost myself,
accused of being someone else.
I heard Japanese steps, saw Japanese tracks.
I ran forward, not looking back.

Day and night I worried that I would be found.
I left no trace, and made not one sound.
Endless wonder of who gave my name out and why,
creates fear and resentment as time goes by.

With few options for my future and not one clue,
the rest of my life is a mystery, one that is strange and new.
A new place, a new name is what I must face.
A new people, the new streets
I am not ready for change.

Kristina Liwanag, Grade 10
Abraham Lincoln High School, CA

New Day

A wait the perfect hour to arise,
B efore we make peace with ourselves,
C ounting the time hour, by minute, by seconds.
D oing it will not make it easier but longer to think,
E very chance we get, trying to make a difference,
F or those you love may not know or just met.
G oing the extra mile blesses you and helps others.
H ate is but an ugly feeling towards others,
I n all thy doings so calmly well,
J ust as you've seen elders react.

Obnette Woodward, Grade 11
Merit Academy, UT

The Pattern of Its Leaves

Sitting beneath
An ancient tree,
A wild tree
Wedged between its knees,
Where its searching feet
Delve into the soil,
I look up.

I look up and I see
A canopy high above me.
An ant I feel, so small against
Its waving arms,
Whose arcs shade me,
So far beneath it.

But in its dappled shade shall I rest,
And gaze upon its cathedral
Bows,
And wonder if the secrets
To the world
Lie within
The pattern of its leaves.

Courtney Haibach-Morris, Grade 10
Helix High School, CA

Can't Escape

Can't escape,
The love,
The fate,
The hate,
These things that revolve,
Some stay,
Others dissolve,
These things that pierce your skin,
And soothe within,
Beat in your head,
Instead,
The thoughts prevail,
Pound in your heart like hail,
Can't escape the war of heart and soul,
Only one must take control.

Colby Giovacchini, Grade 11
Granada Hills Sr High School, CA

Routine

He stared me down maliciously,
His hand about to strike.
I looked on in fear,
But he knew I wouldn't go down
Without a fight.
I wanted to wait, to put off the pain,
But each second gripped my heart
For what was to come was another day
When my alarm began to start.

Kelsey Fletcher, Grade 11
Merit Academy, UT

It's Not What It Seems

I may seem full of joy and bravery
When in reality there's something tearing me down.
The roller coaster I'm in is eventually everlasting.
There are certainly more downs than ups.
I'm in this insane ride that just makes me nauseous.
The ride is pretty intense while others see it enjoyable.
As the ride is finished I say to myself "I made it!"
The uncomfortable feeling is still present.
Overtime the feeling is gone and it's a huge relief!
Having that tranquility in me is priceless
I enjoy as much as I can this peace I have in me
Before I realize I'm in this horrible roller coaster line again.
All these emotions are running through my head
Knowing that I'm not okay the joy in my face portrays otherwise
The courage I build makes me hide the emotions that are killing me inside
Everyone before the ride is outspoken about their feelings towards it.
When they ask me I just stand back and say "I'm okay"
I'm on the roller coaster praying it finishes it soon
All the people around me are asking if everyone is okay
Once again I just stand back and say "I'm okay"

Aida Duran, Grade 11
Animo Leadership Charter High School, CA

Wonder

When there's nothing left to say.
No one wants to wait another day.
They say there's always other fish in the sea.
But that special one already stole the key.
All the lies, thought they would really sting.
But no need for lies and you'll hear my heart sing.
The way you feel no one can understand.
Never had to ever complain.
When they bring all the smiles without any pain.
Got your head in the sky, hugging the clouds.
End up they're the only one you always wished for.
Being with them you can't help but wonder what the future has in store.
Get the butterflies in the stomach, head-over-heels crush.
Because before them your heart was all mush.
A feeling like this you don't want it to go away.
So they say don't worry, they're here to stay.

Marielena Marin, Grade 11
Lucerne Valley Jr/Sr High School, CA

The Space Needle

Being up so high you can touch the sky, and still see all that's below
It's something quite neat when you're up 520 feet
I'd say it's a great place to go
You can walk all around; see the things on the ground
Buildings, busses and planes
There are oceans nearby with birds in the sky, and I'm sure I even saw trains
There's no place finer than the 360 diner
It has seats you just can't beat
So sit yourself down, keep an eye on the ground
While they get you something to eat

Jacob Chittenden, Grade 10
Sycamore Academy, CA

Two Become One

In the still of the night when all sound is asleep,
I hear a faint echo when I listen deep.

I hear not one beat but an echo of two,
One beating for me and the other for you.

Mine beats out a rhythm that says "I love you,"
The other beat matches as my heart beats for two.

The echo flows soft like footprints in sand,
It beats out a message only our hearts understand.

The message is simple as it calls out to you,
"I will love you forever…Our whole lives through…"

With every beat I hear you inside,
With a voice that's strong and can't be denied.

With every beat of my heart I hear a faint sound,
An echo of a heart beat with love all around.

I am never alone when I feel my heart beat,
For your heart is in mine and I am complete.

Two hearts that beat forever as one,
An echo in time as two hearts become one.

Jacqueline Kutner, Grade 11
Heritage High School, CA

Greatness

Standing high, god of the land he perceives;
Beliefs founded upon a neuron gap;
The falling brown bark and the luscious green leaves.

Essence of vanity, only receives;
Wishing to rule, veins filled with beating sap.
Standing high, god of the land he perceives.

Stagnant, shielded. Draped in bark coated sleeves
Of flowing crisp night. We struggle to map;
The falling brown bark and the luscious green leaves.

Decadent tree, causing subjects to grieve,
Tyrant of his own, can't withstand the trap;
Standing high, god of the land, he perceives.

Fibers invincible, the Great believes
Though in truth, only an ax needs to tap;
The falling brown bark, and the luscious green leaves.

Pack of termites, gnawing, at last achieves
The 'great' being shall at last take his nap;
Standing high, god of the land he perceives;
The falling brown bark and the luscious green leaves.

Scott Henry, Grade 10
Chandler Preparatory Academy, AZ

This Is for You

Every day, every single day they ask
"Why do you do this to us?"
I wonder if I ever have an answer.
Is it really that hard?
All they ask is for me to have
a promising future.
But do I even care?
It's not that easy for me.
I struggle with hardships that are
Difficult for a girl like me.
I want to be successful, I do.
It's not that easy for me.
I love school, I really do.
And I am going to try to be the best I can be.
Well what do I tell my parents when
I walk through that door after school?
Hmm well I don't know.
As I learn from life,
I will eventually answer them simply.
Here Mom, Here Dad,
This is for you.

Vanessa Villacorta, Grade 11
Animo Leadership Charter High School, CA

Radical Dreamer

Radical dreamer, asleep like gold of leaves
Awaiting in the wind, in the wings of trees;
Like hidden light in long years of Chimera's hands
Thou is lull'd by swift droughts of time's endless sands.

Radical dreamer, my song of the stars,
List'n I thou, a name unknown of a melody;
Gone are my worries! Just salt's bitter scars,

Radical dreamer, Farewell! Farewell to me.

Radical dreamer, my sun of old heart
E'en shard is jolly on the banks, the sides of sea
Thou shalt morn our dearest worlds apart.

Radical dreamer, Farewell! Farewell to me.

Polina Kamalova, Grade 10
Moon Valley High School, AZ

Necessity to Life

There are many necessities to life,
such as air, shelter, and food
those are all important and good
but the most important and good of all are friends.
They make your day brighter every day.
They keep you company and are there for you when you need them.
They can make you feel better, perhaps like medicine.
So imagine a life of loneliness without friends
and be generous and thank them while they last.

Hyeokje Kim, Grade 10
Cypress High School, CA

Upon a Summer Night

Sitting on the porch,
As time goes by,
A light peach color
Sets across the sky.
Deep red rose petals,
Blown by the breeze,
Scatter apart,
'Midst spiraling leaves.
Within a second
They flutter down at last,
To a small field
Of hazy green grass.
A plump orange sun,
Hangs heavily in the sky,
Upon this summer night,
I let out a sigh.

Imani Todd, Grade 10
St. Joseph Notre Dame High School, CA

Ode to School

It's a land of wonder,
Impacts you like thunder.
A land of learning,
A land of yearning.
A land of many friends,
A land that transcends.
A land of teachers,
A land of preachers.
A land of friendships,
A land of relationships.
A land where you spend a lot of time in,
A land that will eventually fin.
A land from kindergarten to college,
A land where you gain knowledge.
A land which is cool,
A land which we call school.

Mario Moreno, Grade 10
St Francis High School, CA

No Regrets Whatsoever

so tell me
why am I wondering
about what happened to
those idyllic days of
innocent childhood
at the time
did we ever treasure
them enough
because if times keep on
changing as they seem
should I cherish these
painful waking hours
in case the future
is worse

Amanda Trinh, Grade 11
Notre Dame High School, CA

So It Appears

Boy likes girl, Girl likes boy
Or so it appears.
A weak smile from the boy, a small gesture for a hug.
A blush colors her cheeks, She accepts.
The start.
Or so it appears…

Girl talks to the boy she likes, The boy comes to life.
She notes everything he does, He never takes his eyes off her for a second.
They could stay like this forever.
Or so it appears…
Couple of weeks passes…
Girl can't stop thinking about him, Boy slowly disappears,
She starts to worry — He starts to walk away.
The first "time apart"
Or so it appears…

It' Over…

Girl cries…Boy could care less.
She gave him her all, He gave her nothing in return.
She was used. He was entertained
I wish, I wish I can say, "So it appears"
But I would be lying…

Victoria Casillas, Grade 10
Bradshaw Christian High School, CA

Stranger in Hawaii

Arriving here one short month ago,
I thought life would be an unrealistic show.
It isn't only sandy beaches and bright sun,
but perhaps even more fun.

Living here in a host family,
even though often very funny,
We must make the best of our time together
so we make trips in spite of the weather.

Historical museums, long dead volcanoes and nice beaches we have visited.
Counting only SOME things we did.
Flying and long shopping…and stopping —
in Honolulu's Chinatown and in nice restaurants we ate
so we are tired, our feet hurt and we go to bed late.

The start here in Hawaii was very fine,
it is promising to continue to be a good time.
The sun on my skin I cherish and enjoy,
back home, my spirit the gray clouds and cold would destroy.

To find and make friends,
to be a stranger never ends.
Although I have overcome many fears
to leave this wonderful place will be difficult as time nears.

Annika Behm, Grade 11
Mililani High School, HI

I'm Here, Just as Nothing You Can See

I will still be here with you, in your tears and in your heart.
I love you, dear, but we now have to part.
I am still here, but I am nothing you can see.
I am sorry it had to be this way, but that is life — and death.

I will be here, taking care of you,
keep in mind that this is true.
Waiting up here for you,
I will even save you a spot.
Don't try to make yourself be here soon;
or maybe you won't make it up here at all.

I promise I will try to make it go by fast,
just like I did in the past.
You just have to be patient and wait,
I promise death won't be late.

The last thing I ask of you is to never forget me,
because I know deep down in my heart,
no matter how far apart,
that I will never forget you.

Alina Ruiz, Grade 10
Orem High School, UT

Like Flower Like Machine

Sunken in serenity
The notes share the wind like the leaves of a falling tree
Singing with passion and screaming pain away
Laying in a field of flowers and grass
As the bombardiers of war parade angrily
Up and down the burning forest

Under a purple sky with a blood-red moon
Ears excite by the violin-like notes
A sound as sharp as a knife with a message
Wishing to somehow change the world

Spreading hope and erasing misery
Lending a hand to ignite infinity
The flower and machine join the harmony

Jorge Vielma, Grade 11
Bradshaw Mountain High School, AZ

Life

As we enter the world crying, our life begins
Our youth began in the glorious success
How way leads we can never predict
In the cold and dead we stay in one place
The rain attack us with its bleeding drops
Scars on our body will never fade
But it is a prize to receive
For there our mind is awaken,
Awaken to the glory of mankind
And we are now aboard the endless train of life.

Yen Ly, Grade 11
Alhambra High School, CA

There Is Nothing No Nothing Outside Of This Moment

It's all closing in
It's all there
Yet there is nothing
Sleep is anxiety
Wakefulness is struggle
There is a surplus of fear and destitute
There is a famine of ecstasy and even contentment
I am residing in a foreign land
I've never been here before
Yet it's been inside me since the air touched my lungs
I am not changing
I am only discovering
I understand
But don't see
It is new
It is old
It is my mind
It is developing
It has found a sense
That sense is a trigger
It is a warning

Francine Jaramillo, Grade 11
Chino Hills High School, CA

Refined

Tears are not evidence of our weakness,
But yet they show the words the heart can't speak.
For there the proof is for human kindness,
As well as for man's overwhelming grief.
For unspeakable love can be the cause
Of broken hearts that bleed for broken love.
You think upon the joy that there once was,
And know that it will never be the same.

And like a rock becomes a precious jewel,
To be refined we must go through the fire.
For only then can our hearts be renewed,
And selfless love become our one desire.
And though the time it takes to heal is long,
What doesn't kill you only makes you strong.

Grace Fawcett, Grade 10
Chandler Preparatory Academy, AZ

Innocence

What happens to the innocence in this world?
Is it stolen…or
Preserved in one's heart?
Do we take along this journey we call life?
Or does that innocence we once had become corrupted
and fills what was once pure with poison
Or maybe it's just there
Watching with disgust
seeing who we once were
become completely unrecognizable.

Carolina Gomez, Grade 11
Animo Leadership Charter High School, CA

In the Heat of the Moment

We were like ants,
Trapped under a magnifying glass,
With nowhere to run.
Our desert hike had turned tedious,
As soon as the molten sun arose.
My water had long since lost its lush icy flavor,
And now tasted like boiled cardboard.
Even the shade offered no solace,
Its false pretense of chilled air
Seemed to torment all who gazed upon it.
The only sounds to be heard
Were the constant crunching of rocks under our feet
And the occasional sigh of exhaustion.
Our daydreams turned to savory scoops of ice cream
Filled with delicious chunks of cookie dough,
All ready to be eaten in a blissful air-conditioned room.
A room where one could simply bask in the cool breeze.
But our dreams were shattered,
For the only thing to breathe in was the thick dust-filled air.
Our dreams of deliverance and savory ice cream would have to wait,
For at least another hour that is…

Amanda Ewell, Grade 12
Emery High School, UT

Daughter of Mine

Words can't explain how much I love her, but I'll try my best.
You can say she's like my little chick in my nest.
Her mind is so curious and she babbles on and on.
And I miss her so much every time she is gone.
When I'm having a bad day and we're together,
She looks at me, smiles, and makes everything better.
Her laugh makes me laugh and her kiss makes me smile.
For her, I would cross the desert a thousand miles.
She's very unique and has her own personality.
She brightens my day; I can't believe it's my reality.
I'll be there for her when she cries or when she's afraid.
I'll guarantee that my love for her will never fade.
She's opened my eyes which made me a good mother.
For all it's worth, I'm happy she's my daughter.
I can't thank her enough for giving me a chance to feel loved.
She is truly a bundle of joy and a personal gift from above.

Hazel Estrada, Grade 11
Wilson High School, CA

The Roaming Thunder

As you sit there quietly listening,
thunderous hooves pound the plains.
Over the horizon,
the magnificent buffalo roam.
Out of sight over the horizon,
you can still hear the thunderous pounding of hooves.
Before you know it,
that roaming thunder is once gone again.

Colton Peart, Grade 10
Orem High School, UT

Joy of the Lord

If joy was as attainable as the air I breath,
there would never be the instance or need to grieve.
Just like the flowers that bloom in the spring,
there is a time for everything, including the joy it brings.

People put us down,
But we never give up.
Life gets us down,
but joy builds us up.

Is joy in the people, events or circumstances,
or is joy found in taking our chances.
To win, to succeed, and to yet overcome,
is joy found in all or in only some.

But joy is not attainable like the air we breath,
it's up and its down, it comes and it leaves.
Yet there is one joy you can take every day,
it's always there, it leaves no dismay.

With every melody it strikes the perfect chord,
It is the greatest of all, it's the joy of the Lord.

David Wahlman, Grade 11
Redding Christian High School, CA

Deep

Sometimes I wish things could be different
The things I regret I never seem to forget
Shut down from anything new
Like a shadow that came out of the blue
A silence from the past
That seems to always last
Like a breath to keep you alive
That is what I think of you
A breath that lets me know you're still here for me
That I wish I could do for you
My everlasting wish which is my last
A starless night in which I could not make my wish
The endless tears which flow from me
At once I think of the breath
And it looks like I will always be
Just a wishing breath

Jamie Fowler, Grade 10
Lucerne Valley Jr/Sr High School, CA

Words*

Some words are never
said, laying in the heart forever,
never knowing what could be.

I say speak those
words and set your
heart free.

Analisa Miyashiro, Grade 11
Valley Christian High School, CA
*Inspired by Emily Dickinson's "A Word Is Dead."

The Stress Rises, the Stress Falls

The stress rises, the stress falls
The homework gets sent out, the projects are assigned
The kids wake up at sun rise to go to school
Once they see their friends, they feel a burst of relief
The stress rises, the stress falls

The stress rises, the stress falls
The students go to class and sit and dwell
Thinking I can't wait for the bell
They can't wait to get home
Their minds roam
The stress rises, the stress falls

The Bell finally rings, we rejoice
You can hear excitement in every voice
Once arriving at home we feel the stress
Wishing the homework was less
Trying to sleep with school on your mind
Wanting to put that day behind
Finishing the homework, not remembering when you began
Realizing tomorrow it all starts again
The stress rises, the stress falls.

Kyle Paskett, Grade 11
Valley Christian High School, CA

The Dance

Tonight I danced under the stars with you,
Holding you close, your body next to mine,
Thoughts exploding in rainbow colored hues,
Caught in the rapture of your beauty, so divine.

Fragrances, swirling and drifting into my mind,
Dancing together — till the moon struck dawn.
Hiding from all, while wrapped — one intertwined,
Embracing as the wings of a golden swan.

My feet and yours never touching the ground,
Quiet murmurs coming from your only sound,
With the soft, silken caressing finger tips.
We held our breath as a lunar eclipse,
Followed by an uncertain sigh,
Knowing that this was the last good-bye.

Veronica Padilla, Grade 11
Socorro High School, NM

The End

The gentle swishing of leaves rustling
caressing your skin.
Brilliant white specks across the inky black sky.
The sky.
With its never ending vastness
it beckons to me.
Each step I take, closer and closer until
it swallows me whole.

Naomi Sjoquist, Grade 10
Mililani High School, HI

One Heart

Through happiness, through tears, through wishes and fears
We've stuck together, as we will forever
Through the laughs and the smiles, celebrations and trials
We've stuck together, as we will forever
With advice and compassion, through phases and passion
We've stuck together, as we will forever
Through the tough times, through the hardships
Through heart throbs and sorry sobs
We've stuck together, as we will forever

We've lived together, we've lost together,
We've laughed together, we've cried together,
As we will forever

Our bond is greater than friendship
Our bond is thicker than water
Our bond runs through our veins and lies within our heart
And Our bond keeps us from being apart
One heart, One soul
One life, One lesson
We are sisters, we are cousins, we are family
We've stuck together, as we will forever

Maysa Awadalla, Grade 11
Wilson High School, CA

Spring's Gift

I sit in a classroom and feel my mind crack,
As I sit near the window my life is in lack
I watch as the clouds pass and the wind fly on wings
And I wonder why do birds, sing during spring.
As I ponder this notion I suddenly see
The reason for song is the beauty of spring.
The bright, yellow sun with its golden ray beams
Brings life to the earth with its pulsating rings.
The children all play and the kites paint the sky
While adults tan and talk and comfortably sigh.
The wonders of spring are numerous and plenty
And the benefits it brings are never spent nor empty.
It is a time of hope and a time of birth
And a time of celebration and merriment and mirth
But besides the parties and the sunny jubilees
The true gift of springtime is the joy that it brings.

Keegan Kienzle, Grade 11
La Serna High School, CA

L.O.V.E.

Listen, overlook, value, encourage.
Love is something to cherish and enjoy.
Have loyalty to your love all the time.
Make sure your love for someone is the truth.
Love is your destiny to happiness.
Happiness in life is enjoyment.
Enjoyment in life leads to your comfort.
Use major integrity with your love.

Kail Seely, Grade 12
Prospect Continuation High School, CA

Life Is Short

Life is short, so make the most of it.
You and I are only here for a little bit.
Living each day like there's no tomorrow.
Living each day with or without sorrow.
Sometimes living is a pain.
Sometimes life, we cannot sustain.
We all have one life.
Make the most of it.
You and I have one life.
Seconds of time go by,
Another person dies,
Another person cries.
Seconds of time go by.
One less me in the world.
One less sight to see in the world.
Live life how you want to.
Remember, life is short
We only have one life.
Once you're dead, you can't come back.
Once you're dead, there's no coming back.

Sean Cooper, Grade 10
Minarets High School, CA

I

Healed I've become
broken I was
glued together I am
torn I stood
bandaged and casted I sit
beaten and stabbed I laid
rebuilt I have become
destroyed and in ruins I fell
I stand before you a man
broken, hurt, and dying
but nonetheless a man
pick and choose your battles.
me?
I fought for life.

Jaime Chinchilla, Grade 11
Hughson High School, CA

Beacon of Light

Across the water and beyond the sea
Through all that could and might be
A lighthouse is all that most would see
It means so much more to me.
Between the clouds and painted on the sky
As from heaven or the angels from on high
A glorious beacon that shines its light
That leads me both by day and night
Assuring me that I will find my way
That I will reach that light one fine day
I hope you see why I always think of you
For the very same words hold true.

Damon Johnsey, Grade 10
Mountainair High School, NM

Winter

The air is crisp and cold whenever the wind blows
Instead of a nice relaxing, warm comforting breath
It is cut short.
As the cold air slashes down your throat like a thousand knives
You are blinded by white almost
You think it's like heaven but you are mistaken
As the wind whips through your hair
And across your face turning your nose red
White falls almost like rain but not so loud
With no wind it is peaceful
Everything is still, no sound can you hear
The mist is thick and covers the sun
Leaving a golden tint among the fresh powder
Tints of pink are here and there as the snow lays thick over the land;
Trees and branches are drooping as if sleeping
With a white blanket customized just for their shape.
As the fog lifts like a small cave, the view is truly breathtaking
As the bottom of the clouds are painted with shreds of gold and orange
As if God had painted a picture
White snow is glittering with the colors from above and even a silver tint
Snow really is beautiful you just have to look at it with beauty.

Morgan Christian, Grade 12
Lincoln County High School, NV

Alone

Going into our relationship, I didn't think it would be any different
Just another girl, nothing special to me
But then my thoughts had changed and it has become plain for me to see
How sometimes love can be a mystery
You overcame your fear of being hurt again
And you finally decided to just let me in
You let down your guard and life became exceedingly delightful.
Then you shot through my heart, just like a rifle
A .50 cal that nobody could survive
Over and over again
I would ask you why
Why would I try so hard for something
That could be gone so fast?
And it kind of makes me smirk, when I think about our past
My heart was broken.
I had finally attained everything I was looking for
And now that everything seemed to be there no more
I was empty, lonely, not knowing what to do
But in the end I realized, I'm happier without you.
No more pain, no more tears
My heart was full.

Rashawn Mosley, Grade 11
Wilson High School, CA

A Spot Atop the Podium

Practice, practice is your life.
The days seem all but good.
Then hard skills become routine —
That spot on top seems real!
Still then the greatest challenge —
To overcome your fears.
You try and try but only fail.
Tears well, but you can't cry.
Coaches talk and teammates cheer,
You take in one deep breath.
With all your might you cease to think
And let your body fly —

Then your time to compete is here
The music starts, all nerves flee.
You finish boldly and salute
Before the hugs and tears.
That top spot is yours to claim!
Remember all your work.
Each hard day well worth its price,
Today the gold is yours.

Lauren Speers, Grade 11
Valley Christian High School, CA

Parking Lots

I hate pulling into the school parking lot
To find the same white car
Parked at the end of a row.
There are no lines painted there,
No numbers.
Nothing to say 'this is a parking spot.'
I know if I tried that,
I would get a ticket.
Do they?
No.

Every day, the same car, the same spot.
The spot that doesn't exist.
I want to leave a note,
"This is NOT a parking spot. Thanks."
Passive aggressive, non confrontational,
Note.
And maybe the day after the note,
The white car will be parked
Safely between two yellow lines.

Andrea Rodriguez, Grade 12
Woods Cross High School, UT

Huntress

In the darkness
The huntress lies
Hidden, amongst the leaves.

Connor Shutt, Grade 12
Alta High School, UT

Discarded Wings

"There's no place for me here." You said those words to me while
Standing in the midst of a tempest that was your troubled heart.
The spiteful winds stormed about us as you told me the truth,
And finally I could see your tormented soul.

You could never be content here, where people judge and wound,
That sweet heart of yours is too good for this world.
"You can escape from this; unfold your wings," I pleaded.
But that wasn't what you chose to do.

"These are no use," you said concerning the wings on your back,
Even as I insisted that you use them to fly from this forbidding place.
You shook your head resolutely.
"These wings have to be shed."

Now as I gaze upon the broken, discarded wings on the ground,
The tears come, and I let them fall.
From my mouth flies to the unsympathetic skies a question of "why"
Why did you shed the wings you could have used to leave this harsh place?

"You have it all wrong," I hear you say; I look up and see your smiling spirit
With wings more perfect than the ones you abandoned.
Finally I understand that this is your escape from the world that imprisoned you
Now break away to those sapphire skies; you're free.

Melissa Young, Grade 10
St Patrick-St Vincent High School, CA

The Ambush

Heart and lungs in turmoil, you wait for your prey.
Eyes grope the void of space as you see,
two legs, two arms, a human face, a human heart.
You know them, you know what they are.

Without thought of it, and without knowing of it, you yell, "Suppressing fire!"
On legs of flame and thunder, you ride,
pulling the grenade pin, arcing your arm back,
feeling the strength grow there, feeling the hatred spark inside, where,
gristle-faced and eyeless, your human heart screams for vengeance,
Letting the grenade fly, then, without knowing of it, and without thought of it,
you yell the command, "Assault!" And. Time. Stops.

All the moments, slowly coalesce.
Every trigger pull. Every brass shell.
Every splash of blood. Every dead man.
All together, no start of one, no end of another; but together, as in a cauldron. Then.

It is all over. Soot-faced, through tear-gilded eyes, you see,
the objects you've wrought, the carnage, the death,
Your enemy, and your friend, dead together, blood admixed,
No end of one, no start of another, and you wonder, "Will they be sorted?"
Just as you did so many times before, just as you will forevermore.
And with full knowledge of it, and with full thought of it, you utter, "We're moving on."

Abraham Jarque, Grade 11
Mount Everest Academy, CA

Light

The sun, the night, the dark and the light:
Complete opposites that are quite alike

The qualities are different but some how the same
The effects they have tend to make you think about
Life from a different view and rethink the rules

The way of the sun, it's a great source light makes the
Whole world seem happy and bright as if it were perfection
But when the dark appears the goodness fades and
Innocence slips away never to return

They show aspects the other cannot but you can never
Fully understand life for all that it is until you open your eyes,
Open your mind and unveil your heart and capture your soul

The person you are is who you choose to be
You cannot have both, your either the darkness of night or
The light that makes the world bright there is no middle no
        In between,
Never let your insecurities change who you pretend to be

Sarah Hernandez, Grade 11
New Life Christian School, CA

The Top of the Ferris Wheel

I am at the top of a Ferris wheel
Sitting among the clouds.
I am flying, rising, falling, accelerating at will,
Lingering to consider my tiny shadow
On the speckled landscape far beneath me.
I am skiing along the crystalline surface
Of the open sea, feeling the dense sea mist
Against my neck and hair,
Wondering but not worrying
About how far I will speed before
My euphoria has been satisfied.
I am the brilliant morning sun
Rising above the horizon and
Casting hope and light over the waves
Of the gently rippling sea.
I am aware that I sit at the apex,
That I will eventually descend again,
Allowing the euphoria and soaring speed
To settle into normality,
But for the moment I am at the top
Of the Ferris wheel.

Tayson Holzer, Grade 12
Woods Cross High School, UT

It Has Got Me Now

I need way more time
The element of surprise,
It has got me now.

Kayla Bermillo, Grade 10
Mililani High School, HI

Dead and Never Died, Alive and Never Really Lived

I am human
But was never born.
I am dead
But have never died.
I am alive
But have never really lived.
I am here, but have never really existed.
You say I'm in your memories
But I was never there.
I am a part of your present
But you may forget I'm here.
You want me a part of you future
But I can never be there.
You sometimes want to forget me
Since you know I won't always be there
And while that may be true
How I can never stay with you,
For now I shall continue to stay with you
Up until the crossroads of our lives go their
Separate ways and you go to your happiness
And I shall go to mine.

Nicholas Turner, Grade 10
Arbor View High School, NV

Shattered Glass

Cold heart, steady glare
The glass shows angry eyes that could never care.
Who could ever love your touch of ice?
The growl in your voice?
The glass shows grasping claws tearing down last hopes
that tomorrow might bring a sunrise.

Broken heart of a frightened boy
They can't see tear-filled eyes that refuse to cry.
Not even you can see past the mask
You've worn to hide.
They can't see the trembling hands reaching out for help
praying tomorrow might bring a sunrise.

Swinging hand breaks his courage down
He can't stand to see the eyes of the man he loves.
His heart can't take the pain he still endures
From time he's lost.
He can't stand. He's given up on any hope
that tomorrow might bring a sunrise.

Emily Virginia Simonson, Grade 11
Xavier Charter School, ID

obsession

i must make a confession
you are my obsession

i think about you day and night
and no my dear i'm not all right

Sarah Buxton, Grade 10
Clark Fork Jr/Sr High School, ID

Torture

Everything is great, or so it seems as I pretend to be happy and smile.
You act like I'm not sad to make everything seem worthwhile.
We both know it's all become a lie,
And all I can do is wait on standby.
It's been over for a while now and yet,
I stood here waiting, willing to forget.
It's all becoming blurry as you pull me back in,
Then the smoke clears and I've realized you've done it again.
I'm finally not blind to all the things you've done,
My freedom is bliss, it's almost like heaven.
And now, after everything you put me through,
I've finally had my breakthrough.
You won't ever stop torturing me not even for a second,
But I guess this is what I've bargained for, getting to know you.
I've pondered everything and left nothing unquestioned.
All I can beg for is to take back everything from the moment we met, a redo.
I gave and gave until there was nothing left to give,
Why can't you leave me alone when I've finally found my reason to live.
All of my newfound happiness is taken away
By those hateful, burning words you say.
I refuse to be like you and say harsh words, all I can do is hope you will learn that I won't fight back. I'm done with you.

Jenifer Schwartz, Grade 12
University Preparatory School, CA

Hope

Would you say hope was found within yourself? Do you have a supply for those dark nights when your candles go missing? For when the news drone on about death and destruction? Can you pull it out of drawers and give it away? Is it grown or man-made? I'd say it comes from the sky. I watched it one day as it perched on the edge of the sun. It drew clouds onto the blue canvas with a steady stream of its own white hair. It laid across the sun and lazily stretched its fingers, then dangled glistening drops down onto my head. Those silver and gold drops had splashes of blue in the middle, as cool and calm as the water's surface. It hung above the ground, sifting through the smog and poverty, casting away death with a single glare. The birds had it all over themselves, trailing it on their wings as they lifted into the sky. The moons alabaster face had shiny smears of it pasted around its eyes and mouth. The trees wore it as fancy party skirts, swirling it across the grass, painting strings of it in between the stars. It saw me watching as the hope created something beautiful out of nothing. It bent over to look me straight in the eye, as if to measure up my strength. It handed me a slice of gleaming silver, and I tucked it deep into my heart. I held onto the swing tighter then kicked my legs, watching the dust rise up around my ankles. A small child came closer and bravely stole a handful from the sky, formed it into a colorful bracelet that she could wear around her dainty wrist. Soon others came to snatch some for themselves. The smart ones picked it off the tree's lowest branches and tucked it away for safe keeping. The desperate one's fell upon their knees and sobbed for an ounce of the precious drops when no more could be found. I simply swung back and forth, watching the empty and dirty faces gape and moan for some hope to hold onto.

Jessica St. Martin, Grade 11
San Marcos High School, CA

Confusion in the Stars

I have met my match. The one person that can confuse me more than anyone else in the world. The perplexity intrigues me and draws me closer to him, however it's only an illusion for I will never gain the opportunity to be truly close to him within his bubble of confusion. Confounding series of words stream from his mouth, they reach my ears and enter my mind but they can never be processed. His sharp words can never be decoded within my brain. It's not that my intelligence isn't on the same level as his, just that he speaks his heart instead of his head. The words flood upward they never reach his thoughts. A completely different dialect and I have to say that it's a language I want to learn more than any other however a question comes to mind. Will I still feel the same way about this oddity after I've found meaning in his words? I can't answer that question but I know that he is definitely unlike any other that I've met. Even though I know him I figure I will never truly know him and for this I am strangely content because knowing him takes away from the mystery that this unnatural being radiates and that's something I never want to take away from.

Marshanna Valrie, Grade 11
Gardena Sr High School, CA

The Stone

The pain next to your heart
Grew a stone that turned black aches inside
The stone that will not escape the misery and heartache
The stone needs to come out before it breaks through your heart
You can't stop it, it's stuck inside
The thumping of your heart makes the stone grow
The more it grows the faster it thumps, it won't stop growing
It's crushing your heart, a stone that turned black
It pushes harder on your heart the more you think
Trying to stop thinking, makes you think harder
You see a memory. Your heart races. You can't stop it.
The stone grows bigger and deeper
You want to pull it out before it is too late
It aches against your heart, the stone, it won't come
it just keeps growing, it pushes deeper against your heart
there won't be a space to keep growing
trying to pull, it won't come
the stone starts to shatter
piercing your heart, taking a part
the stone that was by your heart that turned black
Took a part of your heart you can't get back.

Jessica Jex, Grade 11
Merit Academy, UT

Music

The belief that life is based on music
Is it true?
Is it true?
We know music is entwined with our emotions
Having a bad day
To plug your headphones into your iPod
Scroll down to the artists
What are you feeling right now?
Feeling depressed?
Play some Jack Johnson
Feeling mad?
Play some The Devil Wears Prada
Feeling lost?
Play some Chubby Checker
Music is deep
Music is sweet
Music is you.

Jared Nelson, Grade 10
Bradshaw Christian High School, CA

You Make Me Feel. . .

You make me feel like I just won the lottery
You make me feel like a little kid who won a Teddy Bear
You make me feel like I just beat the world record
You make me feel like I'm one in a million
You make me feel like the world will never end
But most of all you make me smile like never before

Amber Nakamoto, Grade 11
Mililani High School, HI

The Soldier

The soldier stood and faced his family
Saddened to the bone
He knew that they would miss him
But from tears his eyes still shone

To face the foe and fight its vice
And protect what he held true
He knew his burden would be heavy
But he knew what he must do

The soldier knelt and did his best
To console his dying friend
But he knew that it was futile
He could not prevent the end

The soldier felt the bullet enter
He felt all the fear
But his heart was saddened for his friends
He knew his death was near

The soldier stood to face God
His judgment God would tell
God said to him "Walk peacefully in heaven,
You've done your time in hell."

Kevin O'Toole, Grade 10
St Francis High School, CA

The Powers That Be

To these morning sounds I wake,
Am dressed on the bus by half past six
I dance and sing and prayers make
A marionette of string and sticks

I turn when hands turn
I sit when hands rest
And sometimes burn
Inside my chest

May I step, I ask
May I talk, I cry
My life is a task
My life is a lie

I walked a museum, and saw life in still frame
Each life by an artist, some famous, most not
I saw mine one day, but could find no name
And the colors bled through while the canvas rot

I took the bus home, the next came at five
I sat in my box all alone
Held up by the strings that kept me alive
But had turned my heart to stone

Michelle Choe, Grade 12
Mililani High School, HI

Red Balloon

I am holding a red balloon
That is the truth
It is an absolute truth.
Hey, nice soccer ball
What are you talking about?
It's a red balloon.
That is the most pretty green balloon!
No, it's a red balloon!
No, it's soccer ball, come here and look
Why are you saying it is soccer ball when it's green balloon?
I see purple ball from here
This is red balloon and it's the truth.
The truth should be what fits our life the best.
I see green balloon and it works perfect for me, so I see green
I love soccer! Soccer ball is perfect for me!
No, you cannot just choose what fits the best.
Red balloon was and is and always will be a red balloon!
You can't just change the truth into something that fits!
Rather you choose to believe it or not.
I am holding a red balloon.

Seung Hoon Han, Grade 10
Cypress High School, CA

Growth

I am forever done with this cruel pain,
Led on, destroyed, cannot begin to feign
That selfishness deployed on his behalf
Has not totaled the wholeness of my soul.
Let go, move on, the damage has been done,
Oh, great relief, oh, freedom come to me —
I cried these tears, which endless torrents flow,
Those months, those years, oh, centuries ago,
Think I; when did it start? When did it go?
Love turn'd to hate beyond all repair,
The consistent beating of this despair
Will pass, will pass, with hope and love and faith

To sleep, to sleep, no, not another word,
Oh light, lead the way, bring the peace of May.

Julie-Anne Gabelich, Grade 12
Mary Star of the Sea High School, CA

My Booty

I am a pirate of the sea,
Guarding the treasure
Underneath my bed.
A chest of secrets:
    Photos in sepia of my family, school awards, old
    ballet shoes, books with yellowing pages, a small tooth, and
    a doll with only one eye.
Riches like gold
Hidden from looters.
Treasure buried in a sea of dust
Waiting to be rediscovered.

Francesca Zambrano, Grade 12
St Joseph Notre Dame High School, CA

New Life

Time is running out,
    no time to pout.
All around kids in their caps and gowns,
    the sun beating down.

In the fall a new life will start,
    family all far apart.
Many miles away,
    in the city you will stay.

Breaking the hearts of all,
    promising to call.
Holding in the cries,
    saying your good-byes.

All alone from now on,
    no where to call home, it's gone.
This was your plan,
    make it work, do as much as you can.

Your worries amplified, with no one to help you through.

Rachael Cram, Grade 10
Cypress High School, CA

The Torturous Storm

Drip, the slow trickle continues to drip,
Splash, they grow into giant drops of glass.
With clouds so gray the sky becomes one mass,
Jolt, the lightning makes the earth's heart beats skip.
Boom, the thunder makes most anyone trip.
Wild and untamed they work together with sass.
When added in wind almost nothing lasts
Things will get destroyed, and lives completely flip.

How then, can hurt lives ever be restored?
What can be done to bring back people's homes?
The love of a brother can help bring back,
The things that a torturous storm can discard.
Somewhere for you a kind loving soul roams,
He'll find and help you start over and unpack.

Margo Poissant, Grade 10
Calvary Murrieta Christian School, CA

Unknown

The unknown appeals to curious eyes
Like life after death or the stars in the sky.
We rush the time, seeking endless answers
The hunger to know spreads like a cancer.
We find ourselves unable to understand
The simplicities of life at every demand.
Like the desired heart or the subtle glance
We go astray from our wants, never grasping the first chance.
As the wind whistles of comfort and the trees sway peacefully
The unknown slowly conceals itself within the beauty completely.

Haley Meyer, Grade 11
James C Enochs High School, CA

Rise and Shine

First thing in the morning
I'm gliding down the street
It's not boring
Cause I know who I'm going to meet
I'm going to pick my friends up
We're going to go real far
Who cares about tomorrow?
I've got a car
Crusties in my eyes
Cause I just woke up
Everything's all good
No need to try to rush
I'm in my hood
The ground is lush
My windows are frosty
My radio's turned up
The air is clean and crisp
The sun's coming up
It's my favorite time of day
I'm going to live it up

Ashley R., Grade 11
Diamond Ranch Academy, UT

Rain

The big black blanket is hanging in the sky,
As I leave the safety of the porch,
The sting of the drops hit me,
And I am instantly soaked
They are cold and wet,
These clothes I wear
The sharpness
Of the drops,
Bites
Through
To my skin,
And chills my bones.
When it stops falling down
And the stars fill the sky in all directions,
I go back inside, sad that the rain is gone.

Eric Shute, Grade 10
Orem High School, UT

Disconnected

I'm talking on the phone
With my friends
My dad comes in and says,
"What are you doing?"
I say, "Nothing!"
He comes back, five minutes later.
"Do your homework."
"Later."
"NOW!"
I keep talking on the phone.
The line goes dead.

Crystal Carrillo, Grade 10
St Joseph Notre Dame High School, CA

God's New World Order

Eyes of potential fire and the mouth as a lighter
God gave me the gift to forever ignite a path into a deeper understanding of life
"Knowledge as the spark and discipline the light" says Mike
His words forever branded into my brain
Creating a new outlet
A release for pain
An imaginative way to embrace the fall
The rise
The iron fisted dictating thoughts as they come, and taming them to positive use
Because there is no more of a place for devastation in this time
It's slowly being demolished by the unlimited fires
From the eyes, the mouth, the knowledge, the discipline
The new voices and the rebirth of engineering creative heights
God is breathing into the lungs of the world new life
And he is molding and sculpting new words into our vernacular
Such as love and might
Steady forth shall the soldiers of God's army fight
Incorporating the new insight
Using the pen against the sword
And the tongue as the most powerful weapon in this arsenal

Semaj Earl, Grade 10
View Park Preparatory Accelerated Charter High School, CA

Seconds Trapped by Minutes

Why would someone stare at a broken clock?
A useless wreck stoned by its lifeless appearance
Distorted by its unusual silence, and perplexed by its locked hands
It holds only a single moment, a unique time
A time that tells me it is exactly 11:59
One minute before tomorrow
One second before she leaves
Her hand gripped by his hand
Together, they lie on the same number
Fingers intertwined, and tangled by love knot
He seizes not only her hand, but time as well
And as I stare at this clock, it is not time that passes my life
But my life wasted on time
Only to know a second later, she will leave, and he will chase
A minute later, he will stop, and she will fade
Disillusioned by this strange clock, I wish time would never take its course,
As every second that passes by is one less second as I stare at this clock
Now I look at the time
It is one minute before tomorrow
This is why I stare.

Jonathan Wu, Grade 11
James Logan High School, CA

A Pessimist in Love

Fie, Fie, I fly
This hot beating in my breast!
Please, listen, I do not lie

Fie Fie, this wondrous admiration
Deeply ingrained! Oh how it grates irritation!
The want, dare I say the need
The hold, to feel, to be touched
Nay! Fulfilled
Nary a scorn or contemplation
I concede to the feeling
A celestial gift of great elation

Oh the sensation or spiteful liberation!
Weakness surfaces, strength diminished
Must I repeat this revelation?

I love and love
And am loved and loved in turn
When push comes to shove
I Fly, Fie, Fie, I fly!

Emily Cutler, Grade 12
Merit Academy, UT

Younger Daze

I remember
Those days long gone when we would dance together
Without fear of being judged
Before adolescence gave way to teens
Bringing with it the crippling disease of
Wallflower syndrome
Summer afternoons
Fred and Ginger in the living room
In my grandmother's old shoes
Your father's old suit
Too large for either of us, but
Comfortable
We were younger then, weren't we?
Years have passed
We have grown older, taller
And we have grown apart
You have changed
No more dancing
My shoes fit
Your suit fits
While we try to fit in

Ashlyn Thomas, Grade 10
Helix Charter High School, CA

Believe It or Not

You stand there thinking this is real
But you get caught up in the ways it makes you feel,
  Can't eat, can't sleep
You're thinking to yourself if this is all a crazy dream

You take a minute,
    Regain your thoughts,
But you're still here looking at the same stupid watch

It's said time is supposed to heal all things,
Yet time is the real reason you feel such things,

Maybe this feeling is real,
Maybe it's only in my head,
Love, Live, Life
  Are the only things that are stuck in my head…

Nate Navarrete, Grade 12
North Hills Christian School, CA

Human

I've suddenly realized how
Fragile a human is
A few breakable bones stand guard over
Our heart, and this
Delicate collaboration of tissue and muscle
Can be severed in a moment
Yet we are so beautiful and strong
So much packed into such an easily broken box.
I've suddenly realized how
Insubstantial, like butterfly wings
We truly are…gossamer whispers here for a season
Drifting flakes setting fire to dreams.
Still, we are so complex and stunning
Iridescent colored eyes
Fragile, crackable, like porcelain…like glass
A heart beating with passion and hope.

Allison Woodruff, Grade 10
Glacier High School, MT

Puzzle

When you met me I was a puzzle
A mystery
While with you the pieces put themselves together
And for once I knew who I was
The day you left me
Pieces began to fall out of place
And with it my life

Kyle Jensen, Grade 11
Preston High School, ID

Poetry?

I always thought poetry was boring
I found one poet who wasn't
I read his poems a lot
Almost the same way I would lap up a sappy romance novel
Now I know poetry can be exciting
And I also know that I'm not good at writing
Poetry

Sofia Prokop, Grade 12
University Preparatory School, CA

Lost on Valentine's Day

I was alive then…
I collapsed
Black wind and darkness
Lost direction
I was alone
Shamed, tormented, and pained
Leaked through a song that no one sings
Try to walk a mile in my shoes
Know what its like to have the blues
Wasted days and wasted nights
Why should I keep loving you
When your to blame for making me blue
For you don't belong to me
I was so lonely
I prayed for you
My love…
I'm torn into pieces
My insides turned to ash
Rich men beg
Good men sin
A hopeless romantic dies lonely

Keanu Herrera, Grade 12
Red Mountain High School, AZ

Appreciation

Lovely Sweetly Movely
You are my melody
You made my mood happily
You gave me greetings appropriately

Strangely Quietly Abruptly
You are in my creative story
You are in my secret diary
You are in my dreamful fairy

Actually
You let me feel proudly
Exactly
I never want you to be lonely
Gratefully
We get to know each other early
Luckily
We are together till now since that day

Well we enjoy our simple happiness
Just like so —

Hui Liu, Grade 11
Karl G Maeser Preparatory Academy, UT

Everyone Needs Love

We search our whole lives
To find just the right person
To love and cherish

Cassidy Couture, Grade 10
Temecula Valley High School, CA

The Savior, Just Confirming the World, Presents All Humans Glorious

Don't trust what's hidden before your eyes.
Porta, even Louis, fooled the scholars.
Modern knowledge, philosophers despise.

The subconscious is privately guised,
Encoded with secrets for you to find, but
Don't trust what's hidden before your eyes.

Letters, numbers, and simple symbols disguise
The ciphers passing unsuspectingly by.
Modern knowledge philosophers despise.

Through the ages many have plainly lied
To avoid suspicion of their report.
Don't trust what's hidden before your eyes.

Tritheim's innocence none could devise, and
Spartans' methods failed to make you think;
Modern knowledge, philosophers despise.

People decipher the unending lies
To the gibberish passing by, but they
Don't trust what's hidden before your eyes.
Modern knowledge, philosophers despise.

Amanda Minchella, Grade 10
Chandler Preparatory Academy, AZ

Me vs the World

From days end to days break
The roots and trees within the city quake;
Millions of people together in happiness
But only one me alone in sadness

The wanting of acceptance
But only the gift of absence
I see people walk by, but are we the same?
Our eyes, our flesh, our stance resemble
But I, I feel only the pain
The whisper in my mind only a mumble
Wanting to be heard as strong and humble

What else is there in this so called "Happy" world
When it is a place of sadness, pain, and a joyless pearl
But others are blinded by the lies and what they see
When the truth is it is all just a bad dream

Now my time is almost up
Seeing the world leaving me in the dust
Knowing that I'm gone revealed my life only in pain
Always felt alone, unwanted and nevertheless the same
Now that I'm gone I hope I am not forgotten
But remembered as the person I once was in this dream contradiction

Christopher Hinojosa, Grade 11
Edison Sr High School, CA

The Shot

I walk away from the bench,
The crowd is roaring my name
The scoreboard reads 57 - 57
7 seconds.
I look at the crowd,
Then I smile, confident.
Excited to win.
Knowing my shots will go in.
I walk to the line,
Wait for the ball
I dribble three times
Take a deep breath and shoot
Swish!
But I couldn't celebrate just yet,
I wait for the ball
Still smiling,
Still confident,
Still excited
I shoot again!
SWISH!
WE WIN!

Trent Webb, Grade 11
Temple Baptist Academy, NM

Unspoken Words

Secretly he thinks
Thoughts to dangerous
To be uttered a'loud
In his mind he whispers
Words of truth
Which frighten him
A daily lesson
Each one new
But just as painful
Hidden within his head
The temptation of evil
And sinful regrets.
The soul he lost
Floats behind
Lurking in his shadows
Waiting for him
To turn around
And extend a hand;
But that would return
Memories he'd stored away
Where even his mind, remains silent.

Elizabeth Martin, Grade 12
Westview High School, AZ

Spring

As spring dawns with time
may Cupid work his magic
eternity brought

Evan Ishiara, Grade 10
Mililani High School, HI

The Good Old Days

How I miss the good old days when with my friends I'd fly,
Because the hub caps that we found were UFO's from the sky.

How I miss my Pokemon. I caught more every day,
But I can't find them in the grass, they must have gone away.

And someone, who I do not know replaced my trusty jet
And of all the things to take its place they chose an old swing set.

I lost my ninja powers too and how to shoot hand beams,
But, I think, the worst of all, I've lost those silly dreams.

The good old days, the good old days when no worries were bestowed,
Except that dumb mathematics thing I wanted to explode.

But I should not worry so, I should not think of loss.
For my memories wave to me from the other side of times long cross

And cheerfully I wave to him while he innocently plays,
Seeing things that I once saw, back in the good old days.

Josh Bladh, Grade 11
Merit Academy, UT

Nervous Quirks

Tonight tainted breath will taste like burnt grounds.
Posing in flannel plaid, playing Chuck Taylor games.
Mouthing moments when blind concentration, and tuned lives were cut short.
Never thinking twice
Instigating battles when abominable giants.
Acquaintances of jukebox fans.
New found hobbies of colored smoke,
Consequences or clumsiness result in burnt tongues.
Concentrated hours of affection worded with wool.
Frantic searches for runaway inanimate objects.
Found, cracked, unusable, for now.
Epiphanies of stored memories yet to be photographed.
Watching aimlessly in cramped closet space.
Porch lit, growing tolerance of second hand underage infractions.
On the last drag breathe you in.

Piper Bradford, Grade 11
Merit Academy, UT

Green Relief

A green like the trees
and a breeze like the wind
puts my mind at ease
and happiness begins
slow motion scenery when water is clear and still
pulling out a fresh crisp new ten dollar bill
but always know that this feeling is not permanent
and when it fades you're in the shade yet again with flames burning it
and when it fades again your angry tempers scary
for the peace we attain from this is only temporary

Justyn Stokes, Grade 12
Wilson High School, CA

A Lost Love

We use to have a connection
All I wanted was to show you some affection
I thought we would have something real, but I guess your love pointed in the wrong direction
I really wanted your love and your protection
And my heart was in pain like an injection
So I asked you if you wanted a second chance but I dealt with the rejection
I can see that you no longer want my affection but if I'm wrong please make a correction

Even though I let you go I still had determination
Because I wanted our story to have a continuation
We were just lacking communication
I really wanted you out of all the boys in the population
The only reason I asked you if you wanted to be friends is to see if you wanted something serious
But you agreed so I guess I don't make you that delirious

I thought you would've said something to prove me wrong
That the feelings you have for me are strong
And my heart with yours is where we belong
But I guess six months for you was too long
So I'm moving on because it seems that our relationship is long gone

Cindy Alvarez, Grade 12
Corona Sr High School, CA

A Poverty

The struggles in life aren't what they seem to be
We are taught to believe that our lack of material possessions mean that we lack the ability to succeed
But success is a bias state of being,
The media and the government put these objects on a silver platter for all to feed
They drill these ideas into our brains; Bombarding us with images of inconsequential substances
We need to stop fighting each other,
Black, Mexican, Arabian, Muslim, Jew — we all come together in a slew
A competent force, far greater than what they know.
What they see now is not what they will see forever
The greatest revolution of all time has begun,
Those who they have shut down will rise from the dead
Ghandi, King, Che, Chavez…will never again be silenced
For the day will come when ignorance is no longer a factor of our demise
But it will be a disguise of our potent eyes.
The all-seeing Eye? — It's not in the back of the dollar bill
It's in the back of our minds
We must resurface these eyes
This is a shout out to all my people
DO NOT be ashamed of the poverty that surrounds you
Keep your head up; our shame is a reflection of unsuccessful attempts to become them.

Veronica Vargas, Grade 11
Animo Leadership Charter High School, CA

When I First Saw Her

When I first saw her she was a broken hearted girl with her head in the clouds dreaming of a better world when we first met the words didn't come out right she laughed then smiled and said hey that's life then she told me a story of a little girl who'd been beaten by her mom then passed from home to home next time I saw her she was crying in my arms wouldn't tell me what was wrong but I wish she would next time I saw her she was dead last time I saw her I had flowers at her grave saying goodbye which I didn't want to say I could feel her spirit in the wind as I stood by her grave and I knew she really loved me never want me to give up last time I saw her I changed my ways

Tifarrah Miller, Grade 12
Laguna Creek High School, CA

Too Bright, too Dark

I wake up in a room that is blinding white
Where is the sun
There is no light
To my right there is a hole
I peek down
There is darkness down there
My mind is getting madder
As I focus on a really long ladder
I climb down to see what is going on
Something is up, what's wrong?
I see nobody
Where has the color gone?
At first it was too bright
Now it's too dark
This isn't right
The world is too bright and dark
I liked it better in between
So does everyone else
It seems

Shelly Senter, Grade 12
Ramona High School, CA

Time to Go...

This small town's full of memories,
I don't want to leave behind,
I'm not sure of which way to go,
Feels like I'm running blind.

I had a plan in front of me,
I thought it would work out,
But the day is here, but I wait still,
My mind is full of doubt.

"Is this the end?" I ask myself,
As I drive on down the highway,
Then I realize this is the beginning,
It's time to do it my way.

Stormi Allen, Grade 11
Burlington High School, WY

Dance

Dance, where movement and music meet
Feeling the sounds of the beat
Having a story in your head
Movement from your head to your feet
Jumping out of your seat
Sometimes tears could be shed

Leaping, jumping, spinning
Going across the stage
Having no fear hold you back
It is like the feeling of winning
Or an animal trapped inside a cage
Creativity, something you can't lack

Kara Kirmse, Grade 11
Valley Christian High School, CA

Atlantic

I am ageless and old, I am depthless and deep,
I am breezy and torrential, I am your friend only sometimes,
Clouds churn above me, fish swim around me, rocks beat below me,
You may find a friend below my enchanting surface,
Explorers have tempted my temper,
Entrepreneurs have risked my wrath,
Persecuted have dared my anger,
All for the higher ground I haven't yet claimed, it was mine once and now they call it theirs,
They dare to claim me conquered,
They presume to be the master of me,
They cut through me with their wooden and iron and steel hulls,
They use me, they abuse me — and to what end?
I grant them a calm breeze, them deem me conquerable,
I grant them a safe harbor, they only see opportunity,
I grant them my children, they catch them in their ungrateful nets,
I grant them freedom, they try to chain me,
I give them a gale, they remember my might,
I give them a tsunami, they quiver in fear,
I give them a hurricane, they call me a monster,
They must be put in their place now and again,
They must know I am not to be conquered, they must learn to be grateful.

Sarah Wendel, Grade 11
Golden Sierra High School, CA

Near-Death Experience

I thought I could do it.
My friends convinced me to.
As I was standing in line, I told myself it will be all right.
I'm not so sure.
I see other people waiting in line; talking, laughing, smiling.
How could they be so calm?
I was terrified.
As I tried to calm down, I realized there was no turning back.
We stepped onto the roller coaster and I shook as I tried to get comfortable.
My friend looked at me and smiled.
She had no idea I was completely terrified.
As the ride started, I cringed.
It took off and we were soaring through the air.
It felt like nothing was keeping us from falling.
We rolled, tossed, and flew.
Finally the ride came to a stop and I was changed.
I walked off the roller coaster and wobbled onto the next ride.

Carol Winkleman, Grade 10
Orem High School, UT

Slipping Down

The world is a darker place without you.
Some might not see it, but it's there.
A slight, but significant shadowing around the edges of life.
Proof that there is more to the human body than simple elements.
Once that bright spirit passes onto wherever it will go, it leaves its shadow.
It doesn't belong in that place, here it seems to stay.
And for what? Does it haunt? Does it mourn?
Or is it simply your way of letting us know you've truly gone?

Jordan Sharp, Grade 11
Golden Sierra High School, CA

Fear

When I look into your eyes
All my fear is disguised
The fear of losing you
The fear of everything being untrue
Don't leave me now, no way no how
'Cause without those eyes, everything demise
Can you feel my love? With every touch
That you love so much
With every kiss
That sends bliss
With every stare
That shows how much I care
So why do I have this fear
This fear that makes everything unclear
When I know you're sincere
Yet this fear is severe
Just look into my eyes
And clear these ties
Clear this fear
And hold me my dear

Olivia Vasquez, Grade 12
Watsonville High School, CA

I Am

I am motherhood and responsible,
I wonder about my son's future.
I hear my son sleeping through the night.
I see my son on his first day of school,
I want a good career for him.
I am motherhood and responsible.

I pretend to see him go to college.
I feel sad to see him leave
I touch the hopes my son sees in me.
I worry about his attitude.
I cry when I see him get hurt
I am motherhood and responsible.

I understand he'll grow up.
I say he'll grow up to be a good buy
I dream to see him graduate from college
I try to give him the best I can
I hope he loves me and has confidence in me
I am motherhood and responsible.

Karen Jimenez, Grade 11
Pioneer High School, NV

Embrace Me

Your hand laced in mine
Our love floating in the air
I've found my true love

Lindsay Cahill, Grade 11
Temecula Valley High School, CA

People Are Strange

How long until mankind will realize?
During the day we all look up at the same skies

It is not the difference between us
But how much we have in common that creates a fuss

Are people ever truly naive?
Or is it that they truly cannot perceive?

Why do parents just not embed into their children
That being nice is the only trait of a good human?

Does money ever really change a thing?
Or does it just lessen the sting?

Emotionally we're destined to suffer
Sadly, we believe are troubles harder than any others

Can humans be classified as the same species?
Because we all seem different to me...

Kyle McCue, Grade 12
Millennium High School, AZ

Scolding the Weeds

There is only dullness left,
Washed out people,
Ungrateful for the sky, the mountain, and the star.
Deeply superficial, artificial,
Conformed to their roots.
They drink tainted water and soak in tainted sun.
Absorbing not truth nor understanding,
But false information.
Raising stillborn plants with weak, spindly roots,
That begin the life cycle as infertile,
Thus corrupting and ruining the whole system.
Our water has another additive,
Our renewing, endless ignorance,
Which diseases our society, our humanity,
And remains incurable,
Spreading and adapting to plague what we know.
Prevention's will not be sold, chaos will commit,
Till we evolve our world,
Till we begin to see the difference between,
What is familiar and what is right.

Heather Mazzarella, Grade 12
Sunrise Academy, UT

Fall

Fall is almost here
colorful leaves all around
trees gently swaying

Cody Colello, Grade 10
Mililani High School, HI

I Have Not Seen

I have not seen so much in life
I have not had a major strife
I am still young, I do not know
I still have time for me to grow
I am not yet the person I wish to be
I am simply just trying to find me
I do not know much about this world
I am just a simple girl
I have not yet left a big impression
I am just starting my life mission

I will start a fire
I will watch it grow
I will watch it spread to all I know
I will start new changes and support the old
I will not live under rules I am told
I am the past, future, and today
I am whatever I choose to say.

Katelynn Sasaki, Grade 10
Cypress High School, CA

Moving On

I it's what she said
what she was
what she became
I it's what he listened to
what he knew
what he watched
ME it was thought
it was said
it was all she cared for
HER it was in his head
it was always there
it was the open wound
LEFT a warning had rung
good bye never said
a door closed
FREE a new life
a new view
a new smile upon his face

Kelsey Long, Grade 12
Dobson High School, AZ

Means to an End

Death lists, crazed fists
Who'd have thought it'd come this far?
Boys dying, mothers crying
Guns as bright as blazing stars.

The nation's taken, with such mistaken
Zeal that I've ever seen.
And so it leads, as young men bleed
To the death of a nation, as it seems.

Ethan Lie, Grade 11
Valley Christian High School, CA

Patterned Shackles

Abandoned by the dearth eternal night and shaken by the brother of sleep,
I seek for the realization of accustomed vision.
For the ambiance which floods each shrine, outbursts a phantom of silence.
Each shrine hovers the void of entirety.
Each shrine stammers — the implored — of pitiable, idyllic want.
Now all damsel ghouls defy principle, unbalancing fools' domain.
But there is no domain which heeds unsurpassed.
Everlasting altruistic regard is not one which breathes toxic squander.
It is that of forsaken regard which breathes deeply,
And lathers itself within this foul venom.
This venom which is the savoring spice reeling within each shrine,
Out bursting a phantom of silence.
The silence shadows the sound,
Emitting no true voice among all who heed falsified divinity.
Abandoned by the glaring beacon, and incomplete of eternal night,
I romp stiffly between shackles of madness and patterned vision.
I romp stiffly within the void of grim dusk.
I seek not to heed a falsified divinity, but that of reliance.
Not reliance edified among the ambiance of patterned shrines, but the reliance within me.
And I stay abandoned by the dense heedless pitiable fools,
To shield uncertain instinct within.

Katie Kraychir, Grade 11
Desert Hot Springs High School, CA

Friday Night Lights

The noise rises, the noise falls.
The sun starts to set in the west, as the darkness turns into walls;
Outside the tunnel they are summoned from the crowd
And the cheers become incredibly loud.
The noise rises, the noise falls.

Everyone awaiting the beginning,
With the hope of winning;
1st 2nd 3rd and finally the last quarter,
The forces continue to collide to earn a "W" and earn the respect as a supporter.
The noise rises, the noise falls.

Our hearts racing,
Down set ready go, chasing…
The dream I have that I may leave it on the field,
That I may have the talents to wield.
The noise rises, the noise ceases.

Zachary Vaiana, Grade 11
Valley Christian High School, CA

Modern Day Cannibal

Glinting skin, vulnerable flesh is to dire hunger;
Desperate hunger, a product of desired outcome.
Targeting the helpless soul to claim hold integrity's might;
Innocence, sacred, weak is foraged at pedal's first blossom.
Art of meaning, twisted and succumbed to the hellish belly of the beast;
Light's beam over perspective life gives way for reality's darkened teeth.
Meaning, perspective, life,
All for the inhumane monstrosity of society.

Michael Wilson, Grade 12
TMCC Magnet High School, NV

All Over Again

Understanding clicks
it finally makes sense
I was right all along
I never moved on
but still — the rags and the dolls can all just go die
I can keep on denying
I don't have to tell
I'll push it back down
my one secret I'll not tell.

Once upon a time, I thought it was done
and once upon a time, I was very wrong.

The bittersweet acceptance now won't go away
the deed is now done, and from the end it's begun.

Somewhere inside, I knew all along.
From somewhere outside, I'll find the strength to go on.

Korbie Fowers, Grade 11
Viewmont High School, UT

Ode to My Memory

I would tell you my life, and my name,
but I seem to have forgotten them.
I think I had a husband, maybe children too,
but I cannot recall their names either.
At some point I had parents, a childhood,
at some point I fell in love,
I went to school, had jobs, grew up,
but all that left me somewhere along the road,
I don't remember when.
Little details, like my first kiss, my wedding,
my children's birth —
Did I ever even have all of that?
Did I ever smile into my loves eyes?
Did I ever cry over something I thought was important?

Why are tears cascading down my face now?
I would tell you
but I seem to have forgotten the reason.

Cori Bowles, Grade 12
Willow Canyon High School, AZ

But Still

I am in despair
But never lose hope
I fight with desire
And never tire
Lies surround me like smoke
But still I see hope
Threats are heard all around
But still I am ready for another round
People turn their faces without care
But still the hope is there

Eric Guerrero, Grade 10
Alta Loma High School, CA

The Dress

As I hang here, all alone and untouched,
I will never forget the memories
How you moved me so much.
Dancing skin on silk, together but yet alone,
You gave me legs
But my strings you still own.
Remember my silver? How it shined so bright,
Like rippling water waves
Dancing in the moon light.
My blue tinted green, like the scarf you always wear.
Was held so tight together
By the zipper below your hair.
Your favorite thing, was my black lace and bow,
How every time the music played
You body moved with the flow.
But now your days are done, your dancing comes to an end.
But then a new hope,
Your daughter to begin.

Breanna Lovato, Grade 10
Mountainair High School, NM

The Perfect Place

The waves splash against the sand
leaving seashells for people to collect,
making a sound that is like music to the ears.
The sun shines against the water
making it sparkle.
Such a view makes anyone be relaxed.
The softness of the sand,
while covering yourself with it.
It's so soft that it makes your toes tickle.
People stand in their bathing suits,
holding their surfboards,
ready for the big waves to come.
Little kids are making sand castles
with their little pails and shovels.
The lifeguard peers with his binoculars
making sure everyone is safe.
The view, the sound, the peace,
it all makes you never want to leave.

Elizabeth Chavez, Grade 10
Orem High School, UT

Racism

Racism is a first reaction
You see them, you hate them
You can be hurt
It is a feeling of anger
A feeling of hate
But you can always change it
When someone looks at you
They may hate you
They may like you for your differences
But they can always be your friend.

Kong Vue, Grade 12
Prospect Continuation High School, CA

Our Love Was Forever Lost and Taken

We shared our love for one another,
Felt as if we would always be together,
But then we got separated from one another,
That took and lost our love forever,
I wish we were in love again,
But I don't know where to begin,
So I play songs on the guitar,
Hoping it would bring you back from afar,
To join us together once and for all,
But our love for one another was taken,
Our love was forever forsaken,
I know our love would unite again,
Hoping that time would again begin,
I write this poem in song,
For love was always like a song,
It warmed my heart from inside,
It formed love from outside to inside,
Our love was taken and lost,
But love can be found and found again,
Our love will forever rise again,
This will make love happen again.

Erik Rodgers, Grade 11
Crossroads School, CA

As Endlessly I Line Up Iron Clocks

As endlessly I line up iron clocks,
I recognize the cage that has been formed.
While hanging from a string, they form a box
Of crystal faces beautifully adorned.
Rhythm, despite a soothing, constant tick,
Now overwhelms and aggravates my ear,
An overlapping monotonous trick
Reminding me that I am always here.

Yet why would I so readily oppose
The beauty that surrounds my open mind?
Though physically I'm bound, my wisdom grows
As there are bars; at least I am not blind.
It does not matter what I hear or see,
For every clock, though close, is dear to me.

Pamela Osborn Popp, Grade 10
Chandler Preparatory Academy, AZ

Nishikigoi

Middle of the day, sitting on the grass under a
Cherry Blossom's cool shade. I look over the water just as a
breeze rustles the leaves. There in the water moving to and fro
are the graceful Koi. Their scales shimmering in the sunlight.
They are as numerous as the stars.
The ducks quacking and searching for food.
How graceful the koi as it moves through the water.
How peaceful the koi not having a care in the world.
This place how tranquil, I wish I could stay.
But I have to go back to the stress and noise of the day.

David Ascencio, Grade 11
Valley Christian High School, CA

Truth Lies Beyond

Life is gullibility,
Believing everything we hear,
Or read, or see, or even speak,
To be unarguable truth.
But truth lies beyond:
Beyond our reach, our grasp.
We feel it slip away,
Out into the cold, heartless unknown.
Until our dying day the truth
Will be just beyond the limits of our feeble minds.
We advance upon it, slowly,
And yet, antagonistically, it seems,
Through our cold, unaccepting fingers,
It slips away once more.
We reach for it,
Trying futilely to grasp it in our hands.
And yet we hope:
We hope that a new day will dawn,
And we will somehow find it.
But this day will never come,
Because life is but a lie, and the truth lies beyond.

Loren Forrester, Grade 11
Westmont High School, CA

Winter and Spring

Winter is the coldest time of the year.
Flowers close up and hide themselves away.
Small children go home and there they will stay
As the icicles fall down tear by tear.
Then outside they go to let out a cheer.
They laugh and play in the barn on the hay.
The picture almost looks like a cliché.
Winter will end and spring is coming near.

Spring comes around and birds start their singing
As the bells in the steeple start their ringing.
Roses and lilies come when the ground thaws.
The flowers will make people want to draw.
Trees will stretch their branches to the warm sun
And bask in the glow until they are gone.

Laura Popplewell, Grade 10
Calvary Chapel Christian School, CA

The Deceived Flower

My mouth is filled with the words you say
Disgust is burning with the words you betray
This seed of my mind has become a flower
That appears to be decaying by the hour
Must all good things come to an end?
Or happiness to be brought by a dying friend?
Now you shall see why I spit on your word
For the words you speak are completely absurd
I must reap the deceiving lies from my head
My once strong flower seems to be dead

Samantha B., Grade 10
Diamond Ranch Academy, UT

'Tis a Dream

'Tis a dream merely a dream?
Is it just a thought?
Or the moment of enlightenment.

An epiphany of reality to whom it may hold.
Or perhaps a dark cloud of a curse.
As you slumber in the cold.
Shall it only get worse?

Whether the dream is simply a play of the mind.
Or the play of your inner self to be kind.

Let it be known.
That a dream is as real as our Lord.
Never simply a clone.
Never created when bored.

As marvelous as can be.
As limitless as the sea.

'Tis is the Dream.

Brandon Zavala, Grade 11
Knight High School, CA

On The Way To See God

Two children met
On the way to see God.
But the pathway was dark
And so they joined hands.
Now hand in warm hand
They walked through Life's land
Each hand a prayer answered.
Still looking for God, still lost
Both children strain their meager eyesight;
Straining to see through darkways.
"I'm lost," the boy said
"I can't see a thing."
"Help me look for the light," the girl asked
"I know it's here somewhere.
I just don't know where to start."
Another hand joined with
Them then, Warm, and
Reassuring, was the hand.
"I know the way, My dear Children,"
The Voice came like a parent's soothing
Touch. "Come follow Me, and all will be well."

Amanda Bird, Grade 11
Merit Academy, UT

The Shot

I slowly roam through the eerie wood
with my heart thumping through my chest.
Snow falls, fog is all around and painful silence
which could break with a tweak or a shuffle and nothing less.
I just gaze around the intimidating darkness
and hold my rifle like a newborn infant.
My breath billows and swirls in the gray abyss
and then appears a silhouette cold and bent.

I knew this was my only chance and my heart quickens,
I hold the cross at the breast of the beast
and shock the world with a devastating pulse.
The smoke and rolling echo gurgle down the canyon.

The dark figure jolts and stumbles into the awakened forest.
Though my body is buzzing and alive with excitement,
the earth and air return to their dull, silent peace.

Derek Tuttle, Grade 12
Emery High School, UT

The Game

O, what a fright this day has been to me
Tears mixed with sweat as we finalized drills
Within the hour I would be in the grass sea
Fighting on a field within the hills

My heart raced as the ball rolled to and fro
The crowd wild with anticipation
Feet kicking and running, breaking flow
The noonday sun lighted the situation

Determination pulsed through my veins
My team put forth all effort they had
I shook from fear, fighting to avoid shame
For a moment all I felt was sad

But then the ball rolled in
We had scored the final win

Allee Alverson, Grade 10
Shelley Sr High School, ID

Time Ceases

Time is a void from which nothing escapes
The inevitable black hole of endless flowing space
To fight it is useless unless immortal, then time is nothing
Nothing more than someone else's forever, to ever remain
A maze of endless choices that determine all creation

Julia Stock, Grade 12
Brighton High School, UT

Blue

The nights when the moon turns a melancholy blue
On trails of fire comes a being passing through
A tempest stirred; a wrath incurred
But dawn is the breaking of the chaos referred

Ching-Wen Yang, Grade 12
Troy High School, CA

Summer in Arizona

Summer's callous presence is known today,
All mourn the loss of Spring and Winter's chill
Arizona feels the sun's burning ray.

Breezes are rare, mesquite boughs never sway,
The only sound is the cicada's trill,
Summer's callous presence is known today.

Quails and sparrows, no longer on display,
Seeking refuge in the ground, geckos till,
Arizona feels the sun's burning ray.

In neighborhood streets, children never play,
The desert is scorching, abandoned and still.
Summer's callous presence is known today.

For months summer overextends its stay,
The ground is parched, thirsting for rain's refill,
Arizona feels the sun's burning ray.

Monsoon arrives after lengthy delay,
The desert, replenished, after rains spill.
Summer's callous presence is known today,
Arizona feels the sun's burning ray.

Alexandra Filkins, Grade 10
Chandler Preparatory Academy, AZ

The Love of God, Salvation to the Heart

The love of God is shed abroad in our hearts.
    He separates us from darkness, and gives us a new start.
As we search the Bible through and through,
    We find that Jesus is the only way, and His words are true.

God reaches out His hand to all mankind.
    Everyone that has breath can see His sign.
Even from every country and to every nation,
    He opens up the door of salvation.

There was a man who I knew was God-sent.
    He told me of God's love and my need to repent.
With all my heart and soul in Jesus I believe,
    And from all of my sins I repented indeed.

Then down into the water I was baptized in Jesus' name.
    In my heart I knew I was washed from all sin and shame.
So I began to praise the Lord with the heavenly hosts,
    And God gloriously filled me with the Holy Ghost.

Now to let others know that the love of God is in us,
    We must keep witnessing, and that is a must!
We are God's children, and Satan cannot stop us.
    So let's keep winning souls in the name of Jesus.

Jerry L. Farley, Grade 12
Christian Life College, CA

Arms Outstretched

Arms outstretched toward every apple
With no apparent bruises
All are out of reach

For I have not eaten in months
And my wretched stomach bellows
And I know the best of fruit
Fall into the hands of the hungry
Yet I reach until my limbs detach
For fear of death by starvation

I'm not alone amongst the apple trees
But no one with arms as long as mine
Has been standing here since dawn
They're three feet tall, I stand at eight
Yet their silent stomachs sit contently
Protruding, and my ribs are exposed

And my arms fall to my sides, my knees buckle
My fragile body weeps, but my eyes are thirsty
And the sun begins to fall
I lie sprawled across the earth
Humiliated, impotent, meager and I pray
To a god I don't believe in for an apple to fall.

Corina Ahlswede, Grade 10
Chico High School, CA

Bad Day

It started with the annoying boys in my first period class,
Then, oops — forgot my planner and had no hall pass.
My teacher accused me of writing a note.
My classroom was cold and I had no coat.

I lingered with friends too long and was tardy,
Then the kids in my class made fun of me, calling me "smarty."
Went to eat but left my lunch at home.
My hair was a mess and I forgot my comb.

My imaginary dog ate my homework assignment.
My favorite sweater was covered in imaginary hair and real lint.
I lost my writing utensil.
Writing an essay is hard without a pencil.

With ankle sprained, had to go see the school nurse.
And just when I thought my day could get no worse,
The bell rang — I ran from the school as fast as I could,
Darting out of the school faster than most sprinters would.

I fled the building and headed for the car.
Almost home I didn't have too far,
But flying feet fell into mud.
My books fell to the ground with a sickening thud.

Natalie Prawitt, Grade 11
Merit Academy, UT

Summer Heat

I could feel the clouds
When I woke that morning,
I thought it was so nice
The last summer day.

My parents drafted me
To clean my Great Aunt's home.
Ten years
Of memories, covered in dust.

I took a photograph
In the low light;
Of the gray clouds.
The home purged.

I could feel it,
One moment before,
The last of the summer heat
Rise to the heaves.

I felt it.
Rain began to fall.
The telephone rang.
Angela: Rose died in an accident.
Sergio Gonzales, Grade 12
St Michael's High School, NM

Anniversary

And so you are
the bloodsucking paperboy
filling the void
left by the death
of my hyacinths

o
I know who you are:
you mosquito you,
gorgeous garden suckler;

I smell of animal
or connection
I revel in vice
I rebel, I entice
I rot

there are astrological changes
and minor alterations
in the cycles
of my humans
but I remain
stagnant
and foul.
Zoe Tambling, Grade 11
New Roads High School, CA

Silence

I stood upon a Westward shore
Of dawn's aurelian sea:
Descried the sun to heaven soar,
When Silence beckoned me.

I saw her dancing under moon,
As sonance she allayed,
Her garment was with lilies strewn,
In silver light arrayed.

I watched in awe as she dispelled
The voices of the day,
The wind and gulls and ocean quelled,
Amid her dance's sway.

When all was silent as a void,
And I in noiseless peace,
I sought to ask of what employed
Could cause a sound to cease.

"O Silence, dost thou weave thy web?
Wherefore the absent sound?"
But once my voice her lull did ebb,
She could no more be found.
Eric Bernard, Grade 10
Sky Mountain Charter School, CA

Fading Sunsets

Fading sunsets,
Dimming stars.
Questions asking,
Where you are.

Flashing lightning,
Stinging rain.
Pounding feelings,
Burning pain.

Wanting fingers,
Asking much.
Aching feelings,
Seeking touch.

Passing people,
Breaking hearts.
Whispers of love,
Torn apart.

Fleeting moments,
Times so sweet.
Sea of faces,
Cannot meet.
Alex Montgomery, Grade 12
Temple Baptist Academy, NM

Addiction

I close my eyes
And imagine you
Wrapping your arms
Around me

I smell your scent
Mingling with mine
I feel your warmth
Just one last time

I hear your voice
Whispering in my ear
But it starts to fade
Can you feel my fear?

It seems so strong
As you slip away
I open my eyes
That's all I get today

You're my addiction
That I can't satisfy
Every part of my being
Longs to defy
Andee Dawson, Grade 10
Nevada Virtual Academy, NV

Death is a Robber

Missing, gone, irreplaceable.
Interrupting each day's balance,
halting the inhale, ending the exhale.
Stealing color out of a face.

Leeching the warmth
like frost to a flower.
Taking away color
created by life.

A clear reflection in the mirror
becomes clouded, bleak.
The end is drawing near.
It takes, but does it give?

Giving relief from daily toil.
Gone is now pain.
Halting agony, ending grief.
Leeching sorrow from a face.

Death is a robber
stealing, taking, thieving.
Yet giving, halting, ending;
does the robber of life.
Emily Cummings, Grade 11
Viewmont High School, UT

The Beach

You hear the ocean roaring,
You feel sand between your toes.
It's peaceful like a bird soaring,
It's like another feature of the ocean flow.
You feel the warm sun basking on your skin,
You feel the light cool breeze.
It's like another connection to earth, within,
It puts your soul and body at ease.
You smell the light salt air,
You see the little sand crabs playing,
You see a dolphin splashing, which is simply rare.
You see the coconuts swaying.
This scenic view melts your stress,
You feel like you're part of the earth.
As the rolling waves and soft sand caress,
It's like a new dawning of a new birth,
This is where my happy place is,
This is where I rest my mind and soul,
It's where I don't have to take a test nor a quiz.
This brings my mind and body together as a whole.
This is my happy place

Tiani Naholowaa, Grade 10
Campbell High School, HI

Damage Is Done

Don't look at me.
My mind is crowded with things to say.
Uncomfortable, frantic words try to rush from
My mouth but are caged.
Why do you lie?
Confused, becoming stale,
Abandoning your words,
Disappointment spills down my face.
Why do you lie?
Your thirsty words I will not quench.
Empty, tasteless meaning tries to satisfy
My hunger for the truth.
Your changed, hurtful eyes are sticky,
Clinging to my memory still.
Why do you lie?
Your old phrases aren't getting any younger.

Calley Paxton, Grade 12
Merit Academy, UT

High School

designer clothes, fresh kicks
cheerleaders, jocks, smarties, and the cliques
smiles and cries every day
sometimes the pain and love will never go away
stressful classes
just hoping that we all can pass
sports and championships
friends and never ending relationships

Joseph Anderson, Grade 10
Cypress High School, CA

Juliet's Cry*

Why do you sleep my love?
All color is fleeing from thy cheeks.
What strange water flows through thy veins?
Thy hands clutch at the vile.
Open thy misty eyes, my love,
To look into my soul once more.

Why do you sleep my love?
Thy face has turned to ice.
What strange water flows from mine eyes?
My heart cries with endless pain.
Come back to my side, my love,
Or I will follow you in sleep.

Why do you sleep my love?
Dark sorrow overcomes my strength.
What strange water flows from my side?
Crimson rain stains my hands.
I tremble with the knife, my love,
But death is sweet, for you are my life.

Haley Beckstrand, Grade 11
Viewmont High School, UT
*Based on Shakespeare's "Romeo and Juliet"

The Dawn

I dream at night of a little girl
in my dream she has blonde curl
I look at her and see myself in her eyes
I watch as she falls in pain and as she dies
I cry out wanting to help her but I soon hear
"no darling girl you must let her go dear"
I look around seeing nothing as I look down
I see nothing not even her pink gown
I soon realize the little girl is my past
and I need to let her go and fast
I am growing up but I will not go far
if I hold on to the past like life's bar
I know it hurts to let her leave me here
but in God's eyes I am in his arms no fear
I feel better letting her go and move on
I am still confused but I can see the dawn

Maryann Dodge, Grade 10
Westwood Charter School, CA

War

War against race is a disgrace
War with one another is like a brother fighting against a brother
Black, White, Mexican we're all the same
When we fight each other it makes us go insane
Why don't we just relax and ignore the pain
Peace, love, unity, and respect that's our game
So why don't we just quit fighting and love one another
So let's just quit the games that we're playing against each other

Christopher Moses, Grade 10
Cinnamon Hills School, UT

Of the Life That Is Ours

Every experience in life
Is a lesson to be had.
Each love that comes by
Is part of the clad.
Days that go by
Like waves on the shore
Each having something different in store
With all of the things
That come and go by
Remember them all
With an open eye
Whether it be
Of the night or day
Remember them all.
In your heart they'll stay.
Cherish that night
We danced under the stars
Recall those times
Our hearts flew through the bars
Never forget those times that we had
It was once in a life time and for that I am glad.

Sapphire McFarland, Grade 12
University Preparatory School, CA

Nature

Nature is what we call a gift from God.
He gave us the plants that are on this earth,
The animals you see at death and birth.
There is also a fish that we call cod,
Even when time began he was called God,
He created natural life and birth.
In the ocean we see the creation surf,
God also created a discipline rod.

When God created man He let them sin,
But by His grace He sent His only child,
A son that in the end we all know will win,
For his hearts wild, but he himself is very mild.
Heaven was created and we are in,
And we got in when God sent His son, a child.

Andrew Todd, Grade 10
Calvary Chapel Christian School, CA

I'm Meant For You

My lips were meant for your kisses,
My eyes were meant to see you,
My hands were made to make you music,
My heart was made to be broken,
My soul was made to live,
My personality was meant to make you smile,
Just a little brighter...
And from head to toe,
I'm just a little rebel,
Who would do anything to make you happy.

Claudia Molina, Grade 11
Lucerne Valley Jr/Sr High School, CA

What I'm Thankful For

Every day I thank the Lord for making me a guy
In this short poem I will tell you all my reasons why
I'm glad I'm faster, stronger and able to play football
When girls pee it takes longer they can't use a urinal
I get up in the morning there's no need to comb my hair
But they spend hours poring over theirs it's just not fair
I'm interested in guns and stuff not lame books like twilight
I'll never read a page, but if I was a girl I might
The notebook is a film that makes me cringe, it makes me tense
You see I like the type of films with action and suspense
I eat all that I want and never have to watch my weight
I'm glad I'm not intrigued by shows like Glee or Kate plus eight
The shoes I wear are comfortable and not six inches high
What's the point of wearing those please someone tell me why?
My cell phone bill is less than any average high school girl
And I don't put weird objects in my hair to make it curl
I never have to go through all the pain of giving birth
These are my reasons why it's great to be a boy on earth
But If I was a girl by chance I'd make a list of why
I'm glad I'm not a stupid thinking, rude and stinky guy!

Colton Irvine, Grade 12
Central Valley Christian School, CA

Words

Parity of possibility and dormancy
inability to function, yet constantly thinking;
working towards the goal.
Goals are but limits.

Focus on finishing.
Reach the satisfactory end.
A race to the end leaves no interpretation.
Between the lines exists infinity.
Termination of equal chance
for there are more ways than one.

Do you read from the beginning to the end,
or from the end to the beginning?
In the end, the sun always sets in the West.

Olivia Puckett, Grade 11
Encore High School for the Performing Arts, CA

The Bride That Wore Red

"A tragic crime"
A day to mourn
Black was the deed
Red were the tracks they found her on
"Who could have done such a thing?!" they cried
"Why it was he," said I. For I knew her well
"He?" they queried
"Yes. The soldier who went to war."
"The bravest of us all."
"The boy who broke her heart."
"The boy that never came home."

Jodee Rosendahl, Grade 12
Wheatland High School, WY

Your Path, My Heartbreak

You are blinded by shame
For all you have done
It hurts me so bad
That I was never number one.
You understand my pain
Or at least you claim that you do.
But how can you understand something
That you have never been through.
I try to accept your reasoning
Though my heart breaks in half
I know who is more important
You chose the right path
Still I can't grasp this concept
Of you being gone
My feelings never die
I know this is wrong.
I say that I'd do anything for you
That's a promise I can no longer make
Loving you is inevitable
It's something that I can't fake.

Chantal Vincent, Grade 12
Shadow Ridge High School, NV

The New Year

It comes like a midnight train,
There is no stopping it.
The best thing you can do is
Just let it take you away.
The New Year brings a new smile
To the man in the moon.
Time seems to go by faster and faster
Why can't we make it stop?
Can we make it stop?
No! We cannot.
As long as the next day arrives,
The new year will follow.
Just embrace each one,
And prepare for the next.

Meredith H., Grade 11
Diamond Ranch Academy, UT

GaGa Ooh-LaLa

Luxurious lovable Lady Gaga
Takes the stage with proud and poise
Like a tiger ready to attack its prey
Her head is held high
Her eye on the prize
She is a predator
Out to kill the show
The stage is her field
The audience want more
Fierce and fabulous
Leaves us speechless
Converts us to monsters

Kimberly Vieyra, Grade 12
Saddleback High School, CA

The Meadow

The waves crash, the wind screams across the open sea
the salt water rushes into my mouth, I am drowning.
I try to scream, my cries stolen away by the wind.
Tired of fighting I give in and let the storm have its way.
A great roar splits the heavens, fire fills the sky;
I am lifted from the water by strong arms,
He has come, I am safe.

I awaken to sunshine gently warming the earth
The trees dancing as a sweet breeze rushes across the cool grass.
Wild flowers dot the horizon — all is quiet.
He is there arms open, waiting…
I run into His arms, we sit, I listen
He tells me He loves me and whispers words of comfort,
"My princess you are safe."

Life goes on and I am still in the meadow
I go on day by day and slowly I forget He is there.
I move away from His side and pursue other things.
The clouds grow dark, rain pours in sheets, lightning breaks open the sky
I run frightened, I panic, where is He?
I turn around and there He is, He always has been, He never left.
I press into His side and He says, "I will never leave you or forsake you — you are safe."

Christy Haase, Grade 10
Bradshaw Christian High School, CA

The Light

I am a boy who faces his fears
There was a time when I was scarred
People were jerks
They'd say "You can't do anything"
That was a time of great depression for me

I had a dream last night
In that dream I had a vision of someone I knew
And in the Darkness I saw a voice that said, "I'm you"
Inside of me a light was turned on — then I was alive
I can only see it if I just close my eyes

That morning I had the light by my side
It gave me the power to say, "I can do it"
And guess what? My dreams came true
The light gave me the strength to destroy the darkness within me
Now my life is brighter and will never be taken over by the darkness again

I could make believers out of all of you
Some are born to sweep delight
And others born to endless night
Join me with the light by my side
Or continue being slaves to the Darkness

Jorge Aguilar, Grade 11
Animo Leadership Charter High School, CA

Morning

My alarm chirps, a digital bird.
It's morning, dreadful morning.
Another day has arrived.
Will power builds inside of me.
Building and building,
it rises up.
Enough to get me out of bed
on this morning, dreadful morning.
Milk and corn flakes combine
in the shining bowl
to form my meal
of this morning, dreadful morning.
Warm water splashes on my back
going pitter-patter pitter-patter
like rain on a tin roof.
Awake and now alert,
I am ready for this morning,
not-so-bad morning.
Roylance Bird IV, Grade 10
St Francis High School, CA

Priorities

Stacks of books, scattered papers
What a mess.
Jolly Rancher candy wrappers in a bag
My workspace is cluttered.
Empty mug and drained water bottle
I think I should organize
Open sketch book marked with thoughts
Assortment of pens and pencils
Why do I have so much stuff here?
Unconnected cord and lifeless watch
This really makes me feel clean.
Untied ribbons and empty cases
Sentiment makes discarding hard.
Scriptures and lifetime journal
Reminders of life's necessities.
It may look like a mess
But there are more important activities
Than organizing and tidying up.
Gregory Plaizier, Grade 12
Viewmont High School, UT

Running

Running
When exhaustion hits you like a truck
Your lungs are straws, shrunk so small
Every breath taken becomes harder,
"Run, Run Faster" is the only thought
That passes through your head,
The crowd cheers you on,
Nothing seems to get in your way,
All you see is a dream and a light of
Hope.
Gio Fata, Grade 10
South Pasadena High School, CA

Falling

I look at the sunset;
its colors entrance me;
and I jump
off the edge.
My chest tingles with fear;
I close my eyes and concentrate.
I feel the rush of falling;
I look down and see the water,
closing my eyes again, I hold my breath.
I sink like a boulder
then
shoot back up
out of the water.
My brother is smiling.
Daydreaming, Bro?
He asks.
A.J. Roque, Grade 10
Orem High School, UT

Rain in the City

Rain
pounds
staccato on sidewalks.

Streetlights
provide
misty illumination
through flickering haze.

Umbrellas
drift by,
enclosing people in
their
own
tiny
worlds.
Caitlyn Foster, Grade 11
La Reina High School, CA

Night Glittering Stars

Night glittering stars
Dark clear night,
Street sidewalk flickering,
Like the light glittering sky
Sleeping lonely in buildings
With stars and dark night,
Rolling clear in with light…

Old bench and dirty street,
Rolling over in sleep
With sigh and hum,
Rusty sidewalk street
Rolling over in night
Glittering stars…
Antonio Breedlove, Grade 10
Redwood High School, CA

Strong Enough

This world is ridiculous,
In so many ways,
Just keep your eyes open,
I'm not in a daze.

Why do we take the easy road?
Difficulty brings success,
My path continues forward,
Bypassing all the mess.

Life is my obligation,
Never do I let down,
I'm already so far,
I just can't quit now.

Inspiration is around me,
Take from what they give,
Others scared to finish,
I'm strong enough to live.
Erik Dulock, Grade 10
Bradshaw Christian High School, CA

Forever Winter

The winter breeze
Carries the memory
Past is remembered
It will never be forgotten

Carries the memory
With its biting chill
It will never be forgotten
Because of their strong will

With its biting chill
It burrows into forever
Because of their strong will
They can't ever overlook

It burrows into forever
Past is remembered
They can't ever overlook
The winter breeze
Samantha Porras, Grade 10
Youngker High School, AZ

Pain

pain is a can opener
stabbing at the can
till it gets hold
it cuts all the way
around the edges
till all the contents
spill out
Ellen Carr, Grade 11
Viewmont High School, UT

God's Song

The flower lived
And it died,
All to provide a new life.

"Mamma, why does
This lovely creation
Wither and be gone?"

"Oh, my dear child,
It is merely God's song.

The grass and the trees
Live for sometime
But in a while, they slowly die.

This is his plan
To give life
And to take away;
To be with him
For the oncoming day."

Sadie Ann King, Grade 10
Agua Fria Union High School South Campus, AZ

Anger

Anger, built up inside me
Trying to claw its way through my chest
I can feel my body heat rising
Adrenaline pumping
I need to find a safe way to unleash the animal within me
I need to tame the beast
My fists clenched into balls of steel
I can feel my nails digging deep into the palm of my hand
I just want to scream
The anger feels like it will never end
It suddenly starts to subside
I feel myself getting weak
I feel the energy draining from my head
Leaking down my body to my feet
I caged the beast

Kyle Terry, Grade 11
Roadrunner High School, AZ

Appreciate

Because of you, I've learned to appreciate.
You're always running through my mind.
Us meeting, well I call it fate.
You make me feel so happy,
You got me set straight.
The lock on heart, you have the key.
And that smile on my face, will never be erased.
The words you say, the jokes you tell
Within a second, put me under a spell.
Never shall I mention the word hate.
Because I've learned to appreciate.

Falak Jandga, Grade 10
Fountain Valley High School, CA

This Is My Reality

I gazed out of my window this morning.
The hot, blinding sun of China,
the calm village fields of Zhongshan
and the village women getting ready for manual labor in the fields,
every day is always the same.
I watched the birds as they soared through the air,
filling the sky with freedom.
Nothing tied them down
and nothing troubled them.
I wish I was a bird.
Or at least a leaf,
being carried by the soothing breeze,
or a cloud,
appearing and disappearing throughout this small world.
This way, I can explore the world,
with comfort and with freedom.
However, that is just a dream, a simple wish.
Reality is reality
and my reality is within the village walls.
I hurried and ate breakfast
and ran to the fields to begin my daily work.

Jenny Zhou, Grade 10
Abraham Lincoln High School, CA

A Simple Reminder

To many it is just a scar
Maybe a conversation starter
Or perhaps nothing at all
To me it is the reason
I wake in the morning
And work until my eyelids shut
Some may ask why such
A simple scar means so much
I tell them because every time I look
In the mirror I remember
A friend who cared, loved, and respected me.
This friend raised me up in my darkest hours
Always allowing time for me when I needed it
Brightened my days by a smile and a few words
But overall they always believed in me.

Ben Doxey, Grade 10
Alta High School, UT

Morrison's Asylum

A universe constructed beyond his skull
He lost control
He fled the boundaries of what seemed to be real
Gave pain to those who could not feel
Resurrected a world with the tools of his mind
Conquered the imprisonment of all time
With an image he wrote down there is no attendant in danger
As we roam the streets of darkness, preying upon strangers
A diffused melody of notes in an asylum of pain
A feeling so unbearable, how can I refrain?

Jordan McIntosh, Grade 10
Nevada Virtual Academy, NV

Defective

Peculiarities you love, picking and picking away
at your flaws,
sewing up the ends with barely any fray.

Another day
passing by and you think too much for life to be put on pause.
Peculiarities you love, picking and picking away.

Life just may
be too much for you with its laws,
sewing up the ends with barely any fray.

I know the things you say
for some people are simple too raw.
Peculiarities you love, picking and picking away.

See yourself decay
and leave the rest in awe,
sewing up the ends with barely any fray.

The way we convey
ourselves can only draw
peculiarities you love, picking and picking away,
sewing up the ends with barely any fray.
Melissa Schell, Grade 10
Encore High School for the Performing Arts, CA

Potential

Come forth you adventurers
Come to my side and we see the future
We see that things are not as they seem
We understand that it has to be that way

Leave what you have
Leave what you own
For they do not matter
For they are trivial and meaningless

Who told you that you have to live life by the rules?
Who said that all was concrete and understood
Why they focus on reproduction I'll never know
Why they care about their bank account I'll never understand

Throw your diction and syntax out the window
Throw your blind faith into the toilet…and flush valiantly
Face your fears and laugh at them…laugh hard adventurer
Face yourself and be comfortable with the difference you have

Ignore those who doubt
Ignore those that care about a 401 K
Be what your potential wants you to be
Be there when your animal instinct reveals itself
Dylan Davis, Grade 12
Davis High School, UT

My Devourer

Guilt relentlessly suffocates my mind
Torturing me with unimagined thoughts
Wrapping my stressed heart with coils unkind.

Guilt distracts me, occupying my time
Tangling my spirits into obscured knots;
Guilt relentlessly suffocates my mind.

Hurting my friends like a boasting magpie,
Watching taut lips tremble, tears run uncaught
Wrapping my stressed heart with coils unkind.

Apologies to guilt, lemons to limes,
Because guilt by ignorance can't be bought;
Guilt relentlessly suffocates my mind.

Seized by its hazardous grip, I may find
Guilt to be an acidic vile pot
Wrapping my stressed heart with coils unkind

My vulnerable mind can't now resign
With the devourer that I've failed and fought;
Guilt relentlessly suffocates my mind
Wrapping my stressed heart with coils unkind.
Divya Amrelia, Grade 10
Chandler Preparatory Academy, AZ

Hard to Believe

Open your eyes and try to see
This whole wide world in front of you and me
People are dying, they have trouble surviving
Because of problems
Just Imagine. Isn't it hard to believe?

But in this land of liberty
We only care about what we've got to achieve
With school, money, popularity
That's what's important to society
Turning away from people in Pain
Hungry, Hurting, going Insane

Watch that holocaust in Turkey.
Feel the earthquake strike Chile?
Another girl died from Orange County?
Met a North Korean who cannot get free?
Still, doing nothing is so easy.

Please, open your eyes and try to see
This whole wide world in front of you and me
People are dying, they have trouble surviving
Because of problems
Just Imagine, Isn't it hard to believe?
Diane Kim, Grade 10
Cypress High School, CA

Sakura (Cherry Blossom)
The spring has come.
The flowers bloom,
The birds are chirping,
The cherries blossom.

The sakura sway
with the gentle breeze.
Their pink pedals wave
as they fall to the ground.

They stick to the shoes,
and people let the sweet beauty
get trod on and forget,
how peace lives in cherry blossoms.

Ethan Kikuchi, Grade 10
Orem High School, UT

Playing With Fire
Your eyes hold the fire
Of promise and surmise.
Of desire
And surprise.
A looking glass,
An open pool,
In an open land,
Our eyes, they duel.
They meet at once,
They lock, we'll see,
Which of us
Will be first to flee.
It's eerie how I know your ways
From just the cast of your fiery gaze.

Jennie Christensen, Grade 10
Woodside Priory School, CA

Come Back
Please don't leave me here alone tonight
I want you now more than ever
All it was, was a stupid fight
Don't walk away now, not ever
Please don't throw away all this love
Our love is too strong for it to end like this
I need you more each and every day
Believe me when I say it's you I miss
I won't let go of what we had
At school it's hard to see you
Sometimes seeing you makes me mad
Sometimes you make me blue
Come back and we will forget the past
I know our love will always last

Kayla Webster, Grade 10
Shelley Sr High School, ID

Best Friends
So there's this girl I know.
She's funny, weird, cool and all the good things you can think of.
Never stops from having a smile on her face and hates sadness.
She's one of a kind.
She's my best friend named Lizette
Fights come and they go,
Making it through them and working it out is what counts.
Friends are there to make it all better when problems seem to come around.
Best friends are the good kind of people to make you smile just at the right moment.

I'm the kind of girl that will laugh at her mistakes,
So excuse me if I laugh in your face.
I tend to have so much care for the closest people in my life,
You have to prove to me you're worth it and not just another mistake.
Things in life happen that I hate,
That's just how life is so I have to accept it.
Life is life, it never stops,
We all have to find a way to go along with it
Live happy with no regrets.
Like people always say,
Live life to the fullest.

Vicky Luna, Grade 11
Animo Leadership Charter High School, CA

You
How I feel about you
There is no way to say my feelings
But here I will try
You are the light in my day
And I have never seen a beauty like you
For you are more beautiful than any girl I have ever seen
The way your hair flows down on your face to your back
Is like a running stream with the light shining making the water sparkle
Your beautiful blue eyes reflect me staring at you in a star struck gaze
For when I see you my heart stops
And I lose control of myself
The only thought in my mind
Is there anyone in this world that can compare to you
For you are not only beautiful
But kind hearted
Intelligent
And gifted at anything you do
You are the love of my life

Trenton Halstad, Grade 10
Glacier High School, MT

"Everything" Is Confused...
Everything is not only a word or a figure of speech.
Or something that can be done daily.
My poem is based on everything in the country.
In the streets, the city, the neighborhood.
A change that can take place.
I'm talking about the liberty, the passion, the encouragement.
I'm saying the decisive challenge of misunderstanding against another's.

Eduardo Mercado, Grade 11
Animo Leadership Charter High School, CA

Memories and Tears

Remember life as a kid?
Backyards, and swing sets; all the things that we did?
Dreaming about later in life,
Thinking about big things; living without strife,
I never thought,
Someday I'd look back distraught.
How did this happen?
Just yesterday I got time off for nappin'.
The next step's coming,
I'm going straight from crawling to running.
It all seems great,
But when I stop to debate;
What is going to come,
And what's already done.
I realize that life's too short,
People may try but life's impossible to extort.
Life slips by man,
So slow down, and enjoy it as much as you can,
Before it disappears,
And all that's left are memories and tears.

Carlin Jones, Grade 11
Burlington High School, WY

My Undeniable Angel

You are much mistaken by the love you portray as a beautiful
fantasy. Oblivious you pour your heart out to me, laced with
hope you wait, but I am full of duplicity. Deprived of a strong
love, I am fearful that I will not allow you to be allocated to
me, because it can only bring me grief and pain. I am dreadful
and left here crying isolated. This stupidity of mine holding me
back from the glorious feeling I get when your arms wrap around
me in midday. This struggle is turning the love in front of me
transparent. I want so longingly for the image of everlasting
serendipity to be within my grasp. Though your intentions are
embarrassment of a shattered heart and reject your incredible
love, with torture in my soul. And though it will seem immensely
heartless I must smother this love before it has begun, for I
would rather drown in despair than watch you turn your back and
abandon me here.

Samantha Bingham, Grade 10
Preston High School, ID

Love?

love.
what is love?
love.
is something you cannot have.
love.
is a feeling in which two people share.
love.
the dominant power over hate.
love.
the peace of mind that satisfies from within.
love?

Milinda Kendrick, Grade 11
East Nicolaus High School, CA

Touch the Stars

Even through the worlds toughest wrath,
we always enjoy each others laugh,
when times grow hard
we'll go so far, together we'll touch the stars,
in the beginning or the end
no matter if your paper's thin,
there's no need to pretend
all you need is a friend
who's prepared for war,
and never budge or bend
when the odds are poor
knock knockin' on heaven's door,
we gotta choose a new path to explore
because there was no answer,
sittin' reminiscin' within' that time went faster
all we have now is each other's laughter,
all the good times that pass, all the good times to come
are the memories that last and our most cherished ones,
Even through this world's wrath
we can still have our fun
thy will be done…

Ruben Navarro, Grade 12
Lucerne Valley Jr/Sr High School, CA

Unknown

I hope to see you one day soon,
Every night under the bright moon,
I lay there crying,
Because I feel like dying,
Ever since the age of 8, I've had no meaning,
Life was empty, cold, and dark.
To me, there was no spark.
As I get older I see more opportunity,
But I still hate my community.
If I could run away,
I would never look back to any day,
For why would anyone, if they knew what I know.
Most are just for show and go on about their day.
As for me, I try to be understanding,
But I hate this witch you are handing.

Nicholas Pauls, Grade 12
Crossroads High School, CA

Everlasting*

Time ticks away before our eyes
As we sit inside ourselves
And let it walk away
Thinking we will always have tomorrow —

The emotions that we have
The thoughts we keep hidden
That will collect dust because we think
We will last forever —

Taylor Rush, Grade 11
Valley Christian High School, CA
*Inspired by "Funeral in My Brain" by Emily Dickinson

Summer

It is almost here just a few months away,

I can't wait to go out and swim all day.
The sun will shine and it will be hot.
Oh but wait, I almost forgot.
I have my bathing suit, sunglasses, and sun block ready,
but I need to be patient and try to hold steady.
For three whole months there will be no school,
and all I'll have to worry about is laying out by the pool.
No more homework and no more books,
all that's on my mind now are my tan and my looks.
The teachers will be gone and won't need to teach,
so we will all meet up and go to the beach.
The days will be fun and we will have a blast,
the only problem is it will go by fast.
Summer is not here yet and we have to wait,
we need to focus on school and try not to hate.
It will be here soon and I'm getting excited,
I'll have barbeques and parties and everyone will be invited.
The count down starts now, so save the date,

this will be an amazing summer, I just can't wait.

Valerie Shahin, Grade 10
Cypress High School, CA

Criminal Instinct

Revelations of discrimination.
Injustices of the ones we trusted.
Crimes against humanity.

The wrongs of you.
Of me.
The people of the world are separated by more than
The sea.

People harm themselves.
They hurt one another.
Society enables,
Yet no one disables.
Even though we can see
How our actions affect all of
Humanity

Diamante Smith, Grade 11
Mojave Sr High School, CA

Regret

Alone by a window I sit,
Watching the clouds turn gray,
While the sun slowly fades away.
As fleeting memories rush through me
Of flowers long wilted, of photographs forever faded,
Teary-eyed, I realize I tried to run and hide.
I mourn and cry for deep inside
I need you by my side.

Angelica Cadalin, Grade 10
Cypress High School, CA

Soundless Words

Words fly in the wind,
Echoing through soundless waves of air.
Can you hear the lovely melody?
Happy thoughts turn into nightmares,
Daylight turns into darkness.
Melancholic darkness can't see the light.
Far beyond the abyss, eyes meet the eyes.
Eyes like no other.
Dim lips, dreadful like venom,
Speak soundless words that fly in the wind,
Echoing through soundless waves of air.
Want to hear the lovely melody?
Clouds are pushed away by the wind's peaceful rage.
Hysterical laughter fills the air,
Suffocating the mind,
Leaving the heart deaf,
Leaving only its sight.
Sight that sees far beyond the horizon,
Sight that hears soundless words.
Words that fly in the wind,
Echoing through soundless waves of air.
Finally the lovely melody was heard.

Gabriela Mendoza, Grade 12
Centennial High School, CA

The Chosen of Jehovah

The voices of justice inundate the earth
Voices of worship enlighten everything
They are the faithful of our God
The chosen of Jehovah

The saints come
To exalt the greatness of the King
And the light will shine
As everyone worships the King of Majesty

They come to worship the only one full of light
See them draw near finding themselves with their King
They are the faithful of our God
The chosen of Jehovah

Hosanna the King, Hosanna the King

Christopher Turcios, Grade 11
Animo Leadership Charter High School, CA

Final Frontier

The sun was in my eye
It was in the sky very high
How long since I've been out here
Been so long since I've breathed fresh air
How did we end up like this
Destroyed the Earth's kiss
I could see the Earth's tear
Oh how underground became our final frontier

Chris Ko, Grade 10
Cypress High School, CA

Remember

Wind in your hair
Rain on your face
A breath of fresh air
Memories that you cannot erase

A smile to go a mile
Sitting for a while
Pictures worth a million words
Friends who sing like birds

Sitting around a fire
People to admire
A sunset to embrace
With a smile on your face

From playing the guitar
To gazing at the stars
Sitting by the lake
With friends in your wake

Make an escape
Find your place
Sit for a while
Stop and smile

Jessica Gough, Grade 10
Cypress High School, CA

One Moon, Two Sides

I was jealous of you
    When I first saw you

Your ever-happy face
Your ever-true smile
Your ever-glowing eyes
    Were so fake

I saw your friends
    And how happy you were
But you weren't truly happy

Everything you said
Everything you did
    Was totally fake

But I never saw the falseness
    Behind you
I truly thought you were happy
    But you weren't

I truly thought you were doing well
    Yet you longed for home
I truly thought you didn't need me
    Yet you pulled me there

Nanibah Showa, Grade 12
St Michael High School, AZ

My Run

The freedom,
So calming, fast.
Sending the wind, whispering,
Through the fibers of my hair.

With the striding of the twin pistons
Pumping in eternal unity,
Pumping, pounding, soaring.
Nothing to stop me,
Nobody to slow me down.

True freedom.
Free from bonds,
Like a slave, released by his master,
Feeling the wind, wisping.
Over the hills,
Throughout the war torn lands,
But not to fight;
Just to run.

To escape hate, to become released
From the worldly ways of hate and sorrow.
For no sorrow can come from the running.

Only freedom.

Christian Gregory, Grade 10
Bradshaw Christian High School, CA

I Don't Know

Follow the
Yellow brick road
During the time of war
When in the time of war
It cease to exist and all that's left are
The leaders of this flock.
Point fingers if necessary.

Wander into the forests
Of foreign land in which we claim
Is of our kin, is of our duty, is of our nature
Like the red hood girl.
Point fingers if necessary.

Reap the land
As in conquer, as in gain
As in what we did with the women in
The My Lai Massacre.
Point fingers if necessary.

Who are we? What are we?
I never agreed,
But the term is we.
Point fingers if necessary.

Phuong Truong, Grade 12
El Monte High School, CA

Chalk

Rain peels away
the plaster of the past,
folding along rainbow chalk lines.
Where there was hopscotch
and colored outlines
of our youthful silhouettes,
there is a Flood.
Downhill slide of childhood scribbles,
to the gutters, the ocean below
that we've barely learned to swim.
Red lights reflect off the car window,
fluorescent warning signs

but we skid.

Where there was color, now I know gray.
We've traded chalk for
powdered faces,
stars
for tattered dreams.

In the morning, puddles
of elementary school laughter
evaporate.

Cosette Gonzales, Grade 11
Cathedral Catholic High School, CA

Dear Brother

Dear Brother,
Your shoes are still sitting there
right in the middle of the hall,
I miss your smell, your voice, and
arm on my shoulder probably most of all.

When I fall asleep on the couch
and you guide me to my room,
You whisper words of "goodnight sis"
a gesture that will always loom.

I feel so cool when you're around
I want to shout out loud,
Take you everywhere I go
to show people why I am so proud.

I love to step in your size ten shoes
when you leave them at the door,
The big laces feel so soft
each shuffle I take lets me soar.

You're my big brother
and my big shoes,
Someone I will always cherish
and hope to never lose.

Kaitlin Skopec, Grade 11
La Costa Canyon High School, CA

The Reality of Dreams

I bet you can dream of anything
I know you can wish for many things
While you were sleeping it seemed real
The diamonds, clothes, and gangster grills
You wish you can have this or that
But, wishing is an opinion,
Not a fact

They say a story has a beginning and end,
But, while you were sleeping
You dreamed of the beginning but,
Awaken before the end
You strive to get that dream again
Instead reality breaks your train of thought

Great minds have wishful thinking
Come back to reality and it's all gone
Good things come to those who wait
Let your dreams also become enduring
Before it's too late
You have to take life day by day,
Dreams and wishes may sound great but,
As soon as you awake they fade away.

Autumn Theragood, Grade 11
Mojave Jr/Sr High School, CA

Dreams Unfulfilled

Do they rot in the dank corners
of the apathetic soul?
Waiting indefinitely to fulfill
their goal?

Do they haunt you like
ghosts waiting to kill?
Reminding you of things
you haven't done still?

Does their memory linger?
Their echoes repeat
the promises that they made,
now incomplete?

Do they give you a purpose?
Something to work for?
Something to cling to;
Something to hope for?

What becomes of dreams unfulfilled?
What is their fate?
What happens when
they come true too late?

Travis Athougies, Grade 12
St John Bosco High School, CA

School

Tell me not, yet more page numbers?
Having a life is but a dream.
So much homework hits like lumber.
And work takes longer than it seems.

Work is hard! Work takes time!
And a good grade is but a goal.
So much work should be a crime!
A crime against one's soul.

Not enjoyment, only sorrow.
Is the only thing we feel.
But just wait, there's more tomorrow.
We'll probably have to skip a meal.

Assignments are long, and time is flying
And our attention begins to fade.
Some approached the verge of crying,
While others sat and prayed.

It is one of our constant struggles,
We face every day.
A load we must learn to juggle,
And keep our mind from going astray.

Richard Gonzales, Grade 11
Valley Christian High School, CA

Walking Away

Walking Away
If you looked into my eyes
You would see the pain
I've buried so deep,
Covered by the smile on my face.

If you peeked
Behind the surface
You would find
The tears I've never shed.
The love I'll never give.

Walk on by my love.
Don't stop to turn around.
Don't try to help me,
No one can.
I'm too far gone.

My tears burn my eyes,
Fear wrenches my gut.
But all is not lost,
I can walk away
And be free.

Brandi Sealander, Grade 12
University Preparatory School, CA

Around the World

I have been all around,
From the East to the West,
From the North to the South
To Hawaii, the best.

From the waters of Mexico
To Canada's magnificent water fall,
To the streets of London
With Big Ben so tall.

From Disneyland on the West Coast
And Disneyworld on the East Coast,
To Arizona down south
Where their weather, they boast.

From the Gateway Arch of Missouri
To Wyoming so dull and flat,
From Chicago to Colorado
To watch my sister swing a bat.

Someday I will travel all around the world
To 50 states and Fenway Park,
To Australia and Spain
I hope to leave my mark.

Camille Thornley, Grade 11
Viewmont High School, UT

I'm Not Saying Good-bye...

There's one path to lead us here,
All that matters is that you care.
I hold my troubles in my hand,
Help me bury them in the sand.

I want to hear your voice in the wind,
When can our lives finally begin?
I try to hide away the truth,
You're just the person I cannot lose.

I face the wall, I can't back down,
Even though you're not around.
I look into the sky at night,
You stole my heart, you are my light.

Even though you are now far away,
You make all my notions sway.
I hold onto your love tight,
I can't tell if we are right.

I can't stand saying good-bye,
You said forever, we can at least try.
One last wish, one last chance.
Why is it that you make my heart dance?

Chloe Garcia, Grade 11
Rio Rico High School, AZ

Time Keeper

The sound is rhythmical, a constant drone;
The tempo beneath life's busy clatter;
Pleasant the sound, for you're never alone;
Tick tock is universal in measure.

And with the heart beat of a metronome;
Suns rise and set with the moon all aglow;
New children are born, and old ones leave home;
The clock's pulse is an infinite arrow.

But it's a commanding creature of strife;
Panic to old and impatience to young;
With tension that you can cut with a knife;
That's broken only when the hour's sung.

Lofty the statuesque silhouette stands;
The keeper of time with his many hands.

Amanda Levy, Grade 12
Dobson High School, AZ

Piano

Thine ebony keys, so soft to the touch,
Have power to unlock the darkest heart.
Thy simple melodies, almost too much,
Seem to tame, to claim, to divide apart
The many thousand souls who crave thy sound.
Thy tender lover with the trembling hand
Thy fortes and pianos know no bound
The trills and staccatos running like sand
Thy gift to mankind, gives life to the world,
Burning brighter than Prometheus's fire.
Through ages thy hope has twirled, whirled
Given the deaf their ears, joy, without tire.
Oh! Sing loud thy sweet songs to young and old.
Bring forth thy dear music, treasure as gold!

Andrea Cutler, Grade 11
Viewmont High School, UT

Joy to Life

As humans, we all go through struggles.
Through the black of day and dark of night, we still remain faithful.
Even though in life there are things we need to juggle,
What's the purpose, if you still can't feel joyful?
Was joy determined by our attitude towards this life?
Or was it just given by luck?
Are we humans challenged by God, to strive
for the success of finding his love?
Or are we punished by the wrong doings
that we've brought into this Earth?
We may never know what it will take to bring
in the peace that the universe has already offered.
And forever more,
true happiness is what we'll always be pursuing for.

Jared Munemitsu, Grade 10
Mililani High School, HI

The Untold Story

I always looked at you from across the room
you were the girl that all the boys wanted
I was the guy who was feared by all
you sat next to me and talked to me
I responded back and smiled
you always liked to talk to me
I always felt the same
you had a boyfriend
I walked alone
you could tell me anything
I couldn't
you always talked about your boyfriend
I wanted you to be happy
you disappeared one day
I knew what other people wanted to know
you left before I could say something important
I have long since forgotten those three words

Shane Hosokawa, Grade 11
Mililani High School, HI

Serving*

My passion, I cannot impede it,
Service with several callings in it,
And when I continue to grow,
I feel remorse in my heart, and what I see through it,
No shame or discredit,
But through worship I continue to sew.

Prolonging my faith with encouragement,
My soul lasts much longer
Aiding those in need
To my LORD I go,
Augmenting my love stronger
Needing to lead!

Camille Holm, Grade 11
Valley Christian High School, CA
*Inspired by "Auspex" by James Russell Lowell

You

Your laughter drives the stormy clouds away.
Your voice makes that great ball of fire smile.
Just imagining you makes me so gay.
I would die just to stay with you awhile.
No one could ever imitate your style.
No man is worthy to pursue your hand.
You are faultless, incapable of guile.
You're perfect, too good to come from this land.
Ask and I will meet your ev'ry demand.
Angels are envious of your beauty.
Other women would kill to be as grand.
To hold your hand is a sacred duty.
I have sold my heart to you, so be kind.
Now, I just need to get you off my mind.

Bryant Dixon, Grade 11
Viewmont High School, UT

Demon, Diablo, Akuma

Everyone blames the devil
The devil did this
The devil did that
The devil possessed me
The devil made me do it
The poor guy
I think the devil has far better things to do
He's not looking over the shoulder of every person
Whispering sinful words of persuasion.
He's not possessing you to do anything,
Whether it be to steal something from that store over there,
Or kill that guy who just dissed you,
He's not conspiring against you
To make your life as miserable as he can
The devil is much too busy to deal with anyone personally
We've made him into a scapegoat for our wrongs, our sins
If we truly wish to know where the devil lies
We need not look any farther than our own hearts.

Felicia Mello, Grade 11
Golden Sierra High School, CA

The Many Purposes of a Flower

A flower is full with delicacy;
It fills your soul to a full sensation.

A flower is found in a young hand on a date;
This hand also belongs to a person with a worried face.

A flower stands at a nightstand;
'Tis there to celebrate a new baby.

A flower lies on old wrinkled hands,
For it is given from a person who cares.

Soon it is residing on top of a fresh mound of ground;
to honor a woman who is buried safe and sound.

Maureen Hunt, Grade 10
Orem High School, UT

The Sound of the Strings

Magnetic coils picking up the sound,
From shiny steel strings so tightly wound;

Electric signals through the cable
Will eventually enable

Vacuum tubes inside the amp
To cause the sound to ramp, RAMP, RAMP!

The air explodes with blasting sound —
Like bombs from planes striking the ground!

And all because two hands dripping with sweat
Were picking strings and selecting frets.

Kevin Dorn, Grade 11
Valley Christian High School, CA

They Fell

I was watching TV.
It was a regular Tuesday afternoon
Then it happened
They fell, said the News
The towers crumbled in a matter of seconds
They fell, said the Paper
The planes hit them like a ice cold knife
They fell, said the World
The US was shot in the heart, thousands dead
I sat there and watched what happened
They fell, said I
I could see the people screaming in my mind
They fell, said They
They tried to get out of their coffin
They fell, said Them
The Streets were chaos, no one was safe
They fell, said US
Our limbs were being torn apart
WE fell, said the fallen.

Christopher Rodriguez, Grade 10
Whittier High School, CA

Civil War in the Eyes of a Soldier

War means naught but death from the start.
I have seen my countrymen fall
With tears in my eyes and grief in my heart;
And for the murder I've done, myself I appall.
For those men of honor who I fought
Stood tall for naught but their way of life.
While in my cause I have put little thought
Other than orders from those who feed on our strife.
These men we have slain,
Nay, these brothers we've betrayed.
For this we shall bear the mark of Cain
As our brothers' blood makes red this glade.
Our actions weigh down to choke my heart in sorrow
As the eyes of our brethren look not upon the morrow.

Kyle Crowley, Grade 12
Spanish Springs High School, NV

the hard life

why do you treat me so different
you always yell at me
you keep me away from society
why do you put me in a box
I want to see the world for what it is
through my own eyes

you always tell me to grow-up
yet you treat me like a child
I can't stand it
sometimes I need space, to get away
and you wonder why I go behind your back
but its just to show you I'll be ok, and how I grew up

Melodee Ajifu, Grade 10
King Kekaulike High School, HI

Page of Truth

It's not easy being an undocumented student
This year is the year that students get their freedom and
What can I do?
Can't drive, go out to far places (out of state) to visit my love ones
Especially my grandparents who I adore and desire to be next too
My grandmother is extremely sick, and the only thing I can do is sit down and wait for a call.
Perhaps I can sit and watch everyone.
However I don't!

I know I might not be able to go farther than high school, but there is a little chance I can.
And as small that chance is I have my hopes
I know that one day I will be able to go back and see my marvelous grandparents
These 10 years with out seeing them will one day pay off.
I didn't ask my parents to bring me to this country, however I'm glad they did

I am proud of who I am even though I'm not number 1 in the school ranking I'm number 8
I have manage to stay above the bad influence and I can assured I never done any type of drug
If you see me you will not be able to tell what is my economic status or legal
However if you take time to really get to know me I can be more than a friend I can be someone to trust.

Oralia Pacheco, Grade 11
Animo Leadership Charter High School, CA

War

Only one winner
Thirty opponents desiring that sole title.
The prized and underlined position of Victor,
Insinuating guaranteed fame, ephemerally permanent.
Setting: battleground on wooded terrain, undeniably white as snow.
Thirty different heights, thirty different lengths, thirty different depths,
Troops in ordered formation, in perfected alignment, properly spaced,
Exposed but clothed in ebony black uniform, stolid and tacit, but full of emotion.
Armed with arched shields and rigid swords, they stand boldly.
Who is the enemy? Who is the foe?
Definitions are ambiguous yet standardized. At once, each body takes control
To shortcut the task at hand. Destination in mind, they clash without guilt, cut without pain.
No escaping allowed; all thirty are locked in a shift of motion.
Awaiting their Almighty, anticipating their fate, one by one they disappear,
Defunct, as if they never existed, deleted into obscurity.
But the winner is determined. The clock maker has chosen.
It is Time for the New Roman era:
This is war.
The War of Words.

Stephanie Kha, Grade 11
Red Mountain High School, AZ

Rabbi

The Rabbi is not a person
The Rabbi is a friend, a listener, anything you can think of and times that by two is still not the Rabbi
This thing I'm writing is not a tribute nor a snare
It's more of a notice so that novice's can see the Rabbi
As a thing and not a monster that dwells inside and strikes when only you're sad or mad
It's a thing made of pure happiness that catches dreams and makes them free and grow at last
The Rabbi is my hero and my tree sitting still in the open field of my dreams
The Rabbi is a part of me

Joshua Enciso, Grade 10
Elsinore High School, CA

In the Time You Need It Most

Why won't you let me be your hero?
The one to pick you up when you fall,
And take you to that happily ever after.
In the time you need it most.

Why won't you let me be your savior?
The one to be there forever,
And always love you.
In the time you need it most.

Why won't you let me be your guardian angel?
The one to hold you,
And save you from all your troubles.
In the time you need it most

Why won't you let me be your friend?
The one with a steady shoulder,
And utmost loyalty.
In the time you need it most.

I crave to be all these things for you,
But you don't think I can.
So I'll keep waiting and I will be here,
In the time you need it most.

Jake Rapp, Grade 11
Boise Sr High School, ID

Volleyball

Getting ready for the game
My nerves are driving me insane
Ankle braces check
Knee pads check
We walk out onto the court with
All our blue and pink
Seizing up the other team
I think that we can take them
We gather in a circle to wish
Each other luck
We have the first serve
I hold my breath I hear the whistle
She serves the ball it's an Ace
Only 24 more to go
Running and jumping
The only thing that is in my mind
Left, right, left
The ball is set to me
I smash it on the ten foot line
That's it we have sweet victory
We win a trophy that all of us get to take home
It's not shiny 'cause a
Volleyball players trophy
Is our floor burns

Janai Johnson, Grade 10
Bradshaw Christian High School, CA

My One and Only

Every time that I am with you, you take my breath away
You are perfect in every single way
Looking into your eyes is like a look into heaven
Talking to you is my favorite thing to do
I used to be lost in this world
But since I found you, I found my place in the Earth
You are the BEST thing that has happened to me
I do not know what I did to deserve you
Because you are so amazing and deserve the best
I hope that we will last forever
Because I cannot imagine you not being in my life
If you were ever taken from my life,
You would be bringing my heart with you
I love you now and I will love you forever
I only have one fear in life and that is losing you
You are the breath that keeps me alive
Without you, there would be no purpose for my life
Everything you say, everything you do is right
Just writing this poem isn't enough to show my feelings
I now know what love is
Love is the wonderful feeling I get when I am with you

Nadine Brinson, Grade 10
Great Oak High School, CA

Potential

In God's world, nature changes each minute,
Constantly showing me God's great power.
By a beating heart, or a small cricket
Or a bright sun or a drenching shower.

I wish I could be like a beating heart,
Constantly beating, its duty, fulfilled.
For if so, I would be a work of art
And my iniquities would be distilled.

I wish that I could be the rising sun
Constantly bright, and rising in Glory
And conquer life like a strong Mongol Hun.
My life would be a glorious story.

Life, being lived to its fullest potential
Having my soul live in a Gold temple.

Cayce Jones, Grade 10
Calvary Chapel Christian School, CA

I Wish Upon...

I may or may not always come true
I visit my yellow and geometric self to each and every one of you
I am yearned upon on 11:11
Dimensions away from Heaven
You blow the lit waxes of wonders for me on your scrumptious cake
Now waiting and waiting for me to quake

Desa Yadegarians, Grade 10
Cypress High School, CA

Invasion

As we crowd down the hidden tunnel,
I see lives slowly being despaired,
teardrops from the pain of sorrow.
I stayed breathlessly invulnerable.
Though, not for long…
I sensed the scrimmage beyond my ears,
guns firing, bombs exploding,
lives being taken away.

I prayed as the day goes by,
suffering from hunger and dehydration,
but nothing seems to change.
More blood has been shed,
and so has tears…
I closed my eyes tightly,
as I waited and waited…
I started to sense emptiness in my surrounding.
And I realized,
my prayers have been answered.
"It's over," I said.
We are free.

Stephanie Chen, Grade 10
Abraham Lincoln High School, CA

Vacation

Eyes open, too early to rise,
The sun hasn't even poked its head up
Throwing things in the car, and away we drive.
Long drive, it has fighting and boredom.
Finally we arrive, and unpack.
Hanging with our cousins talking, running around.
Ocean waves rolling as the golden sun turns red.
Drifting to sleep to the peaceful white noise of the water.
Soccer, extreme competition with family, drive to win.
Running, fouls, and goals.
Score, and the taste of victory floods to my mouth.
Emptiness as we pack to leave.
Bitter goodbyes fill the air.
Won't see these cousins until next year.
When we step foot in our home once more,
Drift to sleep to continue life after a wonderful vacation.

Travis Willis, Grade 10
Orem High School, UT

How

How could you do that, how could you get so low?
Is it because you thought I'd never let you go?
Why are you walking around full of anger and lies
I told you tell me the truth or you'll hear goodbyes
I thought you were sweet, but I just wasted my time
Who knew you could be so rude…
That's why I left you behind

Leah Kinores, Grade 10
King Kekaulike High School, HI

Lost Boys

Lost boys have no home,
on the streets where they roam.
Sitting on city streets,
wondering who they will meet.
Talking to the homeless man,
digging through the garbage can.
Maybe they will find a home.
On the streets that they roam.
Maybe they will stay forever.
Living on and on together.

Running from their troubled past.
Hoping to find a better life at last.
Wishing mom and dad were here,
but they've been dead over a year.
Moving from home to home.
Is this the reason that they roam?
For what the future they may hold.
Lost boys stories must be told.
So that they may find a home,
and be released from the streets that they roam

Josephneal Harrison, Grade 10
Mountainair High School, NM

Voice of Tints

I hear noises in the woods.
I see nothing but the sky's tint,
nothing but the tree's shadow.
The voice is angry, demanding.
A black bird perched on clawing branches.

It glares at me with piercing eyes,
seemly embarrassed at something,
raven or crow not too sure
I get a closer look.

Much too small to be either,
but the brightness is making me squint,
Then it chirped and trilled
it wanted an audience so now it has one.
I sat listening to the nightingale sing its song.

Winson Zheng, Grade 10
Radford High School, HI

Sleeping Willow

Chewing his last bit of tobacco
the old man's last two teeth fall out.
His gaping despair lost his wisdom
as the decaying gum deteriorates into bones.
He soon finds himself unable to speak.
With his hidden grin and loose jaws
he buries his teeth by the wisdom tree.

Briana Moradel, Grade 11
San Diego Center for Children, CA

Beautiful Spring

Spring,
it is a time of change.
The grass turns green,
when once it was brown.

The flowers blossom,
when once they were dead.
The tree grows new leaves,
where it was bare.

The sun rises from the east
and becomes the dawn of a new spring.
The snow melts and becomes rivers
Lakes become a place of paradise.

The animals wake from their long sleep.
They see the beauty of spring.
The world is reborn
from its dark, cold death.

Then you wake
and see the beauty of spring.
You feel renewed and relaxed,
as you realize spring has come.
Josh Cooley, Grade 10
Orem High School, UT

Warmth

Heat appears as if from nowhere.
Spreading its warmth.
Thawing.

Feeling returns to fingers and toes,
Softened hearts beat faster.
Slowly but surely melting.

Pure joy runs through the veins,
Heating everything in its path
Until it bursts into flame.

The fire dies.
The heat subsides.
The warmth is gone.

Ice takes over.
Freezing the body; creating
Blue lips and white knuckles.

Blood draws deep to the core,
Trying to keep the heart beating
Until the next encounter with the warmth
That fuels the fire.
Erica Potts, Grade 12
Spanish Springs High School, NV

I Heard You Through the Rain

I heard you through the rain.
And even through the snow,
Kept hearing, hearing, as you spoke
Your ideas going to and fro.

And then your voice continued,
Very loud on my telephone,
Kept speaking, speaking, till you stopped
Your phone-line is now alone

And then I hear your silence,
And thoughts across my heart
Will soon be spoken to you, again.
Then silence will be no more

As all the words are spoken aloud,
And that is all you hear,
And I tell truths you don't want to face
Unpleasant, to your, ear.

And then that's when your emotion, broke,
And you dropped tears down, and down —
And I stopped my words, to make amends,
And finished speaking — again —
Emily Faulkner, Grade 11
Valley Christian High School, CA

Suffocate Me

The walls of my high school —
aquarium tanks.
The water fills.
The stress of trying to belong,
drowns.

But for some reason,
we like drowning.
We like letting this water,
fill our lungs. We love it.

And for some reason,
we start surfacing.
We become our own person,
and learn to let go.

But we hate the oxygen.
We hate the oxygen that fills our lungs,
because only then we are not like the rest.
We form gills. We adapt.

So we suffocate when the glass breaks,
and only those that stayed afloat
can handle the air.
Diane Eykholt, Grade 11
Valley Christian High School, CA

She Smiles

His heart has stopped,
His breath no more.
She knows what comes,
Must always go.
Oh she knows quite well,
Yet she still smiles.

A smile plastered upon her face,
Neither tight nor forced.
Her heart is breaking,
But, I wouldn't know.

This battle is over,
The enemy has prevailed.
Cancer, they call it,
Takes him away.

Her eyes threaten to pour —
Her unshed tears.
Rushing overhead,
Drowning her,
But still, I wouldn't know.

Yet, she still smiles.
Amber Poon, Grade 11
San Marino High School, CA

Divorce

Hush my dear child not another word
I'm not mad at you, that's just absurd
It's the days that go by
That makes me sigh

The stress that I feel
And the heart that he steals
Came shattering down
And in the sorrow, I drown

This was foreshadowed,
When our loves decode
Faith was lost
But at what cost?

Live our life together?
That's a false header
I promise though
That you will grow

Well my dear child
For words reviled
But just know this for true,
I will always love you.
James Lim, Grade 10
Mililani High School, HI

Meadow

My mind is set
On the field over there,
Across the highway,
Without care.
This field is grand
With lots of space.
Away from the town,
The people, the cars,
When you lay in the field,
You can view every star.
I can't believe I live in a place
With no fields, no moon, no room, no space.
Grass reaching to the sky,
Flowing with the wind,
Discovering my thoughts,
As I sit with my horse.
I realize I'm alive,
There is nothing to lose, with everything to gain.
I feel as I can fly,
In this heaven-like meadow,
I wish I could stay…

Brandon Hays, Grade 11
Merit Academy, UT

Do You Remember?

My head on your shoulder,
Smelling your sweet gray hair,
You hold me tight
I knew something was going to happen, but when?
Now no more watching Andy Griffith,
No more grits on Saturdays,
Only memories.
I was so young,
Why'd you have to leave?
A little girl always needs her grandma.
Now I look at your pretty purple doll,
And go back to the times when you were here.
Do you remember?
I remember your wheelchair and medicine collection.
I wish I could remember the better times,
When there was no chemo or tumors,
When there was me and you.
I will see you again someday,
And you will take me back to us,
My head on your shoulder,
Do you remember?

Cynthia Burnette, Grade 10
San Diego Met High School, CA

Who Will Help?

Who will come help the little girl crying?
When really deep down inside she's dying?
She has asked for help for several years.
She is dying and it feels like no one cares.
She has been through hell and back.
No one cares and that's a fact.
The little girl is still crying, what do we do?
Do we help her, or do we call you?
We all have our little break downs.
We've all had our depressing moments, with our frowns.
Who will cry for the weeping girl on my friends shoulder?
Who will make it warmer, when it is colder?
Who will help the little girl who is crying?
Who will help the little girl who is hiding?
Who will attempt to help my friend in need?
Who will do it just for a good deed?

Cyra Cox, Grade 11
Palo Verde High School, NV

I Am

I am joyful and outgoing,
I wonder why people are the way they are,
I hear birds in the trees chirping away,
I want to earn money to get a car,
I am joyful and outgoing.

I pretend to do my work sometimes,
I feel overwhelmed with all the work at school,
I touch my long light brown hair to make it how I want it,
I cry when my family and friends get hurt or injured,
I am joyful and outgoing.

I understand that we need family and friends to live,
I say that blondes do have their moments but so do others,
I dream about getting pulled over with my friends' car,
I hope my dad gets better very soon,
I am joyful and outgoing.

Amber Mitchell, Grade 10
Shelley High School, ID

A Forever Friend

F or someone to laugh with you
R espect and stand by you
I n moments of sadness when you're feeling blue
E verlasting friendship will keep you strong
N ever will you be alone
D rawing from memories together

Yareli Alejandro, Grade 10
Wilson High School, CA

Society

In that twist of wayward fate; those with everlasting designer hate
Following those who stray; in that instinctive, insufferable way
This ephemeral outlook of each passing day
Seen through clouded eyes
Watched over with indulgent buys

Denali Kemper, Grade 11
Mount Everest Academy, CA

It Hurts to Say Goodbye

I never thought it would end like this
In silence.
I never imagined us not talking.
It hurts,
Losing the one person who changed everything.
The one person I could talk to about anything.
The one person I knew would understand despite everything.
You were that person.
We got each other through a lot,
But when it came to our own problems…
We couldn't do anything.
Now everything has fallen apart.
Like Rome, our friendship wasn't built in a day.
But it sure was ruined in one.
It hurts.
It hurts to say goodbye to my best friend.
I never thought it would end like this.
I never thought it would end at all…
In silence.

Haille Van Patten, Grade 10
Roy High School, UT

I Wrote You This Sonnet

Oh my soul, I have to write this sonnet,
Ah my dear, I have to write it for you.
You are a diabolical culprit,
Because without mercy you told me to.
I used to pleasantly think you liked me,
You're my inspirational favorite one.
You are really picking on me clearly,
Because writing loving sonnets is dumb.
I do not like creating in this style,
I let my truthful thoughts on it be known.
You promised me that it would be worthwhile,
My head and my heart are beginning to groan.
But, oh my soul, here it is you have it.
Ah my dear, I wrote your Bloody sonnet.

Amereece Sterba, Grade 12
Sequoia Village School, AZ

Running

Running a long route that can tire you out
But in the long run you'll have a bit
Most of the day and rarely get out
More energy than if you choose to sit

Running in the street out of breath
Exhausted with the sound of feet stomping
The sound of your heart pounding at your death
During races people are cheering
Battling for the finish, tired
Fear of losing is running through your head
Finishing with no breath and all wired
Sweating at the end with your face all RED

Anthony Murguia, Grade 10
Whittier High School, CA

Zebra

Glossy zigzags of ebony and ivory
Juxtaposed on my striking silhouette
My hooves, they dance
As I prance and trot through fields
Not a horse nor a mule am I

I am an intrepid adventurer
From an arid palace, the Sahara
I am bound for greatness
Like Columbus, I sailed for America
Oh, the diversity I have discovered

In my new kingdom, I reign supreme
I flaunt my lustrous locks before my subjects
Intrigued, they gape
They know I am their master
They wish they could be me
In my new castle, a place they call the Z-O-O

Katherine Riley, Grade 12
St Joseph Notre Dame High School, CA

"So Taken Am I"

So taken am I by the sight above,
So passioned am I by its strength and hue;
The sunset curls about the eye of Jove
As liquid light flows over me and you.
Entranced am I by all the heavens high,
My eyes both catching all their falling stars,
And seeing, feeling, how the sun does cry
When he must dip behind the blue earth's bars.
And early stars shine brilliantly like jade
That long after the sun they dance and sing;
Unfortunately, all begins to fade,
The colors to me no more pleasure bring,
For once from heaven to you my eyes turn,
My love, rekindled, never stops to burn.

Alessandra Balsamo, Grade 11
Rio Americano High School, CA

Egypt's National Team

Confederation Cup 2009
Beat Italy the world champs!
Had a Great chance to go to the World Cup
But they lost the death match against Algeria
That don't Matter though
They put that behind them
Had a different mission now
Had to defend their African cup trophy
2006 and 2008 champs!
Went to Angola and came back with the trophy
Set world record
Three African cup trophies in a row!
Six in total!
African kings of soccer!

Osama Abdelrahman, Grade 11
Wilson High School, CA

Dream Love

You held me tight
And kissed me all night
You grabbed my hand
And said you had a plan
You'd take me away
And promised You'd stay
You said you love me
And forever we will be
Always in love
Just like a dove
My heart soared
And I felt adored
Then everything faded
And everything you stated
Slipped from my mind
The world is so unkind
It was just a dream
I didn't scream
I just cried
It felt like I died
You were my world
Brittany Rhoades, Grade 10
Blackfoot High School, ID

Enjoy the Ride

Death can affect you so much.
You don't realize
how much someone really
means to you until they're gone.
At first they seem
just perfectly fine,
then the next moment
you're saying your
last good-byes.
Be it a friend,
an uncle, or a
great grandfather
it's going to hurt.
You have to live
with what you have
and remember
what you don't.
Life comes at you fast and
sometimes it's hard to catch on
But once you get there
enjoy the ride.
Christine McMaster, Grade 11
Fernley High School, NV

Nostalgic Thoughts

Pour a little salt
On sleeping nostalgic thoughts
Wakened, they linger
Lauren Jonker, Grade 10
Calvary Chapel Christian School, CA

Airplane

There is an airplane (up, up) in the sky (sky, sky)
and I wonder if it's you as you fly
right back into my life (my life) and my heart (my heart);
I miss you missing me missing you.

Whatever happened to those moments where we'd spout old clichés?
Those were the days...
And what ever happened to just lying in each other's embrace?
Those were the days...
I guess time had them erased.

That little plane (so small) passing by (so long)
and now it's out of sight and out of mind (my mind) and my heart (my heart).
I won't miss out on life from missing us.

Whatever happened to those moments where we'd spout old clichés?
Those were the days...
And what ever happened to just lying in each other's embrace?
Those were the days...
I guess time had them erased.

But whatever happened now has happened, done and gone;
But I won't, no I won't,
miss out on life from missing us.
Rodrigo Silva, Grade 12
Bourgade Catholic High School, AZ

Welcome to the 50th State

Welcome to the 50th state
We may be last but we're equally great
We may not have the bright lights, big city
But if you need that then it's a pity.
So, all the haters can just sit there and hate
Because deep down you know; you can't beat the 8-0-8

Where lush green mountains reach the sky,
Where the beauty of waterfalls can make you cry
We're the land where palm trees sway to and fro,
And fields and fields of pineapples grow
Catch the bus up north, you'll see what I mean
The rolling waves; the never ending days,
Like nothing you've ever seen

All the locals know, everywhere we go, the Aloha will come with us
There's no fuss; 'cause no amount of miles can ever erase the spirit
Where ever we go we make people feel it, hear it,
Stuck like a tattoo it'll be written on our face; we can never forget this place.

So E Komo Mai,
Welcome to the H.I.
We know you'll enjoy your stay,
You'll fall in love with us every day
Jaycie Ige, Grade 10
Mililani High School, HI

To Live Your Life

I wander
And I ponder
What is the meaning of life?
Is it to come out on top, or to be our very best?
Before we die,
We are all given a chance to fly.
Not all of us will be stars,
Or even make it to Mars.
But, one thing is for sure
And one thing only.
We have each been given one life
And one life only.
86,400 seconds in a day.
220,752,000 seconds in a year.
What will we do with them?
To play in the rain.
To read a good book.
To bake chocolate chip cookies with your little sister.
Life your life
Before it's gone
And you will be happy

Samantha Hansen, Grade 12
Viewmont High School, UT

My Life

Waking up, living it up
Another day I get to live.
Talking to my dad makes my day
I feel so light through the day.

The sun shines; it gives me time
Life goes on and things change.
I need love like other people do too —
My dad gives me love every day and it's what I need.

I ask myself what I want to do
Its like a game — I have to make good moves to win.
I like my life but something that I want is missing
I need to live life to the fullest.
Thinking of my dad makes my day go well
Because I know he's always there.

Jose Garcia, Grade 11
Animo Leadership Charter High School, CA

A Little Rusty —

Breathing— in and out — it calms me.
I think of the ocean pulling back and forth,
The tide rising.
The words wash through me like a purifying salve
And beach themselves upon this paper.
Ah — it feels good to have the rotor running again,
To have the stagnant water flow like cascades once more.
My Moon, my Moon!
May the tide be never-ending.

Qun Zeng, Grade 11
Diamond Bar High School, CA

One Last Week

One more week of being seventeen
One last week of being a kid
Not many more chances to be irresponsible
Those lazy days of summer that were
Filled with running through the sprinklers
And eating ice cream are gone
They're being replaced with days filled with
Work and taking care of yourself
This is your last chance to be a carefree child
When your birthday comes around,
You now have to make the change from a
Dependent to an independent
All of those childhood memories have come
Crashing in around you like a flood
The suffocation of growing up is making you
Want to cry. This whole time you have
Wanted to grow up, and now you wish
With all of your heart, you could be younger again.
After this last week is over, there is no turning back.
Crying won't help you to go where you're going.
We all got to grow up sometime, might as well be now.

Sarah Aplet, Grade 12
Lucerne Valley Jr/Sr High School, CA

The Woods

The Forest full and bountiful and green,
It bursts with life and silent emerald glee.
You sit and stare little one gleans.
One lies on moss and stare to leaves and trees,
And falls unto the trance of the billowing grass.
Then watch my dreams and hopes flow to the sky,
To see the world as through the looking glass.
The world so bright where 'ere the sun's up high.

Then when the stellar bodies dance and switch,
And as the unknown fear begins to rise.
You're startled by every movement and twitch,
And all the trees will bring about your demise.
And though the winds might seem so full of fright,
I know by light that I will be all right.
The Forest in the night.

Ethan Wingett, Grade 10
Chandler Preparatory Academy, AZ

A KISS Beyond a Kiss

K nows how to Rock 'N' Roll with
I nsane guitar solos.
S pandex and face paint.
S immons, Stanley, Frehley, and Criss,

A legacy that will never die
R ock 'N' Roll idols and
M emorable concerts.
Y ears and years of rocking and they aren't stopping anytime soon.

Gigi Silva, Grade 10
Campbell High School, HI

Earth

The earth is cold
A small cube of ice
It's full of darkness
Making things hard to recognize
Our souls full of hatred
Our hearts full of fear.
Nothing but a living pain
Lies in me, as my eyes cry out a cold tear.
Love is lost
The evil has won
We all act as many
When together we're supposed to be one
Cries of pain
Fly through the cold air.
Big smile on the kid's face
Are no longer there.
Find yourself
Before it's too late
Spread love with others
Until your expiration date.

Cesar Sanchez, Grade 12
Pine View High School, UT

Warming Sun

You wake the world each morning break,
Your face so bright and round.
The cold and chill from night you take,
And warm me all around.

The children laugh and run and play.
It's such a sugary sound.
In your golden light they do as they may.
It warms them all around.

The day must finally come to end.
Once more you hide in the ground.
But, Sun, tomorrow's round the bend,
And you'll warm me all around.

Alicia Pedneault, Grade 10
Cypress High School, CA

The Empty Room

Alone I sat in an empty room
Sitting silent in the dark
I see the shadows dance around me
Covering every corner
Upon me they came
Taking me away to the world unknown
As I follow the shadows of the night
I stumble across a man
Sitting in an empty room
Sitting in the dark
As I went forward towards the man
I awaken

Seth Bowen, Grade 12
Madison Sr High School, ID

Like the Wind Across My Face

Like the wind across my face, that came so quickly, and left the same
Leaving me wondering forever, leaving me with a lifetime of pain.
Questions I can't ask, and the love I can never show
Makes me feel lost in my days, because my father, I will never know.
All this time you were so close, but you seemed so far away.
Alone I felt, numb, the space grew bigger with every passing day.
But the world kept turning, and the wind kept blowing
Further and further away I felt, and I finally gave in to not knowing.
I heard one day you asked for me, and I couldn't imagine why
You had never been here before, finally being without you was all right.
And then I thought to myself, this is what I have been waiting for
Maybe you deserve a chance, maybe just one, but no more.
So again I sat waiting, for you to come home
But the home in the sky you returned to, left me even more alone.
My heart broke instantly, I couldn't even cry
Despite all my time waiting, once again, you left my side.
This time I know you're gone, and I know I'll never see a smile on your face
Once again you're so close, but so far away
I'm sure Heaven is a much better place.
Even with my goodbye, I'll hold on to your memory, with what little I have
I know one day we'll make up for lost time, until then, I love you Dad.

Evan Miranda, Grade 10
Mountainair High School, NM

Vacation

I am going on vacation,
Or so they told me,
I was young it sounded exciting,
I started to pack,
I chose my favorite suitcase,
Shiny, black, small,
I packed the toys I would miss,
I began to throw my clothes into the suitcase,
Only the ones I liked,
Not the ones with frills that made me itch,
I admired the clothes with the little stars on the pocket,
My family didn't like them but I thought they were pretty,
I continued to do so until my suitcase was a balled up mess of clothes,
But they told me it was too much and they gave me a smaller suitcase,
I told them I didn't want this suitcase,
But they ignored me and began to fill my Suitcase with only a few clothes,
They took us away in a hurry, the men had guns but I don't know why,
After a few hours, we pulled up to our vacation spot,
There were letters on the gate but I couldn't read,
I asked my sister what it said and she whispered one word to me,
"Auschwitz"

Alia Pyatt, Grade 10
San Diego Met High School, CA

I Wish I Knew You

I don't know you
And I wish you knew me
If God only gave you more time
You could see the young lady I have grown to be
We all miss you down here
And daddy's hurting so much
Every so often we drop a tear
We just wish we knew your touch
No good night kisses, no tucking into bed
We all could have been so happy
But God took you instead
I wish I remembered your smell
Or the hugs that you gave
But instead I cry a lonely tear
As I sit and talk to your grave
I wish I knew your love or seen a smile on your face
God took your hand so early
I wish that wasn't the case
So now I write in the hopes of our future hello
I pray He holds and keeps you, because we asked him so.

Haley Wilson, Grade 10
Valley Charter High School, CA

Would It?

Would it work, if I was to tell you I was sorry?
For all that I have done.
Like leaving you all alone;
To get embraced, ready to have a son.
Would it fix it, if I could take it all back?
If there was any way I could.
I would do anything;
Just tell me and I would.
Would it help to know that I am simply trying?
To do my very best.
To show everyone;
You and all the rest.
Would it work, knowing that I have really changed?
Turned my life around.
I'm going to be a great father;
We can live our lives, safe and sound.
Would it bother you, if I didn't understand?
What happened between you and me?
But I am changing;
For everyone to see.

Daniel Crawford, Grade 12
Rite of Passage Charter High School, NV

The Stoic Tree

Big tree in the woods
Tall, dark, swaying in the wind
Strong, standing its ground.

Jessie Marin, Grade 10
Wilson High School, CA

I Am

I am from the tears my mother shed
and the lies my father told
from leaning into the wind
wishing it was enough to hold me
I am from summers on the beach
and flip flop tan lines
from Janis Joplin Sundays
and Sinatra lullabies
I am from never being enough
to give the love they deserved
from endless nights of contemplating
my place in the world
I am the girl who read Shakespeare
because I liked the taste of his words
I am from the laughter that covers tears
I am from hours in the library
and Audrey Hepburn films
The girl who climbed through the looking glass
and didn't want to come back

Jessica Williams, Grade 11
Grossmont High School, CA

Consequences of a Storm

The rain brings new life,
But also causes a lot of strife.
The howling winds rip at the vulnerable trees,
Stripping them naked of all their leaves.

The lightning flashes,
As the rain splashes,
And the air is frigid,
Causing my limbs to become rigid.

The pouring of the rain,
On the, now satiated, terrain,
Becomes a normal sound,
And loosens the ground.

Flash floods and mud slides,
Cause hordes of people to go inside,
But they often pout,
Because their electricity is out.

Matthew Negri, Grade 11
Grossmont High School, CA

Pretty and Small

The gentle wafting whisper
Of the sweet pollen trees
Of tender singing berries
Hanging on the breeze
The scent is melodic
The tiny creatures dance
In swirls of the small things,
Little planets in our hands

Paula Barteau, Grade 10
Socorro High School, NM

This Poem Isn't for You

I want to be 112 feet tall
So that you cannot look away
And whenever I sing
The notes will ring
All the way to the tip of South Africa.

But — alas, I am only 5 foot 6.
If I exaggerate an inch.
You are handsomely tall
I feel 8-year-old small
Standing in the shadow of your ego.

I wanted you to be happy.
I wanted to spill a truckload
Of daisies on top of you
Just to give you a few
Reasons to be alive.

But roses and lilies are
Poisoned by the weeds of regret
Even the soil of forgiveness won't
Forget that which we don't
Have the strength to loosen our grips on.
Ashley Allison, Grade 11
Desert Vista High School, AZ

Moon Walk

I went to the moon, but there was no air.
Permanent footprints, in this foreign sand.
Someone stop this foolishness.
Because Earth.
Was so clear to me.
But I couldn't breath.
I couldn't breath.
I went to the moon, but there was no air.

We're letting go.
Your pull was getting too weak.
Didn't feel.
When I was heading straight down.
The pain hit me harder.
Than the Earth could afflict.
We thought of everything.
It didn't matter.

I went to the moon, but there was no air.
My footprints, in this foreign sand.
Please don't make the same mistake.
Because Earth. Was so clear to me.
But I couldn't breath. I couldn't breath.
Anissa Livas, Grade 11
La Serna High School, CA

Goodbye

As her smile disappears,
Her tears start to fall
He doesn't know what's coming,
So he asks her, "What's wrong?"

Her thoughts turn to words,
And her words turn to pain
Her words become spoken,
As her tears start to flow
She tries to stay strong,
But she feels so much pain

He looks deep into her eyes,
And quietly tells her, "Please, no…"
Her voice slow and sad says,
"I'm so sorry, we just need to let go."

After walking for a while, it's that time,
One last kiss and a hug to remember
The last words spoken,
"I love you and I'll miss you…"
But still I can't believe,
"It's our time to say goodbye."
Eryn Kim, Grade 11
Mililani High School, HI

Questionable Love

In a dream
I see a girl
With unique qualities

Is it?
Can it be?
Is it meant to be?

I have words to say
But they won't escape my lips
My shyness cuts me off
It doesn't let me communicate

I know one day
I will overcome this
All in due time
Sooner or later she will be mine

But for now
She will have to wait

A questionable love?
Or a true soul mate?
Efren Castaneda, Grade 10
El Monte High School, CA

Nobody Cares

I got an "A" on my assignment today,
But it doesn't matter now,
Because no matter what you do,
No matter what you say,
People don't care

I made a funny joke today,
But nobody laughs,
Because no matter what you do,
No matter what you say,
People don't care

I'm in a jolly mood today,
But now I'm depressed,
Because no matter what you do,
No matter what you say,
People don't care

I was ridiculed by my peers today,
But it doesn't matter now,
Because no matter what they do,
No matter what they say,
I don't care.
John Lee, Grade 10
Cypress High School, CA

The World Is Mine

The world is mine,
I must shout it
from the mountain tops.
As I blast by,
the whole world stops.

They set goals for me
and I burn them down.
Yet they stand astounded.
I never look back.
My mind is firmly grounded.

But if I did
take just one glance,
I know what I would see,
hordes of people
Too scared to be me.

As I look forward
I face new challenges,
I know I'll overcome.
And I'll shout the world is mine,
until I reach the sun.
Ian Fowler, Grade 10
Bradshaw Christian High School, CA

Yan-Shegonalack

Screaming from the depths it comes,
Yan-Shegonalack
It haunts the very souls of men
Yan-Shegonalack
It breaks the mind, the soul of God
Yan-Shegonalack
It sees not the puny man things here
Yan-Shegonalack
Breaking civilization down
Yan-Shegonalack
Yog Sototh fears his face
Yan-Shegonalack
Cthulhu sees him not
Yan-Shegonalack
He eats up stars and breathes black holes
Yan-Shegonalack
Scion of old Azatoth
Yan-Shegonalack
The beast that flies, the hate that screams
Yan-Shegonalack!

Thomas Johnson, Grade 12
University High School, AZ

Love Is

Love is like a bird taking flight
Sweeping you off your feet
With an unimaginable might
And causing your heart to skip a beat

Love is like a rock
Pounding a fragile heart to the ground
While attempting to block
What is lost from being found

Love is like a rainbow
Sometimes it can be seen
Sometimes it does not show
But it is never purposely mean

Priscilla Chan, Grade 10
Cypress High School, CA

out of service, out of mind

my heart is not fluent in Dishonesty.
this is why i feel: disconnected.
dejected. rejected. unexpected.
press 2 for Amnesia; 3 for Truth.
sorry the number you reached is
in hiding. in flames. in love. in-
visible. in America, not Fakeville.
please recheck your information,
and dial again. and again. again.
hang up. tear up the power bill.
slam your phone in the wall. four
calls to me is four calls too many.

Devin Mize, Grade 12
Basic High School, NV

The Silence

And all she can do is sit. Still.
And all she can do is sit. Still. Quiet.
She can't feel herself breathe.
She is so still. So Quiet.
The waves are coming slowly now, each with their own cruel intentions.
One by one they crush her until she loses sight of why she came here.
Here, the waters are so deep, so blue.
The feeling is too surreal.
Treading water.
Trying with all of her broken heart to find her way back to the shore.
She screams "Why did you bring me out here?"
Now the waters are high.
She watches herself being dragged through the currents.
She is helpless.
By way of miracle she watches the storm pass her.
Moving to bigger, brighter, happier places and leaving her with nothing.
Nothing but the silence.
The water is calm.
Her head above water, but she is still miles away from land.
The end of so much pain isn't here and yet, she still finds comfort in all this silence.

Catalina Lopez, Grade 11
Foothill High School, CA

Ombre De L'avenir

And smiles part the clouds as seagulls become swans.
The faces, they float through the air
A thousand pieces converging, becoming one.
The multi faceted memories swarming like an angry beehive
As waves wash away the grains of sand, marking the passage of time,
Cleaning the slate to start anew.
Yet memories persist, ingrained within the mind, within the soul.
Darkly lit foreground upon a glowing mountainscape
The ticking of eternity smashing your control with
Each and every second.
Try to run and try to hide
Your demons and nightmares may never find you but
Memories will always be
Right. At. Your. Doorstep.
And even as you lock the door and swallow the key, they enter so swiftly.
Time is the enemy, memories, death
While ideas are figments of a fractured mindset.
As the day draws to a close, darkness creeps into every crevice
Drowning out the light, and with it, the illusions.
Now, faced with reality, those fond memories give way to betrayal
The darkest hour of light.

Cheyenne Oliver, Grade 12
Darby High School, MT

Godiva

Like a work of art,
Fragile and delicate
Almost too pretty to be touched,
It melts in my hands.
Detailed, with abstract designs and patterns,
Molded into different shapes
And casings,
Always handcrafted with love and care,
The smell of it is divine.
Sweet, with a hint of bitterness, fruitiness,
And maybe even spice.
Anticipation awaits me
As I find the courage to pick one up.
Suddenly it breaks open,
Exposing a liquid paradise of
Caramel, ganache, cocoa, and pure sugar
That tickles my taste buds.

Saturated fat, you kill me!

Sarah Su, Grade 12
St Joseph Notre Dame High School, CA

Drowning in Debris

My soul wanders through this cold desolate world.
I'm a hunter stuck in a world without prey.
I ripped the knife from his hand once curled.
Is there nothing left to say?
Take the pieces out of my heart.
I'm sick of storing them inside me.
You see that you tore my world apart.
Through the scattered piles of debris,
I sit here drowning again.
My mind is a jumbled mess.
You have forever ruined men.
Now I'm only miserable at best.
How am I supposed to live when I'm full of lies?
Just kiss my cheek and say goodbye.

Avalon Albro, Grade 10
Youngker High School, AZ

You and I

You and I, we dance trough time.
You and I, we sing,
No matter what the song or rhyme.

We run outside when it thunders and pours,
Just so we can say "We danced in that rain!"

Our bare feet splash through thick mud as we dance, hand in hand.
We laugh so hard we cry.
We sing so loud and strong that our throats give out.

If the world ended here and now it would be all right,
As long as we could dance together, friends forever, just you and I.

Whitney Chapman, Grade 10
Wheatland High School, WY

Under the Influence

Why is my car crunched at the side of the road?
Sitting there, threatening to explode
My body's strewn across the floor
After being lobbed out through the front window
Twenty yards, to the right
I hear my lady start to cry
Sobbing after she watched me die
I wish I could make it all all right
As she's yelling out with terrible dread
"Oh my God! My boyfriend's dead!"
Babe please calm down, no more screaming
Why is your face all bruised and bleeding?
I want to live and be with you Dear
Going to that party wasn't worth damn near
But since there's nothing I can do
Please remember that I'll always love you
So go on, move on, and live your life
While I fly away into the night
One more kiss to say goodbye?
Oh yeah that's right, I'm a ghost tonight.

Brandon Bader, Grade 11
Dobson High School, AZ

The Gun Rises, the Gun Falls

The gun rises, the gun falls,
The runners ready for the guns call;
Along the track ready to race
Ready to get out at a hasty pace,
And the gun rises, the gun falls.
The air is filled with the gun shots call,
But the runners forget about it after all;
They remember to breathe and keep their form,
With each step they sprint; for God they perform,
And the gun rises, the gun falls.
The race is over and they are out of breath
Forgetting about the gunshot that made them deaf;
The race is done and they have won
The feeling of a win is second to none,
And the gun rises, the gun falls.

Jeremy Thompson, Grade 11
Valley Christian High School, CA

Electric Lions

My mother once told me
a lion lived in the tunnels of the subway,
prowling the electric tracks,
bounding over the concrete cracks,
she told me his roar was the beat of the train
and the grinding sparks the hair of his mane,
my mother once told me that
a lion lived in the tunnels of the subway,
growling and prowling underneath
the streets which he tore
with his razor-like teeth.

Shay Christine Larsen, Grade 11
Preston High School, ID

Her Hell on Earth

She escapes her mother's wrath once again,
As the woman acts upon her with disdain.
Merciless strikes,
Painful slaps.
She wonders what she did to deserve such pain.

She shivers as she lets out a sigh.
Thinking of the bruises makes her cry.
No one to see, no one to believe.
Inside she feels herself begin to die.

Her life has been a living hell for years,
As her mother fulfills her greatest fears.
So much misery and sadness
Is she forced to endure,
So many sleepless nights and endless tears.

Despite her pain and suffering each day,
Inside herself she finds the strength to pray.
For someone to come, to take her away
From the Hell on Earth she lives in every day.

Clara Hayles, Grade 12
Sacramento Charter High School, CA

Wars

Wars were going on between countries.
We were restless.
We were unable to sleep.

I regained my consciousness and I noticed that I was surrounded.
I knew who they were, the Japanese.
I saw that they were all armed with guns and rifles.

They challenged me to a hand to hand combat.
They respected strong fighters and I was lucky to be one.
The vice captain was unconvinced and prepared to shoot.

The leader suppressed her underling and I was set free.
Oh! How blessed I was.
But my wife was not as lucky.

Claudia Chau, Grade 10
Abraham Lincoln High School, CA

The Photograph

The photograph upon the wall is hate,
For all who look outside for more to care.
The photograph upon the wall is fate,
For those who never push themselves to dare.
The photograph upon the wall is key,
For those who will to dig down to the core.
The photograph upon the wall is glee,
For those who learn to give it all and more.
The photograph upon the wall is strife,
And just as soon, the photograph is life.

Madeline Sell, Grade 10
Veritas Preparatory Academy, AZ

Hidden

She is hidden for what feels like a life time,
Fear of the truth and the pain it brings,
She lies to everyone, even herself for safety,
She is not the person in the mirror,
Threatened for being herself, doing no wrong,
Threatened with the eternal flame,
Mocked for what she cannot change,
Once loved, now the love has become hate,
Hated by those closest to her,
Betrayed, hated, hurt,
What did that love mean
Why has it changed, she hasn't changed,
Same human, same person, same soul,
We are all created equally,
We are all His children and His love never ends
His love keeps us safe,
Why can't we love like He does,
You call yourself a believer, yet you judge her,
Why spend your life hating what you cannot change,
We are told to love our neighbor,
Why does it matter who they are?

Mikey Pappas, Grade 10
Bradshaw Christian High School, CA

Hoping Every Day

Down that sweat drops through my nose
tiredness is in my soul.
Cropping, planting the whole day,
bright hot sun beam on top of me.
Yesterday, today, tomorrow,
every day is the same.
Being sold from place to place
I wonder when it will be the day
when I can be free.
A little bit of hope,
a little bit of faith
can bring me up daily joy and happiness.
Waking up every day is not something new.
Past, present, future always may be the same,
but that little bit of hope will be unchanged.

Vivian Chiu, Grade 10
Abraham Lincoln High School, CA

Through the Lens

Close at hand, not far from my reach, always in sight.
rested around my neck, the weight is never a burden

light vibrant with color seen as I look through.
the world changes, nothing has ever seemed so perfect

everything in my version, that no one else can see,
you come with freedom that nobody else can offer.

your weight is never a burden.

Maddie Villalobos, Grade 11
La Serna High School, CA

Somewhere

The first snow of winter
Bathes me in white
Embracing me in its arms
While whispering promises
That it cannot hide

Flurries of diamonds
Rain from the sky
Covering the earth
With a breathtaking sigh

Diamond trees throw rainbows across the snow
Branches rasp the wind
As they shudder the burden of winter
Unto the gossamer powder below

The soft, simple, snow, sends shivers down my spine
Goosebumps race across my skin
Showing me that I'm alive

As I look upon the mountains
Thundering with rage
The knowledge of winter
Turns my heart to stone
On this pale, white day

Dea Flores, Grade 11
Francisco Bravo Medical Magnet High School, CA

Contrast

Green is of life, nature and all things connected.
Sprouting from almost nothing,
growing, reaching for the sun.
Red is of death, blood and all that disappear with it.
Seeping from what was something.
Leaving, turning that something cold.

If green is of life and red is of death,
Then every year they lay side by side,
decking those dreary, gray walls.
Death with life and life in death.
As though the two could intermingle.
As though life could triumph by death.

That was wrong.
She knew, and so she tore the green,
burned it, letting the red consume.
Letting the red win, as it always would.

Yet spring comes, the green retakes the landscape.
The sprouts struggle from the red dirt.
Again, the verdant color dominates.

Quietly mocking.
For not all green can arise from the red.

Laura Mo, Grade 10
Diamond Bar High School, CA

My Other Half

Seconds, minutes, hours go by
But you're still on my mind
I just can't stop thinking about you.
You're always on my mind
I dream about you,
I think about you,
It's like you have become part of me
And I just can't stop picturing your dazzling eyes
It's like every time I look into those eyes of yours
It's almost like staring at an angel from above.
And your beauty is that of no others
Whenever I'm with you
If feels like nothing nor anyone else is important
I can spend hours with you,
But the second you leave my side
It feels like half my body has vanished within me
Your absence leaves an empty hole in my heart
That can only be filled by your love.

Chris Cortes, Grade 11
Animo Leadership Charter High School, CA

Familiar Stranger

I've seen you almost every day.
Heard and watched and listened,
but never really noticing the person that's inside.
I raise my head and see you smiling down at me,
I freeze, not exactly knowing why.
My heart starts thudding heavily when I hear you say my name.
I don't know who you really are,
just know what other say.
But now as we begin to talk and I come to know the real you,
you are more than just what you do, and what other say you are.
You love, and think, and know, and feel.
You have hopes and dreams just the same.
Now I can see I never really knew you at all.
You were just a familiar stranger.

Chelsie Pyne, Grade 10
Orem High School, UT

Father, Please Come Back

My life is now a misery
That's all I can say
All I wanted was for you to stay.
Was it so hard for you to understand?
Night after night all I wanted was for you to take my hand
I looked up to you like you would never imagine

But you left us
Abandoned us here in this empty apartment.
I see my mom cry herself to sleep
She says it's her fault,
Saying you'll come back.
Who can I turn to if…
It's you I need?

Macarena Astudillo, Grade 10
Orem High School, UT

I Dream

I dream of a day when the world as a whole is at peace, a time where people of all color can lead.
I dream of a day When the gun fire stops.
I dream of a day when the bombs do not drop.
I dream of a day when the cops stop accusing.
I dream of a day when the parents stop abusing.
I dream of a day when murder is gone.
I dream of a day when rights are not wronged.
I dream of a day when the world keeps growing.
I dream of a day when people keep going.
I dream of a day when poverty is of the past.
I dream of a day when jobs come so fast.
I dream of a day when energy renews.
I dream of a day when money is no issue.
I dream of a day when race doesn't matter.
I dream of a day when religions aren't battered.
People ask why dream when no dream comes true?
I dream for the future, why not you?
Why is it that dreaming is a myth or a hoax?
Is dreaming a dream that one should not dream?
Though dreaming is an expression no one is denied, so why can't I dream what I'm feeling inside?
I look at today and all I can say, is I dream that tomorrow is not as today.

Noah Zubeidi, Grade 10
Visions In Education School, CA

Two Heads Are Worse Than One

A war in my head that only I can see, that only I can hear, that only affects me.
One side losing, one side winning, one side hoping, the other side sinning.
I'm feeling emotions that I shouldn't feel, I'm hiding scars that can't be healed.
The War is between my present and past, the fear, and pain is coming so fast.
My past has made me what I don't want to be, it's blurred my vision, so now I can't see.
The emotions of both sides are tied together, it seems like this war will last forever.
The people around me don't know what I'm seeing, they don't understand, the emotions I'm feeling.
No one but four, can see the scar on me, The scar that tells a painful story.
This scar is the biggest, and the one I hide the best, I hide it so much, I have no time to rest.
It's built on my heart, its almost crushed to death, I can feel the pressure, when I take deep breaths.
I sit in a corner, surrounded by fear, feeling so bad, that I shed a tear.
I walk in the rain, willing to see, that the water can't wash away the memories.
When you look at me, you see the mask I wear, the mask that's glued, and unwilling to tear.
The next to you see me, see more clearly, that way you can see, my painful story.

Albert Breton, Grade 11
Dos Pueblos Sr High School, CA

I Miss You Daddy

It was just a freak accident that I can never forget from the day you were born your path was set.
The truck pulled out and you hit the brake but you couldn't stop and the bike began to shake,
Your body flew forward your helmet cracked and your head got a huge impact,
You were rushed to the hospital but you died halfway there and till this day I think it's unfair. There's plenty of bad people that could have gone instead but you were nice why did you have to be the one that's dead.
Now that you're gone I miss you so much I look forward to one day feeling your gentle touch.
When I get a nightmare I keep wishing that you are there.
I miss hearing your voice saying I love you even after all the hard times we went through.
When my wedding comes around I will never get that chance to have that one father daughter dance.
I'm going to miss you so much daddy and you'll never even know, I feel so sad daddy that you'll never watch me grow.
I miss you so much till this day and in my heart you will forever stay.

Jasmine Barney, Grade 10
Nevada Virtual Academy, NV

High School Cliques

High schools are fake with all the cliques
People fade into what others think they're supposed to be
Stereotypes fill the halls and classrooms
No one really can see

Cheerleaders are skinny and blonde
Band members carry their instruments everywhere
Football players are always homecoming kings
Nerds won't come near to the light even if it was a dare

The media has brainwashed us
Making us think this is how it's supposed to be
Categorizing us by appearance and ethnicity
But luckily, I can still see

In my school the cheerleaders aren't all skinny and blonde
The band members are actually in the homecoming court
Our population is a huge melting pot
Here, fitting in doesn't have to be a sport

Hawaii has gone against the odds
The melting pot has shown us the light
That what is on TV isn't how it's meant to be
Fitting into high school shouldn't have to be a never ending fight

Kelsi-Ann Matsumoto, Grade 10
Mililani High School, HI

A Girl Caught in the Thrashing Sea

I hate that there are no stars,
no stars to shine my way,
for veiled are they by the fog of the thrashing sea.

Lost are the stars to me,
a girl caught in the thrashing sea.
Lost are they and lost am I,
no way for me to see.

To be where the stars shine bright,
would offer me the light,
to become the girl who escaped the thrashing sea.

With eyes open,
tears fell,
and with her hands the girl parted the fog of the thrashing sea.
The girl had set me free,
she opened her eyes and let me see,
that I and she and she and I,
had parted the fog of the thrashing sea.

I am where the stars shine bright,
and they have offered me the light,
for now I am the girl who escaped the thrashing sea.

Robin Nigro, Grade 11
Poway High School, CA

Beauty

I hear the noises
Which other people find clamorous.
I hear the separate notes
As the warmth enters my body.
I hear it get louder as my smile grows.
I can hear beauty.

I see my reflection
Upon the polished wood.
I see the frets
Imagining the sound of each separate note.
I see each beautiful bronze string
Which shines like the gold under the sun.
I can see beauty.

I feel the metal under my fingertips.
I feel the music as it flows through my body.
I feel the music as it is a part of my soul.
I can feel beauty.

I am the noise that gets louder and louder.
I am the bronze strings that shine beautifully.
I am the music that is a part of my soul
Because the beauty and I are one.

Andy Kang, Grade 10
South Pasadena High School, CA

Raining

Plip, plop, drip drip drop,
The world is wrapped in a misty haze,
as a flurry of wet little drops engulfs the city,
and every head pauses, turns,
to gaze up and listen to rain.

Poky skyscrapers that snatch at the sky
fade into the pastel heavens,
indistinguishable from the clouds,
as their sharp corners and shrill screams
are muffled by faint pitter-patter,
hushed into a long, eerie echo draped above the streets

Where a sea of umbrellas
bob up and down
like a sailboat tossed dizzy by the sea.

And children, dry in matching yellow boots,
splash to the syncopated rhythm
of drumming drops on dripping gutters,
their mouths wide open to the rain
as they chase the clouds' sorrow-laden tears —
chilly but surprisingly sweet,
like a scoop of vanilla ice cream.

Tiffany Chen, Grade 10
South Pasadena High School, CA

Destruction

The loneliness of Destruction
taking lives she does not own
seeing the pain and hate she causes
everyone hates Destruction
living a life she didn't want
caused by her hating parents
pushing her around without a voice
she finally burst out
no one tried to give her hope
no chance to show her love
she lives a nomadic life
obliterating everything she passes by
floods with her sorrow filled tears
her anger pent inside is finally released
an earthquake killing
but finally her voice is heard
a booming thunder leaving desolation
Destruction all alone causing pain
maybe if just one person dared
to love that girl named
Destruction
Caitlyn Runyan, Grade 12
Taylorsville High School, UT

Always Gone

Time is
Cold as the west wind blowing
Always moving, never slowing.
It pushes forward. Not forgiving
What I need. Want. Feeling.
I use my hands, pale and thinning
To grab time up
Stop. Moving.

The wind comes crashing, thrashing
Against my house, sill standing.
The yellow paint gone and chipping,
The windows once wide and open
Now are dark, dim, deceiving.

The sky is smiling, beaming
Light. I close my fist extremely
Tight. Millions, billions of threads of lives
All weaved perfectly in my time line,
My body weak from age cannot keep
Fighting.
Madeline Burton, Grade 10
Las Lomas High School, CA

See the Sea

Calm breeze in the air
Blue, salty, ocean water
Smooth sandy brown beach
Chad Roberts, Grade 10
Wilson High School, CA

Upon Growing Her Wings

Daybreak and dew brushing lightly against her face
Her heart and soul redefining the human race
The sweet sound of her voice is one to never be replaced
So innocent, young, and so full of grace.

Nothings so pure as the smile from a child
Hers creates peace in a world gone wild
A caring being is she, her courtesy travels miles
So smile my baby, for me just smile.

Someday she'll grow her wings, and I hope that I'll be gone
Because that day will be the day that God will sing a song
He'll rant and rave about the day that her wings come upon
Her fragile being is a one time thing she can do no wrong.

So Lord I beg if I'm around when her time has come
Take me instead I'll plead and beg until my heart has won
But if you take my light away I demand the sunshine to be shunned
Because the Earth will be dark and lonely and my mind spun.

And when she enters your gates I guarantee you'll give her her wings
Believe me when I say you can't replace her fragile being.
Alexandrea Villa, Grade 12
Options for Youth Chino School, CA

The Sacrifice

Here in the shadows I wait.
Here I watch and learn, waiting for my time.
You gave me a chance, when the world said I would never exist.
You have guided my footsteps and seen my days.
Your son, you sent to die so I might have life.
They spat upon his brow and gambled for his tunic.
At any moment your hand could have taken him down,
but you let him hang.
The precious lamb sacrificed.
One for countless millions.
Do I deserve this love? No.
And yet you still give it freely.
Now it is my time, to come out of the shadows, and shine,
Shine for your glory and show the world the gift I have been given.
Lord let my life be worthy of your great love.
Let not they say "Whom does he live for?"
Lord I long to hear the words "Well Done Good And Faithful Servant"
Guide me and let me give you the glory from these shadows.
Ryan Tucker, Grade 11
La Serna High School, CA

Calm Is...

Calm is the aromatic smell of odorous flowers
Calm is the sound of rain trickling on my window pane
Calm is the sight of a radiant candle flickering with light
Calm is the taste of a crisp apple, juicy and sweet as you take a bite
Calm is the soft and warm touch of a blanket wrapped around your body
Abigail Hubler, Grade 10
Wilson High School, CA

The Best Things

When I was younger
I wanted it all —
A house and a car
And a man who was tall.
And then I grew up
And I started to see
That the best things in life
Are the ones that are free.
Friendship and love
And music and words —
These are the things
Of which I am sure.
Things of this world
You can lose or can break,
But our love is so true
It can't be a mistake.
Your love is a gift,
That much I can see;
And that's how I know
That the best things are free.

Aryana West, Grade 12
Elsie Allen High School, CA

Time

Time is fleeting quickly,
Trapped in this hourglass,
I can feel every second go by.

If given the chance,
I would go back to the time,
When life passed in slow motion.

To go back to when,
Summer was warmer,
And ocean waves roared louder.

But not even a miracle,
Could send me back in time,
It can only move me forward.

Megan Jones, Grade 10
Long Valley Charter School, CA

Success

Where is they key?
Hidden underneath all this worry?
Experience awaits me at each corner,
Inciting my inner potential, making me
Stronger, filling me with ambition.
Lay out a path for me that I can see and
Grant me an opportunity that I can seize.
Behind the cloud lies my future,
Behind my future lies my past,
Will the clash unlock the door?
Or will I need to use a key?

Tiffany Palmer, Grade 11
St Joseph Notre Dame High School, CA

Father Daughter

My father's love for me is forever lasting, from opening hearts to closing bad behavior
For all the things he's done for me to show me how much he cares
Never lets me forget what he's done for me
I'll never forget all the tears you wiped away or the time you told me you love me
The times you try to look at me your hardest but only darkness you will see
You hear my voice tingling in your mind for you should one day see your daughter
In a burst of bright lightness I shall never fade away
When I'm in deep sadness
Or if I'm built with anger you will always be there in my heart
No matter what crisis we put up for each other
You taught me from good and bad that's why you were put to be a dad
As I became a young lady now, you taught me how to be strong
Mother is away in her own little world, for you have to take the mother's spot
I'll always be grateful for all the struggles I get put through
Or even for the times when I need you most
I know that you will be there, always and forever.
I know we fight which keeps us in times to be apart
We will have that struggle stage
And we will learn how to jump off of it into a great stage
For we shall not have rudeness, tearing our lives apart
For we shall have faith and hope which will keep us together for eternity.

Seqcora Pena, Grade 10
Shelley Sr High School, ID

Remembering Pearl Harbor

The date was December 7, 1941.
All the men were still asleep, just waiting for the sun.
In just a short time, Hawaii would see
The day that would forever live in infamy.

Japanese bombers made a surprise attack.
It was so sudden that we couldn't even fight back.
It was Germany that they had made a pact.
They would leave no U.S. naval ship intact.

In crippling our fleet, they did succeed.
But that caused us to fight and make the heart of Japan bleed.
Of the United States, they had hoped to see no more.
Instead we became engaged in a second world war.
For four long years we met our attackers on a battlefield.
They finally surrendered, but too many men had already been killed.

A memorial stands today to honor the dead.
It also honors the country with the colors blue, white, and red.
It's history that is remembered by everyone.
The date was December 7, 1941.

Misty Lyn Inglet, Grade 11
Preston High School, ID

The Flying Dutchman

There was a tempest
On the seas,
Around Cape Horn
The captain hit his knees.
With a loud voice
The captain cried,
Knowing without help
He would surely die.
It was the devil
Who heard his call,
With a way to survive
Through wind, rain, and all.
Around the cape
His ship went;
Now for her, all eternity
On the seas will be spent.
Black mast, red sails
This ship flies
The Flying Dutchman
Will never die.

Louis Correia, Grade 10
Bradshaw Christian High School, CA

Starry Sleep

Eyes so bright,
Eyes of hope,
Shine with pale moonlight,

Show me the stars,
Show me my home!
On Venus and on Mars,

Feed me! Oh my Milky Way,
With sweet Ambrosia of the night,
Burn and wash away this miry clay,

From my former shell,
I sprout my wings,
And fly away — from Earth and hell

Take flight from this earthly nest,
And join the great heav'nly host,
Soar! Fly! Away!
With nightly bliss, I rest.

Timothy Lee, Grade 11
Desert Vista High School, AZ

Trees

The trees are pretty
Blowing in the wind at night
Green, yellow, orange, and brown

Chelsea Walley, Grade 12
Lucerne Valley Jr/Sr High School, CA

waiting

If she counts to ten, will the audience still be there?

Crystal beads smeared against a faux feather
gleamed into sullen eyes turning black against the spray painted bangs.
A cracked mirror revealed glowing freckles beneath her powdered flesh,
trapped in recurring anticlimactic charades:
choking glamour for bleacher entertainment.
Her claustrophobic surrounding consumed the exit behind,
revealing peacock lingerie stacked upon potpourri wigs.
Charcoal boots lay nearby amongst rugs and spandex,
leaking purple onto Louis Vuitton, just spilled bottles.
Whispered laughter taped across yesterday's snapshots
covered her wallpaper while the repetition of sighs
echoes against nothing, a few petite façades.
Masquerades hung to the right, slowly exhaling each breath
until an eyelash twitch dropped a bead into her hand.

"You're on, bubblegum lips."

Victor Kolyszko, Grade 12
The Meadows School, NV

The Dream

My life, although not interesting to some, is filled with massive amounts of fun.
My friends help me through every day, and they ensure I will never feel gray.
My life is full of many important things, but none are as important as my dreams.
Soccer is my life and my dream. To me, it is everything.
The wind, as you run toward the goal, feels as strong as my forever happy soul.
Dew from the early morning seeps through my shoes,
And a chill runs through my body like an electrical fuse.
The ball, rolling fast, leaves my foot and I watch as it sails into the nook.
Top left corner, my breath is weak. It flies into the net and my whole team freaks.
The final whistle is heard across the field it is as piercing as a wound not yet healed.
We had won the game and everyone was thrilled, but my heart was less than filled.
This wonderful place feels more like home every day. And I wish that I could forever stay.

Lindsay Russo, Grade 11
Grossmont High School, CA

Life

Step by step you climb up the ladder,
Gaining strength and learning about what matters.
As years go by your mind starts to deceive you,
You fall down a few levels and hurt because other people see you.
Guilt joins the rush of troublesome emotions,
And you get back on your feet as if you had drank a potion.
You continue up towards Heaven while passing many trials,
Only hoping to make it the last few hundreds of miles.
Stumble after stumble you pick yourself up,
And make note of mistake so there will be no more mess-ups.
Finally, you make it clear up in the clouds,
And you shout to the world of God's wholesome and amazing warm house

Cameron Nuckols, Grade 10
Viewmont High School, UT

Friends

Friendship is a beautiful thing
Like nature all around
Can you hear the blue bells ring
While giggling friends fall to the ground

Sometimes it is gentle and mild
Like daisies dancing in the breeze
At other times it's harsh and wild
Like snapping branches in an icy freeze

Sitting and laughing until the day is done
Running and splashing into the lake we wade
Having great friends makes life so much fun
Watching as the sun begins to fade

Seasons come and seasons go
Bringing many changes along the way
Our friendship will forever grow
Until our dying day

Coradawn Cates, Grade 10
Shelley Sr High School, ID

The World I See...

I opened my eyes to the world and seen what it has become.
I look to my right and then to my left.
I searched in the eyes of my most loved ones,
And saw the shadows of pain that lurks deep within.
I see the sadness and tears of a soldiers mother,
The hope in her eyes but the heartache of death.
I see hunger and starvation.
And the baby that dies because there is no one to care.
I see the man living on the streets,
With no shelter or soft pillow to lay his head.
I see the cuts and bruises of rage among my friends,
The hurt of pain and fright shown in their eyes.
I see the tragedies of the world,
Leaving millions with nothing but death and memories,
Having to start life all over again.
I see it, Do you?
Stand in their shoes,
Look through their eyes,
Feel what they feel, Then you will truly SEE...

Shanea Barickman, Grade 12
Waimea High School, HI

Live

Trillions of stars to live under,
6 billion people to live with,
1 million reasons to live on,
1000 experiences to live through,
100 years to live,
3 rules to live by,
1 world to live in,
1 God to live for.

Nathan Nguyen, Grade 10
Bradshaw Christian High School, CA

Caged

I live my life in an iron-bar cage.
I do things when and where I'm supposed to.
I focus on others' needs more than what I want.
I wonder what it is that I like to do.
Is there more to life than this?
Is there more meaning in my life?
I am meant for greatness.
But can I be great when I am caged?
When my hands clasp around this
Sweaty, rusted, hard, iron,
I contemplate getting out.
Getting outside my cage and seeing
The world. The hope drives me.
I finally have meaning in my life.
This faith in myself that is willing me to escape.
And then I, as a good little girl, refrain.
I take my hands off the iron bars that I'd so like to break.
I curl up in my cage.

Amanda Ricks, Grade 11
Viewmont High School, UT

Life's Summer

I'm swaying back and forth on the swing.
My feet brush the ground
As I listen to the rhythm of the birds sing in unison,
They sound like nature's orchestra.

Early in the morning the air is nice and brisk
I smell the aroma of tulips
As the squirrels tisk, tisk, tisk.

I arch my back to look up at the sky
I feel like I'm floating as the clouds go by.
What glorious days the summer brings
I can sit forever in this swing.

Eventually winter will come and take these days away
No longer will I hear the orchestra
No longer will I feel or smell or play
The games of summer.

Chelsea Nunez-Padilla, Grade 10
Mountainair High School, NM

Life

Life's struggle tugs and pulls on me.
Failure's waiting patiently.
I hear its call from far away,
I've seen the obstacles it portrays.
Obstruction is what it seeks from me,
But success is in my destiny.
No way I'd give into its demands.
No way I'd let it bring me down.
I stand alone strong as ever,
It's my life and I'm not a quitter.

Makenzie Wingfield, Grade 10
Youngker High School, AZ

Life in My Dreams

Life as I know it just isn't right
so I dream a new life when I sleep at night,
I dream the sky colors so there's always a light
and I dream the dogs nice so they never bite,
I dream the thoughts pure so we can't do wrong
and I dream the love real so you'll never really be gone,
I dream there are no laws so there's none to break
I dream there's no war so no more lives they'll take,
I dream there's no hunger so that everyone's fed
and I dream at night everyone has a bed,
I dream enough parents to go around
and no more kids "lost" that'll never be found,
no more innocent souls lost to cancer or pain
no more heavy hearts whose tears flow like rain,
I dream there's honesty left in this world of mine
no more double shifts won't need over time,
I dream enough money to go all around
no more hard times we're goin' up not down,
so that was a flash of my dream world you see
cause reality hold us back and I'd rather be set free…

Ortencia Trevino, Grade 12
Tulare Technical Prep Continuation High School, CA

Drag Race

The quarter mile of asphalt lies ahead;
The red line spray painted across the road,
The combustion's sound rolls out the tailpipe's heads,
How long the road looks, how fast it will go.
As the tires spin, the smoke fogs up the sky,
Front tires jump, while carb shoves fuel into engine;
Off the line so fast, I couldn't see the other guy;
The power under the hood helps the win.
For those ten seconds or less, I am free.
All worries and stress in life fade away,
While the other guy starts to catch up to me;
I push the pedal more and show him the way.
The sight of my muscle car speeding fast,
Has surpassed the other car, which came in last.

Nathan Gomez, Grade 10
Chandler Preparatory Academy, AZ

A Thousand Pieces

His heart cries out to the one he adores.
The only response he receives is rejection.
Now he has a heart of glass
Not similar to a wound that can easily heal,
Or a sea star's limb, which can grow back,
But is rather fragile,
And shatters like a broken mirror
Every time he hears the words, I don't love you.
A thousand pieces crash to the floor
With no hope of being fixed,
Only to be thrown away.
Who has not had their love go to waste?

Sarah Reimann, Grade 12
Lucerne Valley Jr/Sr High School, CA

Time Changes

Once upon a time you were a little boy
Now you're 17 years old
Grown man
Life living ain't so good
Nobody knows what you've gone through
They ain't seen what you've seen
They don't know what its like to walk the streets
And deal with the fiends
People try and say that the game I'm in
Is all talk no play
Well how's this people how
About you come walk in my shoes
Come pay my dues
This boy is 17 years old
Breaking all the rules
Don't deal with no fakes or wannabes
You want to know a little something about me
Why don't you come ask yourself
Come slide through sick city that's where you'll
Find me hustling the streets

Nate Roderigues, Grade 12
Wilson High School, CA

Rust to Gold

Stormy skies scream aghast,
As golden strands stream through the past.
A sparrow's soft song rides the wind's billow,
Calming the cries of the weeping willow.

Time and time again, there is a new day.
A day to start again, a day we will not pay.
Not pay in money or tears,
Not pay in pain or fears.

It is when rust becomes gold.
It is when this beauty unfolds.
At last, breakdown to breakthrough.
At last, the sparrow flew.

Stephanie Escobedo, Grade 11
Covina High School, CA

Is This Love?

Tell me it's real
This feeling that I feel
I feel like I can fly
But sometimes as if I'm going to cry
Yes we have our ups and downs
And a share of smiles and frowns
But it always works out
Then we start joking around like a couple of clowns
She always knows how to make me smile
Makes my life worth while
Is this really love?
Somebody tell me…

Bronson Soukhaseum, Grade 12
Prospect Continuation High School, CA

My Brain

Playing house and climbing trees
Learning to read and count up high
Adventurous and with car keys
Around the world I plan to fly

Computer learning and brand new pets
Camping memories with all our cousins
Finding friends and joking about the Mets
Eating doughnuts by the dozens

Fantasy and magical books
High school life and A-B days
Flowing creeks and trickling brooks
Less time for freedom and free days

My life's escapes are found within
My brain you wouldn't want to get lost in
Bryn Godfrey, Grade 10
Shelley Sr High School, ID

Pace I Like

I'm slowly strolling down
the wide, filled hallway.
Everyone else is rushing
shutting me out, shooting away.
They are transient wind
in the world of me.
They all seem to have
somewhere important to be.

I let them all past;
they're going a bit too fast.
For me I like it slower
though it means I'll be last.
Because I'll have seen
all the details to see.
That'll help me learn and be more precise
that's the most important key.
Gorden Chang, Grade 10
Cypress High School, CA

Drawing

Holding a pencil
Grasping art itself
Not knowing
What you will draw
By focusing on the paper
But in your mind you see
An image building
As if nothing else matters
On the white paper it suddenly
Transforms into rays and shades
Of Color
Aaron Rakes, Grade 10
Wilson High School, CA

Dance in the Sky

We danced under a simple canopy of floating wood,
the golden sun gently caressing our faces as we twirled
to the rhythm of flighty bees enraptured by
the yellow-gold flowers, vessels of sweet nectar,
spilling over the edges of our canopy.

A breeze rustled through the delicate flowers
and they blew to the ground in a hurry,
waltzing around our feet, as we, carefree,
laughed, ecstatic at the perfection of our scene.

Your face reflected everything I loved and
I would have sworn that you were summer itself
come down to greet mortal me in a tangible form.

The promise of a rare and perfect evening hung in the air
and we lingered, dancing, laughing, comfortable
in the embrace of a foreign but welcoming sky,
content to let nature be our guide.

Your eyes shone like golden honey and I imagined
that they were sticky and sweet [the perfect complement to my
almond eyes]. Rainbow irises splashed across those shoes of yours as
the sun bounced off glass beads on my dress of yellow daisies.
We smiled innocence and danced under a simple canopy of floating wood.
Ridhima Vemula, Grade 11
California High School, CA

A Wondrous Thing Called "Girls"

Those eyes are like oceans of whatever color, that hair like fine silk bested by no other.
Her body's a beauty that I have discovered, yet I lack the courage to tell her I love her.

I love her like most athletes do love the ball,
This love gives me wings so that I'll never fall.
I cannot explain, it seems I lack a brain.
But love keeps me dry when I stand in the rain.

For her eyes are like seas of this entrancing color, her hair like sweet silk second to no other.
Her body a sanctum that I have discovered, but I still lack the courage to tell her I love her.

'Tis real, maybe so. That would be my joy.
But her beauty can use a man's heart for a toy.
I pray and ponder this love will prove true,
I am eased and at peace when she gives me such clue.

For her eyes are like oceans of whatever color, her hair a sweet thing bested by none other
Than herself. A beauty that I have discovered, I gather the courage to tell her I love her.

What was once admiration became a deep crush,
Which became sweet affection, which became a rush
Of emotions longing for her body and soul.
Now that we're together, I at last feel whole.
This wondrous, entrancing, beauty I've discovered
Does truly love me. And I truly love her.
Trenton "King T.R.E" McCullouch, Grade 10
Cypress High School, CA

Spring Time

Spring is the most desired time of year;
It paints Nature's delicate creations.
Enjoy this time, spring quickly disappears.

Flowers rejoice, winter is no longer here.
Nature is alive with animation.
Spring is the most desired time of year.

Cool wind ruffles resurrected green leaves,
Ground welcomes rain with anticipation.
Enjoy this time, spring quickly disappears.
Spring colors and smells give natural cheer.
Clouds forcing open sky with dedication.
Spring is the most desired time of year
Sleeping animals suddenly appear;
Nature greets their return with celebration.
Enjoy this time, spring quickly disappears.
Spring grows fainter, murderous droughts draw near.
Wanting spring spreads heavily across nations.
Spring is the most desired time of year;
Enjoy this time, spring quickly disappears.

Jessica Lara, Grade 10
Chandler Preparatory Academy, AZ

A Vibrant Love

The vibrant sound of an inclination so pure…
A love unified by a small infatuation…
The pitch ringing throughout an undersized world…
The darkest moments approached…
Through those moments that tone of love cherished…
A heart frantically searching for a place to hide…
Amassed by the sound of a love so untainted…
Upon the sunny day the sound carried strong…
Through the tears of a kin so alone…
Like a broken whisper upon the wind…
A love shattered but not forgotten…
A tone not only in memories…
But…
A tone echoing in a heart…
That sheds tears for…
That vibrant sound of an obsession so pure…

Corey Amsden, Grade 12
Horseshoe Bend High School, ID

His Eyes

Green, that is the color that is seen in the morning.
A light, yet dark color, different from others.
There is only one other place I have yet to see it.
His eyes, his green-amber-ish eyes.
Everyone says, eyes are the window to the soul.
His eyes, oh so curious am I to what is behind his eyes.
So deep, yet I can't find what's in his eyes nor his mind.
So clear, yet kept so controlled, are his eyes.

Cheyenne Nokomis Romero, Grade 11
Duchesne High School, UT

One Life

One life, one chance is all I got.
Won't let my potential go to wrought.
Have a goal in life, is all I need,
To make my life the best fit to succeed.
Don't play life like a silly little game.
There's no starting over in an attempt to fame.

Writing is the thing I enjoy all the time.
It takes pure creativity to write and rhyme.
Writing is like a unique piece of art,
It all comes together part by part.
Writing for feature films is my true dream,
Making stories however they may seem.
Screenwriting seems intriguing and broad.
Anything can happen and become quite flawed.
Scripts can vary from all different kinds.
Mine, requesting viewers to use their minds.
Developing characters deep as can be,
Brings viewers in along with the reality.
Screenwriting requires creativity too,
That is why it is what I seek to do.

Kurtis Gefrom, Grade 11
Grossmont High School, CA

Not Just a Sport

It's not just a sport, but a mental game,
Requiring strength and agility.
While striving for the goals in which we aim,
We do the impossible gracefully.

The hours of hard work and frustration,
Which leaves the body tired weak and pained,
Are both elements of dedication,
And results in the mental toughness gained.

This sport is simply not just a hobby,
But a lifestyle chosen ten years back;
It is the one sport known to my body,
And life long confidence I will not lack.

Gymnastics is the sport for which I live,
One hundred percent I will always give.

Allysa Larson, Grade 10
Chandler Preparatory Academy, AZ

Who Am I?

No one knows who I really am.
I don't even know who I am.
Can anyone help me?
Help me find out who I am.
Let me know what I'm supposed to do
Anyone tell me what is my future
So many choices, so many opportunities and yet only one destiny.

Nichlas Ornelos, Grade 11
Animo Leadership Charter High School, CA

Losing a Best Friend

Drowning in my misery…
Wallowing in my pain…
This has never been easy…
Left crying in the rain.

The deafening silence, tumbling…
Over my perfect world…
Words not clear, but mumbling…
Thoughts in my head become swirled.
Craters in the walls, created…
Fists flying sporadically around…
Memories all become faded…
Life has lost all sound.

The hardest part of life crawling near…
Losing grip of a best friend…
Has always been my greatest fear…
I'm sorry for the hurt I've caused…
The heartache you've felt…
Time to put *my* life on pause…
And make sure yours doesn't melt.
Jessica Pownall, Grade 11
La Serna High School, CA

Tsuru

With one mate to last a lifetime
Tsuru represent good fortune and longevity
Yet they are losing hope themselves
With few left alive in the wild
Tsuru are graceful and rare
Living amongst many
On that voiceless list
Tsuru is a quiet fighter
Tsuru is a peaceful creature
Yet you wouldn't notice
If you saw Tsuru sushi
Invisible to many
Tsuru lives quietly among the plant life
As if in spirit
Watching our old or sick
Some believe that the
Tsuru guide us to heaven
To live amongst gods
To fly soft
To fly free
To fly as the Tsuru do
Cierra Taylor, Grade 10
Wheatland High School, WY

Waiting

Standing still, waiting
Staring at the horizon,
Waiting for the one.
Mary Stufflebeam, Grade 12
University Preparatory School, CA

My Fate Echoes

It tickled my toes in infancy,
I clumsily crawled on it.

It cushioned my ankles in childhood,
I gently trotted through it.

It crept up my leg in adolescence,
I kicked it in annoyance.

I knew I could dominate it in maturity,
It could not hold me down.

I felt the gradual strain at the midpoint of life,
It was tugging me lower.

I realized age could not outrun an eternal opponent,
It relentlessly dragged me further under.

I foolishly believed I could overcome it,
My fate echoes those who fought it in vain.

Struggling hopelessly with ambivalence at its power,
Caught in stagnant perseverance,
I now glean this truth:
"Death alone fees us from the sands of time that inevitably engulf us all."
Hansel Weihs, Grade 11
Schurr High School, CA

Art of Fortitude

Exhausted muscles surge triumphant heat,
Battled relentless regiments of fear
To achieve a foreign, glorious feat.

An art of fortitude with motions neat
Run by a system of silent gears;
Exhausted muscles surge triumphant heat.

The brazen rhythm of the gymnast beats
Louder than pulsing drums which seal the ear
To achieve a foreign, glorious feat.

The arduous skill is strange while incomplete;
Which Time does shape familiar and clear.
Exhausted muscles surge triumphant heat.

Tough iron rising from the act complete
Soon is forgotten rust held nowhere near,
To achieve a foreign, glorious feat.

Once held high, common skills now lie near feet;
Cast down to make more exalted acts near.
Exhausted muscles surge triumphant heat
To achieve a foreign, glorious feat.
Joseph Mattern, Grade 10
Chandler Preparatory Academy, AZ

Poetry

Tear, rip, and throw; the sounds of poetry
Paper glides, birds on unsatisfied wind
Frustration, hopelessness suffocates me.

Start with narrative; simple, flowing
Plot lines, emotional maps envelope my mind
Tear, rip, and throw; the sounds of poetry.

Dramatics; costumes, characters charming
Lines, scenes, pressure intensifies. Your fate signed.
Frustration, hopelessness suffocates me.

Searching for a subject, lost and wanting
Nature represented in a few lines?
Tear, rip, and throw; the sounds of poetry.

Hear the music escaping and dancing
From my pen. Ears collapse, eyes blind
Frustration, hopelessness suffocates me.

Repeat your lines, have end words rhyming
Keep the count, aim your pen to land
Tear, rip, and throw; the sounds of poetry
Frustration, hopelessness suffocates me.

Alicia Magrini, Grade 10
Chandler Preparatory Academy, AZ

Un Alma Encerrada

Sitting in my bedroom chamber,
Head within my hands,
A scream lodged within my chest,
I stumble to the window sill.
There they gently sit
Colonies of butterflies clustered at a rest
Till the friendly wind wakes them
And in a dance they begin, to and fro.
Upon a gentle breeze that comes hither this way,
A butterfly beats.

Oh taunting butterfly!
Free to fly to your desire
While here, here I am enslaved.

I fling myself away from the spiteful sights,
Anger coursing through my veins.
I see within the corner a caged swallow, solemnly perching.

Pray-tell me dear bird!
How is it to be like man?
As you do live caged
My wings are clipped from free flight
Ever seeking to taste sweet freedom.

Stacie Sanchez, Grade 11
Cypress High School, CA

Art in Motion

Performances take up all their blank space.
The stage bright with lights and colors everywhere.
Each ballerina dances with such power and grace.

The audience blown away by the delicate chase.
Their faces filled with happiness that no one can compare.
Performances take up all their blank space.

It seems as though the dancers move without a single trace,
Of any place their feet had gone across the stage they share.
Each ballerina dances with such power and grace.

They all move as one, move as though they were in a race.
Movements swift and clear making it difficult not to stare.
Performances take up all their blank space.

Their costumes made with care and such exquisite lace.
Everyone knows that these makings are quite rare.
Each ballerina dances with such power and grace.

Dancers abide to keep up with the pace,
For all the lovers of art that came to watch this snare.
Performances take up all their blank space.
Each ballerina dances with such power and grace.

Alissa Roseborough, Grade 10
Encore High School for the Performing Arts, CA

The Scribe

From my muted pen, blue impatience drips,
With an aching palm inspirations cease;
Pressure whitens my slaving fingertips.

Under my oppressive hand paper rips,
Ink smears and bleeds in vain attempts to please;
From my muted pen, blue impatience drips.

Desperation's fixed, choking, vengeful grip
Clutches the mind's will with frightening ease,
Pressure whitens my slaving fingertips.

Disquiet and I form a cursed friendship,
My faltering hopes it hungers to tease;
From my muted pen, blue impatience drips.

Snap! Crack! The beckoning roar of the whip
That ever demands more than masterpiece;
Pressure whitens my slaving fingertips.

I scribe to gain of success but a sip,
Convinced the ideal page still bears a crease.
From my muted pen, blue impatience drips;
Pressure whitens my slaving fingertips.

Kelly Peyton, Grade 10
Chandler Preparatory Academy, AZ

Finding Home

These creaky steps they groan
As I walk out of an empty house
Another lost home
An empty flight of stairs
Half empty glass of tears

Just another place
Where I can spend the night
Then I'm out of this disgrace
The love was never there
It wasn't anywhere

But I'll keep searching
For a place to call my own
I'll keep looking
For that love
For the place that fits like a glove

I'll find my home
Paige Foreman, Grade 10
New Mexico School for the Deaf, NM

Snow

Snow is a wonderful thing…
When it's falling.
But once it sits and freezes
that is another story
you can walk on top of it
without making a foot print
When the sun finally comes
and the snow is no more
the mud starts to take its toll
making everything soft and wet
My shoes are all muddy
my socks are all wet
I can already hear my mom yelling
in a little bit.
Steven Beard, Grade 12
Lincoln County High School, NV

I Am the Wind

I am the wind
Mysterious
Nowhere to be seen
Feel me on your skin
Over the mountains
In the cool air of the Rockies
Rather be free in the scenery
Then in the musky city of sin
Breathe me in
After the sweet rain
The sweet smell of a light summers breeze
So awesome of a smell
I love to be me.
Skyler Howes, Grade 12
Pine View High School, UT

City Girls and Me

City girls think pets and see a teacup chihuahua that fits in their purse
I see my bull mastiff sleeping curled next to me

City girls think guns and get scared
I see clay pigeons in the mountains

City girls think vacation and see California
I see camping with my horses

City girls think cars and see Mercedes
I see a muddy 4x4 truck

City girls think jeans and see True Religions
I see dirty Wranglers

City girls think sports and see hot football players
I see diving into second base

City girls think shoes and see Steve Madden high heels
I see bare feet walking through the mud

Thank heavens I'm not a city girl; country girls have more fun
Shelly Brinkerhoff, Grade 12
Westwood High School, AZ

I Love You More and More*

I never thought that love could hit me in the eyes
The more I was with you, I came to realize
I felt so much I can't describe the things I felt inside
It was a strong and growing feeling I knew I couldn't hide
There's something more every time when I find myself with you
The feeling is love plus so much more there's no one else I'd rather choose
Silently admitting to myself, my whole heart is yours for sure
I find more of my heart to give, I love you more and more
It has to be a dream looking at moments we've shared
"I praise the heavens high that I'm permitted to walk on air"
Thinking of you, and the songs that I've been listening
The tingles I get inside, now I know exactly what I've been missing
There's something more every time when I find myself with you
The feeling is love plus so much more there's no one else I'd rather choose
Silently admitting to myself, my whole heart is yours for sure
I find more of my heart to give, I love you more and more
Eliza Wilson, Grade 12
Lone Peak High School, UT
*This is something I wrote for my boyfriend, I love you Chris!

Trees

Silent sentinels guarding their realm.
Ancient giants casting long shadows upon the Earth.
Standing, ever-standing defiant to the roar of the wind, and the bite of the cold.
Symbols of steadfastness and strength.
Sheltering all who journey beneath their outstretched arms.
Silent sentinels watching over the children of the Earth.
Porter Jones, Grade 11
Burlington High School, WY

The Sweetest Goodbye

Here we are again
Staring at the end
Trying to say our goodbyes
It's crazy how time flies
I can't leave your side
I know cause I've already tried
I meet your smile with one in return
Your existence in my heart will forever burn
Like a broken heart
Except you never tore it apart
You kept it together and sealed
With you, my darkest secrets are revealed
Never have I found a friendship like this
Laughing together are the moments I'll miss
Even though how much I care for you doesn't show
I'd do anything for you but of course, you already know
You in my life I can't live without
When I'm with you I lose all doubt
You mean so much to me
I don't know how to tell you not to leave.

Sasha Van Horn, Grade 11
Diamond Ranch Academy, UT

A Voice Inside

I found a voice inside of me,
One I can call my own.
I let go of you, my spirit's free.
All along I should have known.
I am my own person,
You don't tell me what to do!
I'm telling you right now, I'm done.
I'm walking out on you.
Honey, may God bless you,
And here's something you'll want to pay heed,
I'll even wish you good luck too.
Trust me, that's not all you'll need.

My dear I wish you well, I do,
But believe I won't be missing you.

Erika Johnson, Grade 11
Encore High School for the Performing Arts, CA

I Love My Babe

All I ever wanted was to be part of your heart,
And for us to be together, to never be apart.
No one else in the world can even compare,
You're perfect and so is this love that we share.
We have so much more than I ever thought we would,
I love you more than I ever thought I could.
I promise to give you all I have to give,
I'll do anything for you as long as I live.
I hope that one day you'll come to realize,
How perfect you are when seen through my eyes.

Sierra Archuleta, Grade 12
Prospect Continuation High School, CA

Do You?

It's hard and It's tough.
Who said life wasn't rough?
Though my mind's full of stuff,
I play a smile and a bluff,
but I'm done…I've had enough.

How can I smile for hours,
when I've seen what happened to the twin towers?
How can we ignore our mild fires,
when I've witnessed San Diego's Wildfires?
How can the donation box remain plain,
when I've seen the damage from the Katrina Hurricane?
And how can I empty my leftover steak,
when people are starving from Haiti's earthquake?

I knew that Life wasn't fair,
and although it's good to be aware,
just watching gets us nowhere.
It's time to show that I care.
…do you?

Linda Gonzalez, Grade 11
The Preuss School UCSD, CA

I Don't Understand

I don't understand,
Why people can't get along,
Why people choose to kill,
Why they choose to stay quiet when discrimination
Happens and speak up to what they believe
But most of all,
Why there is war between us people
Why people must die
Why the day must end so quickly
BUT what I understand the most is,
Why I was born,
Why the sky shines every morning,
Why there is a rainbow after a rainy day,
Why GOD had to make Himself human, Him being KING
AND WHY I BELIEVE IN GOD my Savior!!!

Mariela Miguel, Grade 10
Valley Vista High School, AZ

Friendship

Friendship is a bond that two people share
For the remainder of the lives because no matter where
You go in life or what you do you'll always remember that
Special friend, who was always by your side
When you were happy or sad and meanwhile
You were doing the same for them.
A friendship is a promise spoken
By the heart not by a pledge written on any paper.
I'm sure it would survive anything and anyone
Who would want to mess a bond that strong.

Carmen Rodriguez, Grade 10
Pioneer High School, NV

Letter to Mom

There is a path that splits, like broken fragments of glass,
into thousands of visions and theories.
What path is the felicitous choice,
When every road leads but only backward?—
Violence, kindness, rebellion, submission,
Which is the true answer that is to be sought?
But you had heard of this place,
Where murder does not blend with the diurnal happenings of life;
You had told me of a story,
Where diversity coexists as one entity;
You had given me a dream,
That our frustration will one day engender change in the future.
And how far away is this future!
How worthwhile is this vision,
That can compensate for those lost to time?
But your final voice merely told me to thank,
The inevitable fact that humans exist
In pursuit of happiness—
A truth wherein lies the source of power and destruction.
For all the change, ambition, and revolution,
They are born from Despair.

XingTing Gong, Grade 11
Monta Vista High School, CA

Only He

No one cares — only he,
A relationship not of rivalry,
Too good to be true,
My best friend,
A relationship I know will never end,

Trading stories on the shore,
Sharing diversions with no discipline,
Bursting exuberantly with tremendous delight,
He is my best friend,

Saved my life,
Changed my direction,
Lost my way,
He directed me home,
Best pals, best friends,
No one cares — only he.

Dominique Terry, Grade 10
Bella Vista High School, CA

Loving Memories

On these happy days I can not be with you
Remember me in the memories we've made
And just know my heart is with you every night that I pray
I cherish the moments we've once made
And just because I am not with you
It doesn't mean we are not together
Because our love is as one and will remain so forever

Nickolis James Knabe, Grade 10
Rite of Passage Charter High School, NV

The Sad Father

Look at me now!
I am the father who through fate and misfortune
So many sons and daughters
Cast into the void of death,
Lies on the ground with my
Dearly beloved in the bleeding rain.
Do you see my tears?
I am so distraught — my
Family has torn itself, divided
Against each other with so light a cause
Look around, there is nothing
But sadness for these men marching into battle
Horns and trumpets bellowing
And I will stand on that
Shining hill calling out for sweet beloved peace. Oh!
　　　　there will be peace.
There will be silence.
For in that peaceful sleep of
　　　death, I will be there to pick up the fallen,
　　　wasted away in the cold.
Are my sons happy now?

David Suh, Grade 11
St Michael's Preparatory School, CA

Fame

When conformity and uniqueness meet,
It then creates a certain status quo,
Of that where everyone's wants are to greet,
Their "love" for you they are willing to show.

They like you until you're irrelevant,
You are simply just one of them again,
Once demand is gone you're not prevalent
You're just another already has-been.

It's a euphoric and a surreal state,
People thinking of you as a god,
So glamorous and everything is great,
They share the dream without knowing it's flawed.

Be grateful to have it while it wants you,
It never needs anyone to remain true.

Andrew Ball, Grade 10
Chandler Preparatory Academy, AZ

Apple

Cut an apple in half and use it as a hat
Peel the skin of the apple and wear it
Throw an apple and use it as a baseball
Put an apple in a cannon and launch it
Take a bite of an apple and use it as spit wads
Chop the ends off an apple and use it as a chair
Tickle the apple and a worm will crawl out

Emily Matthews, Grade 11
Golden Sierra High School, CA

Gone…But Not for Long

My name is Alexandra Barba, I am 16 years old,
And up to this point in my life I had never known the feeling
Of losing another human being.
Her name was Lucy; she had the sweetest name;
perfect for the sweetest person
She was my oldest aunt
When I was young she lived in Mexico and when I would visit she always took care of me
but when her only son that was mentally disabled died she came to California
she was finally here to stay I remember hoping she would never go away
My other aunt took her in and I'd always go visit
As I matured into a young woman my daily visits tuned into hardly any visits at all…one day my mom got THE call
The shocking call that told us my aunt was in the hospital
They told us my aunt's condition was fatal
Slowly but surely, day after day and day she got worse
My aunts time on earth had run out
July 12th marks the day my beloved aunt passed away
When the memory of her rushes back in to my mind
I smile a great smile Because I know that life here on Earth is only truly a short while
And if she's looking down at me from heaven at this very moment
The only thing I want to say is "I miss you and look forward to every day because each day brings me a day closer to seeing you again."

Alexandra Barba, Grade 11
Animo Leadership Charter High School, CA

Seasons of Grief

When I learned of your death, I was speechless.
I will admit, I did not cry.
I instead locked myself in our house for a year of utter silence.
I sat in that old chair peering out the bay window you loved overlooking the front yard.
And I watched as the trees blossoms bloomed brilliant colors in the spring.
I watched the kids in the neighborhood run through the sprinklers around our yard in the summer.
I watched as the trees lost their leaves and the sky turned from the brightest blue to gray in the fall.
I watched the first snow fall, covering our yard with a blanket of sparkling white.
For sixty years, I watched these seasons pass by with you.
It felt like in that spring, when you died, I'd lost everything.
Now, I realize that you're still with me every day.
You're in the brilliant colored tree blossoms blooming in the spring.
You're in the air around the kids in our neighborhood as they run through the sprinklers in the summer.
You're in the trees as they shed their leaves and are ready to re-grow and start fresh.
And finally, you're in the snow that fell the first winter without you.

Jessica Ring, Grade 11
Golden Sierra High School, CA

The Drum of Life

I am the drum of life. My music sustains the flow of the fluids that allow you to function.
I beat so that you live. My rhythm supplies you with the ability to breathe and with that the ability to be. There is no you, when there is no me. I beat to the symphony of your emotions. To songs of your triumphs and tribulations. I've played to many sweet victories, many sad situations. I have beaten to love. Love is the sweetest symphony to play to. I beat faster with anticipation as you join hands and peer into each others' eyes. But you enter so completely. For when in love, you are not very wise. I have been broken. Battered by the sad songs of lost loves. Disappointed with the outcome, for she was all I have dreamed of.
You depend on me. You completely rely on the music that I play. For it is what sustains you, what helps you stay. Keeping you alive, that is what I do. For when I stop beating, you stop beating too.

Matthew Reyes, Grade 12
Bishop Montgomery High School, CA

The Tiger in the Dark

Watching from a shadowed place,
You harbor no ill-will.
But when they see your golden eyes,
Like candles in a haunted place,
Watching, waiting, seeing the unseen.
They fear the unknown twitch of legs,
The unwilling tense of jaws.
You are too much like them.
But not enough; no, not enough for them to understand.
You fancy an escape from them,
And the cruelty they possess.
But they know the power behind your eyes,
Beneath your body of cracked alabaster.
And they see your beauty like a thing of fire.
A gorgeous, enticing, danger.
And there's something about it, beauty and alarm,
That turns men into monsters.
The same monsters that they fear.
But not like you, White Tiger.
You're the monster you were born.

Sarah Rosendahl, Grade 11
Wheatland High School, WY

Ode to Shattered Dreams

They said she wouldn't do what she dreamed.
She thought she could prove them wrong as it seemed.
She wished to accomplish her dream.

Always trying her hardest to be better,
Though the tears seemed to only be wetter.
She wished to accomplish her dream.

She was given a choice to make,
An option she just had to take.
She wished to accomplish her dream.

She made the world full of laughter
Her dream was accomplished thereafter.
She finally accomplished her dream.

Miranda Stokes, Grade 12
Emery High School, UT

Save Me

Can you save me from the pain?
Can you help me see the light again?
Can you heal my broken heart?
Can you bring the light back into my life?

You have saved me…by talking to me
You made the pain go away…by being my friend
You made me see the light again…by showing me the way
You've healed my broken heart…by believing in me
You've brought the light back into my life…
through being a good example and a role model for me

Chelcee Judkins, Grade 12
Fremont High School, UT

Soccer

Soccer, my life without a doubt
It's more than just running fast
It's thinking fast. Passing fast.
Maneuvering fast. Shooting fast
It's striking the ball before the competition ever sees you coming.

It's never on one person alone.
It's acting like a team.
Playing like a team.
Passing like a team.
And talking like a team.

No matter how hard you practice
You will always go out on the pitch to give it your all
You may fall
But your teammates will always be there to pick you up.
I play hard, I work hard, it's all about teamwork in soccer
Soccer, my life without a doubt.

Jason Park, Grade 10
Shelley Sr High School, ID

Night Time

Laying in my bed
With darkness surrounding me
The voices leak down through my ceiling
Like wet garbage, sludging out the pipes of a garbage disposal
The screaming
The yelling
The never ending
Night
   After
Night
   After
Night
I lay there all alone
Another night surrounded

Megan Peterson, Grade 12
Woods Cross High School, UT

The Law of Politics

I am the state, I am the Law.
I only debate the innocent's call.
Corruption is an ally, bribes are a friend.
Eruption of the courts lies in lies and the pen.

Guilty! And Guilty! Poor Mr. Poor.
Oh, a pardon for you, Mr. Money my lord.
One is presumed guilty, of notorious poverty
Until proven rich, of aristocracy.

My kingdom stands proud, built on countless dollar bills.
I am the duke, the noble, the king of Silent Hill;
Area triple six, alien immigrant convicts.
I am what I am, sick human politics.

Andy (Hak Joo) Kim, Grade 11
South Pasadena High School, CA

Solace

I wander these empty halls of porcelain shadow
Searching through the endless chasms of my minds
Making my neon red heart glow under insufficient lighting
Biting my nails until they bleed white empty bone
Tearing at my hair until my delicate and convex mind is that much smaller
Running on my legs until they will carry me no more
Work myself nearly only so near to the breaking point that I may wake up tomorrow and do it again
Let my temper flare until it pushes away all that once held dear
Breath so hard I give myself convulsions
List stupid things I do all day
Then
Out of nowhere
I think about all the great things I've accomplished
And I find solace
No peace
No understanding
No happiness
No love
Just Solace
And I think to myself
Is this all there should be?

Zakary Fisher, Grade 10
Las Vegas Academy, NV

Good Intentions

Through innocence I knew you. Though at the time, I thought I knew it all.
Never would I let somebody help me up, no matter how many times I'd fall.
Through blindness, I knew you. My eyes always closed but my heart wide open.
From the outside it looked like I was properly digesting my food, but from the inside I was really, choking.
What I thought was true love was always…only just puppy love.
Something that I thought was sent from above was just established through a push and a shove.
Through immaturity, I knew you. Because I didn't know anything better.
And then I was receptive, but now I'm just a beggar. Through rumors, I knew you.
When the things that people said, were more important than my thoughts.
Trying to put together the stage that I am in, but can't seem to connect the dots.
Finding myself sitting here, eyes steady, head still, jaw dropped, in awe about how much I am finding how I don't know you.
Because you're being defined by just another "crew"
All this time I had been hoping that you grew…
But I've grown out of my immaturity, innocence, and blindness but your still laps behind me that has become the larger issue.
I tried waiting, but I've been waiting for far too long.
It scares me to finally understand that you and I just don't belong.
I've tried praying, but clearly it wasn't meant to be.
Seems there is no future for you and…me. Because my feelings expand far beyond physical attraction.
My stomach getting worked up, heart skipping beats and head aches galore…it's more of a chemical reaction.
You lack passion but perfect in action. No can do. That doesn't fit the description of my "boo."
But ultimately I…recall that…it was, through truth…that I realized how I didn't know you at all.

Kailea King, Grade 10
Campbell Hall School, CA

The Riverbank

There is hope for everyone, cynics just don't see the sun. Though much is taken away, true survivors often stay. When life seems worthless, don't give up. Circumstances, people, or places don't add up. Keep going, learn for tomorrow. Ignore the income of deep sorrow. You are stronger than the world, you can handle troubles it hurled. The phantoms of the past, forget the mass. Keep pushing with strength and you may see a beautiful riverbank.

Chelsea Christensen, Grade 12
Hillcrest High School, UT

The Lost Sister

When I first saw you.
I couldn't look away.
When you smile you light the room up.
When you are sad you bring the clouds.
When you are sick we are all sick.
When you die we will all miss you.
I wish I had the opportunity to meet you.
You passed away before I was born.
Years have past and Dad has missed you.
But we don't know what to do
ever since you left us
I felt that I caused your death.
Every day I walk with the guilt.
I wish I could be a better person
but I can't since you passed away
I want to see your beautiful face.
Well sis
Your brother has a bad life since you left me alone
I will love you no matter what

Steve Rosales, Grade 10
Lucerne Valley Jr/Sr High School, CA

Creeking

I see a happy, tumbling creek
with slippery moss-covered rocks
and clumps of broken sticks trailing
in the water

I hear the water's cheerful splashing
and exultant birds chirping and singing
while warm sunlight shines through vibrant greens
and clear water

I roll up my pants and I roll up my sleeves
I step into the creek and feel it numbing my feet
I wade down the stream, a purpose in mind
I feel like exploring

Kayla Nielson, Grade 11
Madison Senior High School, ID

Moonlight's Glow

The glowing moon hangs low
A luminous lantern in the warm night
The lake is lit with a silvery gleam
Lilies rise for their midnight fun
Glowing like fairies' homes
Silence rings across the lake
Clear chimes through Night's fair ears
Scent of lilies hanging low on the air
Touching nothing upon the silky smooth lake
As calm steals over all around
A fairy maybe two, it seems
Flit over moonlight's glow
For us to see

Stacy Haroldsen, Grade 10
Shelley Sr High School, ID

Fantasies of a Fractured Heart

I searched throughout the land,
Wandering from man to man.
That which I searched for I did not find,
I did not find that man of mine.

On the beach I sat and cried,
My tears as salty as the tide.
Over the sea, a voice called to me,
It echoed from across the briny.

'My love, my love, at last I have found you,'
I peered into the vapors wishing I could see him too.
The vapors swirled, pushed aside,
By a man with a steady stride.

He walked to me,
Fell on one knee
Kissed my hand,
And returned to sand.

Mercedes Rothwell, Grade 10
Keystone Academy, CA

Blossoms

As all the Flowers are to days and life
Each type unique with all imperfections,
Like no day or life is lived without strife;
All nights and deaths must show off their sections.
Though beauty cannot always be seen
When influenced by the other senses;
The beauty that no longer remains green,
With life and all its other pretenses.
Even when dead, beauty can be perceived;
Life given anew, as though one will transform,
Like the Flowers have forever received
Their past through their roots letting them reform.
And again the Flowers always will be
A portrayal of eternal beauty.

Hannah Wall, Grade 10
Chandler Preparatory Academy, AZ

I Believe

I believe in the wisdom of ancestors,
The influence of friends and family,
Being against the terrible evil that one can put upon another,
The effectiveness of elbow grease,
Accuracy, strength, hope
But I don't believe that "trying" is good enough…
"Try" is the intention to fail.
I believe that honesty is stronger than anything.
I believe that true love does exist, even when it seems impossible.
I believe in the golden rule
Respect, honor, freedom
And I believe that "with every golden hour that God gives us is a gift.
That's why it is call the present."

Theresa Gustaveson, Grade 10
Shelley Sr High School, ID

Hoping Is Hopeless

I missed 11:11 again,
And I'm starting to wonder
If maybe it's a sign
That we're not supposed to be together,
Because all I ever wish for is you.
It drives me crazy to maintain such distance,
But I don't think you want me near
So I tell myself this is what I want, too,
And I've become so incredibly adept
At (self) deception
That I almost believe it…
But I can't fool 'em all.
They love me, so they hate you,
Shaking their heads at my hopeless cause,
While I plead your case and sing your praises
…And keep on hoping.
But the jury's out, indefinitely
And the chances of a pleasing verdict
Are slim to none.
And, even then, I can't let go,
Because I always finish what I've started.

Iva Weidenkeller, Grade 12
University Preparatory School, CA

Hurt

I feel as if my bald head is there for everyone to see.
I feel my heart breaking.
What will they do when I'm not here?
Long walks down this hospital hall…practically memorized.
Good days, bad gays.
…But every day is another day.

I know a good attitude is everything…
But it's slowly fading and hard to be happy.
I'm getting through it, hour by hour, and minute by minute
Every day gives life to a new beginning…
And that is what I try to remember,
walking down this long and winding road.

This cancer. Eating me alive…
It hurts. But I know the love will help heal.

Laura Morrow, Grade 11
Viewmont High School, UT

Exhausted

I can't sleep at all.
No matter how hard I try.
It's incredibly late,
But stressed and alert, there I lie.
I'm a tired horse; I've been running all day.
Worn out and broken, I can't wait till the end of May.

AnneMarie Holt, Grade 11
Viewmont High School, UT

Eyes of Another

A flicker of light. No, it was
a moment of truth, that ultimate
elucidation plaguing the heavens. A face so pure, so
beautiful, so welcoming, as though
only meant for me. A black night,
a moon full and bright. My milky
shadow tiptoes in the sky. Toes
hit clear crisp water one by one,
step quietly splashing away, quarreling
with the water. A skirt,
blouse, scarf or midnight blue so only
the pale face with roving dark eyes and pink
soft full lips stares beneath the decking of my
scarf. He calls, an amorous beckoning, a wondrous object
illuminating the night. Shy away but reach, reach
toward that calling hand, that promising figure. The perfect
meadow, the wet feet, the
beautiful image of him —
eyes fly open and the garish reality dawns.
Feet dry, eyes wet. The lump in my throat caresses me to
sleep. Will it always remain a dream?

Aashrita Mangu, Grade 10
South Pasadena High School, CA

To God

In my life you play a huge part
So here is a poem straight from my heart.

I praise you here and see your love
As you Lord over my life from above.

I cry out to you and spill my heart
But little do I know this is only the start —

Of you love, eternity, promise and us
You are the only one who has ever loved me enough.

An enormous hole in my heart you fill
Full of sin, you love me still.

The cost for my sins you did pay
I'm overjoyed to call you mine on this special day.

Melissa Lyznick, Grade 10
Saugus High School, CA

Sunny Sun

Bright sun you wake me up every morning
The light shining through my window
I begged you to let me sleep just this morning
Dawn is so beautiful I would love to hold you
I wonder if one morning you would not wake me up

Daniel Jauregui, Grade 10
Lucerne Valley Jr/Sr High School, CA

Splendid Things

Life's a many splendid thing
It can make you cry
It can make you sing

I don't want to leave this Heaven on Earth
All my precious friends and memories
Through the good times and the bad
You've been through it all

I don't want to leave my home
Although it will be hard
I won't be alone
My family is here beside me
To look over and to guide me

Just be brave and take life as it comes
The morning sun will always rise
It's up to me to win the prize
It may seem tough but in the end
It's all so worth it
Thanks for always being there
For being a great friend.

Emily Northway, Grade 12
Lone Peak High School, UT

Finals

One hour, two hours, three hours, four,
I've been studying so long,
Yet I need to learn more.
You may want to know,
What I'm studying for,
But if I told you,
I'm sure you'd be bored.
I'm studying novels,
And an ancient war,
Algebraic equations,
And so, so much more.
I'm studying for finals,
That's why I've learned so much lore,
Soon they'll be over,
And I'll have to learn more.

Matthew Wellnitz, Grade 10
St Francis High School, CA

True Love

The way you look at me
and how you make me feel
makes me really see
that this is truly real.

I had never thought I could feel this way,
until you came around
I thought my love had gone away
but somehow it was found.

Hector Luna, Grade 12
Lucerne Valley Jr/Sr High School, CA

Every Night

Every night I lay in bed trying to figure out how life began.
Hours pass and I'm still awake trying to figure out what life was like in 10,000 BC
Have stress and anger always existed, or were people once living in perfect harmony?
I guess I'll never know.
Meanwhile, my little boy sleeps silently, occasionally smiling
My boy, a beautiful miracle of life, I can only imagine what it is he is dreaming
I secretly wish I am a part of it, and that he is smiling with me
I ask God for strength, I ask God for faith
But most of all, I thank God for letting me have this perfect little angel.
People are always trying to bring you down…
I've been told I ruined my future, I've been told it will be too hard, I've been called a sinner.
So just in case God's mad, I also ask him for forgiveness.
Am I expected to hide under a rock, should I be ashamed of myself?
Shame is for those who kill
Judge those who hurt another being.
I have acknowledged my responsibility
I have devoted the past year to my son, to my studies and to my family.
I will have a home of my own, with a white picket fence.
I turn my head to the clock, 1 am
I finish analyzing the excellence of my life, and fall fast asleep

Viviana Navarro, Grade 11
Animo Leadership Charter High School, CA

The First Step!

She's home, she's finally home.
Our hearts are filled with the strength of this little baby.
Our prayers have been answered, we praise our Father in Heaven.
After four weeks of being in Primary Children's Hospital,
She returns home, to her loving family.
She struggles to breathe, her lungs ache with every breath she takes.
We wait and watch silently.
She stares into her mother's eyes.
Presley watches as tears run down her mother's face, with encouragement in her loving eyes.
Presley takes her first step!
She looks up at her mother and smiles.
She looks around the room to see tears filling up in everyone's eyes,
And smiles of joy on everyone's face.
We cheer for our little cousin,
As we all gather for a group hug.

Lindsey Chandler, Grade 10
Orem High School, UT

Forgotten Love

What happens to a hindered love?

Have you really let it go?
Or does having it there make your heart ache?
Is it really done and over?
Or that's what you want to think?
Do you want it back and try it again?
Or do you think not having it is best for you?

Do you think about it day and night and wonder what could have been?
But it's best to love and fail, than to not love at all.

Juliana Cervantes, Grade 11
Animo Leadership Charter High School, CA

Lost

Do you know what I am?
I am an unseen beauty lost in this crowd.
Lost in this see of blue, completely drowned in the sea of repetition.
No one notices me.
Here sitting beneath the sun just waiting.
Waiting for the moment when someone sees me as special.
The day when someone picks me from the crowd.
The day when someone sees how the brilliant blue is highlighted by the subtle notes of yellow,
Followed by a sweet melody of reds, melting to the center to form a delicate purple.
All dripping down to the vibrant green holding me with pride.
Screaming to the sky as I turn my leaves for a savior.
Wishing my petals to call out for help. For someone to see my colors as beautiful.
This is me in all my glory.
Unique in my own simple way, only seen by the sharpest, most caring eyes.
To see me as the most beautiful flower you have to be special yourself.
So I will wait, digging my roots further into the ground,
For when that special person comes to find me.
I will wait until I am stolen away to be admired,
Though it shall be my demise, it will be a happy ending.
At least then, at the end,
I will be lost no more.

Calli Hansen, Grade 12
Villa Park High School, CA

Lost

I'm walking down a street.
It is the middle of the day but no one is around.
The road I am on is unfamiliar.
I don't recognize any of the houses which line this quiet, deserted neighborhood.
I begin to panic.
Where am I?
How did I get here?
Will I ever get home?
Run, I must run to get away from this empty suburb.
My feet begin to move and I can see the houses flash before my eyes, leaving them behind me.
I stop to catch my breath.
The houses are all the same, my running has gotten me nowhere.
I fall to my knees in the middle of this lifeless neighborhood and close my eyes.
When I open them, I am in my bed.
Now I know where I am.

Taylor Betts, Grade 10
Orem High School, UT

If

If I had a star for every thought of you, I would have all the stars in the sky, galaxy, universe
my love for you is like the sun, it keeps growing and will continue for eternity
it will light and give warmth to my world
If I had a grain of sand for every time I love you, then I would have all the sands of all the beaches in the world
my heart will keep longing for you as long as the waves still splash on the shores of this world
and as long as there is water and sands for beaches
If I had a living thing for every time I dreamed of you, then I would have all the living things in the universe
as long as their hearts keep beating and as long as they continue to live, my dreams will continue to live

Jae-Yun Lee, Grade 10
Mililani High School, HI

Tomorrow
For many, today is regular day
But for me it is special, today
I'm going to do something I haven't done in a while I'm going to write a poem
I was thinking yesterday,
That I am going to die someday
Then I thought of the things that I have done and noticed that I haven't accomplished much
I got suspended from school which was a big a mistake; I went to the hospital because I was doing something I shouldn't have. My life is a mess I just don't know what to do. Then I think of what my family has gone through to give me the best life, which I was once had when I was small; I think of my girlfriend when she stayed with me after I got suspended, and she stayed by my side when I went to the hospital. That night I heard her cry because she was scared what I might do next.
I may not have the best life,
But nobody does.
What I do have is my parents, my brother, my sister, my cousins and my girlfriend — which is good enough for me.
Miguel Castaneda, Grade 11
Animo Leadership Charter High School, CA

Mortality's Game
We are hoopers, on the court troopers.
It's a game against sin.
We make every shot clean, pure, and virtuous.
Our defense is outstanding…an immovable screen.
With the ball there is one goal, a celestial and glorious win.
We are belligerent to the adversary, every insidious guise of the offense, a fake right, a fake left, is a feeble attempt at our stolid
    fortitude.
We redress our mistakes, and after we have an entirely new impetus to score.
Yet I am NOTHING…compared to my coach, my savior.
I extol his lesson, his achievement before me.
He sacrificing so much yet impervious to the duplicity of the foe.
He along with many others teaches me the plays of the game, of the world.
I have one game, and one chance. I have ONE game, and ONE chance.

Tyler Kellis, Grade 10
Dysart High School, AZ

My Thoughts
I see myself in the future as a doctor, a mother and wife. I want to make my dreams come true but I know that for that you really have to work hard. Even though I stress out and whine about stuff sometimes I know that if I put my best effort into everything I want to accomplish, my hard work will pay off.

Yeah we're almost there. Where we get to be more independent and live more freely…yes, they say it's not easy but it's worth it. I can't wait to graduate already. I'm excited I really am. But one thing I'm afraid of is not keepin' in touch with my friends. I want to be able to accomplish everything I want before I get married and have my own family. That is something that is going to take longer to happen but still I'm sure it's possible.

I can visualize myself in my weddin' dress and also caring for the little ones omg! They're so adorable. That's why every time I see them I just want to hug them and kiss them and never let go…I've noticed I can't ever see a baby without smiling at them. For me it's impossible…I just wish I could help all those in need to give them the love they deserve but don't have.
Ana Gonzalez, Grade 11
Animo Leadership Charter High School, CA

Oregon
The deep blue ocean crashing against the rocks
The dark green forests swaying in the wind
The amazing rains pouring on the hills
The wondrous waterfalls falling down forever.
Caleb Lee, Grade 11
Viewmont High School, UT

A Young Man's Battle
The lust and temptation that binds his soul,
It plagues him like an unholy cancer,
His conviction and redemption must be found,
Or solitude is his consequence
Eric Bergen, Grade 11
Valley Christian High School, CA

To the Moon

Amidst the diamond studded heavens you radiate a melting glare,
Revealing the flush of my cold, bare cheeks exposed to the rough evening winds

With your celestial illumination you guide me through a mosaic of pearl crusted shells
With each step, the velvety sand beneath my feet retraces a disregarded memory

Yet, tonight you shed light on truth your guiding beam illuminates the path in front of me
Your calm crescent twists into an avuncular smile as you teach me to leave the past in its proper place

I grant gratitude to you, moon, for purifying my entangled thoughts
And leading me from my entranced dreams of the past
Into the present, however painful and rough it may be.

Despite your guidance I find myself irrevocably reverting to once forgotten moments
Traveling in a time machine of distorted emotions musing mindlessly in hopes of enacting a cure

As the evening tide creeps in you sadly eclipse into the shadows of your own sorrows
You hide from grievances and regrets, then why, oh moon, should I follow you?

Forlornly melting off into the distance, you fall back into the horizon, bringing on
A new approaching day full of potential I look to you.

Ellie Shahla, Grade 11
Cathedral Catholic High School, CA

Love

Love is a strong word,
But I am happy that I am sharing that feeling with you baby,
I love you: I tell you!.
And you love me! you tell me!
That shows me that you're really feeling me,
Ups and downs aren't always everything,
But putting up with you is the best thing :)
Listening to you talking to you and even dancing with you is something I love
You show me that you care, you show me that you're there,
Making my pain go away is what you're best at, always have you been there for me, always will I be there for you
Like an angel sent to me from the heavens above, I show you my love
As beautiful as an angel that you are,
I always imagine you flying really far.
No matter what happens now and then I will always be with you till the end.

Damian Garcia, Grade 11
Animo Leadership Charter High School, CA

My Childhood

I remember when I woke up at seven to watch Saturday morning cartoons.
I remember when we didn't keep score; everybody won.
I remember when the only stress in school was learning fractions.
I remember when missing school, because you were sick, was awesome because you didn't have to make up your work.
I remember when I would make sure to be nice so that Santa would come.
I remember when ignorance was bliss.
I remember when I thought that everyone and everything was wonderful, until…
I remember the eleventh of September.

Christopher Kuhn, Grade 10
Eagle High School, ID

All That's Yellow

Nice green ripe bananas turn yellow
Happy smiley faces are yellow
Yellow is such a happy color
The shining sun so bright
The color of her yellow hair shining
Yellow squash growing in the garden
Pineapples on the hot islands
Daffodils in the spring time
Birds with yellow feathers flying high
Sunflowers turning toward the hot sun
Lemons so sour in your mouth
Caution signs so you know where to go
School busses driving on school days
Lions growling in the wild
Yellow yarn strung out by kittens
Yellow roses given to grandmas
Sweet baby girls in yellow painted cribs
Soft wet yellow sand between your toes
All the things of the world that are
    Yellow!

Alyssen Baker, Grade 12
Lincoln County High School, NV

Empty Space Filled

A wind with strong scented flower,
A space where not even
Petals can fill in.

A seat where everyone can sit,
However, is not allowed.
Not with the respect of longing.

Staring at the front and back
Checking left and right.
There is many, but all is nothing.

I start smiling even crying.
But everything I do with the longing,
It is not to fill in the space of you.

Empty space of you
With jealousy, is overlooked by many.
But it is, and will be yours and only yours.

So Hyun Cho, Grade 10
Cypress High School, CA

Destiny of a Kiss

A kiss so gentle and fine
Such a soft touch lingers
Upon my lips
My breath is caught
So long and lost
Losing my consciousness
As destiny takes my place

Jessica Drury, Grade 12
Preston High School, ID

Just Islands and Angels

It's just islands and angels in the world.
For islands of life and the angels free.
For islands that shield and carry, give for thee.
The sky's breeze and grand bliss of the angel's kiss,
So angels choose their island's home to be.
The island's doors must open and accept its soul the angel brings.
As angels sing their song of peace, the island's promise warm days to she.
As they choose their partners in this world of two.
The islands give fortune and themselves for the angels use.
For the angels descend, in their feather soft puff cloud of wings.
The islands gleam like the sun rise sea.
They have chosen their soul to be one.
Now the islands and angels partner's pact is done.
For they are one there is no end,
Life or death, they never split or bend.
Its eternity for them, together always.
It's just islands and angels in the world,
Its just men and women in the world.

Akbar Velazquez, Grade 12
Pine View High School, UT

Picking Up the Pieces

I gave you everything you ever wanted.
You said you loved me. You said you cared
But I guess that was a lie.
You broke my heart into a million pieces.
Each time I try to put it back together, I'm cut a little deeper.

As I try to forget about you, another memory comes back.
Like the time when we used to sit there for hours,
And reminisce about all the good times we had watching the sky fill with stars.
What did I do? Did I push you away?
Or did you just lose interest in me?
Or maybe I just wasn't good enough for you.
Maybe that's why you decided you wanted her that day, instead of me.

You promised you would never hurt me.
Knowing that you lied to me, felt like a knife stabbing continuously into my heart.
I'll be able to forgive you one day,
When I finish picking up the pieces.

Rebecca Moseley, Grade 10
Mountainair High School, NM

The Bassist

He
flicks
on the
power switch,
holds down the
appropriate frets,
and with his right hand,
like a spider, his fingers
walk up and down the strings
as he begins to play his favorite song.

Josh Hale, Grade 12
Wilson High School, CA

A Kiss Is a Kiss

Kiss, a kiss
What is a kiss?
Some are wild
Some are mild
They may be shy
They may even make you cry,
With hysterical babble
Or awkward glare
A kiss is a kiss
And, that's all it is.

Hayden Gregoire, Grade 11
Wilson High School, CA

Remember

Want to remember things that never were want to know people who didn't exist
You want to feel feelings never felt wishing to escape your past that never was and
Scared of the future that may be. You looked for hope and for a moment...
— Why be remembered?

You felt safe, warm, and even loved by someone who was there for you, to actually hold.
You cried and someone held you, and you felt yourself growing inside.
You held someone while someone cried inside, but
— Why do you remember?

A fortnight by half, the well seemed dried up but pressure was only building
What you'd thought you'd found wasn't what it was your growing came to a halt
Your ephemeral hope was burning itself out
— Why remember?

Now you long once more, but now it is different you almost had what you felt you wanted most
You have been broken. The farthest dream was being held, now you are falling in pieces.
— Why describe remembrance to me?

Reality is easy, and difficult to accept when you were so close to a dream.
All you can do is do the last thing you want to do
Remember

Andy Harrison, Grade 11
Viewmont High School, UT

The Suffering Child

Alone and hated by fellow men thinking at night will it ever end
Crying and screaming is all I can do hatred words stick to me like glue
Always trying to forget the pain no matter how much I try it stays the same
Unnoticeable to all mankind feeling I will explode at anytime
Can no longer hold back all the tears that I've kept inside for so many years
Pain is eating at my every breath soon I will have nothing left
When will I break out of this inner prison of mine I think about it from time to time
Then a strength comes over me that I've never felt it's so overwhelming I could almost melt
Finally my prison break is on its way I've waited so long for this very day
I feel so happy and free at last who would've thought this day would come to pass
Then I see the world in vain it brings me back to my suffering pain
The hurtful words come back to my head and all I can do is go back to my bed
I look out my window wondering if people will ever change will the ever stop putting other people in pain
I laugh at the fact that this isn't true so I stay in my room and remain hated and blue
They may have thought their taunts were mild that is not true for it caused the suffering child

Rianne Mitchell, Grade 10
Lucerne Valley Jr/Sr High School, CA

I Am

I Am
I am the type of person that will always give you a smile, if that means I am getting one right back.
I Am
I am the girl many think is perfect but to me that just means imperfect.
I Am
I am that someone who can make you see the sunlight even though, to me, the sun lost its light and the moon turned black.
I Am
I am the person that won't let you do drugs and keep you out of depression even though most of my life is depression and drugs are
    the only medication.

Monserrath Serrato, Grade 11
Rio Grande High School, NM

Love Graced Me Meaning

A man of wisdom came to me
As I walked in this terrain
One question, he said, just one
He would answer for my strain
I asked him what love is
How does one know when revealed?
He just laughed and answered:
No answer, for you, can I yield.
How can you not yield? I queried
Is this wisdom just some theory?
He laughed once more in defy,
Then continued with his reply:
For you see, I have never been in love,
No touch from a gentle woman's finger;
No eternal bound of beauty yet,
Has graced me with her linger.
But I can tell you one piece of reflection:
I have lived my whole life in the Sahara
Never has a typhoon came my direction
But once she drowns me with her being,
I will know then of her meaning.

Victoria Silva, Grade 12
Arbor View High School, NV

The Love Rises! The Love Falls!

The love rises! The love falls!
You meet a boy! And here he calls!
His sweet romances and joyous dances
Your gentle lovings and giddy prances
All is well but you cannot help thinking
When the love rises! The love falls!
There you sit under that tree
You think that this has got to be
He leans in closer and then you kiss
As you hug you feel the bliss
As the love rises! The love falls!
You're sitting there under that tree
You feel the breeze and then you see
His love is gone just like the wind
With no one left until the end
When the love rises! The love falls!
Love comes in! And love goes!
Without telling, no one knows
How long it stays, how deep it flows
How strongly bound, or how it goes
As the love rises! The love falls!

Chelsea Chida, Grade 11
Valley Christian High School, CA

My Eyes

My eyes look through me
Seeking for my shallow soul
Where did my heart go?

Autumn Rose Marsh, Grade 10
Temple Baptist Academy, NM

Sobering Decisions

Events in my life have caused me pain
Family and friends tend to do the same
The way we cope is different to all
But the way I did it formed a brick wall

It harmed me physically and mentally, I can tell
It just made me feel like I was living in Hell
Things got worse and never got better
The sleeves of my shirt continued to get wetter and wetter

While I sat and cried I thought of my life
Do I deserve to live or should I die in spite
As I sat up all night I would sit and ponder
Are the years left in my life worth to wander

I saw the way that things were going and knew I needed to stop
But my choices were heavy and I could not move this rock
I thought of the worst and wanted to finish it all
I thought that this was going to be my downward fall

I saw what there was to live for and knew that things needed to be changed
To stay clean and sober my life needed to be rearranged
To succeed in my goal, difficult the journey will be
But I want the tears to stop from those who care and love me

Peter Johnson, Grade 11
Diamond Ranch Academy, UT

Let It Out

When you thought that everything, has been taken away from you,
The only way to fix the problem is in your actions and what you do.
I can promise you're not the only one that lives with conflicts or violence,
And I lived through that, and so I just sat in silence...

I got into substances, and watched life move right past me,
I put myself down so much, and asked everyone to let me be,
I prayed to God for some guidance.
People say it won't help, because I'm just in defiance.

Even having self-esteem problems can be a habit,
All thoughts kept to yourself, filling up that cabinet.
One day you're going to have to open it up, and let it all out,
That one day, it would just come out in a big shout.

I now feel good, and all seems so real.
I no longer keep to myself, locked up or sealed.
I was confused at first, didn't know what to do,
We would fight constantly, between me and you.

Now the feeling of being able to talk,
Or take a walk.
It's so great, it will just take sometime,
And then, everything will be fine.

Bryan Ferrer, Grade 11
Diamond Ranch Academy, UT

Rugby Life

Whistle blowing, ball in air,
Getting tackled but I don't care.
Running hard and running fast,
Only few guys did I pass.
Ball rolls in, into the scrum,
Bodies pounding like a drum.
Hook the ball, through the team,
Not as easy as it seems.
Tackled hard and now in ruck,
Down on ground, seem to be stuck.
Pushing hard to get the ball,
Some stay up, and some, they fall.
Ball goes out, and ball goes high,
Through flankers in the sky.
Catch the ball and throw it to
The half back player who throws it too.
To the wingers running really fast.
How much longer will this game last?
Run hard, run fast, make it fly.
Good job. You made the game win try.

Ethan Timoko, Grade 12
Merit Academy, UT

Anger

Anger hurts and anger kills
Anger…just a bunch of words
Words that make confusion
Words that stir up emotion
Everybody is blind to see
That anger is just a seed
Just a test to see…
If everybody will blame everybody…
Or take responsibility
There's nothing…
Nothing that we can't do
Make peace…
Live our lives…
The way that we're supposed to.

Tyler Karlen, Grade 10
Cinnamon Hills School, UT

Change

Life is like a speeding race car,
leaving as quickly as it came.
The times of your life don't last long,
and you see life won't stay the same.
Everyone must accept the change,
but some will be shocked at what's gone.
Begin searching for something new;
the best choice is to carry on.
As swift as the wind in your face,
like the swallows that come and go,
the friends in your life will be gone
and you are left here on your own.

Ryan Guevara, Grade 10
Cypress High School, CA

Absinthian Melody

Distant, vague, and empty notes drift through crimson-kissed morning rays,
Delicately, dulled ivory keys exonerate a sweet, absinthian melody.
Diapason ditty skims through my attic, making its presence entirely known.
Sweet chimes most would associate with rapture and euphoria.
For me, silver-tongued misery,
Caressing me with its chilling breath upon my nape.
My heart commences to fall into a yawning rhythmic beat,
Lethargic and unfaltering — a state of awkwardness.
My slight wheezes coinciding with its transparent song.
With no possibility of escape, I scruple to the hickory stained boards,
Sheathing my posts with my naked arms,
Feeling the numbing sensation stretch its fingers across my taut skin.
There, spiritless, I feel the faintheartedness engulf my energy,
Looming the curtains of my eyes to a close.
The notes dancing through my thoughts become even more distant,
Even more exhausted than before.
As the ditty runs,
I release all feeling and surrender to the sweet emotion,
My heart's beat suppressing in the gentle kiss of mornings sun.

Shanoah Pontious, Grade 12
Woods Cross High School, UT

As It Comes Down

Drip. Drop. Drip. Drop.
I look into the heavens to see the sky open up as the rain starts to come down.
It falls slowly at first, one drop at a time,
So gentle I barely notice it.

It reminds me of tears
Like tears, it falls softly, with a gentle grace.
Cleansing and refreshing all that it falls on
And renewing everything in its path.

As I watch, it hits the plants in my yard.
It slides down the leaves and stems and buds and blossoms.
Slipping and slithering as it makes its way to the ground,
Where it hits the hard dirt and is eventually absorbed.

Pitter. Patter. Pitter. Patter.
It's raining harder now; the drops are cascading from the sky.
I hear it pounding on the roof
I suddenly realize I am fond of the rain.

Cassandra Dougherty, Grade 12
Redlands High School, CA

Peace

Peace is undisturbed
It cannot be overturned
Peace is the present, future, and past
It will be all we have at last
Peace is calm
Like the beats of your palm
Peace brings us together
Peace will be forever

Yuri An, Grade 10
Cypress High School, CA

Snow Day

Snow falling all around
Swirling, twirling through the town
Kids sledding down the hills
Showing off their new skills
Building snowmen tall and wide
Waiting to see if he'll come alive
No one has to go to school
All the kids think it's cool!

Caitlyn Carter, Grade 11
Lincoln County High School, NV

Broken Ache

Shavings I give to those who step through,
Glimpsing my world for a moment.
Slivers and shreds, then scraps
To any souls remaining, casting shadow on time.
Souls return them in tatters or never at all.
Regardless, I thoughtlessly give.
And to those leaving gashes —
Deep, memorable gashes,
Upon my history, I give sore, heavy pieces.
They take massive spoonfuls,
Bowlfuls for their hunger;
Pouring tears from my eyes,
Always hoping for the few giving theirs;
Instead watching many as they steal away in
Dungeons, away from my
Tender hand, even my loving gaze,
Leaving me with little,
Nothing to love him with,
Hating those, with
All my lack of heart,
Who stain, reject, and discard me.

Whitney Slade, Grade 11
Viewmont High School, UT

Tears of Joy

My family was always poor.
Living in China,
with my nine children,
and my husband.
I had to face many struggles.
Working hard every day for the family,
starving myself for my children
so they can have full meals.
Watched them grow up
Watched them go to school
Graduating and becoming successful
Getting married, having their own families
Wanting them to have a better life than I did.
My heart is full of the happiness
Yet full of sorrow
It was the tears of joy.

Pinky Wong, Grade 10
Abraham Lincoln High School, CA

Stuck

I'm stuck, forced to perform.
Thoughts of you pass my mind.
We are much further apart now.
Have you forgotten me?
Thoughts manifest into things that are unreal.
Not much time is left.
It's time to make decisions.
Will I break free?
Or will I stay stuck?

Nolan Reimann, Grade 12
Cinnamon Hills School, UT

Living

To paint a facade is simple
To smear a smile and force the imprint of a dimple
Only to hide what's beneath the surface
Depression, frustration, or the feeling of being nervous
Through life all of our flaws can't be hidden
And we must work with
What it is we are given

We need money to live
But it's the root of all evil
We need GOD for strength
Yet some of us treat dogs better than people

What's the purpose of life?
If life itself is lethal.
We all have a purpose
But will we all serve it
I find that through our transgressions
In the end, victory is well worth it
So even with the complex situations we are given
We all have to realize, this is merely the beginning

Amber Watson, Grade 12
Inglewood High School, CA

Picasso Nights

In monotone colors, comes the dark night
When silent time starts seeping to a crawl
Where dreams and nightmares seem to badly call
Close your eyes, and immerse in their delight

In fragrant teases, lies ever so slight
To catch scared teardrops as they fall
They reach for me with my back against the wall
I am crashing into darkness, Fight!

As do by myself I wait best
For your loving arms to reach out for me
From loneliness and nightmares I will excise
When pressed against your comforting chest
We, with love paint the skies, for now I'm free
So that only Picasso nights, fill our eyes

Leia Maichel, Grade 10
Calvary Chapel Christian School, CA

Dear Dad

Thank you for all of the things you've done,
You have always brought me toys so my week will be fun.
From your attitude I can conclude
That to none you are rude.
You help us out when we are down,
And sometimes say, "Why the frown?"
There may be times when times are a bother,
But you will always be
My Favorite Father.

Rishi Kapadia, Grade 10
Gretchen Whitney High School, CA

Always Be Yourself

A lways be yourself.
B elieve in true love.
C an't is not an option.
D on't give up.
E veryone is different. Accept them.
F orget the worries. **G** o for it.
H ope does exist. **I** magine the impossible.
J oy is a good feeling.
K eep your eye on your goal.
L ife is a game. **M** ake new friends every day.
N o one is perfect. **O** pportunities exist.
P atience is rewarded.
Q uestion authority.
R emember to sing every day.
S trive to be beautiful on the inside.
T ake time to dream. **U** niqueness is good.
V alue is important.
W hen in doubt, sleep on it.
X doesn't always mark the spot.
Y ou will fail, keep trying.
Z oos are very happy places.

Nicole Moses, Grade 12
Red Mountain High School, AZ

That's My Son!

Supporting my family was my job.
Keeping them well fed and happy was my goal.
Giving my children a better future was my dream.
I hoped, every day, my children would be successful.
Having them fail is my fear.
Watching my children cry is a nightmare.
I worked in the hot sun every day on the fields.
Knowing this hard labor will get my children fed.
Watched them grow up…
Day by day…
Watching them graduate on stage shed many tears.
On their wedding day,
I cried them a river.
I held their newborn son.
My heart begins to fill.
Seeing how successful they've become…
They completed the meaning of my life.

Dennis Li, Grade 10
Abraham Lincoln High School, CA

What a Fool

I'm always thinking about you
What a fool I am the way I left you
Months passed by, what a waste of time
Stuck here today, for you I pray to be safe
I was the man of the house that paid the bills
Now that I'm away I can't explain how bad I feel

Michael Meza Campos, Grade 10
Rite of Passage Charter High School, NV

My Grandmother

My grandmother sat by the bed all alone,
in a world that seemed so unknown.
Next to her was a door,
that once led to my aunt and father's toy galore.

Sitting by the window,
she dreamt of times that seemed so long ago.
How my aunt and father once sat around her knee,
listening to her stories by the chimney.

Her ears that was once filled with their happy glees,
can now only hear the wind blowing against the lingering trees.
Silently she wiped away a twinkling tear,
knowing that they're no longer here.

Thoughts of how they treated her now,
are knives battering through her frail heart.
She began to wonder how,
and when it all began to start.

She wasn't mad nor kept their neglect in mind,
even if she knew they've left her behind.
She forgave and forgot the attitude they've shown,
even if she knew she's now all alone.

Ivy Pham, Grade 10
Abraham Lincoln High School, CA

Destination

I drive down these paths with
those rifles in the trunk,
these men in their seats,
ready for peace and for war.

With my hands on the wheel,
looking at the rear mirror,
I see smiles on their faces,
but fear in their eyes.

The road frightens me.
Each mission reaches a different destination.
I'm leading their lives to an end,
the lives of courageous men.

They bring their armor to protect themselves,
knowing that their lives are at risk.
We're letting them go,
those brave, brave warriors.

As our flag ascends,
we cheer with joy.
But I could imagine their blood shed
and remember the laughs we shared.

Cindy Chen, Grade 10
Abraham Lincoln High School, CA

I Am

I am dazed and confused.
I wonder if the people in the world will ever keep it real.
I hear the sounds of a brighter day.
I see the footsteps of my past catching up with me.
I want to be a better person.
I am dazed and confused.

I pretend that I can single-handedly change the world.
I feel the pressure of my life crushing my soul.
I touch the angel that God sent to protect me.
I worry if the world will be safe for my kids.
I cry when I think of all the harm I caused.
I am dazed and confused.

I understand that no one is perfect.
I say you have to love yourself before you can love someone else.
I dream that my mom will understand that drugs aren't important.
I try to better my life to ensure a better future.
I hope I can succeed to make my dreams a reality.
I am dazed and confused.

Jazzmyne Glover, Grade 12
Pioneer High School, NV

Puppy

I'm sittin' down all alone in my house
Wishin' I could go outside and play but till then I am
Sittin' here waitin' out the day
I can't resist the temptation anymore
I know I might get into trouble
But it's okay because I ain't stoppin' once I get through that door
I'm gonna have fun while it lasts
Because the time goes way too fast
So I play my big ol' heart away
Till my master comes home and calls my name
And I know I should be ashamed
But it's okay because it was so much fun
And I really love to run
So till next time, I wait for my time to go out to play again

Mitchell Moore, Grade 10
Cypress High School, CA

What Happens to Aged Love?

What happens to aged love?
Does it become decrepit and inactive,
Or is it more treasured and respected?
Is aged love more valuable than youthful love?
Who's to say red passionate burning love,
Is better than deep blue cherished love?
Is love like wine? That becomes sweeter with time?
Can love grow stronger with practice
And weaken when left to fight on its own?
Do we admire mature, experienced love
More than young spontaneous love?
What happens to aged love?

Leah Teters, Grade 12
Merit Academy, UT

The Spark of Enlightenment

Crackle, crackle, the fire goes
Brimming with new life
The quick "pops" and "cracks" of the fire growing
Burning away with ease
As it matures, its sound does grow
A harsh roar commands attention
Yet, hiding the inner beauty
Of the warm and wonderful fire
I hear the fire speak to me
I hear its soothing monologue
I feel its warmth upon my face
As I listen quite intently
It tells of adventures and things of the past
Of the great events it has witnessed
As the story continues, it fades away slowly
I hear the fire taking its breaths
Yet still giving off its warmth
I listen as it dies away, I listen to the end
Although my story is over, another begins
Kindled in the fireplace of an unsuspecting person

Nikolas Barth, Grade 10
St. Francis High School, CA

Transparent teary Teal Skies

Transparent teary Teal Skies
Glassy — Opaque — waters below.
The chatter of the feathers — line
Nature smiles — sowed.

Rustling — of leaves against trees
Blooming dandelions — Flowing away
To the orange Sun — responding to her call.
Glistening — Glossy clouds see.

Aerial — Harmonized together
Stained flowers relaxing
Arising to the top — Yet down below
Sparkles — Glows — Serenity.

Joana Bolivar, Grade 11
Imperial High School, CA

Before I Go

Before I go, I want you to know that I loved you,
You were the one that I could always turn to.
I want you to know that you were the man of my dreams,
But your love for me is clearly not what it seems.
Before I go I want to break your heart how you broke mine.
I can't believe our hearts were once intertwined.
I'll settle for breaking the guitar where you wrote my song.
I don't know how our relationship ended so awfully wrong.
Before I go I'll give you back that broken promise ring,
I no longer want to hear you softly sing.
I'll erase all the good memories from my head,
But I have to go before I take back everything that I've said.

Brittani Cole, Grade 12
Preston High School, ID

One

Hearts beating as one
The sisterhood surrounds me
We are one team
We are one soul
United under one passion
The game
Sweat dripping down our faces
Muscles coiled
Ready to spring at any instant
Adrenaline pumping
Minds focused
We move as one
We are one
Nothing can stop us
Nothing
Alone we stand vulnerable
But together
Together we make miracles
Defy the odds
Achieve the impossible
Together as one

Hayley Huntsman, Grade 11
Lone Peak High School, UT

Voices

They are here again,
The voices in my head.
They make me do what they wish.
I can't hold back.
Help me again,
Like how you helped before.
I hope you will help again.

My poor soulless life depends on it.
Help me to live.
They cannot overtake me,
Not again.
I already have had enough.
They cannot control me.

Even though they left
They will return.
We can do nothing,
Nothing but wait.
We can just hope,
Hope for a way forward.

Quintin Begay, Grade 10
Mesa High School, AZ

The Ocean

Dancing on the shore
the ocean beckons to me
waving back and forth

Jenna Lee, Grade 12
Red Mountain High School, AZ

A Room Full of People

This room full of people so ready to go
I've been here before
It's where I warm up every time
I sit back against the wall
My eyes see everything around
I look at people's faces and the way they move
I feel like the gladiators that once were, they sat like me watching their opponents
This is the room where they come and go
I see some getting ready just like me
Their face is set with iron determination
Others come in with the win still on their face
You can see that they are still tired it was worth every minute they were on the mat
Then you see the downtrodden faces of the defeated
They can't even seem to look up
They pull back on their warm ups and keep to themselves
Then there is me I sit and watch
This room is so full of people so ready to go
And I sit here watching and waiting
My turn will come

Coben Hoch, Grade 12
New Plymouth High School, ID

The School of Life

Tell me not, in doleful voices/ That our break has come to pass
Do not want to lose my choices,/ And return, once more, to class
Life is brief! Should be joyful!/ And the school yard has no fun
Soon be grown, don't be wasteful/ Many things yet to be done
Not studying, and not learning,/ Neither, were we meant to do.
We must spend time without yearning/ For a break that's coming soon
Time is short, and school much longer/ Than anyone would wish for
But our minds are getting stronger/ Though often times, they are sore
But we need it, it is a guard/ From the world we soon will face
And though the path is long and hard/ We will handle it with grace
It is power, and it is strength/ That Knowledge always bestows
Those who are seeking it at length/ Will weaken all of their foes
So bear on through the painful day/ Or that difficult pop quiz
And prepare yourself for the fray/ That the world most surely is.

Silas Walker, Grade 11
Valley Christian High School, CA

The Healing Heart

Time is what it takes to recover this pain,
This pain of yours can be felt like a sharp knife stabbed into your chest.
It takes time to recover this bleeding broken heart,
By then you stitch your wound like sewing machine.

Days, months, and years passed by
Your wound is healed like magic,
Forgetting about the past painful love of yours.
Throwing it away to the bottom of the sea where you buried your love one away.

Till this very day you smile and play
Laugh and say "I'm okay."
This heart of yours can heal one day.

Samantha Lysaythong, Grade 12
Hiram W Johnson High School, CA

Window

The crystallized air hangs heavy outside.
The sky, a silver, twisting trout,
shimmers through the cataract of clouds.
I touch the foggy pane,
letting the cool condensation
fill each groove of my fingertips.
The curtains lie heavy
in velvet and rose-colored dust,
pushed aside like the milk
that no one realized was spoiled.
I press my hand flat against the antique glass,
hoping the mystic rain
will tell the fortune inscribed in my palm.
The corners of chipped white sill
drip with the net of ivy.
With every ounce of force left in my finger,
the one blessed with the embrace of silver,
I lift, tap lightly, and hope
you'll urge me not to
"disturb the animals."

Karina Reed, Grade 12
Centennial High School, ID

Wait…

The tears, they fall,
they fall like rain…
Scattering down the window frame
you sit by the phone
waiting…
Waiting for that call
that assures you everything's all right,
that the war is now over,
there's no need to fight…
Your thoughts are full of hopes and wishes
praying he'll be back soon for those holiday kisses…
The days go by
so fast, yet so slow
and there you sit alone in that old antique rocking chair
patiently waiting for the news.
The bright smile you once had is now only a face of wrinkles
and as for your blue eyes they no longer twinkle…
I wonder why this may be? Why you are so sad?
But then I realize
you never got the call you wish you had…

Taylor Bolin, Grade 11
Arlee High School, MT

Love Lives On

Love lives on through the soul
Past pain, past affection, past the toll,
Of the hands of time.
Love exists outside of us
Beyond sight, feelings, touch
Or a simple rhyme

Haley Green, Grade 11
Valley Christian High School, CA

Who Am I?

I sit in my room and I asked myself who am I?
I come to a conclusion that I don't really know.
And many questions come to my mind
just like do I fit in?
Who really am I?
Why do these things happen to me?
I've been through so much with my family and friends.
There have been times where I just feel like leaving home.
I sometimes feel like I am nobody in this world.
I always try my best but thing are just not the same.
I have noticed that many things are just not going to change.
But I just don't understand why me?
But with this I have started to become independent
and doing my own things.
I lost someone really special in my life that was always there for me
With her lost I have really changed my point of view in life.
Many people don't know me
And they may say I'm ugly
But it's not like I care
Because I am who I am and I am happy the way I am!

Viridiana Barba, Grade 11
Animo Leadership Charter High School, CA

I Will Never Go Through That Again

Do you want to go on another date?
You know that I do.

Do you have anyone in your life that is more important than me?
No, not after getting to know you.

Do you love me?
More than you could ever imagine.

Would you ever break my heart?
I would never make that mistake.

Would you marry me?
In an instant.

Would you break up with me?
Not in a million years.
We're perfect together, aren't we?

(Now read the lines from bottom to top)

Alex Franklin, Grade 10
Red Mountain High School, AZ

Wholly Renewed

Living in the tar
Dirtied yet oblivious
You gave your cleansed hand
You have purified my sin
I'm glad I've met you Jesus

Rebecca Lee, Grade 11
Alhambra High School, CA

Tragic Disasters

Just an innocent little girl
Who was out to change the world
She had a heart of gold
And now her story is told
The chain reaction that she left behind
Helped change the worlds mind

As the grey smoke filled the sky
People all around the world began to cry
As our hearts filled with pain
Next came the other plane
As the first tower came tumbling down
Everyone stared without a sound

As this earthquake took place
It was sad to see everyone's face
The town was filled with joy
As they found that little boy
His hands were stretched toward the sky
Then everyone began to cry

As all the things that happen on this Earth
We all know that it's not worth
A tragic disaster
Dashanna Cureton, Grade 11
New Plymouth High School, ID

Case

A new kind of friendship
Between he and I
We will be friends forever
Until one of us shall die.

We go out back
And have some fun
We play catch
He loves to run

He brings it to me
Again and again
He sits by my side
Until we begin again

"Come on boy!"
You're doing great!
We will go again later
But it's getting late

I lock him up
Till tomorrow
I'll be back
Feel no sorrow
Shelby Chapple, Grade 10
Shelley Sr High School, ID

The Madagascan Sunset Poem

Your shoulders wrapped so elegant,
In a rich and emerald green,
Bound by such deep gradients,
And caressed by subtle sheens.

Red and gold explode below,
And white hot comets pass,
The rest is lined with black shadows,
And all encased in glass.

But *I* see right through your facade,
Not fooled by green and red.
Your plan is very plainly flawed,
It's on your very head.

You quickly curtsy to and fro —
A charismatic cover.
But they don't know what I do know
About what they might discover.

Your mask is very intricate,
But *I* know your full name!
Though don't you even start to fret,
Because I love you just the same.
Amanda Gruba, Grade 10
Bradshaw Christian High School, CA

I Hear Them Shooting

I hear them shooting.
I hear it as I sit.
Sitting in this dark, windowless room,
Sitting on cold cement; constantly

Hoping — Praying — For them,
For those whose duty for the Fuhrer
Is to be shot —
Shot by me.

I hear their screams,
Their cries, their brothers dropping.

Hoping — Praying — For them,
That God has something better,
Better for them.

I hear — I hope — I pray
(As I'm burdened by this,
The dead weight against my side)
That someday,

Some — Blessed — Day,
I can take their shot.
Jeremy Nordfelt, Grade 11
Viewmont High School, UT

Where Has My Anger Gone?

Where has it gone?
My strong emotion
It has disappeared
All my anger

My life was full
With endless anger
Driving my life
In all directions

Now it is gone
And I am lost
I must find my way
Through this mist

A life without anger
A world without pain
Let the peace last
In this world we hold

But I miss it
My anger
I miss my guide
Where has my anger gone?
Timothy Gonzales, Grade 10
Roadrunner High School, AZ

The End

Life is a struggle.
Things aren't always how you want it.
You try to do what you can.
But at times things can go wrong.

Things can crush you or make you strong.
Everything was going good,
I thought it was going to last.
People would talk but, I would ignore.
You could tell you really liked it too.
But there was a little twist,
The story was not going the same.

I didn't feel the same no more.
I think you could notice.
Everything was nice and good,
but that thing killed everything.
Now everyone's doing their own.

I have a new story now,
At times I miss the past.
But everything just helped me,
see and made me stronger.
One thing for sure I'm not going to forget!
Karina Bocanegra, Grade 11
Animo Leadership Charter High School, CA

The Rose

A fire burning in his hand,
the flower grows throughout the land.
Give it as a gift,
to cause her heart to softly lift.

Watching her in the moonlight,
her eyes light up very bright.
Here comes the kiss,
for the life of them will be bliss.

The anniversary of the first date,
the boyfriend came in a little late.
Her heart feels a slight sting
until her lover presents a ring.

Two become one in the blink of an eye,
at first they both were very shy.
The life is great that they both chose,
and to think it all started with a rose.

Nick McNulty, Grade 12
Burlington High School, WY

My True Love

Today was full of surprises,
I feel horrible in my heart
I can't control my feelings,
Even if we are not together
At times I am very happy,
And sometimes loneliness appears
Did you ever lie to me,
Did you ever hide things from me
I wonder why I love you so much,
I am searching for an answer
Did you even care once,
Or was everything made up
Now I see what I thought was wrong,
I am excited for what is to come
In the distance I see what you have created,
Hand in hand we walk together
We promise each other till the end,
You, the only one that receives my kisses
You are my sweet tart

Eunice Banuelos, Grade 11
Animo Leadership Charter High School, CA

The Highway

We got lost in July's hot asphalt
drove-up
through a hole in the sky
searched
for God,
sweetgrass,
the shadows of the clouds.

Kayla Riley, Grade 12
South Pasadena High School, CA

For the Benefit of No One

A female lion does 90% of the hunting.
There is a prison in Ossining, New York named "Sing Sing."
Henry Ford flatly stated that history is "Bunk."
2:20 am, April 15th, 1912 is when the titanic sunk.
Most toilets flush in E flat.

It's information that clogs the brain, knowledge that delays the thought train.
You can't help but hear it. And you will never forget it.

The external tank on the space shuttle isn't painted.
The average human grows 590 miles of hair.
Sounds travels faster through steel that through air.
Baseball's home plate is 17 inches wide.
On a die, 7 is the sum of any two opposite sides.

It's information that clogs the brain, knowledge that delays the thought train.
You can't help but hear it. And you will never forget it.

The Earth gets heavier every day as meteoric dust settles in it.
Robert E. Lee graduated from west point without a single demerit.
Out of 20,000 species of bees, only 4 make honey.
Christmas was once illegal in England and about
30% of Australians have ancestors from Ireland.

It's information that clogs the brain, knowledge that delays the thought train.
You can't help but hear it. And you will never forget it.

Chelsea Allen, Grade 12
Merit Academy, UT

Accepted

Accepted, what do I have to do to feel accepted
how can I be myself and have others respect it
Why do I feel the need to fit into a category
Am I accepted by my family if I don't do as my dad before me

Every time I sin to feel accepted, a nail gets impounded into the Cross
My heart bleeds at the thought that my soul is lost
Bad influences recede like darkness, I am the one who pays the tax
I hate all the inexpressiveness, I just want the cold hard facts

One thousand friends on Facebook, I command the world to see
I have sanctioned myself, and others have neglected me
All the pain I feel, I lock up and let smolder
The rage is unrelenting now that I'm getting older

To be approved of today, means I'm cursed tomorrow
I suffer silently to myself, I am immersed in sorrow
I feel caged in my mind but to you I look fine
God help me to seek truth, without You I feel blind

I go through so much, I go to great lengths
For the approval of another, not realizing my own strengths
Perhaps the road is written already, and I just have to accept it
But still I try and try again until I feel accepted

Junior Crumlin, Grade 11
Diamond Ranch Academy, UT

A Thrice-Minded Star

We may guess at what they are.
He may say they don't go far.
You might guess or try to ask,
What they do, what is their task?

While they question it, I'll say.
Their purpose is a grand ballet.
They walk upon the morning light
When seen, it is a glorious sight.

They dust webs with fresh morning dew.
And raises the rose with it too.
By the lake, they are often drawn
To the sound of a calling swan.

In our dreams, they are essential.
They help lead to our potential.
For through my imaginations,
I forged these bright creations.

Johanna Nielson, Grade 11
Madison Sr High School, ID

Picturesque

It's the oranges I wake up for
The sunshine in my room
The bright blues get me out the door
Showered, clothed and groomed

The greens send salutations
From the grass and trees
Along with red carnations
Blowing in the breeze

It's the deep blues that I love the most
The sheets of sky above
The puffy clouds, white like ghosts
Or the feathers of a dove

The scarlet sunset starts to bleed
Dripping drops of red
Nocturne purple nudges me
And sends me off to bed

Zach Rosenstein, Grade 12
Layton High School, UT

Last Wishes

Bounded to the harsh sentence of death,
I stare at the cold night sky
And plea God with my last single breath:
I pray to you so when I die
My wife will look past my misfortunes
And learn to love once more,
So that our memories can be attune
And not live shallow like the shore.

Joshua Simon, Grade 12
Desert Mountain High School, AZ

Why?

Sometimes I wonder who am I?
Why are we in this world that at times
can be rough and painful?
As I've been here in this so called world, I've learned many new things;
One of them is that time doesn't wait for you, and the older you get
the faster time goes…it's uncontrollable. My life is great, I have everything
someone needs. A nice comfortable house, friends and of course a family. I
wonder why is it that I have this and others don't? I'm thankful, however,
that I have the most important aspect in life: a family. I may not be perfect, no one is, but
I'm happy with what I have in life. You don't have to be the prettiest, or the richest
in the world to be happy. Just be yourself and enjoy life as it comes.
Don't just exist, live. I've also leaned that things happen for a reason and
people come and go. You meet new people, you lose some people.
My mom once told me friends come and go, but family doesn't, and I agree.
The closest people you'll ever have is family, they'll be there through thick and thin
and will love you no matter what. As I look in the mirror, it reminds myself
who I am. A 16-year-old young lady with dreams that one day will come true.
And with the mentality of the world just being a big fairy tale with peace and joy.

Yesenia Gonzalez, Grade 11
Animo Leadership Charter High School, CA

The Hour Is Late

Buildings shrieking,
Blots of fire emanating,
Waves miles high flourish in the distance,
Everyone becomes lost in an instance.

Destruction at your feet,
You feel the immobilizing heat.
The seismic roars destroying all you loved,
The gods use liquid mountains to seize your control.

People finally coming together as one,
But it is too late for the time they have is none.
We abused that, which loves us best,
So the gods punish us without contest.

I want to watch it all go down I want to see the world flushed clean of destruction.
There will never be peace till we all change the function of are most beautiful construction.

Steve Mason, Grade 12
Post High School (Self-Cont), UT

Storm

Poetry is like a
Storm
They are,
    The quick, brilliant
    flashes of feelings,
    The pounding noise of
    the rhythm of the words.
    The soft, flowing words
    that roll off your tongue.
    The endless noise creates music as the
    words create pictures.

Amanda Lew, Grade 10
Cypress High School, CA

Drama

Unavoidable beasts
Flying through the CROWDS
Attacking large groups
Never making a sound
Feeding, Devouring, invisible creatures.
To never quite die,
Drama has such a feature.
Ignore it and RUN,
If you think Drama's fun.
But if you can't risk it,
I suggest that you fix it!

Tiana Song, Grade 10
Campbell High School, HI

The Outdoor Guardian

Churning up the grass
Cutting, slicing, tearing fast
Roaring to life
Clearing out signs of strife
Keeping the outdoors looking first-class

Kept in a shed out back
It is only care that I lack
Sunlight streams through the wooden panels
And when it rains, the water forms channels
And yet, I am covered by potato sacks

Forever scented by grass
And made of plastic, metal, and glass
I keep peace in the neighborhood
Between the HOA and the people — as I should
Hardworking I am as I always have been one for completing tasks

Meera Kumar, Grade 10
Horizon Community Learning Center, AZ

Remember Us

You are one in six billion,
the only star in the night.
You are the sunset that spills into the ocean,
the most beautiful thing in sight.
You are the lyrics to my favorite song,
the beat that makes me dance.
You are the melted chocolate in my pocket,
the reddest rose from my Valentine.
You are the secret that I hold so dear,
the mystery that spins my mind.
You are the kiss on my lips after a fight,
the frantic beat of my heart when you're by my side.
You are the call I make after a nightmare,
the freeing of heavy chains on my fears.
You are the first step I will take towards love,
the single burning candle in the dark.
You are nothing short of my everything.

Emily Kye, Grade 12
Etiwanda High School, CA

Meaning of Life

There is no meaning of life without love, patience, and kindness,
Life is not meant to be gloomy and full of darkness.
Yet it is to be celebrated with everyone's heart embraced,
And learn from all the moments we have faced.
Becoming better as a person and never looking back,
And not looking at the things you lack.
Time is a precious gift in our life,
So we need not to live in strife.
Life is just another journey, just another trial,
And cherish our lives, and go the extra mile.
Use every minute of your time,
And reaching that never ending climb.

Jennifer Packard, Grade 12
Madison Sr. High School, ID

Bulldogging

The gate opened wide,
And with a spur in his hide,
He exploded.
The steer lurched out of the gate.
He ran with his might to get away.
Racing, chasing, I spurred my steed.
My pony took a bound, departing for the lead.
Ready for the dive,
I spurred my horse one last time,
Then I took flight.
I sailed in on the steer, and with perfect grace,
I threw my arms round his head,
And I hit the ground as I went.
I twisted, turned and bent,
And with one last grunt from me,
And a groan from him,
I threw him to the ground,
The buzzer rang, and the crowd gave a cheer,
And I knew that I had bulldogged this steer.

Cort Jensen, Grade 12
Emery High School, UT

On Writing a Sonnet

To write a sonnet you need much patience
The words you speak must be pure and true.
When you get stuck and are losing your sense,
Look in your book at the day it is due.
My brain is on fire and yours should be too.
Nine or eleven but never comes ten,
Syllables stuck together like glue.
When will it ever end, oh when? Oh when?!
But poetry brings such light to these words.
Life, love, laughter, and other things as well,
Maybe something's so simple, such as birds,
But whatever you write, I cannot tell.
Be sure not to rhyme silver and orange,
unless you rhyme it with sliver and door hinge.

Ben Belisle, Grade 10
Chandler Preparatory Academy, AZ

Light

It's strange how
Looking out the window
Tends to hypnotize
Even when the lights
Flash
And chaos engulfs the mind

There's a sanctuary
Where the thoughts tend to hide from the light
And the passenger beside you
Becomes
Untouchable
Because you've already given your hands away

Victoria Lang, Grade 10
San Marcos High School, CA

Moments

One look
One smile
One thought
One moment
Can pull you in
Deeper and deeper
You can't escape it
It clings to you
Like a super glue on your fingers
Struggling to get free
Or
Struggling to stay
The choice is yours
Life
Your heart
They are all risks
You won't get anywhere without taking one or two
But no matter what moment you are in
Remember to live your life to the fullest
And don't let a moment slip you by

Heather Wiese, Grade 12
New Plymouth High School, ID

Dear John :)

I was afraid I would miss you when you weren't near,
But then I realize that you are always here.
In my daily thoughts and my evening dreams,
In my steps when I walk and my smile when it beams;

And so I recognize that you reside in a place as high as can be,
Perhaps the very essence of me.
You are kept close, in my heart, so very dear,
I think of this and my sadness disappears,

Just like you told me on the phone,
So, don't ever think for a second that you're alone.
You have me just as I have you.
I'll be in you're heart, too.

Alyssa Kroeger, Grade 11
Gilroy High School, CA

Rain Storms and Hard Times

Rain is so dark and gloomy,
everything looks so dead;
it makes me think of death.
During the storm it seems like everything ends,
just like hard times in life.
But once the rain goes away,
the sun comes out,
opening my eyes
making me see the beauty of the world
making it so wonderful.
The rainbow shines,
giving color to the world.

Chase Conrad, Grade 10
Orem High School, UT

On Pressing Matters, Version 1.0

The foul beast reaches far
Invading vision hunting wide
Binding you. Constricting you. Dictating you. Suffocating you.

Carelessness has consequences
And the beast feeds on revenge
Capture evokes horrid sequences
Up there on the inquisitive bench.

Lives can change in a second
Each choice you make can matter
With every action, the beast you beckon
Take heed! 'Ere your life becomes tattered!

Punishments are severe
Even for crimes without victims
And, watching, the beast nears
They're your choices, and you picked 'em.

As innocent as they may be
The beast is vicious and unforgiving
It can hardly contain its glee
For bringing misery to the living

It keeps you safe. But at what cost?
Many important elements of life are lost.

Sebastian Chapa, Grade 12
Merit Academy, UT

Mondays

The first day after break is surely bleak,
When everyone's depressed for lack of rest.
Monday is no one's favorite day of week.

As hours go by, the homework seems to sneak
Into our planners, loaded with detest.
The first day after break is surely bleak.

Discussions fill the hours with need to speak
In students who then sleepily digress.
Monday is no one's favorite day of week.

Our fun is gone, no time for hide and seek,
With even teachers heartily depressed.
The first day after break is surely bleak.

Learners hunched, expressions looking meek,
Not ready to put knowledge to its test;
Monday is no one's favorite day of week.

Students braced like soldiers without speech,
Embarking on our petrifying quest.
The first day after break is surely bleak.
Monday is no one's favorite day of week.

Amy Lundy, Grade 10
Chandler Preparatory Academy, AZ

Lights

The lights make noise
Noise unheard by the unseen
Noise heard by the unwanted
Noise that slices my eyes
Tears drop
Tears unseen because I am
I am unseen yet unwanted
Questions no word can place
Unanswered, unseen, unwanted
Scars replace the words, memories
Seemingly impossible to fake a memory
Breathtaking, eye-slicing, ear-shattering
I am left wondering
Wondering, is this me?
What is my world
My world is love but why
Why am I unseen
Why do these scars haunt
This isn't me, but unanswered
Unanswered is love
Love is but a dream in a world unseen

Kaitlyn Kelley, Grade 11
Mililani High School, HI

Life

Life, Life, Life
It's suppose to be fun
There aren't supposed to be guns.
Babies are being aborted,
Teens are making them,
Parents are left with no
Jobs
Budget cuts,
WOW that's something
Everyone is being affected by.
Schools, teachers and students,
It's Crazy
I just wish there was a
Simple solution to all of this
War, Peace, War, Peace
I agree with Peace,
Peace is the key to equality.
I wish I can just wake
Up and realize it's just all a
Dream
BUT IS NOT!!!

Haira Dela Cruz, Grade 11
Animo Leadership Charter High School, CA

Winter Snow

The snow of winter,
Conceals the land in white sheets
A chilling embrace

Kim Pee Castro, Grade 10
Mililani High School, HI

Shanghai Morning

The rosy hue of dawn gently rises
Doors start opening and closing like wings flapping

Pots and Pans start clanking
Bing, Bang, Bing, Bang

Leftover oil and grease from last morning is thrown in to the pot
Pshhh, bubbling

As it approaches 8 o' clock people start streaming out from the apartments
Click, Clack their slippers sings against the concrete
Their pajamas flutter in the morning breeze, swoosh

The air fills with the smell of eggs, dumplings, and fresh rice cakes
5 cents for 1! 2 for a dollar! The vendors shout.

The day has started in Shanghai.

Yan Ming Zhou, Grade 12
University High School, CA

Shock Wave

I want to jump into a gaping, bottomless pit
Where new emotions don't play on the hurt I already feel.
Seeing couples my age disconnected form the real world makes me sick
Because unlike them, I don't have a romance I can call real.
At times I have to remind myself to breathe
And to bury this sorrow down, down deep
As my instability begins to be too much to sheathe,
I try hard my sanity to keep.
As the shock from the fall of falling in love catches me,
Part of my heart still sticks to the one who pushed me to begin with.
I have no voice or person left to recite my creed,
And I'm left to wonder if the concept of true love may be a myth.
My heart is in my stomach where I don't want it to stay,
So I make another mistake in an attempt to find someone new to love it away.

Abbie Sawyer, Grade 10
Orem High School, UT

The Land That Once Was

A chill runs down my spine as I stare into his hollow eyes.
With scythe in hand, he comes to collect his debt of life.
Silently, I follow him down a barren road.
Surrounded by dead bony trees.
No pleasantries exchange (for I believe he is unable to speak)
Besides there is fear gripping at my throat keeping me from speaking.
We stop at a fork; and with a bony finger, he points at path for me to
follow to the land of things that once were.
He cannot guide me forth for this is not his land to live.
Only cold, I feel, as I leave his presence.
Where I go I know: all must change.
When I enter, I am not the same…and never will be again…

Robert Millfelt, Grade 11
Wilson High School, CA

Is This Love?

With every look from your eyes,
my cold, dark world bursts with color.
When I'm lost in my imaginings, I
think of you and no other.
So, I ask myself, "Is this love?"

From the first day that we met,
I've felt nothing but felicity.
I guess it's because you made my dreams
into a reality.

Every time we see each other, my
stomach gets butterflies.
This feeling gets stronger as
I gaze into your wondrous eyes.
Are you the angel sent from above?

I ask myself if this is love,
but I know my answer is true;
I now know that this is love
and the one I'm in love with is you.

Kevin Sanchez, Grade 11
Anaheim High School, CA

Breathing Water

Down
   Down, Down
as I
Drown
   Drown, Drown
water races into me
rolling breakers, roaring sea
Heaving
   Heaving, Heaving
as I'm
Breathing
   Breathing, Breathing
water into lungs and veins
swallowing these liquid chains
Flying
   Flying, Flying
as I'm
Dying
   Dying, Dying
soaring towards the blessèd light
leaving forever eternal blight.

Morgan Blomstrom, Grade 12
Douglas County High School, NV

Poetry

My heart speaks its mind
Smudged lead forms expressive chaos
Poetry is formed

Chelsea Durfee, Grade 12
Red Mountain High School, AZ

The Waiting

One line from one song.
That's all it takes.
That's all it takes for the stitches holding me together to come undone;
for the brick wall around my heart to crumble,
for my world to shatter,
and so goes my heart along with it.
The song goes on.
My mind flashes to days intoxicated with laughter,
with enchantment and adventure;
my mind flashes to days with you.
You are like a poison,
one that I am still trying to find the antidote for.
How long will this go on?
I am waiting.
Waiting for the day when I don't look for you everywhere I go.
When you aren't my last vagrant thought before sleep,
my dream every night,
then my first conscious thought in the morning.
I am waiting.

Kate Balser, Grade 10
Orem High School, UT

Amity's Melody

Beautiful sounds of her instrument
calm me and relax me
her everlasting voice can go on for days
as my heart listens, the sounds begin to decay
her piano keys faded away into an old memory
two years ago was the last time she played for me
now she's gone to an empty box in my mind
trying to remember her lovely melody…it saddens me
looking into a empty casket, dressed in black
attempting to bring Amity's Melody back
by raging on an violent and destructive path
creating disturbing sounds, to bring her back
but I couldn't ever accept the fact that she's gone
when I go to sleep at night, in my dreams I hear the piano keys pressing on…

Christopher Siders, Grade 11
View Park Preparatory Accelerated Charter High School, CA

True Devotion

O' this hateful love!
It is so peaceful, as a dove.
It has brought me sorrowful joy.
He makes me happy, but I fear that it is my heart that he may destroy.
His words are so wise, so full of devotion,
It is like he is making me drink a strong love potion.
I fear for the day we will have to be apart,
For I know although he may leave, he will still be part of my heart.
To think, that when I am down, he won't be there to help me get by,
The thought itself is enough to make me cry!
It is a horrible happiness he brings to me,
As long as I know he is there, I will sleep peacefully.

Karen Angeles, Grade 10
Lucerne Valley Jr/Sr High School, CA

Memories

It started with a smile
Then came the overwhelming laugh
The innocence lasted a while
When someone talked on my behalf

Things seem harder the older I became
The smile drifted into an emotionless sleep
It would never be the same
These memories I would keep

I grew up still
With lessons left to learn
As I tried to do my will
The fire will still burn

Memories last a lifetime
Some of them not always so kind
Nicole Pancheri, Grade 10
Shelley Sr High School, ID

Poison

She created the poison
That slips into my soul,
The toxicity overwhelming hope,
Its old cold hold choking all joy.
Slowly she stops the soul.
Her poison meant to kill,
To destroy, to shatter,
To make life as a fragmented puzzle.
Her poison resides within her
Flowing out and splattering all over
Like a cauldron boiling over.
This poison of hers has trapped me
Leaving me to drown in despair
But as I desperately try to swim
The question enters my mind.
Whose hand let the poison in?
Was it hers or it was mine?
Greg Rutledge, Grade 11
Viewmont High School, UT

Eric

I just don't understand,
Why you did that to yourself
What you needed was a helping hand
But you kept your problems inside
Now I'm wondering what I could have done
Maybe you would have changed your mind
And possibly put down the gun
But it's too late your gone
And everyone misses you like crazy
I wish I could rewind
And show you there was more to life
you just had to find.
Lauren Streich, Grade 10
Xavier College Preparatory School, AZ

The Wind Surfer

I don't do it for the fame
I don't do it for the money
I do it for her
The love shared between me and Clementine
She's soft and warm like a blanket
So smooth, so fresh, so beautiful
She glistens as the suns sets beyond her
She's so quiet and still as it ascends above her
I love when she curls and I softly stroke her
She roars, crashes and throws out the people who strive to join her
She gets violent during dark days with beating rains
But I am the only man who can calm her down again
I glide over her until she attempts to throw me out
But I ride her and show her that I can't be tossed aside
She then will be tame and return to her peaceful state
She begins to make her usual roar and the people come running back
They always get steered away by her because she doesn't want them
It's 'cause I'm the only one she wants
Me, the Wind Surfer
Clementine, the Blue, The Beautiful, The Ocean
Jake ZoBell, Grade 12
Woods Cross High School, UT

Love You Yet

If I sang you lullaby and gave you a hug goodbye
Would you still consider giving me up for another guy
I'm always a step behind you slip me another lie
I wanna leave cause the grass is so green on the other side
But you come to me another time a new demon in the old disguise
But always take control my mind and rest my worries with your golden eyes
You don't know that my whole demise is balanced on a pole of ice
And seeing the truth in your eyes is more elusive than a poltergeist
This whole war's a soldier's fight we march for what we know is right
And all the grey space saves place for me to grow inside
And in the end I hope to die looking out at my whole divide
To see you on the other side I'd get to you if I could fly
We never did see eye to eye all the things you idolized
Made me wish that I knew why you wouldn't wait till I arrived
In the end all the pain and the names at this fire fight
You're my dose of cyanide just make sure that I'm still alive
Jake Nakamura, Grade 10
Mililani High School, HI

Conqueror

"I came, I saw, I conquered."
I came to the battlefield; we came not only as an army, but as a monster. Riding our war beasts painted with blood of the conquered.

I saw the opposing army. I could smell the fear coming from their souls. Their destiny was sealed. It was fate, they would die and I would survive.

I conquered the pitiful enemy. They were a sad excuse for an army. Their bodies seemed to be like magnets to our swords. They were crushed by our massive weapons. They became the conquered, and I became the conqueror.
Conor Keenan, Grade 11
Golden Sierra High School, CA

My Dream

I am hopeful and impatient
I wonder about the bright dazzling stars
I hear a whisper calling me to sleep
I see my dream forming
I want it to be real
I am hopeful and impatient

I see myself as a mother
I feel her warm body in my arms
I touch her beautiful face
I worry my dream is fading
I cry when I wake up and my baby is gone
I am hopeful and impatient

I understand my dream is strange
I say it's fine; it is my dream after all
I dream of my darling angel
I try to sleep and see her again
I know one day she will be in my arms
I am hopeful…and impatient
Isis Serrano, Grade 10
Schurr High School, CA

Fading Dreams

My vision laid not in the plane of life,
Held tight, tenacious under grandpa's sight.
Unthinkable, within, with faithful strife,
May you lead yourself not into the blight.
For guidance is the tool that always fails,
And patience unfolds the box of despair.
With every second wasted with your wails
Your toil and zeal delve in futile affair.
By bells of old, the dream is merely seen
A ghastly blaze so bright of living blight;
With torches of war, in the hills of green,
your fortress falls, before the horrid sight.
Oh, bow and wind please lead it not astray;
My vision's fading, up, up, and away.
Michael Nico Balagtas, Grade 10
Cypress High School, CA

Family

The people who care for me,
The people who are there for me,
When I'm down, they lift me up
The door to their heart is never shut.
They always know when I'm down,
Their arms surround me, I know I'm found.
Together by fate, together as one,
No boring moments, it's always fun.
I came from a past hard to say,
They came to me and showed the way.
With past behind we look ahead.
I thank God with tears I shed.
Katya Eastland, Grade 11
Merit Academy, UT

A Rude Awakening in 1940

Stop shaking me Mom and no, I don't know where Dad is.
What a stupid question to ask —
BADOOOM!
I immediately sat up like a hundred needles pricked my all at once on my back
That mortar was so close to my room that my ears were ringing throughout the night.
It cries like a monster have bellowing yells of no mercy.

Without hesitation, Mom yanked me out of bed out into the hall down the staircase
we're nearly running at the pace she's getting at.
Her hands are sweaty and tightly bound around mine.
I can't see her face but some noise comes whistling in
a sharp crack then a light
BADOOOM!
We make it to the backdoor. Our bags were hastily packed by the nanny earlier.
Mom asks the nanny where Dad is.
She says everything rushed and broken. Constantly repeating words one after another.
Her hands won't stay at her sides rather, they're frantically kneading themselves together.
The nanny tells her the radio announcement from this morning,
the Japanese are taking everyone associated with the government.
Eyes dart around the sky looking for bomber planes. The nanny tells her something else.

At the approaching sound of the mortar's booming call, we run like prey down the road.
Mom tells me with a quickened breath, we're going north. To Allied China.
Chantal Cong-Huyen, Grade 10
Abraham Lincoln High School, CA

If I Could Go Back

Wishing I could go back…regretting what I have said
Not knowing this would happen
Wanting and wishing I could go back, hoping you'll forgive me.

Feeling sad on the inside, but not wanting to show it…deep down sadness
And scared to lose a friend like you
Deep down you don't wanna know how I feel
I don't know how to explain myself
Mainly feeling horrible and how bad I hurt you…

How you were to me…feelin' loved and happy
Only person who understood me
And who really knew what I was going through
To feel you were unwanted.
But to me you meant a lot…
Makin' me feel special because to me,
You knew how it feels and how it feels to be not wanted and horrible

So quiet and now showing what you really feel…
Only wanting others to be happy before you
Always knowing if they're happy or not…
Knowing how to cheer someone up
With no problem…
Megan Fowler, Grade 10
Leupp Schools, Inc, AZ

Wetback

I open my eyes
And what do I see
An imaginary land full of family and trees
As happy one can be
I did not know it will all come to an end
Traveling for days
We reach a river
Thinking it's all fun and games
My uncle picks me up and begins to cross
Soon I realize we're not going back
For we walk into a brown abyss
With snakes slithering behind our backs
We hear a sizzle, and begin to run
Run away from the brainless snakes
For they change from blue to red
Into the steep hills we go
For a dark green van awaits
Pitch black inside and as hot as the devils den
We make a stop, all gasping for air
Quickly noticing this weird new land
For I have never dreamed to see

Mario Rojas, Grade 11
Animo Leadership Charter High School, CA

Only If…

Only if I were a genius
I would be able to use my intelligence to help the sick.

Only if the world had no wars,
there would be more peace and less deaths.

Only if there was more school fundings,
then our innocent teachers would not have to leave.

Only if the kids in poor countries could eat three meals a day,
then maybe they will live strong and have an amazing future.

Only if…
Speaking will not make any changes.
The actions of yours and mine will change what is wrong —
Let us all change the world and make a difference!

So Eun (Gloria) Oh, Grade 10
Cypress High School, CA

Silent Tears

Withering roses fall to the floor
My heart is a beating so soft and assure
I wander around with lips still stained
From the layers of lipstick put on from before
The bells still chime in the chapel below
And little white dresses fall freely like so
Hearts are forgotten like rocks on the shore
And a beautiful scene is vaguely adored

Kelsey Chappelle, Grade 10
Hamilton High School, MT

A Life*

A life can be saved
A life could be taken.
Give a life aid,
Or it is forsaken.
A life can be plain, plain as paper
There isn't no shame in a savior
A life cost more than all the money in the world
Her life could be saved, if you helped this little girl.
A life is born every minute of the day.
A life is taken every second they say.
A life is good, a life is bad.
A good life is more than some have had.
I know my life was worse and better than others.
But I'm glad I've had a life, a life from my mother
So be grateful with the life you have.
And know it could have been something bad.

Daniel Dadeppo, Grade 11
Rite of Passage Charter High School, NV
*Dedicated to my mom

Tear Drop

I am with you every step of the way,
Through the ups and downs of life.
Laughter causes me;
The kinds of laughter that come from crazy friends
That can laugh together after saying one word.
True laughter,
Tear drop streaming down your face.
I'm those tear drops.
I also come with sorrow;
Broken hearts, stressed out lives,
Overwhelming odds.
I am those tear drops.
I am here with you all the time.
I am a tear drop.

Chandler Jensen, Grade 10
Pine View High School, UT

My Mother Always Told Me a Man's Shoes Speak

— Mother always told me a man's shoes speak,
Not of little things, but Life's strange journey.
His shoes can tell you if his soul is meek,
Or if like a Poor Man — God hears his plea —
You can see his cares — easy as the dusk
Of night and the dawn of Day's first light strewn —
The trails on which he has trod, from their Musk
And their Dust, washed away by morning's dew.
Their Holes are a looking glass to his life —
The cares his brow has worn by the Laces
That bind Life together despite its strife,
And through his Soles is seen his Soul's tart spices.
But — What more remarkable 'bout his shoe,
Is the quick glance of his life's strange, sweet dew.

Daniel Bittner, Grade 11
Viewmont High School, UT

Sixteen Years…

With only sixteen years gone by
Writing this makes me cry
I used to be so small and clean
It was a time when my impurities weren't seen
I look back on my life so far
It went from good to so bizarre
I never thought I'd see the day
When my own mom would cry and say
I don't like the girl I see
Daughter you have disappointed me
I could tell that day I broke her heart
I knew I was tearing my mom apart
I had grown up the way she planned
She still reached out a helping hand
Now the time has come
Where all I wish, is to change what I've done
I feel so bad for all the lies, tears so quickly fill my eyes
The pain I've caused might slowly fade
But I can never change the choices I made
I love you I hope you can find it in you to love me too

Trisha Jorgensen, Grade 10
Preston High School, ID

Oceanside Pier

So I go to this beach,
called Oceanside Pier
and yes I do surf
all throughout the year

I ride a 6'2,
a famous Lucas Fish
and surfing this beach
is nothing to miss

I'm not only there just
to surf and eat fish,
but to check out life
and realize how beautiful it is.

Lacie Smith, Grade 11
Encore High School for the Performing Arts, CA

Intact

Mine finds me when I least expect,
don't know how, but suddenly it's there.
I know it is, I feel… intact.
Moments like these are so rare.

Yet I can't help feel that it's worthwhile
to wait, when I find it I feel (alive?)
The world becomes nicer, less full of guile.
I thrive.

Even when I don't have mine,
I know we all have a soul at times.

Mariah Woods, Grade 12
Encore High School for the Performing Arts, CA

Mature

And I never thrummed in the wheat stalks
when God told me my train had left
yesterday
at the hour my shadow peaked.

Bristling as I tread lightly through golden
waves
Inescapable to a lonely eye, so apparent
in the separate plane I call mine.
Pleated became the lengths that rested
    beneath my cold, bruised feet. gliding
amongst a single tree amidst
    my Down falls.

It brings me to admit my regrets took me away
    from you: who are you
Whispering of insecurities too realistic
    to be considered true. I breathe
with it's swaying branches, so sparse
they cannot be seen by the eyes that penetrate
    mine, little do I understand the blue lenses
    I saw are hiding colorless glazed through
pupils
    Branches that thicken with the saplings own
        willingness to survive
                    Flourishing.

Melody Redmond, Grade 12
Brighton High School, UT

What's Left of Me

I'm not the same person I used to be,
I was once full of secret,
Now that isn't who I used to be,
Full of loneliness and isolation, how can that be me?

I won't lie and I will be honest,
I used to be caught in my form of art,
that's past me and I have done my best,
To leave my past and be who I want to be.
I still lie and I don't rest,
From what lies I still hide,
Now that I'm different they all come out of the nest.

My art, my writings, the stories I told,
Are no longer a part of me,
that's left me so cold,
I wonder what would become of me if I never grew,
That could no longer be my goal.

At least I still think,
That I have changed my personality,
I'm not the same person I used to be,
The things I used to be,
Are no longer a part of me, that's all that's left of me.

Katherine Nolasco, Grade 11
La Serna High School, CA

Every Day

He fascinates me
His smile
His eyes
His smell
The way he walks
The way he talks
How I feel when he hugs me
So comfortable
I never want to let go
The way he kisses my forehead
So sweet and caring
The way he looks at me
Like I'm the only one for him
And I've stolen his heart
What fascinates me the most
Is the way he kisses me
Time stops
I lose my breathe
Butterflies in my stomach
He makes me so happy
He is my fascination
Sienna Edmunson, Grade 12
New Plymouth High School, ID

Cell Phone

One minute I have it the other I don't
The other I don't when it's cold
Or when it's hot
Its loud ring when I'm outside
And vibrate when I'm inside
Texting 24/7 talking nonstop
Right when I get home can't wait
To hear the voices of someone
Hoping to have a full battery
For the rest of the day
Thinking nothing but my cell phone
Why my parents don't
Understand
In class texting my friend trying
Not to be caught by
The teacher it's all I can think
About texting or talking
For hours that's all I
Can think about running the phone bill
Up getting yelled at for it but I don't care
That's why it's called a cell phone
Sheleane Nelson, Grade 10
Lucerne Valley Jr/Sr High School, CA

Fresh Smell of Nature

Light breeze of cool air
A wolf's battle cry breaks the silence
Feeling of truly being free
Brock Cherry, Grade 10
Shelley Sr High School, ID

Lisa, Bright and Dark

She flings from the top.
Her many different faces reflect the things she sees —
the creatures and fiends, the people and their dreams,
colors and flashes, a light show that clashes with everyday life
She stands alone, but she's with a million more
you just can't see…happy pleasant distractions,
She doesn't have to be here (she can say, "bye," in the blink of an eye.)
Lisa is bright today.
The many conversations
she listens and replies to with disturbed fascination
Paranoid fears seeping through her ears, the cause of her many tears
Lisa is dark today.
Light and shadows overtaking her world farther and farther
Too tired to continue, too faithful to let go
a worry that doesn't disappear,
makes her scream (or so she believes)
Someone's calling, calling her name…
"Lisa, Lisa come here and stay — "
(She's away.
Lisa's not here today.)
Gloria G. Escamilla, Grade 11
Schurr High School, CA

What Dost Thou Ask?

What dost thou ask of me?
To see a face which has no name.
And thus the sanctity of fairness in her image has no grace.
Dost thou not say, "To look at the wretchedness that has taken control of thee?"
However, beauty doth radiate,
But unfair to that of the kindness by the heart,
Which instead of feeling results to hate.
In spite of fear temptation takes emotion,
Reaching the depth of the sensation.
Fear strikes within. Dost thou ignore the common sense,
The tempest within reason and feeling?
And thou dost ask of me,
To bend the laws of feeling and trust.
But ask what you will,
For I shall not do thy deed out of lust.
Raeni Pehrson, Grade 11
Merit Academy, UT

Home Depot, Dried Rain

It may be cold, but the smell of hot tamales wraps its spicy arms around me
Hugging me tight safe
Stiff concrete I sit on a slab
And watch.
A lady cooks hot tamales in a cart
Stout. Worn.
A crowd of Latinos gather tired jeans and paint speckles
They grin big smiles fleshy clear eyes
They laugh and eat and I sit…on a slab.
I watch. I want.
One day could I be that free?
Asha Grant, Grade 11
Harbor Teacher Preparatory Academy, CA

Treacherous Conquests

How often men crumble
Into the desolate sea
That is perilous and pale
Yet you still sail,
Valiant and true

Helpless I become
As you tear my walls down
Revealing how bitter and flighty
I can be…

How often it is my love
Heaven collides with hell
My reason is not reasonable
Nor is my faith believable

Yet you still captivate me
Fond of my contradicting mind
Your chivalry outweighs my opposition
To the deliverance of my heart

Alyssa Southworth, Grade 12
Reed High School, NV

The Voice

A voice as gentle as a summer's breeze
Drifting over the clear blue seas
a beautiful girl,
my angel with wings
She makes my head swirl
every time that she sings
I want to hold her and kiss her cheek
a relationship at it's peak
but though you are the one I love
a beautiful angel from above
Our lives are just a tragic play
and the scene is at it's end
a love decaying day by day
Leaving two hearts we cannot mend

Tyler Rowan, Grade 10
Cypress High School, CA

The Feeling

Who am I, no, who are you?
As I open my heart and share my
Feelings with you — as you wonder
Ponder if what I'm saying is true.
Ask yourself, why shouldn't you
Love is only a word I use when it's
True well if I didn't say it to you
I meant to. They say love is in your
Heart and the feeling is only the
Start so I hope when you read
This that you know it came from
A poet's heart

Myoho Winston Jr., Grade 12
Cinnamon Hills School, UT

The Way of Life

I don't want to remember that horrible phone call.
I don't want to remember falling to my knees and hitting slick tile,
crying until I couldn't cry anymore.
I don't want to remember the cold house at which we arrived.
I don't want to remember the sorrow that took over my grandmother's face.
I don't want to remember how my heart, mind, and soul throbbed in pain
when I realized I was never going to see him again.
I don't want to remember the numbing, cold, rainy day
that we all mourned his death.
I don't want to remember the rough earth I clutched in my fist as I threw it
into the bottomless pit as my last tear fell to the ground.
I don't want to remember my last good-bye,
as I blew a wish to the wind knowing he would receive it.
I do want to remember the stories he told as he relived his childhood.
I do want to remember being held in his arms, my cozy security blanket.
I do want to remember sitting on the front porch next to him
in his old rocking chair
listening to what he called musica de la Buena.
I do want to remember that he loved me and I loved him.
But most of all I will always remember you, Don Cheto, my grandpa.

Briseida Aguirre, Grade 12
Westwood High School, AZ

Crevices

When thoughts slink through your fingers and fall into a crack,
taking with them the memories you never will get back.
When you peer into the looking glass and see a stranger's face,
and realize that you, yourself have gone and left this place.
When you find that you're as blue as the weeping willow tree
and recognize that there's someone else that you wish you could be.
When you decide that the secret that keeps you hidden within your mind
has no obtainable cure — no antidote to find.
When you feel the way you feel and no one comprehends,
and you stand alone in a crowded place surrounded by your friends.
When your abilities are tested and you just can't be enough
and you think that you are able but you find that it's too tough.
When you are pushed beyond your limit and tested to the end
and you know that you will break if others make you bend.
When it seems that the tunnel you are wading through
is the only one without the light waiting at the end for you.
When you feel that you're unable to be the you, you are
and the exit from your sorrow is simply just too far.
When you think that life's cruel journey is just too all embracing,
know that you will get through the trial you are facing.

Megan Labrum, Grade 11
Pine View High School, UT

Overcome

We see villains,
Things we fear,
Speak of gremlins,
Things we hear.

We never know,
We never see,
What's always in front,
What's always beneath.

Constantly battling inside,
Constantly failing to rise,
But now we are strong,
And now we belong.

Let us stand,
Feel our strength,
Give your hand,
Hear our thanks,
'Cuz we will overcome!

Rebecca Huizenga, Grade 11
Encore High School for the Performing Arts, CA

Nature

Trees are everywhere and they are so green,
Birds like to fly on them and make their nest,
I love watching this beautiful scene,
Making sure their nests are only the best.
Flowers blooming in the spring and summer,
Lilies and tulips are so fun to pick,
When spring and summer end it is a bummer,
When winter starts there is no ice cream to lick.
Pretty butterflies flying high in the sky,
When they get tired they land on flowers,
When they are rested they fly so high,
Butterflies fly north with the spring showers.
Nature is so amazing to comprehend,
I hope it all survives 'til the end

Meagan Downs, Grade 11
Calvary Chapel Christian School, CA

He Loves Me...He Loves Me Not...

Why couldn't I just have stayed away?
I knew he was older but I'd have to say,
He looked amazing, a tan complexion and six-pack abs,
And I knew he couldn't fit into any high school fads.
He had brown hair and baby blue eyes,
And far outranked any high school guys.
I knew I shouldn't, I couldn't help but stare,
And the next thing I knew we were a pair.
He gave me his football jacket, the one with his name,
And I wore it, for good luck, to every last game.
I thought he loved me but I guess I was wrong,
Because he cheated on me with some cheerleading blonde.

Kimberly Barden, Grade 11
Diamond Ranch Academy, UT

The Passionate Player*

Hey babe wanna come over to my place
there's lots to indulge in, it's a palace!
Plasmas, stereos, cars and money
all could be yours if you'll be my honey.

We'll sit in the Jacuzzi at night
and look down at all the lights;
moonlight strolls along the beach,
beautiful songs to our ears will reach.

You will have the best of the best
no more worries, come hear the rest.
You will be my queen, a crown upon your head,
diamonds everywhere even for the sheets on the bed.

Cute belts with diamonds all around
have all you want let the gifts abound.
Stilettos and all of the finest pumps,
they are cheap to me we'll buy them in clumps.

We'll party all night and have lots of fun,
all you want until daylight may come.
So if you have liked all you've heard,
come to me and you'll be my girl!

Bradley Reeves, Grade 12
Bakersfield Christian High School, CA
*In response to Jessica Cardenas' poem

Heroes of America

It isn't about buildings falling,
And it never should have been.
It isn't about planes crashing,
Or it happening again.

It was
And is
And should always, always be
About the people.

About the people, desperate,
Jumping out of broken windows.
About the people clad in yellow,
Fingers clutching heavy hoses.

About the heroes who died
Saving people who couldn't save themselves.
About the passengers who voted in that fated plane
To fight
That others might survive that day.

These and hundreds more
Are the lives,
Are the people
That make America great.

Aimee Davidson, Grade 11
Burlington High School, WY

Mother

Even though you're gone, I know you're alive.
You would run through the orange groves,
And your feet would beat through the beat of the earth.
Your wind would go through the wind of the earth.
And in that endless abyss of such abstract obscurity
Full of vigor and youth
You understood such ancient verse
So foreign to you now.
A dimension of hollow sounds and empty air.
Empty of people.
Yet you still hear the sounds of that endless fountain
And the rustling of the leaves
And like those leaves, you quietly leave
The world you and I share.
In the field of orange orbs
The wind still carries your wind.
Through those fields of light, in the darkness
Your feet still rule queen of the earth
The air carries your essence.
And in your true sadness
I understood only the corners of such a fragile heart.

Alejandra Rivera, Grade 12
Golden Valley High School, CA

Your Very First Concert

Bass. I can distinguish every sensation.
As I breathe, I smell the sweat and
It makes me notice how the music controls.
Forces that are unrecognizable
Move their bodies in synchronize patterns.

At first the groups are obvious.
Friends are hard to come by
Unless you arrived there with them
In the passenger seat of your Dodge Charger.
After an hour in, the mass is a whole.

The music is what brings you together.
For a few hours, as you crowd the stage
Of your idols, you forget that the world is harsh.
You are safe in a sort of innocence that can
Protect you. It cradles you in its womb.

Sierra Hayes, Grade 11
Merit Academy, UT

The Rabbit I Am

In this meadow of liberty and harmony,
I look for the hobbies of jumping and hopping.
Digging for pleasure is not as easy as it seems,
But once it becomes a routine,
It is just like a dream!

Arlene Ngor, Grade 11
Los Alamitos High School, CA

To a Love Departed

To the last stroke upon a face of porcelain
Smooth, creamy
Etched by the wear of years
By the marks of order and wisdom
Shaping her very identity
Dark hands followed such curves

How I looked to that face for guidance
She would greet my every morning
Sun-kissed or dew-lipped
Sharing in my excitement when the hours were short
Yet the same face sternly reprimanded me for my foolish dawdling
Whenever I approached her midnight gaze

And when she lost that spring in her step
She soon ceased to be, and
All that she was faded.
I cried that day
and I laughed, too
At how a clock can be
Such a lover and a friend

Ivan Pyzow, Grade 11
Los Angeles County High School for the Arts, CA

Lunacy of the Insomniacs

Dry are the bones that the sunshine wards steals,
A mount of creations will become his meals.
Strict customs of breeding devour the soul,
The lavender powder is taking its toll.
Great mystics arrive to see the demise,
Still everything's treated with blasphemous lies.
While natural selection provides destiny,
There's only one answer, it's clear, and I see.
The answer's not sloth, nor greed, nor to please,
Nor disposal of freedom, it's not malady.
It's sinking too deep where the woodcarvings sit,
It's finding the pieces that don't even fit.
It's motives divine, thoughts higher than mine,
Conceiving the vengeance of eight men or nine.
Still everything's treated with blasphemous lies,
Successfully breaking monotonous ties.

Melissa A., Grade 10
Diamond Ranch Academy, UT

Love Is...

Love is...the greatest feeling that spreads throughout
Love is...like a play with a fairy tale ending
Love is...what I feel for you each and every day
Love is...a smile that keeps me running wild
Love is...uncontrollable
Love is...my heart and soul given to you

Tylynn Lewis, Grade 12
Wilson High School, CA

I See You

As I wander the deep paths alone,
Waiting to find a true home,
I stumble upon many new sights:

A river that tumbles down below.
Trees that connect life from above.

Secrets that I could not know.
A life that was hidden from my eyes.

A world so new, one could get lost.
A protector so old, only some knew.

A culture so diverse, only some understand.
A heart so strong, none could conquer.

A peace so deep, one could drown.
A love so true, one could die.

A truth that would not be heard by others.
I see you now.
I see you.

Amanda Hewlett, Grade 11
Grossmont High School, CA

Eternally Yours

Walking alone in this world,
no one is around for me.
I get cut down and walked over,
seeking hope where there is none.
I want to find you, to be loved by you.
Wishing I could be loved again,
searching for your everlasting comfort.
Suddenly bright light envelops me,
making me feel like I belong.
I hear your faceless voice deep inside me,
calling my name.
At last I've found you!
All my troubles are set free.
You've wrapped your love around me.
For this, I am eternally yours.

Delsa Romero, Grade 10
Orem High School, UT

Beyond Dreams

What is beyond dreams?
Who really sees these?
The unnoticeable things seen.
Beyond the broken trees.

What is beyond dreams?
Who knows what's been seen.
Strange things that have never been seen.
What things will I see there?

Alyssa Cox-Allen, Grade 10
Pioneer High School, NV

Imagine

Imagine,
Imagine when you first came into this world,
When you started crawling,
And when your feet first stood on the floor or ground firmly for walking.

Imagine when you first learned how to communicate,
When your brain started developing,
And when you first entered elementary school.

Imagine how you've grown up from your childhood to your present,
When you first realized that the world has two sides; bad and good.
Imagine now that you've accomplished those dreams you've been struggling for,
And how you've come to the destination of your success.

Imagine how sad it would be, when you will leave behind
Those dreams, those accomplishment.
Imagine how tragic it is for you, that you came into this world,
Struggled to accomplishing your dreams
But yet you leave them behind by
Your face being wiped out of this earth like dust.
Imagine that.

Ademola Adeniran Oladimeji Jr., Grade 12
Cristo Rey High School Sacramento, CA

Running Through the Crowd

Shooting bullets, bombing cities, fleeing people.
You hold my hand tight,
as we flee with the crowd.
People push back and forth,
until I can't see you any more.
You told me to not get lost,
but I'm sorry I disappointed you.
I run through the crowd searching for you,
but it was like a wall that separated us forever.
I know that I will never see you again.
I walked into a strange city as I am pushed along with the crowd.
Hungry and thirsty, I wish I could be found.
I hear angels singing and see light coming down from the sky.
Singing so sweetly and so softly, I want to go with them.
Suddenly, someone pulls me away from following the angels to heaven.
And the next day, I call them my new parents.

Ivy Cheng, Grade 10
Abraham Lincoln High School, CA

Love's Warm Embrace

Love is soft as silk, sweet as honey and warm as a summer's sun shining upon my face. Love fills me with a burning fire that rages with such desire to please the person I love. You wish that everyday wouldn't go away but you know you must go and complete the days task wearing a mask to hide what is inside for you don't want to hear people say that there will be a day when one will pass while the other lasts and all you have is the memories of your past…those too will fade away into the mist of time but do not cry! You may ask why and I shall say there will be a day when you will see your love again, like Romeo and Juliet do not fret for death cannot separate true love like two doves together forever in this life and the next.

Billy Sickels, Grade 12
Prospect Continuation High School, CA

Giving Up on Love

I'm giving up on love, because love gave up on me,
People say love makes you happy, but I disagree.
But love makes people blind, so they can't see,
So, I hate it when people say love sets you free.
If love was an object, I would throw it down the drain,
I hate love so much because it caused me so much pain.
Every time I try to love, people treat me like dirt,
And I'm getting sick and tired of being so hurt.
But it's okay to like, and that's cool,
But once you love, you become a fool.
I'm playing chess with love, and I'm in check,
Move out of love's way, before you lose your neck.
Love is spreading everywhere, like a terrible disease,
And it is very dangerous, like angry bumblebees.
Love is always fighting me, and it wins,
Love is also as rough as snake skin.
I can't think with so much love in the air,
I'm supposed to love but I don't care.
I hate love because people hate me,
Love hates me with a guarantee.
I'm giving up on love, because love gave up on me.

Christopher Gaines, Grade 11
Cinnamon Hills School, UT

The Moon Is a Dancer

When stranded at heart in open ocean
all lack of integrity, lost passion.
No turning back; just forward motion,
where love sank in an untimely fashion.
And open and barren, blank stares arise
from stubborn come-up-ance of charity.
True character's shown through a frightful surprise.
Your harsh. broken coat was a parody.

Of fizzing new waves from far out at sea
strolling in from a merry, playful night.
Whisper as stardust glitters quietly.
And when from beauty through the spread of light,
and hourglass-faces age the time past.
"The moon is a dancer," said the ship's mast.

Kayla Simoncini, Grade 10
Chandler Preparatory Academy, AZ

My Cat Mariah

Every day I as I sat in my room
my cat Mariah comes up like a bloom
when I held her In my arms
I cherished her with great charm
when I pet her soft fluffy fur
all I can remember is a soft tingle purr
every morning when I brought out her food
I always knew she was in a great mood
I will never forget that day when she
that day when she left me

Gabriel Carino, Grade 11
Alta Loma High School, CA

Animals of the Holocaust

Countless sheep quietly weep as they are driven off cattle cars,
Wolves gawk and admire their newfound prey,
Sadness fills the atmosphere,
As the flock is broken up.

Their wool is sheared to clothe a tyrannous beast,
Some receive numbers to be tattooed into their hoofs,
Others are given showers of oppression and cruelty,
While a small lamb's flesh is consumed.

The ill and emaciated are thrown into pits,
Where their stench will not linger,
Bleating muffled,
In the screaming abyss.

Fires are lit,
The ashes flutter out,
The air turns bitter,
With the taste of death and doubt.

Straton Roberts, Grade 10
Preston High School, ID

Left Forgotten

Dead to the world, dead to me, dead to all
Rejected, forgotten, never again
You have excluded yourself from us all
I am no longer a pawn to offend
From you, for me. There is no you and me.
Making your promises, never for real
All hope has faded, I cannot be free
You weren't there, don't know my fav'rite meal
Why can't I ignore you, I can't forget!
You are a part of me forever more
You come near me now, life full of regret?
Is this happening? Are you at my door?
Don't lift me higher, then let me fall down
I won't survive if you let me fall now

Jesse Argueta, Grade 12
Blair High School, CA

Moving to Utah

I was six years old,
six years old when I moved to Utah.
I was halfway through first grade,
and had plenty of good friends
where I lived in sunny San Diego,
in Southern California and just north of Mexico.
The warm weather and the sandy beaches were great there.

Then I came to Utah with its cold wind and snow.
I froze to death for the first couple of months,
but then I got used to it and even enjoyed it.
They don't have snowball fights, sledding,
skiing, or snowboarding in San Diego.

Isaac Mata, Grade 10
Orem High School, UT

Contemplations

I like it when
Poetry has a meaning
And not a rhyme.
I like it when
Poetry has a beat
And a song.
I like it when
Poetry unfolds the unfoldable
And shows us
What cannot be shown.
I like it when people write
Simply because
They want to chronicle
Their thoughts and contemplations
Until the words
Drone out
And tend
To
Merge.

Allegra Holland, Grade 10
Lycee Francais La Perouse, CA

Hope

The experience of waiting,
was very long and impatient,
I decided to swim to
the island of Hong Kong.

There, I was to start
a new life,
as a worker,
not a farmer.

Ten years passed...
I learned to live
independently, and longed
for America.

Here I am.
In America, with
a big, happy family
of my own.

Amy Leung, Grade 10
Abraham Lincoln High School, CA

Thank You

No matter what gloom
Or feelings of doom
I have on any particular day

In your company I find
My attitude is refined
And my smile always finding its way

Hawwi Namarra, Grade 11
El Camino Fundamental High School, CA

Behind the Mirror

In other people's eyes they see my world,
With flowers, butterflies and with a lots of hearts
They believe that I'm deeply happy and that I have everything I want
I'm not going to deny that I'm not,
But behind what people see from the physical stuff
Deep inside I'm full of madness but most of all full of sadness
They don't know what I've been through
A group of lions attack me in a place where I should feel safe
I stand in the mirror and look at myself
And I feel like I look great but nobody knows what's behind the mirror
A sad lonely girl who needs love from those who say that they lover her
All she needs is trust in order for her to shine
Motivation, not a huge lecture
Behind the mirror everything is different you can't hide the lions that
Roar at you, every second with any movement you do
Behind a mirror is a cold dark place with no light
Nobody see behind the mirror the true girl
And what she truly feels but for now everyone is going to look just at the mirror
Never behind it.

Gabriela Rodriguez, Grade 11
Animo Leadership Charter High School, CA

The Sea

Mountains of water crash onto the sand
Taking with them every existing object that stands in their way.
Wind whips the ocean into creamy peaks,
Only to disappear and reappear once again.
Sun's rays catch the scarlet fishing boats
That bob up and down like a child's bath toys.
Waves lap on the shoreline,
Quietly humming a lullaby to any being that stops to listen.
Snow white gulls soar effortlessly against a dark sky,
Looking like marshmallows held over charcoals in a fireplace.
Children's squeals of delight resonate over the glassy surface
As they splash around in the shallows.
Stripes of white light float on top of the sea
As tears of joy fall silently down a woman's face as her man kneels on one knee.

Esther Brueckner-Leech, Grade 12
University Preparatory School, CA

Morgan Winslow Young

Born into a world half day and half night,
your rosy complexion
made each bright, beautiful day memorable.
There was no rain in your life.
Carefree and loving, you were like our lemonade stand:
always giving, never receiving.
But while shining your light on the dark suburbs of Virginia,
a cold-hearted man showered a hailstorm of bullets in your direction.
Giving you the night —
but you did not take it.
You knew who you were and where your foundation was built:
built upon the rock of your Redeemer.
He did redeem you, and we know you live on.

Ashley Whitten, Grade 11
Viewmont High School, UT

To Write

To write is to bring alive, bring alive and set forth.
Thoughts of the mind, thoughts to be put in place, to organize, to create.
To write is to create, create worlds, create people, create a movement.
To write is to be free, free from physical handicaps, those who hold us down and that which blocks our way.
To write is neither to go over that impending wall or around it.
To write is to blast a hole right through it and to escape
To write is to escape. Get lost in places never before seen, or imagined.
To write is not only to be free, it is to set free.
Not only thoughts of the mind, and places unseen.
See, to write is to set the minds of others free.
To write is to produce change, to change the world, to change the mindset of others and the way that they see the world.
And all with the push of a pen.
So write, and set forth into the world your thoughts and dreams, all that is within you.
Let them flow from your mind, through your veins straight to your fingertips, and just push that pen to paper.
Pen to paper, there is peace in the sound.
To write is to find peace.
Peace.

Lise Ofagalilo, Grade 12
McKinley High School, HI

Summer

The tickling of the warm wind whispered that it was here.
The scent of tanning oil and charcoaled mounds of meat being coated with condiments gave me shivers.

The butterflies and bees, singing in nature's choir sounds like sweet serenity.
The cooling sensation of mid-melted chocolate ice cream rushing down my throat.

Tire swing rope racking against the trees with the thrill of every temptation to leap.
Summer smells of chlorine and sun screen as people try to hide from the golden rays.

Listening to the laughter of the kids by the water as they try to escape the water's cold reach.
Splashing and cheering coming from the pools as the thrilled teenagers take each other out in a game of chicken.

Warm winds of the mid summer nights let me know that it's finally the hour of fun.
Long lasting tan lines and scolding sunburns are all the results of the season I love…summer!

Friends and family of mine all come together around the bonfires for s'mores.
Summer was here to bring smiles to each glistening face.

Jessica Grove, Grade 11
Glacier High School, MT

My Happy Ending

How was I supposed to know things would end this way? Can I go back and change everything how it was? Please, at least give me one chance. Everything has changed since I moved to L.A., I miss my cousins, my family and friends. Eight years have passed and sometimes I think to myself "would everything be better if I had stayed?" My mom and I were best friends. We still are that hasn't changed, I always saw her smiling and that made me happy. Never saw a tear running down her face, well only when my uncle passed away. She met this guy from L.A., tall, curly hair and with five kids that had his name. I hardly saw my mom, since she met this man. She always worked and she hardly went out, which made me glad she had a new friend. At least that's what I thought, I didn't know what was going on, I was only nine. After that, she told me that she had found her true love. And he wanted us to be part of his life. At first I was surprise, knowing that it wasn't only going to be us two, but also we were going to be living in a big crew. Being the only child is depressing, not having someone to play with, and knowing that I was going to have brothers and sisters it was a very good feeling. When we moved in I thought it was going to be like on TV everyone happy and friendly. But instead it was depressing. I saw and experienced things I didn't know about, like when I saw his kids in drugs and gangs. "What's this?" "is this how a family is supposed to be?"

Erika Juarez, Grade 11
Animo Leadership Charter High School, CA

I Feel Safest When...

A bunch of
caring,
dazzling,
enthusiastic,
faces gather
happily around me
in a justifiable,
kindhearted,
loving manner.

Never to stop looking
over the unlimited
quantity of rainbows
hidden deep within the
still yet tremendous
underwater vessels
which have been waiting for the last
XVII years
zealously to be found.

Tawnya Traywick, Grade 12
Red Mountain High School, AZ

Dance with Me

"Dance with me,"
He whispers in her ear.
She looks up at him in his tux,
Her in a beautiful dress.
His mouth is in a half smile,
His eyes show his sincerity.
She wordlessly takes his hand
And he guides her to the dance floor.
A slow song has just come on,
And they are the youngest at the wedding
At the tender age of 17.
He gently places his hand on her waist
As she wraps hers around his neck.
They begin to sway to the light music,
Never parting stares.
Their eyes lock and the song ends.
He softly kisses her cheek
And silently disappears into the night.
She never even spoke a word.

Hannah Jacobs, Grade 11
San Pedro Sr High School, CA

Old House

Seeping sunshine through the walls.
Curly cobwebs, spider crawls.
Whitewashed wood that's weak with age
Dusty dressers in a cage.
That vapid veteran cowers
Midst grasses and flowers
A lost soul behind its walls.

Arianna Rees, Grade 12
Sky View High School, UT

Forget the Fights

Let us forget the world
For this moment let's just celebrate in our own little world
The day I met you I saw strength and knew from that point you were the one
You were a pure man with a big heart
I hope you heard me that night I asked you to be mine not for today
but forever
One thing is my heart will be pure to you for life
I know I might not have everything well, nothing at all
Except for a good future and you to help me find a good path
Being a woman I am sure to make mistakes and hope you accept that
but to keep you I'll do all it takes
I'm a lover not a fighter
but I will fight for what I love
I might not be perfect
I don't try to be something I'm not, I am me and not fake
So love me for what I am and who I am
let's love every moment we are together
at the end
It will be our strength that will keep us standing while others fall

Alma Ledesma, Grade 11
Animo Leadership Charter High School, CA

The Flower

In my life, this little, empty room
Sitting, staring, in my box, soaking up my gloom
And then one day, you came along and pebbles you would throw
At my window, 'till it broke, awakening my soul
And now, I do not sit and sulk, I do not mope and cry
I sit out on my roof with you and watch the world go by
Some days we'd escape to a daydream by the sea,
And we'd dance together, in the moonlight all alone, just you and me
We dug a little hole there, in that daydream where we'd go
There we planted a tiny seed, gave it love, and watched it grow
Now it is a flower, beautiful, and bright
There are words upon it's petals that shine in the moonlight
And every night we're there together, we smile, sit, and read
Our special flower's message to us
"Love is all you need."

Ivy Durio, Grade 11
Oakmont High School, CA

Leader of My Team

The leader of my team is always there;
Through fiery souls and anguished hearts.
While most drown in the deep sea of emotion,
The leader of my team is steady and sure.
The leader of my team gives orders of exactness
"Push forward! Never look down! Always do your best! Run the out."
The leader of my team encourages us with flying words of redemption, faith and logic.
The Leader of my team requires no more than a victorious season;
But what does he get?
Times of trial, pain, tears and doubt.
But until then
The leader of my team is always there.

Samantha Vehrs, Grade 11
Merit Academy, UT

A Life Is a Dream

A life is a dream…
Many dreams of the dreamer…
So high Up…
For me He dreamed many things
Things yet to be seen.
Sweet 16 supposed to be
Treacherous and brain dead.
Pure ambition can bring
one to so many places.
Perhaps to be a special type of teacher
A patient, helpful, understanding type
For children who are
Considered to be unsuccessful
and have no chance in doing so…
Mayhap life is not told
By careers but by the films that inspire one…
At Least that is the way
It may be for this one

Rachel Hiatt, Grade 11
Valley Christian High School, CA

The Mountain Again

in the valley below I'm looking above
the mountain hides what I love
I will take all the pain and sorrow
for them to be waiting tomorrow
I'm coming to get back what I lost
I'll give up my life if that's the cost
I just want to see them smile again
all my lost people that girl and my friends
here I am climbing the mountain once again
the world left me unbalanced
but I'm not falling off a single step
I am determined I have the will to fight
I'll keep climbing with all my might
'till the peak and I see everybody's all right

David Robbins Jr., Grade 12
Monterey Trail High School, CA

My Mother

My mother once told me
That she was very ill
She didn't know if she would make it
She told me her life story
And that she loved me with all she had
That if she didn't make it my sisters would make good mothers
She would always be with me in spirit
That no matter what happened I should never blame God.
The Chemo made her sick
"I'll fight this and win" she would say
I am starting to feel better
I don't want to go back on Monday
Soon this pain will be over
And it was

Sara Kofoed, Grade 11
Preston High School, ID

Falling Over You

Footsteps, moving forward.
Never know where I'm going.
End up at the same place, the same time.
Thinking of you, and me, but not us.
Sit on the swing and wonder, when I'll branch my wings.
Be loving, sharing, keep on caring.
Yet no matter how many times I sit on that swing,
And ponder, look out to there yonder.
The pain in my heart doesn't leave, doesn't stray.
It doesn't feel better, it won't go away.
No matter how many times I say I don't care,
It's really you that doesn't care.
You don't care about the words you say.
You don't get it when I smile your way.
Footsteps, moving backwards.
Know right where I'm going.
End up at the same place, the same time.
Not thinking of you, but me, never us.

Alex Few, Grade 10
River Springs Charter School - Home School Program, CA

Replay

You're a sea of empty bottles.
Lips stained red, you attempt to drown your sorrows
In your addiction, kiss death on the cheek,
You can't talk your way out of everything.

You've got a problem that you won't face,
And through your ignorance, you've become a disgrace.
But these fleeting highs and lows will fade,
Leaving you lost and trapped in your pain.

In bursts of clarity, reality seeps through,
And your sad, desperate melody plays out of tune.
When you're left alone with no one to blame,
You crawl back to numbness and let it replay.

Alana Bramhall, Grade 12
Red Mountain High School, AZ

Letting Go

When we first met we didn't know a thing
About each other but soon we became more.
We wouldn't admit it but everyone knew,
Because the person I ran to was you.
The long nights we shared would soon be over.
We had no clue that the friendship we had
Would soon be something we wouldn't recognize.
On our face it's erased, but deep down inside
We're screaming to let out the feelings we have.
But you're not the same as you used to be
You've changed so much you're a stranger to me.
The pain you've caused isn't worth to rewrite.
I've held back and second guessed myself
But I know now I can do better.

Kayla Clark, Grade 10
Preston High School, ID

Her Prayer

She walked on death roads,
although she was never alone,
She put up one big fight,
Just to get herself through the night.
She cried and she cried,
For the pain to go away,
She cried begging that happiness would come one day
She prayed and she prayed,
For her sickness to disappear,
She prayed and she asked,
OH GOD ARE YOU THERE!
She sits in her bed, body aching and sore,
She'll close her eyes and say,
GOD I CAN'T TAKE THIS ANYMORE!
As God hears her cry and brings her home,
She stands free and tall and all the hurt and pain is gone.
She looks down from heaven
And looks at the shell she lived in and she yells
I'M FREE FROM THE PAIN, NO MORE CRYING
And happiness is what she gained!!

Korrena McDaniels, Grade 10
Foothill High School, CA

Premonition

I feel a premonition comin' on,
I've locked myself inside my mind,
I've declined on the brink of destruction,
This seclusion is my only sanctuary,
From these haunting nightmares,
I plea for your forgiveness,
Will you wake me from this horror?
I'm too caught up in this madness,
These premonitions taunt me nigh' and day,
I locked myself inside my head,
These voices within my mind,
Whispering words of wickedness,
Ripping and shredding me inside out,
How can I stop these fatuous burdens?

Jillian Airaudi, Grade 10
Hesperia High School, CA

Bloom of Oleander

White petals, floating in the soft hush of wind.
Brushing my face with their silky softness.
I smell the fragrance,
It's heavy and coats my throat.
I close my eyes, a soft smile teasing the corners of my lips.
I let the whispers kiss the soft flesh on my eyes,
Lovingly licking them dry.
The hot air fills my lungs.
I lay in the grass letting my body sink.
Feeling Mother Nature consume my thoughts.
Feeling her warm, loving embrace rocking me to sleep.
Tell me it's going to be okay.

Charlie-Marie Bybee, Grade 12
Merit Academy, UT

My Petal

Standing there looking at the horizon
As the fusion of hues decorate my day
Swaying with the reviving breeze
I start to wake.

I stood there in the middle of the field
Looking around me I saw multiples of my image
Everyone seemed to look like me
But yet I felt very distinct!

My color, my beauty, my pedal and my stem
Each with is own identity,
Though similarities are present
There is no one like me.

I am a flower with its own character
Blossoming for the opportunity to be picked up

I am my only self
And the only one I want to be.

Rita Saikali, Grade 11
Fontana High School, CA

In the Dead of Night

In the dead of night, lost and distraught
But mostly confused, I came across a path
Lying in the middle of a thousand tranquil trees.
A trail of light igniting its way through
Delicate fields of sweet unyielding darkness.
Must I follow this moonlit apparition
Which strikes this precious earth like a wild fire?
Although I am in desperate need of guidance
I let nothing point out the way.
I'll step aside and make my own road.
Whether it leads me to a distant sanctuary
Or a close demise, I jeopardize nothing.
This trail of light will always be.
If others fail, I can always come back.

Ruth Castro, Grade 12
El Dorado High School, CA

What if I Could Fly?

Taking a step into my path
Feeling the wind beneath my wings
Having a breath of the cool air
Making a dive into my future
Falling into the light of time
Catching up with everyone else in life
Going through clouds that I call home
Holding on to faith that keeps me up
Going through gates that leads me somewhere else
Saying goodbye and hello to the ones I know
Knowing the way through the sky
What if I could fly?

Marie Consalvi, Grade 10
Knight High School, CA

Rest in Paradise

My heart starts to pound, my smile turns to a frown,
My ears can't believe this message that it found.
My body is weak, I can hardly speak.
My life breaks down, I lose feeling of my feet.
My mind denies, as if all I heard were lies.
I'm blocking out my mother's cries.
It happened so quick I could hardly think.
My soul rots, begins to sink.
I feel unbearable pain, so much on my mind,
So much I need to say.
I never meant what I said, I never wished you were dead.
I should be the one, take me instead.
One day I'll be on my way in a black casket, carried to my grave.
I hope you're happy and free resting in peace,
Not having to live in this inferno and greed.
If only you knew what I'm saying is true,
Rest in paradise Jefe, every day I miss you.
!Forgive me!

Jose De La Cruz, Grade 10
Crossroads School, CA

Blessed Be Your Name

Heavenly Father,
Blessed be your Name,
In times of hopes or despair
When the world is not always fair
Even when there is in my cheek a tear
Or in my heart a scar of fear…
God of the universe
God of my soul
In you I place my heart filled with holes
Which proves my humanity and hopeless goals
To you I give its full control
Mold me and make me into a humble soul
And may you my fears and sadness console
Blessed be your Name
Not only when I am in a good mood,
But every minute and second include
Blessed be your Name, Light of this world
May the world forever proclaim your love.

Judith Kim, Grade 10
Cypress High School, CA

The Club

We're at the club, we scream, we run,
We sweat, we laugh, were having fun.
The sounds, the lights, the melodies,
They all bring joy inside of me.
For which my mind and feet are set,
To dance the night away.
Across the dance floor, I cannot see,
For which the DJ's fog has blinded me.
I close my eyes and drift away,
For which I've danced the night away.

Kevin Garcia, Grade 11
Merit Academy, UT

I Don't Know Why

I just don't know why
I love you the way that I do.
I tell my heart to let go.
But it says "no can do"
Not a day goes by when you're not on my mind
I want to let go because the more I love you
The more it pains me
Watching you with someone else
Aches me like the cramps I get
Once a month
It subsides then comes back once again
I want to not love you, but my heart says I have to
I've learned to deal with the pain
Even though I feel like there's no gain
They say if you really love someone you will let them go
So that's what I have done
But my heart still says hold on
I love you.

Aijalon Range, Grade 11
Christian Brothers High School, CA

Soothing Slushy Slush on a Sunny Sunday

A slight warm breeze blows gently across my face
As I sit on the old brown bench and look at children play
Taking a sip a of cold soothing slushy slush on a sunny Sunday
Till the day ends and my slushy slush says goodbye

Days went by so slowly as I sat quietly, soundless on my stool
The silent room fills the emptiness of a body soul
Coldness runs down my body like icy cube
Where there's no soothing slushy slush to fill a person's heart

I waited impatiently to find this day
I waited until this very moment
As I sit on the old brown bench and look at children play
Taking a sip a of cold soothing slushy slush on a sunny Sunday
Putting a slight smile as simple as seen
Fill this person's heart with love and joy again

Jennifer Lysaythong, Grade 11
Hiram W Johnson High School, CA

Hawaii Heaven

A beautiful patch of land under the sun
Endless hours of electrifying fun
Cruising with friends in the calm ocean
After a quick stop to local motion
Gorgeous shores
Leaving you begging for more
Amazing people
Strong and great, but we're all ohana
These beautiful islands
Our own little slice of heaven

Dominick Lankford, Grade 11
Mililani High School, HI

Rotation of the Earth

Orbited around all,
from winter, to spring, summer and fall.
In the dark,
she is one of my stars.

She taught me rhythms, and beats,
in the cold, and sun's heat.
She doesn't shine in the daylight,
but I sure do feel her might.

Blood sister I have one,
sisters in the Lord I have tons.
In the tons she is one,
share the same Father, and bond.

Husband and child she must think of,
she and I will have it tough.
I must not think of myself though,
for we both have fields to reap and sow.

My star is still there,
it's the Earth's rotations I must bear.
Noealina Tiaseu, Grade 10
Home School, HI

My Passion

When you have such a passion
You do what it takes
To be the best dancer

And dance with such grace.
The hours of practice
The journey you make

Will teach you life skills
And make you feel great.
This is my love

And I've learned so much
I've overcome such trials
And gained so much trust.
Krystal Richardson, Grade 12
Emery High School, UT

The Cow

The cow is sitting
on a blue roof
He's looking over
the sunny canyons
He's hurtful because
someone ate his smooth
beef shoulder
Now he can't play
his guitar at 7 am
David Carlin, Grade 12
Hillsides Education Center, CA

Love and Nature

A wave crashing is my heart breaking,
When I walk down the beach all I hear is the noise of the waves
Hitting the rocks and them swaying on to the shore.

There is a shell, broken in two.
If you look inside me I can bet you that is what my heart looks like.
When I picked it up, it crumbled to more pieces.

I ask myself if this is over yet.
But the truth is, that it will never end.

The birds above me sing a song that is so beautiful.
That all you want to do is sit there and watch them fly, just like time.

The wind is picking up it blows me away.
It brings back memories of you taking my breath away.

When I turn around to look back at all the good things,
I hear the sound of the crashing waves, the birds that sing so beautifully
And the sun setting behind this gorgeous thing that is called the ocean.
The ocean is an image that reminds me of what our love was.
But all I think of is the good times we had, but all I did was waste my time
And gave you this, such thing that is called love.
Melanie Richards, Grade 11
Del Norte High School, CA

Judgment in My Shoes

Am I an outcast because I'm not pretty?
Am I a doormat because I'm not witty?
Am I a leper because I'm not slim?
Am I worthless because I can't spend money on a whim?
Is it ok to tease me just because I'm not like you?
If you were in my shoes, how would you feel about the things you do?
Would you laugh at the jokes made behind your back?
Would you feel good inside when people make fun of what you lack?
Would you think it's funny when you're the butt of people's pranks?
Would you sit there smiling and tell your tormentors thanks?
Somehow I don't think you'd find your actions cool if you were me.
If you were in my shoes, maybe then you'd start to see.
You're no better than anyone else, because we're all the same inside.
We're all human beings, and we're all equal in God's eyes.
So before you choose to judge me by what I have and how I look,
Remember what God said about judgment in the Good Book.
The standards by which you judge others will apply to you as well.
So think about that when you choose to put me through hell.
Nicole Guerra, Grade 11
Cinnamon Hills School, UT

Lion Walk, Lamb Talk

People roar like lions, and walk like lambs. From the outside, it's just an appealing scam.
As we go, we think that no one would ever know it's all just pretend!
We can fool ourselves, walking weakly like a feeble lamb, but is there ever an end?
It doesn't quite look right, but it doesn't feel like a sin…
In a world full of posers, why can't we fit in?
Lyndsay Tidwell, Grade 11
Viewmont High School, UT

Illusion

Men and Women
They run across the desert parched and exhausted
Some can't wait to be back to home base
Others wonder why they're there
When will the disaster be over?
People are running and screaming for their lives
Men and women are losing their lives
And some people are sitting back wondering what's happening
Up in the distance there was a voluminous cloud of debris
There are people firing from every angle
The people can feel the vibration under their feet
Young children are crying frantically
Nobody knows what's happening
As the people up and down the streets
They're finding their loved ones lying below
Our men and women are ready to fight
Will they ever surrender?
They see men running with camouflaged gear
When will the white flag go up?
This is the story of our men and women fighting in the war, in Iraq
Alicia Albillar, Grade 10
Lucerne Valley Jr/Sr High School, CA

Planted and Grown

I am an old comforting home
With faded blue paint and faded childhood memories
Calmed like a deserted battlefield

I am a shattered soul
Of a broken love
Who is haunted by their feelings

I am the isolated relief
Who planted my roots in the soil of my room
Closed off from the world

I am the independent child
With built up anger
But blossomed and released it peacefully

I am rooted through my home
With my battered roots
But have planted them in isolation
And they flourished to make me.
Josue Buzze, Grade 10
North High School, CA

A Book

A Book is Alive
it NEVER Dies
they say
it Lives on
in our Lives
Sean Burns, Grade 11
Valley Christian High School, CA

Regrets for Breakfast

Awake, and I make my way into the shower,
My hopes and dreams are spread wide across the hour.
I have enough to worry about,
Without the eyes that give me a reason to breathe.
Sent away because the feeling makes me weak.
I've seen everything I've ever wanted to see.

Take a look inside my eyes,
And tell me, can you, can you sympathize?
The waterfalls behind them,
They tell you everything I need to hide.
My plate is filled with regrets
That you served to me so well,
And so now I have my story to tell.

My break and I can't help but break.
A silver platter set up just for you to take.
But I never saw through the perforating lies.
I wasn't trained to see through your disguise.
I didn't even have the courage to ask you why.
Ryan Borg, Grade 11
La Serna High School, CA

To My Best Friend, Aubrey

A is for Always being there for me
U is for her Unconditional love
B is for Being herself
R is for being Real with me
E is for her Energy
Y is for the Yummy food she cooks

L is for her loud exuberant Laugh

S is for her Sweetness
C is because she's Cute
H is for her big Heart
R is for her Randomness
E is for her Excellence
I is I'm Incomplete without her
B says she's my Best friend
E is for her Extraordinary personality
R is for her Radiant smile

All of these reasons are why I love her and why she's my best friend
Elysse Walker, Grade 12
Temple Baptist Academy, NM

Beyond

Beyond...
our world
is there anything?
I want to know!
Beyond
Omar Khdaier, Grade 10
Wilson High School, CA

An Eternal Promise

One day, in marriage your hand I will take.
Another promise to you I will never break.
I'll try to show in all that I do
that with all my heart, I do love you!

I know I mess up now and again,
but it's getting better then it was back then.
and I feel so sorry for all that I've done.
But I know for sure that you are my one.

You are an angel in my life,
and one day soon you'll be my wife!
We'll be happy than and it'll all be okay
I'll have you in my arms every living day.

My heart you've stolen and it's yours to keep,
I know one day with you I will sleep.
But until then my angel,
please stay in my life!

And one day soon, I'll take you as my wife.
One day in God's temple covenants we'll take,
This promise to you I will never break.

Tyler Giddings, Grade 12
Richfield High School, UT

Save Me

I know not who you are
My love is afar
Tell me what to do
When all I see is you

I know what I must do in life
Yet how do I rid myself of this strife
You used to be my angel of which I dreamed
Now I see it was all a scheme

Though I have built my life around you
I know now my queue
So I will take my life and flee
And unresistingly take back my glee

Please don't come back and ruin it all
I'm so far up; I don't want to fall
The base of my life is now strong
I will forever remain gone

Tell me that I've made a mistake
That all of this is fake
Tell me you will take me back
So I can tell you my love, for you, has gone black

Crystal Marsh, Grade 12
Wilson High School, CA

Miss You

Falling asleep under the stars
You're not with me, but I know you're not far
Not far away from me, but I miss you

I take you out to the old tire swing
You gave me your wristband, I gave you my ring
I look at that wristband whenever I miss you

Artificial rose sitting on my shelf
I remember that day, it was like nothing else
Amazing the way you know how to make me miss you

Don't know what makes me miss you
Could be the embers that glow in your eyes
It's a wonderful feeling, and sad at the same time
And how fast, how quick time flies
Until I can see you again
Then I don't have to miss you

It's your smile, It's your walk
It's the way that you talk
When you speak, I could listen
Forever not missing
A thing, but you

Savannah Wilmarth, Grade 10
Mililani High School, HI

Depicted

A blowing of the breeze,
creates a stirring of summer leaves
the bending and bowing of trees,
makes a flurry of feathered wings
the birds that take flight
what a beautiful sight.

An icy blast of wintery air,
encourages a snowy flair
the freezing of the ice,
depicts a picture so nice
the snow flashing by,
reflects the glow of the starry sky.

A warm subtle wind,
brushes across gentle skin
with everything turning green, life is bursting at the seams.

A chilly gust of tempest air,
helps a world not so fair
the sharp turning color of leaves,
a slowing of time it seems.
Going into a resting state,
it must be everything's fate.

Loden Holt, Grade 10
Middleton High School, ID

Life and Death

Have you ever thought about life and death?
You will never known when it could all end
Do not be scared when you take your last breath
In the last minute you will know your true friends

For those who will die in a peaceful sleep
Shall be in a better place to dance and eat
No one will hear them not even a peep
For all those out there enjoy your treats

Think about those people who you care and love
Cherish the moment and tell them how you feel
You know they can't hurt you or push or shove
Trust me it's going to be a great deal

So remember enjoy your life while it lasts
Don't be depressed have fun and have a blast

Robert Franklin, Grade 10
Pioneer High School, NV

Faint Hope

I know not where this path I tread will go.
The leaves do fall on this road I follow.
The Wind blows through the treetops strong and cold,
And yet I walk on this road all alone.

The Sun is setting on the horizon.
His golden colors play across the sky.
I stop to see the birds all flying South.
I know now that wintertime approaches.

The autumn colors have all fallen down.
The trees stand bare and shake in the cold wind.
Slowly, the snow starts falling to the ground.
Wintertime has finally fallen here.

But still I push on through the heavy snow,
Knowing that the spring is soon to follow.

Drew Liu, Grade 10
Diamond Bar High School, CA

On My Mind

The sun rises,
I have you on my mind,
You're so beautiful inside and out,
These feelings that I have for you I can't figure out,
When I see you, you put a smile on my face,
I'm so happy around you, I wouldn't want to be in any other place,
You are the friend I have chosen,
Our friendship will never be broken,
Memories of wonderful times,
I can't forget the time you were mine,
I have you on my mind,
The sun sets.

Alejandro Hernandez, Grade 11
Crossroads School, CA

The Sun Rises, the Moon Falls

The sun rises, the moon falls,
The morning brightens, light shines on walls.
Dew glistens on the cold, stiff grass
Looking ever so still, like it were glass.
And the sun rises, the moon falls.

Darkness escapes back to his stalls,
But outside the vastness, the sunshine calls
To little children who are eager to play;
Ones who laugh, live, and don't stress their lives away.
And the sun rises, the moon falls.

The moon does the sun ever recall?
For when the sun arrives, the moon quickly falls.
The morning sights that are too bright to the eye,
Are maybe too bright for the moon, who chooses to fly
And the sun rises, the moon falls.

June Yoo, Grade 11
Valley Christian High School, CA

Miss Mayeli

If I could spend all of my days with you
I would say things to make you laugh and smile.
The sound of your laughter is joy, it's true
No other time spent could be more worthwhile.

Oh, to see your pretty blue eyes twinkle,
As you listen for the funny punch line.
And the way your nose makes a soft crinkle
Just before you laugh at a joke of mine.

No one would I rather be with but you.
For it seems together we are in sync.
I hope that you wish to be with me too,
Will you sign a marriage contract in ink?

This may be an odd proposal for sure,
But know that my feelings for you are pure.

Eric Bocanegra, Grade 10
St. Francis High School, CA

A Broken Friendship

A Broken Friendship, is hard to forget.
A Broken Friendship, you'll always regret.
A Broken Friendship, first started ever since you left.
A Broken Friendship, explains how you feel about yourself.
A Broken Friendship, sets our problems free.
A Broken Friendship, you know, it'll always be.
A Broken Friendship, reminds you of the good memories we had.
A Broken Friendship, warns us that you took the wrong turn.
A Broken Friendship, how could this be?
A Broken Friendship, will take time to heal your broken heart.
So try to stay away from causing a Broken Friendship.
Because, a Broken Friendship is hard to forget.

Tracy Duclayan, Grade 10
James Campbell High School, HI

The Moon Falls, the Sun Rises

The moon falls, The sun rises
Though the night was black, the sky now glows
The dark goes at last
The hills cast shadows
Ember spills onto me
We remember the healthy heat
The moon falls, the sun rises

Light opens our windows
Brings sight to far off waters
The bird sings, welcoming the bright
Night is gone, shade spreads out
The moon falls, the sun rises

Black stains the blue skies
The sun reigns no more
Doors lock shut
Darkness cuts through the valleys, blanketing the hills
Moonlight fills the air
Soon bright the clouds crawl away
The sun falls, The moon rises

Caydon LiRocchi, Grade 11
Valley Christian High School, CA

Watch Me Fall

You watched me fall so many times
But you.
Never helped me back to my feet
I was young and you never let me
Forget that.
I wanted you to see but your eyes were closed
I learned to
Forget you.
I walked alone because I hated needing
But the day I realize I'm happy being
Just me.
A sudden sadness fills me
I don't want to grow up
Because.
The stage I dance on is empty.
Once upon a time you held my hand
Promised together we'd
Conquer the world.
But now all I have are the clay dinosaurs that line my window
And the unfinished thought — that once upon a time
My Dad and me…

Jessica Lin, Grade 10
The Harker School - Upper Campus, CA

Elegy for My Sock

Not too long ago, you were my foot's companion.
You were always on the left and your twin on the
right; and I secretly liked you more than righty,
because you kept my toes just a little bit warmer.
Oh, and who could forget about your material?
Just the right blend of cotton and polyester. And
your simple, yet elegant design. Turquoise, indigo,
and purple stripes; such a beautiful montage of colors.
I want to weep when I remember the wonderful
relationship you had with my knee. Never once
did you slide down to my ankle. Even when I
was running, you stayed true to your name, and you
were my trusty Knee-High Sock.
Some days, I spend the whole night in nostalgia, just
thinking about how warm you kept me. You somehow
managed the great feat of making me look stylish and
keeping me from getting frostbite, at the same time!
Oh dear sock, how I loved you! Until that faithful day
when *holding back tears* I lost you. Losing you was
like losing a sole mate. Righty was no good without you,
my darling lefty. How I misseth thee so…

Neyat Yohannes, Grade 11
Lawndale High School, CA

Missing the Bristles

Summer to fall, what a transition
Green leaves turn color and fall to the ground
I've made my transition
Not a young green leaf anymore
I've changed color, and I'm not supported
By the sturdy tree of childhood
I've fallen to the ground of reality
I hit hard and it hurt…only for a little while
I watch the others get raked up
By the harsh bristles, the obstacles of life.
They are being gathered up, and bagged
Positioned into their place in society
Suffocating in the tight space, crammed in a brown paper bag
Getting crushed and recycled again and again.
I've missed the bristles so far
And I watch the ones I love get raked up. One by one
I don't know if I will miss them all together…but I plan to
I want to make an impact that will be studied later on
Like a fossilized leaf.
The one who missed the rake
And made an imprint in the rock.

Reese Schroeder, Grade 12
New Plymouth High School, ID

Red

The fires reach to heaven
But all I see is ash
As the light of every good man
Is lost within the past

Mark Stone, Grade 12
Viewmont High School, UT

Masquerade

Hides the imperfections
Even a small crack of exposition
Of sinful contradiction
Shatters the identity completely

Jasmine D'Souza, Grade 12
North Hills Christian School, CA

Swim

Gliding through the water…
it feels so smooth.
As you pick up speed
it's as if she is pushing you.
Although your heart is racing
it is all so relaxing…
the repetition
the movement
the breathing.
You keep on following
that endless black line
it seems so natural,
you do it all the time.
Even though
in reality your going slow
it feels as if you're flying…
gliding…
didn't you know?
She's helping you
defy gravity.

Jessica Bish, Grade 10
Cypress High School, CA

Diversity Is Beauty

Lives of monotony are not well lived.
Accept all ways of life and love all shapes,
Many gods, colors, and dances to give.

Vigor is in an assortment of lives,
Elegance is in a medley of faiths.
Lives of monotony are not well lived.

God, Buddha, Mami Wata all forgive,
The Waltz, Tinikling, Banda all relate.
Many gods, colors, and dances to give.

All the prejudices we must outlive,
The myopic views of people misshape;
Lives of monotony are not well lived.

Elegant lives we cannot strongly live,
Until we recognize every landscape.
Lives of monotony are not well lived.
Many gods, colors, and dances to give.

Erica Starr Parrish, Grade 10
Chandler Preparatory Academy, AZ

Where I Live

The ocean is quiet
I can think clearly today
This is where I live.

Maricruz Jauregui, Grade 12
Lucerne Valley Jr/Sr High School, CA

The Burden's Load

I felt the burden's load. I carried it on my back.
Each step I took, another rock was placed inside the pack.
I don't know how much more I can endure.
Boulder, by boulder, my shoulders sag.
My heart is pounding. My legs are aching.
The sweat rolls down my face.
Sweat and tears mix and mix, and fall upon my lips.
The taste of salt makes my thirst unbearable.
Left, right, left, right, left, right, just one more step…
One foot in front of the other… "So close…" "Keep walking…" "Almost there…"
I fix my gaze upon something in the distance.
I may be weak, I may be weary, but I trudge along.
Through the muck and mud; dust and rain, I almost let go of the pain.

I cheer and yell, and suddenly, my pack is lighter — it feels almost heavenly.
The burns and bruises, and calloused hands, seem to vanish like footprints in the sand.
All the grief and pain I suffered, only teaches me to muster.
Muster every might I can, and realizing I am only one man.
I cannot make the journey alone; I cannot make the journey alone.
The pack is too heavy, the mountain too steep, the river too deep.

If only, if only, I would have known then. He truly is my only friend.
My Brother, my Savior, there is no end. He is eternal. He's my best friend.

Elizabeth Hiller, Grade 11
Viewmont High School, UT

March 8th 2010

It's March 8th Twenty-Ten,
I'm sitting in class with a paper and pen.

Feelin' sick, feelin' blue,
All I wanna do is be with you.

You're my medicine when I'm feelin' down,
Always turning my frown, upside down.

All day I've been thinking about you,
Can't get you out my head, I'm missin' you!

Family and friends I don't want to see,
Just that girl, that I'd want to be (with).

My love for you is unbelievable, it's more than how a fat kid loves cake,
Starting at the beginning was never a mistake.

Seein' you is heaven, missin' you is hell,
I still can't believe I fell.

Falling for you is one of the best things that happened to me,
I can't deny it, we were meant be.

Clifford Pagala, Grade 12
Mililani High School, HI

It's Okay to Stare

You'd think I wouldn't stare,
I just can't get myself to care.
The way your hair rolls and your eyes shine,
But it feels like I'm so out of line.

You walk past laughing with your friend,
And I didn't want this moment to end.
I caught your eye and held the glare,
For you, I would fight a grizzly bear.

Seems like such a long time ago,
Back in those days when I had a 'fro.
Oh, how we've matured and grown,
Now it's 3 kids and a place to our own.

You'd think I wouldn't stare,
But to this very day, I don't care.
I love you and no other,
And to that, I could swear.

Leander Loh, Grade 10
Cypress High School, CA

Social Pier

If only society sank at pier,
Selfish sailors bound by formality.
Dark crews are cliffs, slashing, slicing, sans tears.
Still, silent, submerged, sandbars at ships leer,
Neptune sneers at bailers' futility,
If only society sank at pier.
Darting eyes, ears waiting for footsteps near,
Ferrying souls, unknown identity,
Dark crews are cliffs slashing, slicing, sans tears.
Red rusty rivets, disparate dreams, fears,
Forge whole hulls of embrittled unity.
If only society sank at pier.
Grinding groaning gears, at fast covered ears,
Screech, squeal, scream of absent utility,
Dark crews are cliffs slashing, slicing, sans tears.
Fog! fog! No port in sight, no lifeboats here
We sink, swim, slosh in social maladies.
If only society sank at pier;
Dark crews are cliffs, slashing, slicing, sans tears.

Jonathan Hui, Grade 10
Chandler Preparatory Academy, AZ

Life

Life is a twister
It goes round and round
It leads to smiles
It leads to frowns
Never be mad
Never be sad
Cause life's too short
To be like that

Zachary Khan, Grade 11
Wilson High School, CA

Power

The word that hungers the world
Power
It makes the wealthy rich
Makes the celebrities icons
It is what everyone is craving for
The lowly cubicle workers
The starving, sick, and poor
These will never know power
Power is for people who have money
Some abuse this power in every possible way
Some, however, do not.
The philanthropists and the
Charities
There is so much hope for those
Without this word
You don't have to have power
To be successful in the world.
But just about everyone
Would disagree…

Lauren Kemmer, Grade 11
Desert Vista High School, AZ

Seasons of Love

Like a light summer breeze whistling a sweet tune,
Like rays of sunshine brightening the day,
Like the freedom and levity of a Monarch butterfly,
Like a sandy beach offering fun and games.

Like the leaves of autumn whispering witty words,
Like the brilliance of fall foliage,
Like Saraswati sharing her knowledge of life,
Like the harvesting of nature's ripe resources.

Like the ominous warning of a winter thundercloud,
Like deceptively majestic glaciers hosting warfare,
Like a frozen lake concealing the deepest truths,
Like the inexplicable individualism of a snowflake.

Like the scent of freshly cut grass in springtime,
Like a bubbly waterfall cascading off the rocks,
Like a gorgeous azalea opening its heart,
Like raindrops on windows writing letters of love.

Erika Johnson, Grade 10
Homestead High School, CA

Pie

Pie tins clink and clatter
Metal spoons tap, tap, tap,
Beat the pudding mix together
Cream, creamy, creamier
Pour the mix into the shell
Refrigerate for 3 hours
Yummy, yummy, yummy,
In my tummy.

Erica Clopton, Grade 10
Mohave High School, AZ

Love

Heart wrenching as this may be,
There's no other way to express how it feels
Other than to show you so you can see.
There's been songs about it, movies about it, so much that deals with it,
It's truly sickening because…well…it's not like that at all.
No matter how romantic and heartbreaking it was as portrayed in *The Notebook* or *Dear John*,
For whatever reason, I feel like I have to run,
Run as far away from it as possible, because…well…I'm scared of it.
My heart was broken once before; it wasn't very swell.
I've only been in one relationship, and now…I want to run away from it.
Because…well…I crave for it.
It's something so indescribable, so wanting…
That even though I'm scared of it, I want it.
That's why I run away from it…because…well…
Running away from it is one step closer to bumping into the one,
The one who will love you forever and always. Because…well…
All we need is love.

Maxine Baker, Grade 11
Marysville High School, CA

Blossoming Chaos

Tears, Joy, Devastation, and Perseverance is what has become of our world now.
Parched throats unable to grasp the bit of juice that comes from the fruit you admire so dearly.

You say you hear the blood scream and the anger ooze out of your own heart.
Did you ever take the Time to wonder why Anger seems to be the answer to everything we breathe?

You are too oblivious to notice the truth.
Like a glass of wine sitting on the table, you do not know how you got where you stand;
Supposedly from a place of a more peaceful nature.

Boom! There is the gunshot blown by the soldier. Boom! There is the gunshot created by the enemy.
Chaos flies like an angel up in heaven.

Like yesterday and tomorrow,
A bit of juice comes from the Unique and Naive flower
Over there blooming with grace,
Unaware of the negative environment it will soon be a part of, once discovered.

Alyssa Reaves, Grade 12
Wildwood School - Secondary Campus, CA

Depth

Depth is radiance.
It is insight that no one can possibly eradicate
And the light in depth's eyes is a dazzling sun that utterly astounds spectators,
Each intensifying illumination in sync with a triumph.
With every breath depth takes, the more impenetrable its skin bolsters from failure
And for each utterance that passes its lips, the flaming ardor of self confidence is amplified ten notches.
It was once feeble but the delicate structure of feelings is now something of the past
For the present engages immense joy insurmountable by the dark hallway of previous time.
All that depth's mind can envision is resilience, complete immunity to any hurt.
The vision is a ceaseless increase of depth
Because forevermore, depth is present
And depth is radiance.

Ann Tran, Grade 10
Henry Sr High School, CA

Tonight

Tonight I realized something,
As I stood at the bottom stair of my porch,
With a boy, the love of my life.
I begged him to stay with me, to stand with me,
As long as we could,
And as he said "I can't," and walked away,
I could hardly bear to watch him go.
He told me, "Go inside, stay warm,"
I felt warmth as I was near him.
My heart beats for him.
To feel his warmth, against me in a hug.
His lips softly pressed to mine.
You are in love, my heart whispers.
It beats only to the rhythm of our love.
I begged him to stay, hugging me. Forever.
"Please!" I begged.
But he must leave.
I dream of being close to him, but reality is ever afar.
So, I wait.
Impatiently, I wait.
Tonight, I wait.

Taylor Graves, Grade 11
Silver High School, NM

My Brother

My brother never had anyone to look up to that thought positive.
He only had my cousin.
My cousin was a kind of person you'll see in the streets.
He dressed the same way as my cousin.
He thought the same way,
Even did the same things as my cousin did.
He was always doing negative things.
He didn't have any feelings toward the things he was doing.
My brother was lost in the power of satan.
He was trapped and was trying to find a way out.
His next step was possibly in prison,
Till he finally found a way out.
He was enrolled in a confirmation class.
He started following the path of Jesus.
He's now twenty years old and trying to get his G.E.D.

Andrew Negrete, Grade 11
Animo Leadership Charter High School, CA

Spring

The flowers flow in the wind
The trees leaves are wild
The animals are lively
Everywhere life becomes a ball of energy
The harsh weather of winter is over
A new season has begun
Spring is the season of life
The plants bloom and baby animals are born
The cycle of life never changes
For spring with always be the beginning

Madeline Fuchs, Grade 10
Cypress High School, CA

A Disregard of Sanity

Were the days growing darker?
Were the nights getting smaller?
Was my mind...ever so restless it was
Falling hopelessly into madness?
Into the deep ditch of despair.
The finely tuned strings
Snapping away with every breath.
The dark clouds looming eerily closer,
Closer to the scattered bits of mental stability
Somehow miraculously left.
An infinity of crazed subconscious
Surrendering all hope of repair
Following the path promised never to take.
Dreams flaked in tinsel
Nightmares filled with ducks
Fireworks, forever igniting.
And the days growing darker
And the nights getting smaller
And my mind...ever so complete it was
Dancing merrily into madness.

Kristy Boden, Grade 11
Grossmont High School, CA

God's Nature

The nature of the earth shows God's great might
Sunrise and sunset respond to His call
His strong voice created thunder and light.
He painted the seasons like spring and fall.
His voice shook the earth when He created
The mountains and valleys that fill these lands.
His wond'rous creations He never hated.
He holds the whole world in His able hands.
The heavens declare the glory of God;
The skies tremble when He calls a command.
And in His hands He holds a mighty rod,
Capable of ruling from sea to sand.
Thanks to God's profound imagination
The outside world is full of inspiration.

Melissa Chesney, Grade 10
Calvary Murrieta Christian School, CA

Seed

Is a seed as small as it seems?
It is true, but in certain conditions, it gleams!
Hope, nutrients, and proper care,
Are the elements of growth for great results
Sprouting, growing, climbing!
It isn't so small anymore
Like the power of an atom,
At first glance it might not look like much
But you should see the power of such!
Are we not all seeds?
Who, when provided with such needs can grow like reeds?
Life proceeds!

Colton Beck, Grade 11
Viewmont High School, UT

The Doors Open, the Doors Close

The doors open, the doors close
The sun sets, night falls
In the study simple and plain
The student works for future gain
And the doors open, the doors close

Subjects flash through his mind
But past grades call from behind
These little grades, with their ups and downs
Determine his future to be found
And the doors open, the doors close

What's done is done, the past is set
Moving forward the student progresses
Learning and striving for new successes
Adapting and changing to many different chances
And the doors open, the doors close

Ross Martinez, Grade 11
Valley Christian High School, CA

The Hunt

The air was brisk,
The night was cold.
To go out was a risk
To any one old.

But to one creature,
Whose passion was to fly,
You can say for sure
He loved to soar high.

He soared through the clouds
As he searched for his prey.
He spotted the sheep, huddled in crowds.
He quietly descended at the break of day.

And as the dragon swept one up, with his mighty claw,
He licked his chops, the catch was without flaw.

Brian Bloxson, Grade 12
Lucerne Valley Jr/Sr High School, CA

She Is the One

Dying within trying to get rid of this lingering sin,
hurting so bad I don't even know where to begin.
I try to deal with the pain running through my every vein
but in my mind I know that I am slain.
A slave to my heart I will always be,
so full of love I can hardly see, will I ever be free?
but then she looks at me with a soft set look,
my heart she so easily took.
Finally I can see, but there's only one thing in front of me.
It is her, she set me free, my sin finally let me be.
My heart lets up I have finally won,
all because of her, I know she is the one.

Cody Schmidt, Grade 12
Libby High School, MT

this is not about what you think, trust me

i wanted to send you back through the looking glass.
maybe you would come out different.

you were just a phase, one that is always
in the pathology of people like me.

but i wish you weren't

i always had a feeling
you wouldn't be around,
for me or anyone else,
but i hoped i was wrong

i bet even you knew it too

but we kept it hidden, and only with the long
pauses in conversation did we realize it again
but it only made us want to continue talking,
the fact that we wouldn't anymore kept us going

so here we are, well, here you are.
meeting each other again
for probably not the last time.
and once again I am standing
in front of a mirror wondering "what if?"

and i wish i wasn't

Chesalie Loach, Grade 11
Grossmont High School, CA

Swimmer

The race of a swimmer.
The time is up.
It's time to start.
Time to get up on the block.
My body is tense.
I'm ready to start.

I hear the whistle to tell me to get ready.
I'm on the block to prove my worth.
My training is now put to the test.
To see where I stand, against my foes.

The whistle sounds the time to start.
The starting sound is heard; and the race begins.

We're in the water.
It's cold against my skin.
I kick to the surface, with speed to win this race.
My body moves by its own accord.
The movement is swift and sure.
The race is done.
I won the race!
I congratulate the others, and I get ready for my next race.

Jessica M. Oviatt, Grade 10
Orem High School, UT

Cold Winter Day
It is cold
It is quiet
We hold
Then dare try it
A dash outside
We dare not try
Yet birds dare to fly
We must go outside
We pray to the sky
To warm the cold tide
We become sly
A jacket as out the door we slide
A moment outside and we fly
Back in the door
Not so sly.
Delfin Acosta, Grade 10
St Francis High School, CA

L.A. County
Lonely, clear nights
Lights and stars
Sleeping on sidewalk benches

Wondering, thinking
One sigh, one hum
Sangabriel Street, rolling buildings

Dark flickering lights
Over and over
Wondering glittering stars

In darkness and thinking
Buildings rusty with dirt
Lights over night
Alvares Robles, Grade 12
Redwood High School, CA

My Escape
Sad heart please disguise
for I cannot hide
how I feel inside
Tears behind my eyes
my sad hearts capsized
Shipwrecked by the tide.
My thoughts start to slide
into a sunrise
it's there I escape
Like a bird in flight
There I feel the shape
of ships in the night
on a lost landscape
far away from sight
Bequin Everett, Grade 10
Shelley Sr High School, ID

Dreaming
Long night,
Going to sleep.

Starting to dream,
Can't wake up.

Something's wrong,
Having a nightmare.

Can't run,
Can't hide.

I wake up,
Look at the clock.

2:00 AM,
Fall back asleep.

Dream again…
Humberto Rodriguez, Grade 10
Wilson High School, CA

A Day of Darkness
I walked through the door,
to see my house has been raided.
Everything goes black as I fall to the floor,
my sight has faded.

As I wake I see a crowd around me.
Guns, screams, hands tied behind my back.
I get up, and try to flee.
Bang! Bang! Bang!

And suddenly I'm dreaming,
I blame the end of my life on fate.
"We are protectors for him," they're saying
I see my grieving family, "You're too late."
Cindy Lui, Grade 10
Abraham Lincoln High School, CA

Love
Love
Love is strong
Love lives within the heart
The bad side about this love
Is that it can get broken
Smashed, shattered, and hurt
Love is a game
Don't give it to everyone
Be careful who you love
Love comes at unexpected times
So be careful
Because this is how love is
Love
Amanda Lafferty, Grade 12
North Hills Christian School, CA

Optimistic Optometry
Some might say
Life is gray
Like the sky on a cloudy day

Problems will come and go
Making life a daily foe
Do not concentrate on lows
And character will soon show

Even in the darkest room
Where a cloud looms
Sunlight follows soon

Daily put on your armor
To fight its toxic power
And capture a grayless autobiography
With your optimistic optometry.
Megan McKinley, Grade 11
Valley Christian High School, CA

I'll Be Back Soon
Just point me where I need to go
And I'll be on my way
Don't tell me what you know
I'm going adventuring today!

An epic journey it will be
I'll give the world hope
I'll climb tall mountains and trees
And you can't come unless ya got rope.

I'll chase the bad guys
While you run home
Even though that is unwise
You'll leave me free to roam!

Now I see your face is angry and red
Okay, Mom, I'll go to bed.
Cory Christensen, Grade 12
Layton High School, UT

Not Quite Done
I'm not quite finished with my life,
I'm not sure when I'll be done,
But for respect I strive,
When I lay down,
To my family I'll be number one,
I can see myself in the future,
With a good job,
I want everybody to see me,
I see myself with a big house,
Family and dog,
That's just how I see it will be.
James Avampato, Grade 10
Rite of Passage Charter High School, NV

A Farmer's Golden Dream

Burning in the red hot sun.
Sweating my butt off.
Blending and kneeing,
planting and cropping,
selling and trading.
Working from day to night,
night to day,
just to live a better life.
No time to rest,
and still have to fight.
Wishing and dreaming,
hoping it will come true.
A journey to San Francisco,
which became true.
Seeing the golden sun
rising upon the Pacific Ocean.
The day I will never forget,
the day I came to the Golden City.

Joyce Liu, Grade 12
Abraham Lincoln High School, CA

Hidden Appreciation

It's this one thing
I'm trying to tell you

You, who carries
Happiness, help, and hope,

Are an angel always
Watching over me.

Nightmares disappear, and
Never come back again.

Whenever I knock, "creak — "
The knob tilts its head with kindness.

It's this one thing
I'm trying to tell YOU
THANK YOU.

Youna Ro, Grade 10
Cypress High School, CA

Relax

There I was,
sitting on the warm sand.
The fresh cool water
tickling my toes.
The sun shining down,
warming my face.
The waves rolling on the horizon,
the white caps full of power.
My mind at ease,
as was the world around me.

Janalee Willmore, Grade 10
Orem High School, UT

Memoirs of Troubled China

My father had a heart of gold.
His heart was strong when he passed the Pacific cold.
In America he worked so bold,
in China his fortune increased by many fold.
Came back and sent brothers and I to urban education,
knowledge rained on us like precipitation.
Poverty left our family like an amputation,
then war hit China, with no resolution.

The Red Sun bombers came and proceeded bombing.
We saw many corpses, no longer alarming.
Bombing took my father traveling in Singapore, it was heart-shattering.
After the war, wasn't much comforting.
Then came the Communist Mao days.
Where we had to change our ways.
We had to share our father's American pays.
Or risk being shot in the face.

We shared our fortune with others.
I'd rather work in the gutters.
And went to America with my brothers.
When did my father's hard work profit another?

Ryman Ruan, Grade 10
Abraham Lincoln High School, CA

Chloe Shorts

Hey! I'm down here! Yeah, that's right.
In the course of my last year I tried not to think of my blight,
For now even in death I'm still the smallest one around.
I recall this guy named Seth who on my love frowned.
So I was off to prove my love, and he said I had better start to grow
Before I released the turtle dove. And still all I wanted was a beau!

Everything I tried failed from pills, to food, to a crazy doctor
And it wasn't until I saw a man behind me trailed who called to me and said,
"I could be your proctor."
He then pulled out of his bag a pair of stilts.
"These will be sure to win his love."
"I don't know," I said, "It looks like that one tilts."
But he convinced me that they were great for Red Rover,
And with that one blunder,
I went from six feet over,
To six feet under.

Caitlyn Costley, Grade 11
Viewmont High School, UT

As Things Go By

As the days go by quickly, the nights go by slowly.
At times I feel so lonely, and then I think of my family.
They look at me no differently;
I just wish I could start over as an infant.
But all you can do is fix it yourself.
Don't sit there and dwell on the past
Just get your life on track so in the future you can look back and laugh.

Chase Krumme, Grade 12
Rite of Passage Charter High School, NV

Surrender

The suffering face of a depleted, defeated girl reached across to me, precariously. Needing, pleading, not for help, she was beyond that. She needed an explanation. Confrontation. Anything to subdue this confusion. Illusion of care and love. That someone could be there. A frown was plastered to her face. Misery gave her no space. It grew on her like a vine. Entwined in her heart, tearing her apart. Her gaunt face was stretched and hollow. The truth of her lies were too big to swallow. A prelude to her downfall. Black mascara tears fell like a waterfall. She needed, pleaded for someone, anyone, to step forward and catch her in their arms. Protect her from harm. No one did. She met my eyes with defeat. Her face depleted, defeated. I saw now that she was just a child. No more than 17 years of age. Children need to be protected. Who was protecting her from herself? One page of paper cannot describe the agony in her eyes, it was so scarring to me. I reached out, drew back, suddenly afraid. Afraid of the truth. Of the promises I made. Now lying scattered, broken. As if they never mattered. As if they were never spoken. She hoped I could not read the depth of sorrow on her face. To recognize there was no space from it. That it was true. Immutable. I didn't know what to do. Breath caught. Couldn't breathe. Couldn't leave. After a long, incurable moment, she took a step, torpid and heavy. Slow and unsteady. And I wasn't quite ready to face this quite yet. I watched. Saying nothing at all. What good would it be? I watched her fall. She opened her mouth, but her eyes implored what her mouth could not. Her eyes, the color of agony, burned right through me. And weightless as she was, she was too heavy for her unsteady legs to carry. The ache in her heart was too heavy to bury like she did all else. She shook, trying to lift her body. She fell once more. Stared at the floor. Sightless. The girl lived no more. She was dead, but still dying. Still crying inside. Still trying to make the pain escape. I make myself look away from the mirror. Can't stay here. Shaken and taken aback from the image of myself. A tear falls, silent and heavy. I can't look any longer. I'm not ready. Not steady. If only I was stronger. I wouldn't have let myself die. Would have tried harder to live. To give up my addictions. Conflictions. I was suffocated by a lack of love. By the absence of home. Left hated and alone. My heart not intact. I walked away without looking back.

Natalie L., Grade 11
Diamond Ranch Academy, UT

My Son

He is the light of my life,
My diamond in the dirt.
My angel sent from God.
The only one I love.
Since the day he was born, I couldn't let go.
never can be away for more than one moment.
Because when I'm not with him I feel so alone. No one can bring a smile to my face the way he does. It pains my heart when he cries, I never want him to go through, any hurt or confusion. Want to protect him from all harm and evil. So I pray every night to God above. To keep angels protecting my son. Keep him safe in your arms. Show him the way to live right. No one will ever understand the way I love him. Don't understand how people just don't pay attention to them. Neglect and hurt putting their needs first. It's only about him if he is happy then count me in. I would do anything in the world for my son. Since the day he was born I knew God was real. When you see something that precious it can only be a miracle. Don't ever put yourself first. Because when you hold him in your arms. There's no more just you it's all about him. His kiss will take my breath away. His love for me warms my heart, He will never know how much I love him. No matter what happens all I know is God will protect him.

RaeAnn LaPoint, Grade 12
Prospect Continuation High School, CA

Capturing the Moment

In the photograph you will find A day that will always be on my mind
There is a bride and groom that did unite In marriage under the sun so bright
My mom had the camera in hand to capture the moment that was anything but bland
The wedding was full of looks of love exchanged between the couple mentioned above
They said their vows in front of those there as a breeze blew tried to move any loose piece of hair
The exchanged hugs and congratulations from family and friends It seemed that there would see now ends
The year was two thousand and six in the hottest month of the year the though of melting was a great fear
The place was the city of sin yes, it was Las Vegas, Nevada we were in
The picture was taken to remember
The family I just met I had no idea that is all that I would get
I wanted to get to know each one before that memorable day was done
The day was filled with experiences had by all my senses

Nicole Fried, Grade 10
Shelley Sr High School, ID

I Am

My name is Katherine
I am a daughter, a sister, a granddaughter
A niece, a cousin, a friend
A teenager, a student, and a learner,
I am confident and scared, terrified but excited
I am loving and caring, thoughtful, and hopeful
I am careful but careless, broken yet whole
I am misunderstood, misguided, and mislead
I have many goals in my life, I am hard-working and determined
I am a tiny speck of dust in this world, I am a piece of art
I am selfish, but I am also the most giving person you will ever meet
I am a believer of God
I wish on stars, and dream on dreams
I pray to God, and I cry my tears
I smile on the outside, but I am dying on the inside
I listen to others who don't listen to me
I walk on eggshells as well as fire
I believe in passion, but not fairy tales
I am not perfect
That's me in a nutshell
My name is Katherine

Katherine St.Clair, Grade 12
Sierra Charter School, CA

Did You Know?

Did you know?
The one who lost her heart
It still beats inside her chest
But it turned cold with time
And now no warmth flows through her body.
Did you know?
Her eyes have turned bitter, yes
She stares with a cat like glare
Her soft hands have gnarled into a hook
And she stares out from her window alone and cold
Did you know?
Dust flows inside her home
she doesn't open the window in fear of light
For it will certainly ruin her to face the harsh chatter again
All alone and cold
Did you know?

Esther Chun, Grade 12
Cerritos High School, CA

Fall

Turkeys, pumpkins, the crackle and crunch of dancing leaves.
Yellow, red, orange, and brown swirl in the frosty air.
Jumping in piles of just-raked leaves.
Hoarding Halloween candy.
Snowfall spells the end
Of autumn and start of another winter.

Lauren Atchley, Grade 11
Laser Alternative School, MT

Inspiration

The days that I can't see you,
Are just the start of my troubles.
You've inspired my happiness in dazzling ways,
And continue to do so.
You make sure that a frown may never consume me.

Your eyes shift color to the mood of my emotions,
Like a mood ring, as if you understand how I'm feeling;
Just at that very moment.

You bring me the light in the darkest of times,
When I'm trapped in what seems like an endless black.
A black that keeps you in and never lets you go.
You free me from the dark.

You hold my obsessions and share them only with yourself,
No one else should ever know.
I know I can trust you,
As you know you can trust me.

I've found my interlocked place in your arms;
Never let go, never let me fall,
And I shall do the same for you.

Jesse Davis, Grade 11
Tenaja Canyon Academy, CA

Mirror

The world is obsessed with mirrors
You mirror me I mirror you
We constantly look into them
And this is what we see:
I'm fat I'm ugly I'm too short, too tall
What has the world come to?

Mirrors only show our flaws
Because that is all we want to see
So we use the mirrors
To hide those flaws only creating more
We step out of the house with fake confidence
Thinking we're showing a new person
But in reality all we've done
Is show the world who we are not

Have you ever stopped and thought
What if the mirror is controlling me?
Showing me what it wants to see
Making it so I change myself to become who I am not
The mirror will shatter letting him escape
Taking over my life so he is me
And I'm trapped forever inside the mirror

Alexa Nelson, Grade 11
Viewmont High School, UT

The Journey of Fate

The journey of fate was a long one,
the journey of my life in the long run.
I traveled to the vast land of being free,
to experience the feeling of being free,
And I have seen what is there to see.

The beginning was difficult in the sense of change,
I was lucky enough to take part in foreign exchange.
Growing up again in the land of dreams,
faced the poverty and almost lost hope it seemed,
And I have seen what is there to see.

Things built on family foundations of four offspring,
life easy at last it would bring.
Hardships overcome one by one together,
getting through the rain or shine weather,
and I have seen what is there to see.

As I lie on this hospital bed, I have nothing to dread,
no regrets besides the fact,
that I do not know how to act,
to see the tears of my beloved ones but,
I have seen what is there to see.

Norman Chen, Grade 10
Abraham Lincoln High School, CA

Changeling

Under the shade of a petrified tree
A terrified wood sprite said to me
"What do I do when all that I see
Is the malevolent shadow of who I used to be?"
And I stared at her with wide eyes
Thinking, pondering, but about to decide
Then it came to me, and I almost denied
The truth of the thing — that we all hide

We hide from our demons, stuck deep in ourselves
Tucking away our problems so no one can tell
Where the evil comes form if not from Hell
When God has no reason to show himself
"What do we do?" She asked as I explained this
And I told her to simply be shameless
Act in a way you weren't scared to list
To anyone, including the mirror

The reflection of all we've done is a factor
Of course, I should exclude the disaster
Of sins pulled from others outside me and you
And know that there are things we all do
That we can change for a better tomorrow

Anna D., Grade 12
Diamond Ranch Academy, UT

Human

Everyone always puts up a strong front.
Somehow, being sad is being weak.
Sharing what you feel inside is considered overly emotional.
Crying is for babies.
So we try to hide the hurt we feel and try to hold back the tears
And build up these useless walls to tuck away our fears.

Too often we forget, we're humans.
We hold the power to cause chaos, to destroy, to inflict great pain
And at the same time,
We have the ability to create miracles, to rebuild, to love.
We are capable of so many things
And at the same time,
We can be so handicapped when it comes to emotions.

There are leaders who hide and instead become followers.
There are friends who fight and instead become enemies.
There are lovers who split and instead become strangers.

We don't have forever.
Life is fragile.
Sometimes we will fall, sometimes we will rise.
Accept it, embrace it, live it.

Amanda Hsu, Grade 12
Fountain Valley High School, CA

American Soldiers

They stand on those fields
with their rifles in hand.
As this goes on
only few will stand.

These men fight for our freedom
come home with nightmares.
As they risk all their lives
only few people still care

Their screams and cries cannot be heard
drowned out by gunshots and thundering booms.
But many cannot return home
to rest in their rooms.

These soldiers love you so much
they shed blood, sweat, and tears
to show that they care
they hide all their fears.

When you see that red, white, and blue
make sure you stand true
because these men fought and died for you.

Brittney Gill, Grade 10
Excelsior Education Center, CA

Not Meant for All

Love is not meant for all,
You and me are not meant to fall
In love, between you and me,
Why can't you just only see.

That you and me are
Not just meant to be,
You are not my type,
Why can't you just see.

You may think I am mean,
My love for you is never seen,
Because I don't want to hurt you
Anymore, heartbreak can't be undone.

You may think of me,
But, you are my friend,
Hope you can still be
In the very end…

Charnie Doan, Grade 11
Arroyo High School, CA

In My Heart

I cannot help the jealousy.
It's creeping and infecting me.
In my mind, and in my heart,
hating you is the hardest part.

I cannot help the jealousy.
I know it only hurts me.
In my mind, and in my heart,
loving you is the hardest part.

It's the spite in me,
the hateful side of me
in my mind, and in my heart,
that makes wanting you the hardest part,
that makes needing you the hardest part.

Despite all I say or do
In my heart,
I still love you.

Sarah McLernon, Grade 11
Antelope Valley High School, CA

Veil

Hidden Behind a Veil of Deceit
Bitter and Sour
Sugary Sweet
Laughing at Heaven
Shouting in Hell
Forever Remembered
The Girl in the Veil

Karina House, Grade 11
Viewmont High School, UT

Lock and Key

It's not surprising, how everything you knew changed.
It's visible from your face, you're not going to forget him.

I have sympathy for you, 'cause I see the pain in your eyes.
I know you dream of him at night,
And wake up crying because of the heartache.

You're wishing to go back to the days,
When you saw his smile you got butterflies.
And now he is laughing, because it was his mission to hurt you.

You want an explanation, but you realize you won't get one.
You hear people saying you got rejected,
And they give you their apologies.

Then you realize the effect he had on you, and how lost you have been.
You realized you don't need him, that you never did.

You start believing again, he may have broken your heart but,
You can still fix it again, you see the possibilities again.

You no longer feel sorry for yourself,
With a giggle and a smile and a friend,
Your problems are solved,
Your heart was under lock and key.

But you broke the lock, and now you're free.

Montana Hogrefe, Grade 10
King Kekaulike High School, HI

Obvious Rip in My Heart

Painful reminders of the past sneak up and bring the quiet tears of hurt.
Things that never reminded me before,
Now serve as silent sentinels —
Keeping me in the past, keeping me in the pain.

Will I ever be free?
Finally, I think I've freed myself,
Only to be brought back to my knees in apparent anguish.
As I kneel on the ground, fighting the tears that threaten,
I tell myself: Be strong.
Do not be conquered by things from the past.
The past does not matter — keep thinking about tomorrow.

But even as I say this to myself, I know it will take time.
Time that will still have pain and still have hurt.
But for now I'll just try to keep the pain I'm feeling a secret.
Feeling this pain shows weakness —
Weakness I don't want to have.
Maybe if someone else knows, they can help me?
No! It's not important to them and it wouldn't help me for them to know.

The one person I want to tell already knows, but does nothing.
The obvious rip in my heart does nothing to theirs.

Elise Horne, Grade 11
Viewmont High School, UT

This Woman
This woman came from the brightest being that gives us life.
This woman gave birth to the first microscopic beings
And they grew and took until they grew to become men — who took advantage of her
They took from her and extracted what made her profound,
While she made her 365 day journey. Then these men developed industries
And began pulling the roots from her head as she screamed — we used it to write, paint, and waste
Then we spoiled her veins with toxic chemicals and wastes
Her once clear veins have become the poison that circulates around her
When she tried to reach for the sky to ask her mother for help
These men blasted dynamite in her arms to make tunnels
And when she had her moments of pain and she could not hold it in any longer
She cried and wailed causing storms, floods, and quakes
With a finger pointing we dictated it was her natural disaster
DISASTER! Why do we hurt this woman?
Why do we take advantage of this woman? Especially when we all came from this woman?
This woman, I respect her — she needs help — she screams for a savior!
This woman, I met when she was crippled, burning, and dying
She trembled in fear; her head tilted making days shorter-up for help and down to grieve
Someone told me to be grateful that I am not her. But I am here and I have to help this woman
For I love this woman
For I love this Earth

Leonard Chan, Grade 11
Purple Lotus International Institute, CA

Survive
The streets, the hallways, the homes, the people, none are safe anymore; no place can I be at peace.
They laugh, they walk, they carry on their lives, but do they really know what's waiting in disguise?

They think it's hard, they think they know, but they have no idea what's waiting in the dark.
Its fiendish smile, its welcoming gesture, it seems as a monster that no one looks through.

On the outside it's all happy and joy, but no one tells. No one shows you the stress, the work, the pain.
No one strives to achieve more than what's required. If only they told you what all you could be.

Only then would we know. Only then could we grow.

But for now the minimum is all that is asked. For now none are pushed or put to the test.
For now we merely drift and have higher concerns with the outside world and the inside despair.

How can they not know? How can they not see? I guess for now it will all lie with me.
I will go forth, I will succeed, I will shine bright and make all others not only care, but fright.

Sara Byington, Grade 11
Viewmont High School, UT

Love Hurts
Through these past few days, I've been reminiscing back it's the first time I couldn't understand what we had, was it love? Was it passion? Was it all a waste of time? Now it's hate. Now it's pain. Now it's all this stuff combined, I can't force myself to erase all our memories but when I'm thinking back I always feel like you fooled me. Nobody to blame but myself from being blinded, crying in my sleep hoping this hurting passes by. I've been told by my sisters how these guys are all the same, but you had me so convinced that this world suddenly changed, 'cause you always made me smile but a smile isn't forever. I guess it's unpredictable like change in the weather. I thought we'd work this out like those other times before. But the truth had to reveal we can't live a lie no more. I'm still young and i'm still trying to stay true to my heart. My dreams have disappeared and now my life's scattered apart.

Lorena Velazquez, Grade 10
Crossroads School, CA

Love Hate Relationship
Your eyes are like the stars above.
Your hair is like the sparkling sand.
Your lips seem as smooth as still water.
Your smile is as the sun.
You smell as if it had just rained.

But,

Your mind is like a circus.
Your soul is of hellfire.
Your heart is like the darkest night.
Your words are cruel.
Your doings are curt.

But,

Even though you make me cry,
my heart rushes every time I see your face.
So I guess for now we'll have to stay,
in this Love Hate Relationship.
Samantha Morgan, Grade 10
Orem High School, UT

Lost
Making your way through the days
In the depths of hardships and haze.
With struggles that you face
And living life at your own pace.
Trying to find the person inside you
While feeling down and blue.
Within the deep dark world
Lost confusion and swirled.
Hiding the frowns with smiles
While beating at the trials.
Praying for a miracle to come your way
Or even just a "hey"
Overcoming the fears of being yourself
Has found the person hiding inside.
Whitney Draper, Grade 12
Emery High School, UT

Good Friendship
Your kind of friendship
It takes more than caring
To be a real friend;
The nature of friendship
Requires a blend
Of warmest compassion
And love, deep and true,
To reach and to comfort
The way that you do.
I can see
That your kind of friendship
Is priceless to me.
Sean Stephenson, Grade 10
Orem High School, UT

From
I am from the depth of the Earth,
from the earnest warmth around the hearth.
I am from the decay beneath the ground,
from those too afraid to make a sound.
I am from the night after sunset,
the star-less sky and moon on offset.
A reflection of my Shadow that creeps nearby;
Invisible silhouette when I pass by.

I am from the natives and explorers of the past,
all of whom can be made up within a cast.
I am from the gardens and desks of sunlight,
from stories and tales and dreams at night.
I am of the sea; the stream; the river,
from here I belong, there is no need to quiver.
I am of the sleeping dogs upon a lap,
located visibly — Hidden — on a treasure map.

I am from the Voiceless trees being cut down,
defenseless yet visible and Invisible to others,
I am like the thorns on a rose, part of something special yet always ignored. Me.
Valerie De La Fuente, Grade 11
Los Amigos High School, CA

Come Love
Come love, walk slowly and carefully still,
We'll weather the miles, together we will.

Come love, speak softly and whisper your tales,
My heart is yours, like a ship to its sails.

Come love, breathe deeply and waste not the day,
The sun has a secret it wishes to say.

Come love, have patience our night is still young,
We'll sing now the songs that have yet to be sung.

Come love, sleep soundly, and lie by my side,
Grant us a peace only faith can provide.

Taste now, my love, the bittersweet air,
Savor our time, like the lights of a fair.

Feel now my heart, it beats inside you,
I know where yours is, it drums in me too.
Delaney Burks, Grade 11
Northern Utah Academy for Math, Engineering and Science (NUAMES), UT

My Beloved

You needed me, so I ran to you with open arms.
I walked by your side and led you through the valley of the shadow of death.
I paid your debts, But you turned your back and chose another.
I offered hope and a future, but it was never enough to satisfy your ways.

I watch you slowly spiraling down as life pulls you one way as I pull you another.
Your confusion fills you with anxiety, and pain shadows your heart.
You feel neglected and alone and I feel your grief.

Now you have hit bottom again.
You are on your knees crying, begging for redemption.
Through pain and confusion you give your life to me asking for forgiveness.
lifting your voice up to me confessing your sins.

My eyes fill with tears of joy.
Though I hate to see my child suffer, we have been reunited once again.
My love and happiness overflows and pours out into your heart and I watch you lift up your eyes to the heavens and smile a smile
of love, peace and thankfulness.

Then you hear me say, "I love you more than anything, so I will never give up on you.
Though you forget you need me, I will stand behind you and hold you high.
You are my beloved, my child, my life. You have my love, my forgiveness and I will stay with you forever."

Lauren Gale, Grade 10
Brookside Christian Academy, CA

The Unknown

Luminous mist rests heavily on the dark, silent forest
as the mournful howl of a wolf breaks the curtain of quiet.
Fear is the ever-present companion of the lost, wandering soldier.
Dark outlines of jagged trees take on the form of Nazi enemies
as each snapping of a twig reverberates the sound of gunfire.
The damp chill of the unfriendly night air seeps into his bones
like the ungodly memories of war seeping into his soul.

Then, like a flicker of light in the darkest abyss,
Hope appears with friendly assurance as she replaces the foreboding Fear.
The young soldier bounds towards her with mindless desperation, forgetting all caution and stealth.
Without warning, a gunshot shatters the still night air
as the soldier staggers violently to the ground.
His body shudders uncontrollably, then lies still
as Death replaces Hope as his forever-companion.

Natalie Seamons, Grade 12
Emery High School, UT

All the Same

Black, White, Asian, Hispanic, Indian, or mixed color doesn't matter, people are the same on the inside. So why must we be so judgmental? We say that people are all equal, but that's a lie. People are still excluded, treated differently, and discriminated against. But why? We're all so alike, and yet so different. But is that really a bad thing? We're all different for a reason. Life is excruciatingly miserable and difficult for most individuals, and it all happens because they're different.
It's pathetic!
All of these people being so judgmental and looking down on others as if they're superior, it's a false kind of power, like hiding behind a mask, formed from nothing more than hate. Remove your masks and your plastic smiles, open your eyes and see each other as the equal beings you're meant to be.
Because in the end of it, we're all the same!

Bonnie Jean Marks, Grade 12
Riverside Preparatory School, CA

Mad Stage

I remember forming our New Age musketeers of three.
That feeling of "no one could slow us down,"
being completely invincible.
Him: I remember how you made me feel worthy to live,
the new adventures we formed,
kismet played its perfect timing.
Her: I remember the excitement we had.
The never ending sleepovers
chocolate-flour-water-plates-smashing fights
Him: Our lovers' mad stage,
to-the-point I never wanted to leave your side.
I remember the joy of being "family."
That never-let-you-down attitude you both gave me,
how you still fight for me every day.
Her: I remember singing songs out loud,
those goofy dances I made up just to embarrass you,
how you still loved me even after those looks shot at us.
I remember I would kill for you.
Him: That feeling of finally being real,
being with you,
finally being a part of something.

Ariel Alvarez, Grade 12
Westwood High School, AZ

Try

Close your eyes for then you'll see
Fantasy transform into reality
Wake up, and you will dream
It's hard but things aren't always what they seem
Don't reach for the stars; you can get to the moon
Try, try, TRY! You'll be there soon

I've watched your struggles
Can attest to your guilty troubles,
But remember this every time you fail,
The long road to heaven passes through hell

Fly high on golden wings
Float away on silver clouds
Past the azure sky, Victory calls!
And in the end, (I see it now!)
An evergreen laurel adorns your brow.

Sua M. Figueroa, Grade 12
Schurr High School, CA

Surprise Surprise

Screaming colors at first sight, oh my!
The Wonderball has a treat for you and I,
Dig deep, what's this?
A surprise you don't want to miss,
Like it, Like I, I am more than meets the eye.

Dy-Dan Nguyen, Grade 12
University High School, CA

The Ultimate Test

The day has come, our trial to face.
A mighty challenge: a cross country race.
We stand at the line, time slows.
Who will be the victor? Nobody knows.
With the crack of a gun eternity ceases.
The work begins, our tension eases.

From the first step we become machines.
Our lungs are pumps, our feet are wings.
Until the finish we must fight.
Each breath a gasp, each step a flight.

Our coaches call for speed, our muscles for rest.
Mind over body, the ultimate test.
Nothing in our way, save exhaustion.
Those that fall behind are soon forgotten.

Our leap into oblivion, the final sprint.
Of all former struggles, there are not hints.
We harvest the fruits of our labors:
Herculean deeds expressed by mere numbers.

Andrew Evans, Grade 10
St Francis High School, CA

School Days

At first it was crackers, snacks, and toys,
Along with that, friendships were made.
Subtraction and adding soon became joys,
Essays were no more delayed.

Classes advanced to more difficult things,
Like English, algebra, and history.
Talents became more interesting,
No longer remaining a mystery.

Before you know it, high school is here,
Sports teams and groups perform and play.
The crowds and band give a shout and a cheer,
The Shelley Russets again cry, "Hooray!"

Now that 10th grade is almost done
I sure have had a lot of fun!

Christy Searle, Grade 10
Shelley Sr High School, ID

The Stars

I am the stars. Not often seen, but always there.
I am distant, but bright. Be not deceived.
I am your own, so call on me for your deepest wishes.
I am aligned in your favor, so fear not the future. Most of all,
I love you now, and for eternity. Just as the stars go on…

Harrison Stokes, Grade 10
Preston High School, ID

Home

The bells of time,
Have stopped their chime,
And now you must go.
On angel wings,
Your heart they bring,
To your final home.
Your burdens vanished,
Your fear is banished,
And no more reason to cry.
No more you endure,
This earth's evil lure,
Now that you are free.
The dance we dance,
Of loves romance,
Will wait a little longer.
My roads been run,
My life is done,
And now I'm coming home.
And when I'm there,
The love we share,
Will forever be.

Lori Hofer, Grade 10
Moore High School, MT

Bound to Be Outdoors

The sky that wet November day
Poured rain like tears on forests gray,
When the bright sun shone at noon
It gave the promise of beauty soon.
As the pitter patter of the rain subsided,
The beauty of nature stood undivided.
And here in nature I've decided,
In this wondrous world of Pan,
Nothing compares if made by man.
As the blanket of the night fell,
The dancing fire had cast a spell.
The smell of burnt wood stood out clear,
I sat by friends that I hold dear.
The taste of warm campfire s'mores,
Left me wanting so much more.
As I looked upon the starlight,
The veracity of the night
Reminded me of why I adore
Being bound to be outdoors,
Where all of nature makes me implore
To let me stay just one day more.

Myvy Ngo, Grade 11
Valley Christian High School, CA

Summer Breeze

Gentle winds caress
A tender, loving rose in
Calming waves of blue

Sami Wiser, Grade 11
Viewmont High School, UT

Nameless

As children we are told we can be whatever we dream to,
whether it be astronaut, super hero, or even president.
Yet as we get older we lose this imagination,
choosing to fit in and do as we're told instead.
What happened to the imaginations that we once had,
allowing us to be anywhere and everywhere without leaving our house.
The world has told us that our imagination is wrong,
and so we've learned to disregard our dreams.

The dreams we once had and couldn't wait to tell our friends
have become the same ones we shelter from others as not to be looked at strangely.
Even though everyone has these dreams,
we have been told that our dreams are nothing but foolishness.
We are told that our individuality is wrong,
that only working as one is tolerated.
Individuality has been struck down.
We must follow the flow of society.

Even our names are nothing but words.
The names we were given to make us different from one another;
The names we've been given are completely pointless now;
We all might as well be nameless.

Why? Why have we become nameless?

Phoenix Pizon, Grade 10
Bradshaw Christian High School, CA

My Daily Star

Day after day I hope to soon conquer the brightest star in my blue sky,
Night after night I ponder why it shines so bright
If I could only hold you tight and make you understand
That I want you to be mine.

Although there might be cloudy days and dark nights,
My heart reflects the wonder and innocence of your lovable sight.
Seeing you day and night shining in my life,
Illuminates me, I just wish you could be by my side.

So far so close I've seen you shine
I now turn around and walk away with the biggest pride of my life
Knowing that the brightest star in the sky was once in the palms of my hands
Shining my life and illuminating each night of my fragile sky.

Here we stand,
There we stood,
With our feet firmly pressed against the ground we shall understand
That we're no longer innocent kids playing in the rain,
But the coldest rain drop falling from the sky with no destiny.

When summer comes we should remain apart,
Nights will be dark, days will be dry and my sky…
And my sky will be simply the pure reflection of a broken heart.

Carlos Velazquez, Grade 11
Animo Leadership Charter High School, CA

Anybody?

Does anybody hear the hungry children's cry?
Or do you only hear the rich man's lie?
The world is stricken with poverty
But all that we care for is ourselves.
Does anybody see the abandoned children weep?
Or do you only see the cherished comfortably sleep?
The world is overwhelmed with abandonment
But all that we care for is ourselves.
Does anybody hear the crippled call out for help?
Or do you only hear the strong delightfully yelp?
The world is immersed with the disabled
But all that we care for is ourselves.
Does anybody see the sick slowly die?
Or do you only see the healthy happily sigh?
The world is afflicted with illness
But all that we care for is ourselves.
Does anybody feel their pain?
Can anybody be humane?
The world is consumed with sadness and pain
But all that we care for is ourselves.

Hye Soo (Laura) Lee, Grade 10
Cypress High School, CA

Life, Difficult or Easy...

Life has a lot of meanings
People could have fun times or sad times
In their life.
Life maybe joy full, life maybe a dream,
But just live it and have fun.
People just give up in the life they have,
But I'm not going to give up
I want to learn more and more about it.
Life can have love, life can have death
But that's all part of life.

It's more than that. Life is a hard level and
You just have to live life how its suppose to be lived.
Learned from right to wrong or wrong to right.
Learn that things are too good to be real.
You may have had many regrets but things happened
And every mistake is just a learned lesson.
Life is just like steps you have to take
Is just like learning how to fly
And you just got to take one step at a time

Eduardo Tellez, Grade 11
Animo Leadership Charter High School, CA

Moreno

M ore lovable than a puppy
O nly one of a kind
R esponsible and respectful
E nergetic, most of the time
N ever sees the negative side of something
O ther half for my brothers

Luz Moreno, Grade 12
Wilson High School, CA

Hard Headed and Now Blessed

Criminal minded got me in some trouble,
I was a lost soul that had tumbled.
Fell off top, now down another level,
Breaking the law, labeled a rebel.
I finally connected with the Lord upstairs,
I got enemies, that mean, mug an stare.
Stuck in a cage like a horrible creature,
Praying on my knees cuz' God I need Ya.'
I had plenty of friends, but turned their back,
A man on his own, looking for a straight path.
Climbing the mountain I be the first to last,
I chose to be innocent, not guilty in my task.
I'm walking the ladder, to Heaven's gate,
So when I die I don't need to be afraid.
Put me with my cousin who's resting in paradise,
I reminisce when we had those good times.
This lifestyle had infected my head,
Success runs in my blood, that's what they said,
For me, I am God's child,
At times I ended up wild.

Victor Lueras, Grade 12
Crossroads School, CA

A Great Impact

Cesar Chavez and Jaime Escalante
Both made a big change, that was excellent
Cesar's family wasn't doing too good
Although he worked real hard and didn't join the hood
He started up the Farmers Association
And they started up a protest within the nation
Then people got better pay and working conditions
Cesar Chavez has now completed his mission
Jaime Escalante was brought up in Bolivia
He moved to the US without a trivia
Jaime Escalante got three jobs
Instead of going to get some robs
He then started teaching at Garfield High
Where a bunch of students had their heads in the sky
Garfield High's academics shot up to the sky
They even surpassed that of Beverly High
Both of these men had different goals
They worked on them with their heart and soul
Both of these men went through a fight
In the end they brought their people into the light

Rudain Sebai, Grade 10
City of Knowledge School, CA

Brain Freeze

Biting into an ice cream cone,
feeling the rush of the cool summer treat
as it takes over your nerves,
creating momentary cranial pain so intense
as to lend you incapable
of speech or movement.

Deborah Moody, Grade 12
Woods Cross High School, UT

The Trouble with Speech

Writers' block? The term mocks the spoken word!
Text, though difficult, shares silence with thought; but giving minds a voice — now that's absurd!

This block of stone marks graves of speech disturbed,
And loves (O'er pencils stilled) vocal chords taut. Writers' block — the term mocks the spoken word.

Artists give others eyes to look inward;
Portray, in silence, the image they sought, but giving minds a voice? Now that's absurd!

But one displays herself as much in words:
A frame of hidden hopes around the thought. Writer's block: The term mocks the spoken word.

It's simple to record what has occurred;
For one can then destroy what has been wrought, but giving minds a voice — now that's absurd.

While writings, writ wrong, are easily burned,
Words, once spoken, can never be rebought.
Writers' Block: The term mocks the spoken word, but giving minds a voice — now that's absurd!

Laura Stromback, Grade 10
Chandler Preparatory Academy, AZ

High School Dreams

I find it hard to move the pen, across the once blank pages as I look around at this life, and all of its stages
I look around at this school, all the blank memories the ones I once loved, but now hate, yes, these…
I look around at these people, my enemies and friends I find that I wonder: what happens when High School ends?
Where will we be? Who will we still have? Who will we love? And when we look back…
What will we see? Sophomore Slump and Senior mistakes did we do all that we tried? Did we do everything it takes?
Do we dare to look back? And see all we've done? Dare we ask? Was it at least fun?
Did we accomplish, those high school dreams? Were the tears worth it? And were the screams?
Were we all a little crazy? And all a little strange? Are we still ourselves? How much did we change?
Are the dreams the same? Do we still sing a song? Why did it seem to last so long?
What are these high school dreams? Do we still have them, what do they mean? Will we ever be heard!? Were we ever even seen?
And does it matter, now that it's said and done it's all over, and still no one…
No not one of us knows, if we reached for a star took our dreams, and then went far
Will any of us do it, when high school ends I ask myself as I sit here, and laugh with my friends

Aurelleah Formoso, Grade 10
Bradshaw Mountain High School, AZ

Misunderstood

Selfish — Arrogant — Disrespectful — Annoying
Why do you call me these things? To tear and rip and dysfunction my wings?
To see me cry in pain, in shame?
Well I won't, I will stand and take what you have to say then bottle it up and hide it away.
No shame, no pain.
. . .
Not that you can see.
Underneath my seemingly impenetrable skin, something is chewing, is ripping, is clawing its way into my soul.
Deep down under it all I am numb, dying…or am I already dead?
Can you see what you've done? The harm that you've caused.
And why? Because of my flaws
I may not be perfect but I am not evil!
What do I have to do to let you see that?
And all this…because I am misunderstood.

Selena Peterson, Grade 10
Pacific Coast High School, CA

Life

I quickly leave the womb with a thundering boom.
I leave in a jiffy looking nice and spiffy.

This is what I am and I am what I am.

I sadly go to school which I think is uncool.
In school I get all A's and I pass with great praise.

This is what I am and I am what I am.

I become a lawyer known as the "Destroyer."
I achieve immense wealth while I still have my health.

This is what I am and I am what I am.

I grow to be very old, with skin that has many rolls.
My hair starts to go gray and my mind starts to stray.

This is what I am and I am what I am.
Julian Urrea, Grade 10
St. Francis High School, CA

New

I've never felt this way before
I thought you might want to know
This feeling is overpowering me
And all it does is grow

The first time I saw you
I never knew what would come of it
I wish I knew how long it will last
Because this is something I'll never forget

In the night I dream of you
In reality you are my dream come true
Nothing can compare to where you send me
It makes me feel like everything will be okay
Sara Khadra, Grade 12
University Preparatory School, CA

Heartbroken <3

It seems as if I was a toy
You keep playing
Your words don't mean anything
Our relationship has no trust
And it's impossible
Everything I did wasn't worth it
And the love I had, the love you "HAD" was never real
Lie to lie, you threw all the trust I had for you away
Each and every time you hugged me.
I'm tired.

My heart and everyone is right
You and me aren't meant to be!
Martha Villatoro, Grade 11
Animo Leadership Charter High School, CA

Ode to My Orange Folder

It may seem
like any old folder.
Holding nothing but worthless papers.
Cluttered, jumbled, chaotic
and mixed up,
with writing scribbled all over it.
But to me, the folder is everything.
Homework, handouts, and essays
fill the pockets.
In no particular order; just how I like them.
No page numbers, indexes, or tables of contents.
The folder isn't just a folder to me.
Sometimes it's a movie about a boy surviving school.
Or an old journal, with new feelings, thoughts, and opinions
constantly pouring in.
Or a 1000 page novel, exploding with adventure and suspense.
It can be all of these things.
But always,
it's a lifesaver.
Brian Benton, Grade 10
Palo Alto High School, CA

What Is Love?

How do you know what love is?
Is it a feeling is there a sign?
How do I know your love is mine?

How do you know what love is?
Does it make a sound? Maybe a flash of light?
How do I know love will last through the night?

How do you know what love is?
Is it all the flowers?
Spending time together for hours and hours?

I know what love is, now do you?
I know what love is because I love you.
Kelli Horstmeyer, Grade 12
Prospect Continuation High School, CA

The Feeling

As I walk my legs shake like there's an earthquake.
As I arrive I need to sit but cannot sit still.
As I relax my heart beats fast from the close atmosphere.
As I realize my stomach is taking off and never landing.
As I smell my nose opens for his scent to occupy.
As I listen my ears twitch in a focused direction.
As I look my eyes shine dazed in a trance.
As I think my head draws a blank to oblivion.
As I talk I trip over my words and get nothing out.
As I feel a hand touches mine and holds it in a claim.
As I remember the other times this has happened,
As I connect all the times back to the same person,
I know I want every bit of it to be mine every time I see him.
Sarah Vitug, Grade 10
Cypress High School, CA

So What's So Different

We all have a human heart
We all need the light and the dark
We all hurt on the inside
We all have a sense of pride

So what's so different?
We all have eyes that see
We all are who we choose to be
We all love and we hate
We all have no choice of our fate

So what's so different?
We all have a voice
We all need to make this choice
We all should have no shame
We all are exactly the same.
Ashley N. Rymer, Grade 12
Prospect Continuation High School, CA

I don't come with a sword

I can't play the banjo
I can't walk on skies
I can't write
Not even from the heart

A man with a sword is hard to find
For a dragonfly

So I wish I had a sword
So I could fly
So I could be
Thirty-four

Nineteen years
Out of the score
That separates us
Jake Sagadraca, Grade 10
Mililani High School, HI

A Wish

Ripped, smashed, torn apart
Shattered pieces of my heart.
Stitched, stapled and glued
It will never be renewed.
Over and over it will shatter,
It has gotten to where it doesn't matter.
I guess I got sick of crying all those tears,
All 'cause those stupid boys over the years.
It is 'cause of them I have made a wish,
I hope I am not being too selfish.
I wish I could fly away
And make everything okay.
But what I wish for most is this heart
To have a beginning and a brand new start.
Bethany Rogers, Grade 11
Cinnamon Hills School, UT

I Am

A one of a kind individual
A mother to three "littles"
A daughter of five siblings
A role model to my "littles"
An inspiring youth counselor
A person with feeling to consider
A happy outspoken person
An artistic person living life
A respectful classy lady
A phenomenal woman
A strong survivor
Domonique Estrada, Grade 11
Wilson High School, CA

Never Really Had

So much hurt, I can hardly breathe
15 years and I don't understand
Why you just had to leave

You never kissed me or hugged me
Never encouraged, comforted
Or told me you loved me

Let me know, Mom, was I really that bad?
Every day I miss the mother
That I never really had.
Merilyn Stuck, Grade 10
Mission Bay High School, CA

Sunrise

Within a dark corner
a child screams for help,
but no one answers.
Drowning in feelings of death
he raises his blade
and thinks of his last words.
Hands, golden with light
grab away the darkness in his soul,
embrace's him deep within their bosom,
holding him while he cries.
My sunrise has come.
Yukito Daidouji, Grade 10
Mililani High School, HI

The Seed

Now alone in sorrow's spring,
doth I rise, the new dawn bring.
The dust I was, now I see,
is to my roots a melody.

The silence rains upon my soul
to bring me from this dirt filled hole.
From shining sky the clouds do flee,
Has Death's cold grip begotten me?
Dylan Andersen, Grade 11
Viewmont High School, UT

Vile

Into the Alameda lagoon
Water flows from the bay
Into the muddy Alameda lagoon
Dark and mysterious
Algae blooms green
Ducks dive
Into the muddy lagoon
To devour mutilated fish
In the muddy Alameda lagoon
Megan Manning, Grade 12
St Joseph Notre Dame High School, CA

I Can't Forget

It's hard to forget
Because you just regret
What you do will stay with you
They never go away, it's sad but true

But even if your far away
Or if you found someone new
I will never forget about you and me
You're hard to forget…I can't forget
Shaylen Wong, Grade 10
Mililani High School, HI

A Broken Heart

Every now and then
I sit and think
What wrong I did to you
All I did was to love you
So now tell me
Why you left me
With a broken heart
So now all I do is sit
And cry the pains away.
Isamar Morales, Grade 11
Wilson High School, CA

Index

Author Autograph Page

Author Autograph Page

Author Autograph Page

Author Autograph Page

Author Autograph Page

Author Autograph Page

Author Autograph Page

Author Autograph Page

Author Autograph Page

Author Autograph Page

Author Autograph Page

Author Autograph Page

Author Autograph Page

Author Autograph Page